VOLUME 603

JANUARY 2006

THE ANNALS

of The American Academy of Political
and Social Science

ROBERT W. PEARSON, *Executive Editor*
LAWRENCE W. SHERMAN, *Editor*

Law, Society, and Democracy: Comparative Perspectives

Special Editor of this Volume

RICHARD E. D. SCHWARTZ

Yale Law School

SAGE Publications Ⓢ Thousand Oaks · London · New Delhi

The American Academy of Political and Social Science

3814 Walnut Street, Fels Institute of Government, University of Pennsylvania,
Philadelphia, PA 19104-6197; (215) 746-6500; (215) 898-1202 (fax); www.aapss.org

---

Origin and Purpose. The Academy was organized December 14, 1889, to promote the progress of political and social science, especially through publications and meetings. The Academy does not take sides in controverted questions, but seeks to gather and present reliable information to assist the public in forming an intelligent and accurate judgment.

Meetings. The Academy occasionally holds a meeting in the spring extending over two days.

Publications. THE ANNALS of The American Academy of Political and Social Science is the bimonthly publication of the Academy. Each issue contains articles on some prominent social or political problem, written at the invitation of the editors. Also, monographs are published from time to time, numbers of which are distributed to pertinent professional organizations. These volumes constitute important reference works on the topics with which they deal, and they are extensively cited by authorities throughout the United States and abroad. The papers presented at the meetings of the Academy are included in THE ANNALS.

Membership. Each member of the Academy receives THE ANNALS and may attend the meetings of the Academy. Membership is open only to individuals. Annual dues: $84.00 for the regular paperbound edition (clothbound, $121.00). Members may also purchase single issues of THE ANNALS for $17.00 each (clothbound, $26.00). Student memberships are available for $53.00.

Subscriptions. THE ANNALS of The American Academy of Political and Social Science (ISSN 0002-7162) (J295) is published six times annually—in January, March, May, July, September, and November—by Sage Publications, 2455 Teller Road, Thousand Oaks, CA 91320. Telephone: (800) 818-SAGE (7243) and (805) 499-9774; Fax/Order line: (805) 499-0871; e-mail: journals@sagepub.com. Copyright © 2006 by The American Academy of Political and Social Science. Institutions may subscribe to THE ANNALS at the annual rate: $577.00 (clothbound, $652.00). Single issues of THE ANNALS may be obtained by individuals who are not members of the Academy for $34.00 each (clothbound, $47.00). Single issues of THE ANNALS have proven to be excellent supplementary texts for classroom use. Direct inquiries regarding adoptions to THE ANNALS c/o Sage Publications (address below). Periodicals postage paid at Thousand Oaks, California, and at additional mailing offices.

All correspondence concerning membership in the Academy, dues renewals, inquiries about membership status, and/or purchase of single issues of THE ANNALS should be sent to THE ANNALS c/o Sage Publications, 2455 Teller Road, Thousand Oaks, CA 91320.Telephone: (800) 818-SAGE (7243) and (805) 499-9774; Fax/Order line: (805) 499-0871; e-mail: journals@sagepub.com. *Please note that orders under $30 must be prepaid.* Sage affiliates in London and India will assist institutional subscribers abroad with regard to orders, claims, and inquiries for both subscriptions and single issues.

Printed on acid-free paper

THE ANNALS

Editorial Office: 3814 Walnut Street, Fels Institute for Government, University of Pennsylvania, Philadelphia, PA 19104-6197.
For information about membership* (individuals only) and subscriptions (institutions), address:
Sage Publications
2455 Teller Road
Thousand Oaks, CA 91320
For Sage Publications: Joseph Riser and Esmeralda Hernandez

From India and South Asia, write to:
SAGE PUBLICATIONS INDIA Pvt Ltd
B-42 Panchsheel Enclave, P.O. Box 4109
New Delhi 110 017
INDIA

From Europe, the Middle East, and Africa, write to:
SAGE PUBLICATIONS LTD
1 Oliver's Yard, 55 City Road
London EC1Y 1SP
UNITED KINGDOM

*Please note that members of the Academy receive THE ANNALS with their membership.
International Standard Serial Number ISSN 0002-7162
International Standard Book Number 1-4129-4011-7 (Vol. 603, 2006 paper)
International Standard Book Number ISBN 1-4129-4010-9 (Vol. 603, 2006 cloth)
Manufactured in the United States of America. First printing, January 2006.

The articles appearing in *The Annals* are abstracted or indexed in Academic Abstracts, Academic Search, America: History and Life, Asia Pacific Database, Book Review Index,CABAbstracts Database, Central Asia: Abstracts &Index, Communication Abstracts, Corporate ResourceNET, Criminal Justice Abstracts, Current Citations Express, Current Contents: Social & Behavioral Sciences, Documentation in Public Administration, e-JEL, EconLit, Expanded Academic Index, Guide to Social Science & Religion in Periodical Literature, Health Business FullTEXT, HealthSTAR FullTEXT, Historical Abstracts, International Bibliography of the Social Sciences, International Political Science Abstracts, ISI Basic Social Sciences Index, Journal of Economic Literature on CD, LEXIS-NEXIS, MasterFILE FullTEXT, Middle East: Abstracts&Index, North Africa: Abstracts&Index, PAIS International, Periodical Abstracts, Political Science Abstracts, Psychological Abstracts, PsycINFO, Sage Public Administration Abstracts, Social Science Source, Social Sciences Citation Index, Social Sciences Index Full Text, Social Services Abstracts, SocialWork Abstracts, Sociological Abstracts, Southeast Asia: Abstracts& Index, Standard Periodical Directory (SPD), TOPICsearch, Wilson OmniFileV, and Wilson Social Sciences Index/Abstracts, and are available on microfilm from ProQuest, Ann Arbor, Michigan.

Information about membership rates, institutional subscriptions, and back issue prices may be found on the facing page.

Advertising. Current rates and specifications may be obtained by writing to The Annals Advertising and Promotion Manager at the Thousand Oaks office (address above).

Claims. Claims for undelivered copies must be made no later than six months following month of publication. The publisher will supply missing copies when losses have been sustained in transit and when the reserve stock will permit.

Change of Address. Six weeks' advance notice must be given when notifying of change of address to ensure proper identification. Please specify name of journal. POSTMASTER: Send address changes to The Annals of The American Academy of Political and Social Science, c/o Sage Publications, 2455 Teller Road, Thousand Oaks, CA 91320.

ANNALS
OF THE AMERICAN ACADEMY OF POLITICAL AND SOCIAL SCIENCE

Volume 603   January 2006

IN THIS ISSUE:

Law, Society, and Democracy: Comparative Perspectives
Special Editor: RICHARD E. D. SCHWARTZ

Section Three:
International Processes

Section Four:
Quick Read Synopsis

FORTHCOMING

Shelter from the Storm:
Repairing the National Emergency Management
System after Hurricane Katrina

Special Editor: WILLIAM L. WAUGH

Volume 604, March 2006

Preface

By
RICHARD E. D. SCHWARTZ

The vision and generosity of a law dean made this issue of *The Annals* possible. Hannah Arterian, dean of the Syracuse University College of Law, gave crucial support to a project that came to be known as the Syracuse Conference. The conference, held at Syracuse in mid-April 2005, brought together a remarkable group of scholars to consider the topic, Legal Evolution: Toward a World Rule of Law. The papers prepared for that conference comprise the basis for this volume and for a companion issue of the *Syracuse Journal of International Law and Commerce*.

In 2003, Dean Arterian asked me how I would like to mark the occasion of my retirement, after twenty-five years of teaching there. She suggested a conference. Before long, we agreed that I would design the conference in any way I wished—and that she would allocate the funds needed to support it. The volume you have before you resulted from that conversation—and from the planning, writing, and meetings that followed.

In February 2004, I began seriously planning for the Syracuse Conference. Working from a new residence in Connecticut, I had generous help from Robin Paul Malloy, Linda Zimack, and Theresa Coulter in Syracuse and from Jenne Lea Hayden, my staff person in and around New Haven. The conference itself, and the publications that issue from it, evince their remarkably competent assistance. I thank them all for their wonderful work.

Richard E. D. Schwartz is Ernest I. White Professor Emeritus at the College of Law, Syracuse University, and senior research scholar at Yale Law School. He has also held positions at Northwestern University and the State University of New York at Buffalo. He is the founding editor of the Law & Society Review. *His publications include* Criminal Law: Theory and Process *(with Joseph Goldstein and Alan Dershowitz) and* Unobtrusive Measures, 2nd ed. *(with Webb, Campbell, and Sechrest). His special field of interest is in the sociology of law, specifically law and society, the proliferation of democracy, and the world rule of law.*

DOI: 10.1177/0002716205282658

In addition, I want to express my great appreciation to the participants who made the conference work so well. Each one contributed time and attention; each of them took a turn at the podium, and everyone joined in vigorous informal conversations.

Two friends from way back have played an especially important part in shaping the conference. They are Malcolm Feeley and Robert Post. I acknowledge my debt to each of them and thank them again and again.

Professor Feeley, now president elect of the Law & Society Association, then a graduate student at Minnesota, worked with me in the summer of 1965 (I believe) in Evanston to help edit the first issue of the *Law & Society Review*. We have kept in touch ever since. Time and again, I have applauded Malcolm's many important contributions to our field.

Professor Post I have known since his undergraduate days at Harvard—before he decided to go to law school. Over the years, our contacts have been casual but always rewarding. Now that Robert has moved to New Haven as the Boies Professor at Yale Law School, we share a lunch from time to time during which he donates to me, in a few minutes, hours' worth of good advice.

Many of the papers prepared for the conference have been revised for inclusion in this volume. To a rare degree, paper presentations and conversations at Syracuse encouraged vigorous and valuable exchanges in the marketplace of ideas. I hope that the articles that follow will adequately reflect the additional insights arising from this quality of the conference.

My role in planning and carrying out the conference was inevitably limited. Though it took a lot of time, the heavy lifting was done, after all, by the scholarly participants. My job was to set the tone, and to lighten up the atmosphere a bit.

I started as manager, went on as coach, and have ended up as cheerleader. With a team like this, arrayed against ignorance and preconception, how can we lose?

Sociolegal Evolution: An Introduction

By
RICHARD E. D. SCHWARTZ

The articles presented here were prepared for a conference held in mid-April 2005 at Syracuse University. The conference brought together forty scholars, from Syracuse and elsewhere, to provide insight into the paths taken by diverse nations toward constitutional democracy. All of the participants were interested in the interaction of law and society as a factor in the growth and functioning of democracy. They generally agreed that democratic governance, concept, and practice had taken hold in many countries during the past sixty years and that the dynamics of this trend could usefully be explored by bringing together people who had studied those developments in a variety of countries.

The title for the conference, "Legal Evolution," summarizes my own perspective on these changes. Later in this introduction, I will say what I mean (and do not mean) by the term. For me, at least, it is a useful way of thinking about changes in human society and culture and does not imply a Social Darwinist, extreme individualist, ideology.

The phrase in the subtitle "democratic rule of law" embodies several elements: popular choice of leaders, freedom of information, protection of rights of minorities and women, and due process of law. Each of these characteristics can contribute to public participation in the society and to the public having a say in government. Some research has been done, and more is needed, to determine whether and how these characteristics affect public participation in governance.

In this introduction, I shall briefly discuss each of the four elements that contributed to this volume. Because of increases in sociolegal research, the Syracuse Conference was able to bring together country specialists and theorists who shared the view that legal-constitutional democracy depends for its development (or evolution) on the culture and social structure of

DOI: 10.1177/0002716205282661

each society. While no synthetic generalizations emerged from the conference, we trust that the articles will offer useful leads for exploring the dynamics of democratic development.

Law & Society

To understand the evolution of law and constitutional democracy, we need to study the sociocultural foundations on which law is built. This is a central question in the newly emerging field of Law & Society (L&S). As a separate discipline, L&S did not exist in the United States until after World War II. In the early 1950s, it was a dream of half a dozen pioneers who found each other through networking, professional meetings, and publications. Fifty years later, a thousand or more scholars identify their field of special interest as L&S. Their academic degrees come from law and/or several social sciences: sociology, political science, anthropology, psychology, economics, and history.

L&S has been interdisciplinary from the start, using concepts and methods selectively drawn from any source within law and the social sciences and beyond. L&S welcomes and uses the ideas of philosophy from Aristotle to John Rawls, and natural science from Galileo to Thomas Kuhn. The premise of L&S is that no single discipline, in isolation from the others, delivers the kinds of questions or answers that can be generated by combining the methods, concepts, and data from several disciplines. How to bring these bodies of knowledge together is, of course, an arduous task. The conference aimed at that kind of synthesis.

The rapid growth of L&S suggests that traditional legal scholarship had focused too exclusively on statutes and judicial decisions and, as a result, had not systematically covered a number of important law-related topics. Law teachers and scholars took it for granted that law was an instrument for defining unacceptable behavior, resolving disputes, and avoiding conflict. Little research had been done, however, to test whether these results were in fact achieved and when, where, and how. With rare exceptions, law school faculties before 1950 did not study such matters. Instead, law teachers, and the lawyers they trained, assumed what Galanter has described as the "received paradigm"[1]

The pattern as of that time almost justified the observation that "law is an ass." In a pragmatic culture, dedicated to asking the generic question, "What works?" indifference to consequence was an anomaly. Something had to happen to address that question. What happened in the second half of the twentieth century was the development of sociolegal research in the larger context of an L&S perspective.

Sociolegal research has generated findings, particularly in American society, that explore questions of legal organization, legal consequences, and legal foundations. For example, what are the deterrent effects of punishment for various crimes? How do businesses use or avoid using contracts? How do police practices help or hinder the resolution of domestic disputes? Does federal regulation of corporate practice promote full and accurate reporting of balance-sheet reality? Do unions increase or detract from the well-being of workers? Such questions can be asked and at least partially answered by research studies, reports of which now fill academic journals, and, to some extent, popular publications as well.

Also of interest are the practices of judges, juries, and attorneys. Legal personnel are organized in courts, law firms, police, bondsmen, parole boards, and so on. Each of these entities has distinctive organizational characteristics. They have a job to do, and their methods of organization facilitate or impede the effectiveness with which the job gets done.

The legal system does more than impact society. It also relates to society by being influenced by it. In the language of logical positivism, law is both an independent and a dependent variable. In lay language, law is both a force in society and a product of society. Overtly, law-as-product occurs in American society through the machinery of elections, designed to select representatives who come together to generate laws. In principle, the selection of representatives reflects popular needs and evaluations. The reality, as usual, never quite accords with the principle.

This volume of The Annals *brings together the conference papers that focus on other societies evolving toward (or away from) constitutional democracy and a rule of law.*

How well does law in any society express and implement the needs and/or the desires of the population?[2] That is a good question. Even a partial answer for a single well-studied society (such as the United States) is difficult.[3] Conceptual problems abound, and reality offsets the ideal no matter how that ideal is formulated.[4]

Money, organizations, and controlled media exert an influence on who is chosen to represent the public, and incumbency tends to perpetuate representatives once in office. Popular discontent with this state of affairs does sometimes lead to a reaction and marked change, but it takes a lot of discontent to disturb a political system that is well established. Before the population reaches a boiling point, irritation is siphoned off into humor. The third most frequent lie is said to be, "I'm from the government and I'm here to help you."

Studies of an established legal system can identify the pressures that lead to change. Since the American system has been so thoroughly studied from this perspective, the Syracuse Conference paid close attention to the U.S. case. In the context of the conference, several participants were asked to provide insight into the way their studies of American law could help us to understand legal change in other societies. Their observations on this subject, shared at the conference, will be published in a January 2006 issue of the *Syracuse Journal of International Law and Commerce* under the title "Law, Society, and Democracy: American Perspectives."

In addition to the papers that were America-based, many of the conference papers deal with the process of legal change in other societies. This volume of *The Annals* brings together the conference papers that focus on other societies evolving toward (or away from) constitutional democracy and a rule of law. Many of these articles suggest the dynamic forces that determine the direction of governance in the countries described.

Whether this collection will effectively lead toward viable generalizations and policy guidance remains to be seen. Much depends on developments beyond the bounds of any single scholarly effort. But when a president of the United States expresses the intention of aiding democracy in every nation, a clear need is suggested for knowledge as to how and whether such a broad commitment can be implemented. These were President George W. Bush's words:

> So it is the policy of the United States to seek and support the growth of democratic movements and institutions in every nation and culture . . .[5]

Scholarship can at best only suggest answers to the pragmatic question, "What is to be done?" But scholars can be especially helpful if they put together the pieces of the puzzle, derived from many sources. That, in effect, was intended in the design of the Syracuse Conference.

The researchers in these studies come primarily from the United States. Through intense research, they have become expert on the patterns of legal development and governmental change in societies abroad. Studies by these authors inevitably reflect their knowledge of L&S in the United States. At least implicitly, they compare what they see happening in other countries with the American legal experience. What they report and analyze helps us to understand the diversity of sociolegal systems and the divergent paths that have been followed as law develops in a wide variety of societies. Their observations express an L&S orientation, and their results tend to reinforce the idea that full understanding of law in other societies must take into account the significance of culture and society in supporting and changing their systems of law and government.

The relation of the society to the legal system can never be fully understood without a detailed, searching study of the realities in that relationship. Documents may have an influence, and that influence needs to be observed and understood. But the reality goes beyond any documents. To move beyond the documents to the social reality is an important component of the L&S agenda.

In this volume, studies of legality in different societies represent the L&S point of view. In these articles, and in the book-length studies that more fully describe these phenomena, we find a wide variety in the description of L&S systems as they exist and as they are developing. One would like to generalize from this sample of societies, but the diversity of their stories makes such generalization difficult. The more general the proposition, the greater the danger of vacuity. While cautious in this regard, the conference participants, in discussion and in writing their papers, introduced the kinds of ideas that might well enter into some sort of generalizations: things to look at, think about, and use carefully.

An important caution, deserving repeated emphasis, has to do with the relationship between the legal system and democratic governance. While law is a necessary element in democracy, it is no guarantee of it. Law can help in fostering and maintaining democracy; it can also be used to subvert and destroy democracy. The classic example of how that can occur is Nazi Germany, where Hitler used the German custom of obeying the law to support his deadly attack on disfavored minorities.

It would therefore be unwise for legal evolution to be hailed as some sort of panacea for the world's ills. Rather, we should recognize that law itself can reflect those aspects of the society that determine how law will be used. Where power and/or wealth are highly concentrated, law can be used to enforce and enhance that concentration to the point where the capacity of ordinary citizens to affect governmental policies may be destroyed. On the other hand, law can sometimes check the concentration of power and wealth, thus helping to bring about enough balance so that genuine democracy can be established and maintained.

Such issues are neither new nor newly noticed. Aristotle saw that popular rule (democracy, as he defined it) and oligarchy tended to struggle with each other as principles of governance. When the people dominated, giving every advantage to ordinary citizens and minimizing the advantages of the elite, Aristotle noted a tendency for the elite to seize power and establish an oligarchy. But when the elite used governmental power to increase their advantages too far, they provoked such discontent in the society as to precipitate a counter movement toward a democratic extreme. That ancient insight, derived from the Athenian cradle of democracy, retains validity today but with the added concern that dictators, once in control of the state, may become increasingly powerful and difficult to dislodge. Considerations of that kind, clearly envisioned by the Founders as dangers to constitutional democracy,[6] continue to present problems for a balanced system of governance.

In the American situation, our culture assumes the permanence of constitutional democracy. But even in a country that prides and advertises itself as fully democratic, there is a continuing danger that democracy can be weakened if and when elites of left or right use modern means of persuasion to create the appearance of democracy while undermining it. Aristotle might well have said, looking at the American situation, "Nothing too much." Liberty and equality can coexist as principles for organizing society, but care must be exercised to avoid either of them taking over.

Monitoring where we stand on such issues, even with as much research as we have had, is no guarantee that policy will be informed by sociolegal findings. One of the best known of all L&S articles, Marc Galanter's "Why the 'Haves' Come Out Ahead,"[7] convincingly analyzes the connection between wealth and success in court with advantages regularly going to the "repeat players." Yet attempts to balance that advantage, for instance by the development of the Legal Services Corporation (LSC), reportedly at best met about 25 percent of the legal-representation needs of indigent clients. While the LSC has lasted for many decades, its budgets have been regularly threatened and the whole operation vigorously attacked. If sociolegal research, in a country where it is vigorously pursued, has not had much of an impact on policy, why might one expect such an orientation to be useful in other countries?

When we talk about using such knowledge, I must say we are not yet at the stage where we can turn what we know into a valid basis for action. Though there is hope that it will be useful, it is clear that scholars will rarely be policy makers. Perhaps the studies described here will inform people who are, or will be, charged with operational responsibilities. Perhaps it is just as well, however, that these studies tend to be descriptive rather than evaluative. The participants brought to the conference a mixture of intentions that included value-free objectivity and civic concerns.

The Conference

Participants in the Syracuse Conference seemed to me hopeful that their studies could be turned to good account even if not directly by themselves. They reflected the idea that their work might be effective in bringing socially unacceptable behavior under legal and democratic control.

A major underlying issue was whether or how law could contribute to the control of terrorism. What we can expect is that law will be used as one method for responding to terror. In the United States, terrorist activity has led to legal sanction that was widely supported. The case of Timothy McVeigh, bomber of the federal building in Oklahoma City, illustrates how law can work to judge and condemn terrorism. McVeigh's conviction after due process of law was widely accepted as legitimate.

Whether McVeigh's conviction and execution deterred others from such behavior we do not know. General deterrence, that is, preventing others from repeating the punished behavior, continues to be a problematic issue in criminological research.[8] We do know, however, that the law tends to be invoked and socially supported when it accords with the mores. In that circumstance, the combination of social disapproval and legal sanction seems to be effective in the control of deviant behavior. By contrast, where law is clearly at odds with popular sentiment, as in the famously failed Prohibition of alcoholic beverages,[9] law is likely to become a dead letter, observed in the breach. At what point does a conflict between law and the mores render law ineffective? That important question is not likely to be definitively resolved by any of these papers.

Each contribution to the conference, however, constituted one piece of this larger puzzle. Taken together, they at least suggest that change toward democratic governance and the rule of law is not only possible but that it does in fact often occur. And the understanding of how that happens, with what results, is a subject richly deserving careful attention.

Although the Syracuse Conference covered only two days, those forty-eight hours were for me, and I think for many of the other participants, an unusually rich source of ideas. The idea of community among scholars is an important part of the search for truth. This is what science at its best can do for us. Especially in these times, when every normative assumption is subject to dispute, we need to be clear that the search for truth is always tentative.

[D]emocracy can be weakened if and when elites of left or right use modern means of persuasion to create the appearance of democracy while undermining it.

It is with that kind of attitude that we in the social sciences can hope to make our greatest contributions. The process of societal evolution cannot be foretold in advance, much as we might desire it. Given our present state of knowledge, we inevitably face what Robert K. Merton described as the unanticipated consequences of purposive social action.[10] All we can do with any degree of confidence is look to the past to sensitize ourselves to what has happened. Models of what will happen are inevitably subject to error. Does that mean we must give up forecasting? My answer is that forecasts are inevitable but that they must be done cautiously and with an awareness of their fallibility.

The Idea of Legal Evolution

Against that background, I want to explain how the term *legal evolution* was used in planning the conference. To my way of thinking, the idea of societal evolution can have real value provided it is used with two strict qualifications.

First, societal evolution cannot be predicted with certainty. Human culture is so dynamic it can change quickly, generate new conditions, and convert previously unimagined possibilities into live options. Correspondingly, it can lead to dead ends. Societies, like dinosaurs, can become extinct.

Second, whatever projections we might make as to the future, we cannot assume that what we envision, even if it did happen, will inevitably be a good thing, that is, bring about a society that would be widely welcomed as progress, something highly desirable, or an improvement over what existed before. George Orwell put that case strongly in *Animal Farm*[11] and cogently in *1984*.[12] Isaiah Berlin, another British wise man, warned repeatedly of the dangers of projections that would generate the opposite of what its well-meaning advocates predicted.[13]

If, then, evolutionary thinking about human societies cannot predict with certainty or tell in advance that what will happen will accord with decent human values, how might evolution be a useful tool for analyzing social change? In preparing for the conference, I was strongly advised by three people to drop the concept of evolution. Two of them had given me good advice throughout the planning process, for which I shall ever be grateful. Malcolm Feeley urged me to drop the term entirely, and Robert Post suggested that I use it if at all only as a metaphor. A third participant, Larry Rosen, spelled out in detail why he objected to the use of the term.

I shall paraphrase the objections and try to meet them.

Q1: What are the precise mechanisms by which evolution operates in human culture and society?

A1: Societal evolution starts by variation from a sociocultural base. Survival and flourishing of the variation depends on the environment. When the variation or innovation fills a felt need, it is more likely to survive and flourish. If the environment, physical or social, is hostile to the variation, that variation may be extinguished, unless it finds a new, more favorable environment. These two terms characterize biological evolution as well as societal.

Societal evolution differs in large measure from biological evolution in the greater capacity of humans—compared with other animals—for thinking, remembering, projecting, and communicating. Those capabilities can be described as rational faculties or, in a word, reason. Reason does not repeal the significance of base and environment factors although it clearly alters both of them often quite quickly.

Q2: In proposing the use of evolutionary ideas for understanding legal change, are you suggesting that all social change is amenable to this kind of approach?

A2: Perhaps law is more amenable to an evolutionary approach than other social institutions. For one thing, legal principles in many societies (including the United States) tend to change slowly, to retain continuity, and to preserve a record of the decisions made. In evolutionary terms, the base is regularly cited in legal decisions whether or not precedents are followed. Legal change tends to be resisted and limited when it does occur. Thus, the base tends to be preserved. When legal change occurs, it is often justified in terms of change in the environment. With these characteristics in mind, it seems that law might be a distinctively favorable institution for application of evolutionary thinking.

Q3: Doesn't the use of evolution (even as a metaphor) for discussing social change bring us back to "Social Darwinism"?

A3: Social Darwinism as an ideology was used to celebrate the fittest individuals who were said to survive and flourish because of their fitness. It served to justify social practices that were indifferent or hostile to the less fit. Evolutionary models, applied to society, need not support that ideology. In legal evolution, law can be used to advantage the advantaged or to alleviate the problems of the disadvantaged.

Q4: More generally, doesn't an evolutionary model imply that whatever has evolved, or will evolve, is good?

A4: No. Societal evolution, properly applied, describes what has happened and suggests why it has happened. Judgments of good or bad depend on the values and perceptions of the observer. Projections into the future are difficult to make. But the record of past evolution may provide a basis, albeit a chancy one, for what is likely to happen in the future.

Q5: Can you cite examples of the valid use of evolution in studying legal change?

A5: There are some quite clear findings in comparative anthropological data[14] that demonstrate the relation of law as a correlate of economic development: the greater the technological complexity, the greater the likelihood of legal roles[15] (police, judges, and lawyers) being present in a given society.[16]

Q6: How can this evolutionary model apply to complex modern societies?

A6: Since World War II, many nations have adopted the forms of constitutional democracy together with a legal system, constitutionally specified, that follows the examples of European Code Law and English-American Common Law. This trend follows no single path but seems to be a powerful tendency in many nation-states.

Q7: Can one predict that this trend will continue and become increasingly pervasive?

A7: Not necessarily. But for those who favor legality as a promising way of implementing the principled composition of differences, the legal system that has evolved in complex societies might prove to be an effective way of providing a voice for ordinary citizens.[17]

My discussion of legal evolution in this context must necessarily be limited. I did want to provide some explanation of the reasons why the evolutionary idea appealed to me. I hope also that my usage does not invite others to reuse the evolutionary concept in some of the unfortunate ways it has been used in the past.

Before leaving the topic, I want to refer to two writers on this subject who differ markedly in their views on the usefulness of the evolution metaphor as applied to human affairs. Their views are succinctly stated in quotations that Larry Rosen found and sent to me:

> While the absolute types and patterns proposed by earlier evolutionists are no longer accepted by legal anthropologists in view of the diversity of social patterns in human history, the basic evolutionary principle assuming a correlation between the legal and social order of given societies has become a commonplace in social thought. . . . Logic as well as anthropological observation suggest that legal development is related to the growth of social organization. . . . In general, the sophistication of the legal system corresponds to the size and density of the population. . . . The evidence is overwhelmingly persuasive that societies at the same level in their evolution, regardless of their chronological position in history, develop laws that display remarkable similarities.—Theodore Ziolkowski[18]

> Biological evolution is a bad analogue for cultural change because the two systems are so different for three major reasons that could hardly be more fundamental. First, cultural evolution can be faster by orders of magnitude than biological change at its maximum

Darwinian rate and questions of timing are of the essence in evolutionary arguments. Second, cultural evolution is direct and Lamarckian in form: The achievements of one generation are passed by education and publication directly to the descendants, thus producing the great potential speed of cultural change. . . . Third, the basic typologies of biological and cultural change are completely different. Biological evolution is a system of constant divergence without subsequent joining of branches. Lineages, once distinct, are separate forever. In human history, transmission across lineages is, perhaps, the major source of cultural change.—Stephen Jay Gould[19]

Gould's view, given his mastery of evolutionary theory and of biological data, must be daunting to those of us who would apply the evolutionary metaphor to human culture. Gould was a prodigious scholar, whose works I have not begun to master. Still, he may have given some reason to question the position quoted above.

In a book posthumously published called *The Hedgehog, the Fox, and the Magister's Pox*,[20] Gould argues—in opposition to Edward O. Wilson—that different processes emerge as systems become more complex. Still, Gould recognizes that more complex phenomena should take into account that which can be observed at a more fundamental level. Chemistry does not repeal the laws of physics; it acknowledges them and uses them to understand chemical interactions. But inevitably at the more complex level, new phenomena occur that must be taken into account if chemical reactions are to be fully understood.

I think that social dynamics can build on a theory derived from biological evolutionary studies. Those who declare otherwise may be right, but they cannot be proven right. To my knowledge, social science theory can derive from any source and use any metaphor, as long as it develops ways of investigating empirically the phenomenon in question. And these methods, as Karl Popper pointed out, must always be phrased in such a way as to meet the test of falsifiability.[21] Only when the metaphor of societal evolution generates testable predictions will disconfirmation of its predictions provide a test of the theory's plausibility.

Micro-Macro Questions

This introduction is hardly the place or space for developing theory at any length. Leaving that task for others, and hopefully for work I might do in the future, I do want to allude to a couple of concepts that were built into the conference and that are dealt with in many of the papers prepared for the conference. They stem directly from the fundamental idea of democracy. From its origins, sociology of law has insisted on the important part played by the mores, or very strongly held norms, in determining the content of law.

At the present as well as at any other time, the center of gravity of legal development lies not in legislation, nor in juristic science, nor in judicial decision, but in the society itself.—Eugen Ehrlich[22]

Where the gap between mores and law is very great, law is subject to strain. It can adapt by becoming dead letter, or by using force to demand compliance.

The significance of this tension has been emphasized by the first writer quoted above, Theodore Ziolkowski. As a template, Ziolkowski uses the story of Antigone so powerfully dramatized by Sophocles. In defying Creon, the head of state, Antigone insists that her brother receive a decent burial. Ziolkowski uses that story to begin his analysis of a vast range of literature. Antigone is portrayed not only as one who speaks truth to power but also as a representative of a higher moral code, a natural law that pits morality against Creon's man-made decree. Ziolkowski follows this theme through the centuries, as it appears over and over again in literature. His treatment is insightful and impressive.[23]

Where the gap between mores and law is very great, law is subject to strain.

If we use Ziolkowski's work as a starting point, it leads us to notice a crucial tension—the potential and often experienced bind between law and the mores. Not at all inconsistent with the L&S approach, this use of literature increases our feel for the human emotions that are invoked by such conflicts. The literature he cites, from Sophocles to Kafka, reminds us of the emotional tension that moves human beings who are seized with the emotions of belief in the right. What happens when the tension between moral belief and law reaches the breaking point?

Recognizing the power of such a tension, analysts of L&S should find additional motivation for identifying the nature and sources of strongly held empirical and normative beliefs. If social stability requires some degree of compatibility between mores and laws, a major task is to identify the nature and origins of these strongly held beliefs, at both the individual, organizational, and societal level.

In the contemporary world, these strongly held views are often associated with the nation. As Philip Bobbitt points out in his book *The Shield of Achilles*,[24] the nation has become a powerful cultural unit bringing people together in many ways and in many circumstances. Bobbitt, another participant in the Syracuse Conference, traces the development of nations in the West from the period of formation of states following the collapse of the Holy Roman Empire. With the Treaty of Westphalia that ended the Thirty Years War, states adopted the principle of religious toleration. Bobbitt's way of describing the historic process is by using the phrase state-nation as a unit that in general preceded the nation-state. His analysis suggests that states tend to come first and that in giving security, rights, and duties to their citizens, the state contributes to the unity and affective attraction that manifests itself ultimately as an emotional commitment to the nation. Thus, the state-nation, as he puts it, changes into the nation-state, in which national unity supports the state.

Assuming that states will continue to act as the international organizational units, it does seem likely as Bobbitt suggests that no nation-state can, acting alone, provide its citizens with the security and benefits that might have been possible in the past. He therefore speculates on the patterns, which he calls "scenarios," of possible developments in the globalizing world that would affect the way nations relate to each other. In particular, he pays special attention to the economic relations between states suggesting that several patterns could emerge to characterize the relations between nation-states on the world scene.

Whatever patterns emerge, law is likely to be called on to play a part both domestically within the state and internationally. The culture will inevitably include tensions between groups, of the kind found in well-developed nation-states and in those states that struggle to stay together against powerful centrifugal forces. The more we can learn about such tensions, the better the chance that they can be dealt with in a way that preserves a level of civility and a sense of justice.

We can see illustrations of tensions like these in every part of the world. Law is sometimes called on to manage such differences. Recent examples that have riven states are numerous. The severity of such conflicts can be extremely severe and fatal to some of the population groups involved. One need only mention names like Srebrenica, Rwanda, East Timor, Palestine, and Iraq to illustrate the lethal effects of ethnic hostility.

In many of these situations, people struggle with conflicting loyalties. Tribal and religious loyalties play a major part, taking precedence over loyalty to the nation-state. The concept of democracy calls for freedom of the public to choose leaders. Bringing people of diverse background together as citizens of a state does not swiftly or inevitably bring them together as citizens of a nation. In the absence or relative weakness of a sense of citizenship, the state may be subject to internecine conflict, and law may prove powerless or counterproductive in addressing the problem. The Civil War in the United States demonstrated how costly such a division can be to the population, with residues that last for a century and beyond.

Peaceful solutions to such tensions, such as Vaclav Havel's acceptance of the division of Czechoslovakia into two states, are rare. Much more typical are the kind of conflicts that we see between Spain and the Basques, Nigeria and Biafra, Saddam's Iraq and the Kurds. Such conflicts can sometimes be alleviated by peacemakers within the state, and sometimes they are resolved only after long and violent struggle.

Is there a role for law in preventing or allaying conflicts of this kind? Potentially, but not dependably. A legal system within a society can play a part by enhancing minority rights according to principles and procedures that are widely accepted as legitimate. The United States, for example, has had substantial success in dealing with racial inequality through law and the civil rights movement. Perhaps in that example, the two elements, law and society, were both essential as they interacted toward a common goal.

International pressures might also have a positive effect in furthering the democratic principle and limiting the centrifugal power of divisive loyalties. The case of South Africa provides a striking example of the role of the community of nations. Invocation of the boycott provided one of the important factors in the success of the African National Congress. But the effect of the boycott interacted with domestic developments in South Africa in which legal and newly invented quasi-legal procedures for peace and reconciliation played an important part, one described by James Gibson in an article in this collection.

The analysis of such cases can contribute to our understanding of how, when, and in what ways law can play a constructive role in allaying conflict and strengthening democratic governance. We have not yet found a general theory or methodology for analyzing such matters. But if law is to play a constructive role, it must be aided by the kind of insight that can come from social science research into the roots of this kind of intrastate conflict. The rule of law can play a part in such situations, especially I would say if it can benefit from the kind of sociolegal research that tracks the interrelationship between law and society.

In the articles in this volume of *The Annals,* there are many insights into these problems. I do not propose to foreshadow them but leave it to you, the reader, to discover them. I have found these articles replete with information and insight, and I trust you will have the same experience. I do propose in a brief closing note to give a few examples of ideas and findings that have stimulated and gratified me as a listener and as a reader.

Thank you for your attention so far, and I do hope that you will enjoy the reading materials before you.

Notes

1. Marc Galanter, "Notes on the Future of Social Research in Law," in *Law and the Behavioral Sciences,* 2nd ed., ed. L. Friedman and S. Macaulay (Indianapolis, IN: Bobbs-Merrill, 1977), 18-20.

2. Michael Ignatieff, *The Needs of Strangers* (New York: Chatto & Windus, 1984).

3. Daniel Yankelovich, *Coming to Public Judgment: Making Democracy Work in a Complex World* (Syracuse, NY: Syracuse University Press, 1991).

4. Patricia Ewick and Susan Silbey, *The Common Place of Law: Stories from Everyday Life* (Chicago: University of Chicago Press, 1998).

5. George W. Bush's Second Inaugural Address, January 20, 2005. 55th Inaugural Ceremony.

6. See, in particular, Federalist no. 10, in James Madison, *Federalist Papers* (New York: Penguin Putnam, 1987 [first published 1788]).

7. Marc Galanter, "Why the 'Haves' Come Out Ahead: Speculations on the Limits of Legal Change," *Law and Society Review* 9 (1974): 95-160.

8. Hugo Adam Bedau, *Death Is Different: Studies in the Morality, Law, and Politics of Capital Punishment* (Boston: Northeastern University Press, 1987). See M. Radelet and R. Akers, "Deterrence and the Death Penalty: The Views of the Experts," *Journal of Criminal Law & Criminology* 87 (1996): 1-16. See also Austin Sarat, *When the State Kills: Capital Punishment and the American Condition* (Princeton, NJ: Princeton University Press, 2002).

9. Joseph Gusfield, *Symbolic Crusade: Status Politics and the American Temperance Movement,* 2nd ed. (Urbana: University of Illinois Press, 1986).

10. Robert K. Merton, *Social Theory and Social Structure* (Glencoe, IL: Free Press, 1957).

11. George Orwell, *Animal Farm* (New York: Harcourt, Brace and Company, 1946).

12. George Orwell, *1984* (New York: Harcourt, Brace and Company, 1949).

13. Isaiah Berlin, "History and Theory: The Concept of Scientific History," *History and Theory* 1, no. 1 (1960): 1-31.

14. Robert Carneiro, *Evolutionism in Cultural Anthropology: A Critical History* (Boulder, CO: Westview, 2003).

15. H. Wimberly, "Legal Evolution: One Further Step," *American Journal of Sociology* 79 (1973): 78-83.

16. Richard D. Schwartz and James C. Miller, "Legal Evolution and Societal Complexity," *American Journal of Sociology* 70 (July 1965): 159-69.

17. Albert O. Hirschman, *Exit, Voice, and Loyalty* (Cambridge, MA: Harvard University Press, 1977).

18. Theodore Ziolkowski, *The Mirror of Justice: Literary Reflections of Legal Crises* (Princeton, NJ: Princeton University Press, 1997), 9-10.

19. Stephen Jay Gould, *Bully for Brontosaurus* (New York: Norton, 1991), 63-65.

20. Steven Jay Gould, *The Hedgehog, the Fox, and the Magister's Pox, Mending the Gap between the Science and the Humanities* (New York: Harmony Books, 2003).

21. Karl Popper, *Logic of Scientific Discovery* (New York: Basic Books, 1959).

22. Eugen Ehrlich, *Fundamental Principles of the Sociology of Law* (Cambridge, MA: Harvard University Press, 1936).

23. Ziolkowski, *The Mirror of Justice*.

24. Philip Bobbitt, *The Shield of Achilles: War, Peace, and the Course of History* (New York: Knopf, 2002).

The Rule of Law: What Is It?

Democracy and Equality

By
ROBERT POST

If democracy is defined as the form of government dedicated to the realization of the values of self-determination, democracy bears a complex relationship to equality. Democracy requires equality of democratic agency, which is different from the forms of equality that flow from the values of distributive justice or fairness. Indeed, insofar as the forms of equality demanded by distributive justice are defined by reference to philosophic reason, rather than by reference to democratic self-determination, there is an intrinsic tension between democracy and distributive justice. This tension is reflected in the common conflict between rights and legislative competence. But insofar as violations of the equality required by distributive justice impair democratic legitimacy, democracy requires that these violations be rectified. Changing conceptions of distributive justice may thus fundamentally alter the preconditions of democratic legitimacy.

Keywords: democracy; equality; collective decision making; freedom of expression; autonomy; public discourse; justice; legitimacy

I n this article, I shall discuss the relationship between democracy and equality. Consideration of this topic is made difficult because "democracy" is such a notoriously vague and encompassing term. It is often used as an elastic synonym for good government, stretching to include whatever is desirable in a state. Understood in this way, of course, the idea of democracy loses specific content and analytic bite. If democracy means merely good and desirable government, we need not discuss democracy at all but only the forms of equality that ought to characterize a modern state.

Robert Post is David Boies Professor of Law at Yale Law School. He has written or edited several books, including Law and the Order of Culture *(ed.), 1991;* Constitutional Domains, *1995;* Censorship and Silencing *(ed.), 1998;* Race and Representation *(ed. with M. Rogin), 1998;* Human Rights in Political Transitions *(with C. Hesse), 1999;* Prejudicial Appearances *(with K. Appiah, J. Butler, T. Grey, and R. Siegel), 2001; and* Civil Society and Government *(ed. with N. Rosenblum), 2002. An earlier version of this article appeared in* Law, Culture and the Humanities *1:142-53, (May 2005).*

DOI: 10.1177/0002716205282954

In this article, I shall take a very different path. I shall closely examine the meaning of democracy, and, having fixed a definition, I shall discuss the logical and practical connections between this definition and various forms of equality. I begin with what I take to be the unobjectionable premise that democracy refers to "the distinction between autonomy and heteronomy: Democratic forms of government are those in which the laws are made by the same people to whom they apply (and for that reason they are autonomous norms), while in autocratic forms of government the law-makers are different from those to whom the laws are addressed (and are therefore heteronomous norms)" (Bobbio 1989, 137). The question I shall address is the relationship between autonomous forms of government and equality.

I

What does it mean for a form of government to be autonomous? Democracy is not the same thing as popular sovereignty, a state of affairs in which the people exercise ultimate control over their government. Popular sovereignty is compatible with forms of popular fascism in which a dictator carries the genuine and spontaneous approval of an entire people.[1] Nor is democracy identical to majoritarianism, in which a majority of the people exercise control over their government.[2] Although it is frequently said "any distinct restraint on majority power, such as a principle of freedom of speech, is by its nature anti-democratic, anti-majoritarian" (Schauer 1982, 40-41), a majority of the electorate can implement rules that are plainly inconsistent with democracy, as for example by voting a monarchy into office. These examples suggest that popular sovereignty and majoritarianism may be intimately associated with the practice of democracy, but they themselves do not define democracy. That is why it is not unintelligible to conclude that particular exercises of popular sovereignty or majoritarianism are antidemocratic.

Democracy is distinct from popular sovereignty and majoritarianism because democracy is a normative idea that refers to substantive political values (Michelman 1998), whereas popular sovereignty and majoritarianism are descriptive terms that refer to particular decision-making procedures. Implicit in the idea of democracy are the values that allow us to determine whether in specific circumstances particular decision-making procedures are actually democratic. Governments, for example, do not become democratic merely because they hold elections in which majorities govern. Such elections are currently held in North Korea. To know whether these elections make North Korea democratic requires an inquiry into whether these elections are implemented in a way that serves democratic values. It is a grave mistake to confuse democracy with particular decision-making procedures and to fail to identify the core values that democracy as a form of government seeks to instantiate.

The values of autonomy are essential to democracy. In the context of government, these values are associated with the practice of self-determination (Kelsen

1961, 284-86). We must ask, therefore, what it means for a people to engage in the practice of self-determination. This practice is often interpreted to mean that a people be made ultimately responsible for governmental decisions, either by making such decisions directly or by electing those who do (Meiklejohn 1948). But in my view this is an insufficient account of the practice of self-government. For reasons that I shall explain, I think it preferable to say that the practice of self-government requires that a people have the warranted conviction that they are engaged in the process of governing themselves.[3] The distinction is crucial, for it emphasizes the difference between making particular decisions and recognizing particular decisions as one's own. Self-government is about the authorship of decisions, not about the making of decisions.

It is a grave mistake to confuse democracy with particular decision-making procedures and to fail to identify the core values that democracy as a form of government seeks to instantiate.

We can test this distinction by imagining a situation in which the people in their collective capacity decide issues but in which individuals within the collectivity feel hopelessly alienated from these decisions. Suppose, for example, that in State X citizens are provided with interactive computer terminals that they are required to use in the morning to register their preferences about various issues. Each morning, an agenda for decision (composed by an elected assembly) is presented on the terminal. The citizens of State X must decide what color clothes should be worn, what menu should be served for lunch and dinner, the boundaries of the attendance zones for the neighborhood school, whether a stop sign should be placed at a local intersection, and so on. Assume that citizens of State X can get from their computer whatever information they believe is relevant for their votes, including information about the likely views of other citizens.

Imagine, further, that State X has no public discourse. There are neither newspapers nor broadcast media. The state bans political parties and associations. It proscribes public demonstrations and prohibits individuals from publishing their views to other citizens. Each citizen must make up his or her mind in isolation. Decisions in State X, however, are made on the basis of the majority vote of the collectivity, and all individuals are henceforth required to comply: to wear blue, or to serve chicken for lunch, or to attend a particular school, or to stop at the local intersection. Individuals in State X feel completely alienated from these decisions. They do not identify with them and instead feel controlled and manipulated by the external force of the collectivity.

Would we deem State X an example of a society that engages in self-determination? Although in State X the people retain their ability, "as a collectivity, to decide their own fate" (Fiss 1996, 37-38), which is to say to make decisions by majority rule, I very much doubt that we would characterize State X as a democracy. We are much more likely to condemn it as a dystopian tyranny. Rousseau long ago diagnosed the reason for this condemnation: collective decision making is merely oppressive unless there is some internal connection between the particular wills of individual citizens and the general will of the collectivity (Rousseau 1968, 58-62).[4]

Of course, it is implausible to claim, as Rousseau might be thought to claim, that there can exist a complete identity between the particular wills of individual citizens and the general will of the democratic state. It is enough that individual citizens can recognize in that general will the potentiality of their own authorship (Post 1993b). When this occurs, collective decision making is democratic because it is experienced as self-determination. But when citizens feel alienated from the general will, or from the process by which the general will is created, voting on issues is merely a mechanism for decision making, a mechanism that can easily turn oppressive and undemocratic.

It follows that the value of democracy can be fulfilled only if there is a continual mediation between collective self-determination and the individual self-determination of particular citizens.[5] If democracy requires that citizens experience their government as their own, as representing them, they must experience the state as in some way responsive to their own values and ideas. How is this theoretically possible under modern conditions of diversity, when the citizens of a state are heterogeneous and disagree with each other? The focus of analysis must shift from specific state decisions to the process by which these decisions are authorized. Citizens must experience that process as responsive to their own values and ideas.

This is the theory of the American First Amendment, which rests on the idea that if citizens are free to participate in the formation of public opinion, and if the decisions of the state are made responsive to public opinion, citizens will be able to experience their government as their own, even if they hold diverse views and otherwise disagree. That is why the First Amendment, which is antimajoritarian, is nevertheless regarded as "the guardian of our democracy."[6] Han Kelsen (1961), speaking of democracy rather than of the First Amendment, put the matter this way:

> A subject is politically free insofar as his individual will is in harmony with the "collective" (or "general") will expressed in the social order. Such harmony of the "collective" and the individual will is guaranteed only if the social order is created by the individuals whose behavior it regulates. Social order means determination of the will of the individual. Political freedom, that is, freedom under social order, is self-determination of the individual by participating in the creation of the social order. . . .

The will of the community, in a democracy, is always created through a running discussion between majority and minority, through free consideration of arguments for and against a certain regulation of a subject matter. This discussion takes place not only in parliament, but also, and foremost, at political meetings, in newspapers, books, and other vehicles of public opinion. A democracy without public opinion is a contradiction in terms. (Pp. 285-88)

The First Amendment protects the communicative processes by which the American people work toward an "agreement" that is "uncoerced, and reached by citizens in ways consistent with their being viewed as free and equal persons" (Rawls 1985, 229-30). Of course, under conditions of modern hetereogeneity, actual agreement is impossible, so the notion of agreement functions merely as a "regulative idea" (Findlay 1981, 241) for the formation of public opinion. If we use the term *public discourse* to refer to the communicative processes by which public opinion is formed, we can say that public discourse continuously but unsuccessfully strives to mediate between individual and collective self-determination to produce "a common will, communicatively shaped and discursively clarified in the political public sphere" (Habermas 1987, 81).

In a modern democracy, therefore, citizens are free to engage in public discourse to make the state responsive to their ideas and values, in the hope that even if the state acts in ways inconsistent with those ideas and values, citizens can nevertheless maintain their identification with the state. There is much about the constitutional law of freedom of expression that follows from this formulation, but for present purposes I shall emphasize only that modern democracies on this account must regard their citizens, insofar as they engage in public discourse, as equal and autonomous persons. That is why Jean Piaget (1965, 362-63) was profoundly correct to observe that "the essence of democracy resides in its attitude toward law as a product of the collective will, and not as something emanating from a transcendent will or from the authority established by divine right. It is therefore the essence of democracy to replace the unilateral respect of authority by the mutual respect of autonomous wills."

II

We are now in a position to deduce our first postulate about the relationship between democracy and equality. Democracy requires that persons be treated equally insofar as they are autonomous participants in the process of self-government. This form of equality is foundational to democracy because it follows from the very definition of democracy. Democracy requires an equality of democratic agency.

Democracy continuously strives to reconcile the self-determination of individual citizens with the self-government of the state. This means that democracy must regard each citizen as an autonomous, self-determining person, at least insofar as is relevant to maintaining a live identification with the self-government of the state.

Every citizen is equal in this regard. To the extent that the state treats citizens unequally in a relevant manner, say by allowing some citizens greater freedom of participation in public discourse than others, the state becomes heteronomous with respect to those citizens who are treated unequally. The state thereby loses its claim to democratic legitimacy with respect to those citizens. It follows that every citizen in a democracy is entitled to be treated equally in regard to the forms of conduct that constitute autonomous democratic participation.

This definition of democratic equality is of course formal and functional. Its precise content must be established by specifying the forms of democratic participation. These forms are given to us socially and historically, and different forms will imply different forms of democratic equality. For example, equality in the context of voting will be different than equality in the context of public discourse. Voting to select national or statewide officials is understood to be a method through which citizens participate in the choice of their leaders. Because all citizens are affected by this choice, we recognize citizens' equality of agency by the principle of "one person, one vote." The principle signifies that each citizen is to be regarded as formally equal to every other in the influence that their agency can contribute to public decisions.

The purpose of communication within public discourse, by contrast, is not to make decisions but to empower citizens to participate in public opinion in ways that will permit them to believe that public opinion will become potentially responsive to their views. Whereas equality in voting is measured in terms of equality of influence on ultimate decisions, equality of participation in public discourse cannot be measured in this way. Because influence in public debate is a matter of persuading others to one's point of view, the state can equalize influence on public debate only if it controls the intimate and independent processes by which citizens evaluate the ideas of others. Such efforts are intrinsically undesirable when performed by the state, both because ideas are not equal—the very structure of public debate rests on the premise of distinguishing good ideas from bad ideas—and because any such governmental efforts likely would verge on the tyrannical.

For these reasons, equality of agency in the context of public discourse is measured by guaranteeing each citizen the right to express himself in public discourse in a manner that will allow him to believe that public opinion will be responsive to his agency. This function cannot be achieved by offering each citizen the identical quantity of expression because a citizen may well deem a given quantity of expression as inadequate to her communicative needs and hence become alienated from public opinion, even if that quantity is equal in amount to that given to every other citizen. For this reason, the First Amendment characteristically permits persons to speak in the ways, manner, and circumstances of their choosing. The First Amendment rests on the hope that when persons are free to speak in ways that they believe are adequate to their meaning and conviction, they can come to feel that they have been given the opportunity to affect public opinion and hence can maintain an identification with a state that is responsive to public opinion. If the state too closely regulates when and how a person may speak, speech may lose its ability to mediate between individual and collective self-determination. In the context of public discourse, therefore, the relevant equality of agency inheres in the liberty to express oneself in the manner of one's choice.

There is sometimes tension between speech as an instrument of individual self-determination and speech as an instrument of collective self-determination. In the context of election campaigns, for example, there have been frequent calls for regulation of public discourse. Consider the following:

1. The speech of candidates is to be restricted on the ground that the population as a whole has come to view elections as illegitimate because some candidates are so wealthy that their speech is vastly more prominent that that of other candidates. Speech restrictions are justified on the "democratic legitimacy" principle.
2. The speech of candidates is to be restricted on the ground that all candidates should have equal access to the electorate, and some candidates are so wealthy that their speech is vastly more prominent than that of other candidates. Speech restrictions are justified on a "fairness" principle, which holds that each candidate should be allocated the "same" amount of speech as every other, so that no candidate can "drown out" the speech of her competitors.

Scenario 1 points to a genuine dilemma within democratic theory because it postulates conditions in which speech that serves the purposes of individual autonomy has compromised the ability of public discourse to serve as a medium of collective self-determination. If personal autonomy is restricted by censoring the speech of individual candidates, democratic legitimacy is lost with respect to those candidates. Yet the unrestricted exercise of individual autonomy will undermine the capacity of public discourse to serve its larger function of mediating between individual and collective autonomy for the remainder of the population. The state will compromise democratic values either by regulating or by not regulating. Although scenario 1 seems to postulate a question of the relationship between democracy and equality, it actually poses the question of how, within the terms of democratic theory, the purposes of self-government may best be served.

III

In this regard, scenario 1 sharply contrasts to scenario 2. In scenario 2, the speech of candidates is regulated on the grounds of a "fairness" principle that does not derive from the logic of democratic legitimacy but instead from an independent notion of "equality" as between candidates.[7] If in scenario 2 inequality among the candidates has not caused a delegitimation of the election process, censorship under scenario 2 would compromise the autonomy of candidates without a corresponding gain in collective autonomy. The concept of equality at issue in scenario 2 may therefore be in tension with the purposes of democratic legitimacy, which requires that candidates be accorded the equality to act autonomously, not the equality associated with equal amounts of speech (Post 1997, 1534-38).

This conclusion is quite powerful, for it suggests that many forms of equality associated with notions of distributive justice or fairness might actually be inconsistent with democracy. This inconsistency occurs whenever the demands of distributive justice compromise the autonomous participation of persons within democratic self-government, which is necessarily presupposed by the project of autonomous self-determination. From the perspective of the egalitarian principles that underlie distributive justice, the requirements of autonomous self-determination can come to seem regressive and libertarian. The equality required by democracy, which is an equality of autonomous self-determination, can easily be experienced as thin and formal, in contrast to the robust forms of substantive equality typically associated with theories of distributive justice.

The tension between equality and liberty that currently characterizes First Amendment jurisprudence is typically located at the boundary between an idea of equality that focuses on the equality of agency, and an idea of equality that focuses on distributive justice or fairness. Consider, for example, these two scenarios:

3. The speech of citizen A, which consists of fighting words, alienates all other citizens from participating in public discourse.
4. The speech of citizen A, which consists of racist speech, alienates citizens in group B from participating in public discourse.

In scenario 3, state censorship of citizen A, which will alienate A from public discourse and therefore sever A from the possibility of experiencing democratic legitimacy, is justified in terms of protecting public discourse. Whether and how such censorship can be justified as consistent with democracy is a question that must be settled entirely with the logic of democratic legitimacy.

In scenario 4, by contrast, state suppression of the speech of citizen A is justified in terms of protecting the access to public discourse of group B, rather than in terms of the requirements of public discourse itself. Scenario 4 is typical of the tension within First Amendment jurisprudence that characterizes controversies like the regulation of hate speech, which was involved in the infamous march of Nazis through Skokie, or in the suppression of pornography, which is said to subordinate women. In scenario 4, the potential loss of democratic legitimacy to A in suppressing his speech must be weighed against the potential loss of democratic legitimacy to group B in failing to suppress the speech.

This balance can perhaps be struck within the logic of democratic legitimacy, as in scenario 3. But it is commonly said that the balance ought to be struck by taking account of the substantive claims for equality that group B may be thought to press. This is especially true if group B is otherwise subordinated or oppressed.[8] To the extent that the balance is struck in this way, and to the extent that this resolution of the question produces results that are different than would be reached were the question to be resolved solely within the logic of democratic legitimacy, the claims of substantive equality are in tension with democracy.

Much depends, therefore, on our understanding of the logic of democratic legitimacy. This logic requires that citizens be treated equally with respect to the requirements of autonomous participation in the practice of self-government. The nature of these requirements will depend upon our precise account of the prerequisites of autonomous agency. So, for example, Amartya Sen is famously associated with "the capability approach" (Sen 1993, 43), which argues that each person should be endowed with a certain set of capabilities that correspond to "his or her actual ability to achieve various valuable functionings as a part of living."[9] Sen is notably, and perhaps intentionally, ambiguous as to whether the set of capabilities to be accorded to each person are to be measured by the criteria of "justice as fairness,"[10] or instead by the criteria of "autonomy" (Sen 1982, 24).[11] Understood in the latter sense, democracy may require equal distribution of the capability set required for autonomous personhood; understood in the former sense, democracy may be in tension with equal distribution of the capability set required by distributive justice.

IV

The association of democracy with the equality principles of distributive justice is widespread and common. I recently addressed a conference in Mexico, for example, where the question for discussion was, "Does democracy require a broader egalitarian notion that levels all social, cultural, and economic differences inconsistent with the moral equality of all citizens?" This framing of the issue plainly focuses on the relationship between democracy and strong substantive egalitarian principles. I have so far argued, however, that democracy presupposes a different kind of equality, an equality measured in terms of the autonomous agency required by democratic legitimacy. And I have also argued that the egalitarian principles of distributive justice or fairness can in particular circumstances be in tension with democracy.

This conclusion will no doubt be controversial because it is generally thought that implicit within the idea of democracy is a notion of strong substantive equality that flows from the moral equality of citizens.[12] But if democracy is understood, as I have argued, to rest fundamentally on a commitment to collective self-determination, it requires only those forms of equal citizenship that are necessary for the project of collective self-determination to succeed. And, as we have noted, many forms of equality can actually interfere with the individual liberty required by this project. At root, a deep theoretical tension exists between democracy and various notions of distributive justice that seek to protect the moral equality of citizens. Insofar as democracy is a form of government committed to self-determination, democracy must also encompass self-determination about the meaning of the moral equality of citizens.[13]

What counts as "moral equality" will no doubt be controversial, and a democracy will settle these controversies by reference to the self-determination of its citizens. A democracy will decide the meaning of moral equality in the context of public discussion and debate. Advocates of strong egalitarian principles have typically regarded such debate as offering inadequate protection for distributive justice because they believe that the judgment of citizens may be distorted due to the influence of prejudice and bias.[14] They have consequently used the idea of rights precisely to cabin the exercise of self-determination. The substance of these rights is characteristically determined by reference to various forms of philosophical reason. This reason can be in tension with, and deeply antithetical to, the political determinations of democratic legitimacy.

Democracy continuously strives to reconcile the self-determination of individual citizens with the self-government of the state.

It is not the case, however, that democracy and strong egalitarian principles must necessarily be in opposition to each other. Strong egalitarian principles may, in particular circumstances, have significant democracy-reinforcing effects. Democracy requires that persons identify with the state, even if they disagree with the particular decisions of the state. Although free participation within public discourse is a *necessary* condition for this identification, it is far from a *sufficient* condition. Imagine for example a group of citizens who are free to speak and to participate within the sphere of public opinion, but who are nevertheless destitute, marginalized, stigmatized, and subordinated. These citizens are unlikely to identify with the state in the manner required by democratic legitimacy. The unequal treatment of these citizens may well lead to their alienation. In such a case, the maintenance of democratic legitimacy would require that this alienation be ameliorated, which may entail remediating the alienating conditions of inequality.

What follows from this reasoning is not that democracy includes within it commitments to strong egalitarian principles but rather that the systematic violation of these principles may sometimes lead to the failure of democratic legitimacy. The distinction is significant because whereas democracy affirmatively requires that citizens be treated as equal with regard to the dimensions of their autonomous agency relevant for democratic legitimation, it contains no such requirement with regard to other inequalities. Democracy requires only that inequities that undermine democratic legitimacy be ameliorated. It does not require this for reasons of fairness or distributive justice, or because of any philosophic commitments that stand outside of democratic debate and decision making, but simply because such inequities undermine democratic legitimacy (Post 1998, 22-24; 2004). Democracy does not require the full rectification of these inequities, but only the rectification necessary to maintain democratic legitimacy.

The unsettling implication of this reasoning is that democracy is quite compatible with important forms of status subordination, as long as these forms of subordination are not experienced by citizens as alienating. At a time when the disempowering of women was accepted as natural and just, for example, democracy did not require that this terrible form of subordination be ended.[15] But as soon as this injustice functioned to alienate citizens from their government, democracy-based arguments became available to maintain that this disempowerment was incompatible with democratic legitimacy and was therefore to be ameliorated in the name of democracy.

This example suggests that strong egalitarian principles can establish a dynamic and dialectical relationship to democracy. As these principles become politically salient, as they make inequities visible and oppressive, as they prompt citizens to experience these inequities as alienating, they prepare the way for the eventual emergence of democracy-based arguments for the amelioration of these inequities. There is thus an intimate relationship between democracy and strong egalitarian principles. Democracy does not itself entail these principles but is itself substantially affected by them because it must perennially reckon with the threats to democratic legitimacy generated by these principles. Democracy is in this sense tightly connected to egalitarian commitments.

We should not forget, however, that egalitarian commitments can also endanger the autonomy necessary for the practice of self-government. Democracy and equality are thus bound in an indissoluble knot, mutually reinforcing and mutually antagonistic.

Notes

1. On the distinction between democracy and popular sovereignty, see Post (1998a, 1998b).

2. For a contrasting viewpoint, see Dahl (1957, 67).

3. The concept of a "warranted conviction" is meant to signify that a subjective conviction of self-government is not a determinative and preclusive condition for the realization of democratic values. The conviction must withstand scrutiny, which means that it is always open to third parties to attempt to convince a citizen that his or her experience of self-government is delusory.

4. Ironically, Rousseau seemingly contemplated that the general will would be formed through just such an alienated process as I have sketched. "From the deliberations of a people properly informed, and provided its members do not have any communication among themselves, the great number of small differences will always produce a general will and the decision will always be good" (Rousseau 1968, 73). This suggests that Rousseau may have had a finer grasp of the analytic prerequisites of democracy than of the sociological dynamics necessary for its realization.

5. I have elsewhere argued that "the essential problematic of democracy . . . lies in the reconciliation of individual and collective autonomy" (Post 1995, 7). For a full discussion, see Post (1993a, 178-79).

6. *Brown v. Hartlage*, 456 U.S. 45, 60 (1982).

7. For a particularly clear statement of this notion, see, e.g., *Harper v. Canada* (Attorney General), 2004 SCC 34, at § 63. ("The current third party election advertising regime is Parliament's response to this Court's decision in *Libman* [v. Quebec (Attorney General), [1977] 3 S.C.R. 569]. The regime is clearly structured on the egalitarian model of elections. The overarching objective of the regime is to promote electoral fairness by creating equality in the political discourse. The regime promotes the equal dissemination of points of view by limiting the election advertising of third parties who, as this Court has recognized, are important and influential participants in the electoral process.")

8. Indeed, it is commonly claimed that the speech of A should be censored not to protect public discourse but to promote the just demands of group B for equality (Matsuda 1989, 2358).

9. Sen (1993, 30).

10. Sen (1990) developed the capabilities approach as a response to Rawls.

11. In this earlier piece, Sen (1990, 116) labeled his approach "a capability rights system." In later work, Sen (1993, 39) referred to this aspect of his theory as "well-being freedom," which refers to "a person's actual freedom to live well and be well." Sen was explicit that freedom is valuable as both an end and as a means (Drèze and Sen 2002, 1-8).

12. For example, Amy Gutman (2003, 26) wrote, "When I use the term democracy, it signifies a political commitment to the civil equality of individuals."

13. For examples, see Ackerman (1991, 26-27).

14. Ackerman (1991, 10-14); *United States v. Carolene Products Co.*, 304 U.S. 144, 152 n.4 (1938).

15. Although democracy requires that citizens who are participants in the practice of self-government be treated equally insofar as their participation is concerned, it does not itself define the set of citizens who must be deemed participants. As Ivor Jennings (1956, 56) has remarked, "The people cannot decide until someone decides who are the people." Even today, for example, children are not considered participants in the democratic process.

References

Ackerman, Bruce. 1991. *We the people: Foundations*. Cambridge, MA: Belknap.

Bobbio, Norberto. 1989. *Democracy and dictatorship: The nature and limits of state power*. Translated by Peter Kennealy. Cambridge, UK: Polity.

Dahl, Robert. 1957. *A preface to democratic theory*. Chicago: University of Chicago Press.

Drèze, Jean, and Amartya Sen. 2002. *India: Development and participation*. 2nd ed. New York: Oxford University Press.

Findlay, J. N. 1981. *Kant and the transcendental object: A hermeneutic study*. New York: Oxford University Press.

Fiss, Owen. 1996. *Liberalism divided: Freedom of speech and the many uses of state power*. Boulder, CO: Westview.

Gutman, Amy. 2003. *Identity in democracy*. Princeton, NJ: Princeton University Press.

Habermas, Jürgen. 1987. *The theory of communicative action*. Translated by Thomas McCarthy. Boston: Beacon.

Jennings, Ivor. 1956. *The approach to self-government*. Cambridge: Cambridge University Press.

Kelsen, Hans. 1961. *General theory of law and state*. Translated by Anders Wedberg. New York: Russell & Russell.

Matsuda, Mari. 1989. Public response to racist speech: Considering the victim's story. *Michigan Law Review* 87:2320-81.

Meiklejohn, Alexander. 1948. *Political freedom: The constitutional powers of the people*. New York: Harper.

Michelman, Frank I. 1998. Brennan and democracy. *California Law Review* 86:399-427.

Piaget, Jean. 1965. *The moral judgment of the child*. Translated by Marjorie Gabain. New York: Free Press.

Post, Robert. 1993a. Between democracy and community: The legal constitution of social form. In *Democratic community: Nomos XXXV*, ed. John W. Chapman and Ian Shapiro. New York: New York University Press.

———. 1993b. Meiklejohn's mistake: Individual autonomy and the reform of public discourse. *University of Colorado Law Review* 64:1109-37.

———. 1995. *Constitutional domains: Democracy, community, management*. Cambridge, MA: Harvard University Press.

———. 1997. Equality and autonomy in First Amendment jurisprudence. *Michigan Law Review* 95:1517-41.

———. 1998a. Democracy, popular sovereignty, and judicial review. *California Law Review* 86:429-43.

———. 1998b. Introduction: After *Bakke*. In *Race and representation: Affirmative action*, ed. Robert Post and Michael Rogin. New York: Zone Books.

———. 2004. Sexual harassment and the First Amendment. In *Directions in sexual harassment law*, ed. Catharine A. MacKinnon and Reva B. Siegel. New Haven, CT: Yale University Press.

Rawls, John. 1985. Justice as fairness: Political not metaphysical. *Philosophy and Public Affairs* 14:223-51.

Rousseau, Jean-Jacques. 1968. *The social contract*. Translated by Maurice Cranston. London: Penguin.

Schauer, Frederick. 1982. *Free speech: A philosophical enquiry*. New York: Cambridge University Press.

Sen, Amartya. 1982. Rights and agency. *Philosophy and Public Affairs* 11:3-39.

———. 1990. Justice: Means versus freedoms. *Philosophy and Public Affairs* 19:111-21.

———. 1993. Capability and well-being. In *The quality of life*, ed. Martha Nussbaum and Amartya Sen. New York: Clarendon.

Reflecting on the Rule of Law: Its Reciprocal Relation with Rights, Legitimacy, and Other Concepts and Institutions

Arguments concerning law and social change call for a relationship between legitimacy, the rule of law, and respect for rights. To the extent that a government is subject to the rule of law, the human and civil rights of its citizens are advanced. When citizens can bring disputes concerning rights to court rather than fight in the streets, the rule of law is enhanced. Respect for rights and the rule of law are likely to make a government more acceptable and hence more legitimate. A basic requirement of legitimacy is that government advance everyone's share of primary social goods, their opportunity to participate in society and hence their basic rights. Rights are not only statements of ideals or entitlements but goals and tools for pursuit of those goals, means for pursuing law reform, advancing the rule of law, and enhancing society's legitimacy.

Keywords: personalism; legitimacy; rights; horizons; rule of law; primary social goods

By
SAMUEL J. M. DONNELLY

Introduction

Great progress has been made in the establishment of the world rule of law since the important seventeenth-century developments in international law. Since the end of World War II we have had one of the great periods in the development of international law and the world rule of law. The development of the European Union and the progress made under the European Covenant on Human Rights has been particularly remarkable.

Samuel J. M. Donnelly is a professor of law and senior scholar of law and jurisprudence at the Syracuse University College of Law, where he has taught since 1964. He graduated from Harvard Law School in 1960, served as a clerk with the New Jersey Supreme Court in 1960-61, a teaching fellow at Harvard Law School in 1961-62, and an associate with Carter, Ledyard and Milburn 1962-64. His books include A Personalist Jurisprudence, the Next Step *(2003) and* The Language and Uses of Rights *(1994).*

NOTE: This article originally appeared in the *Syracuse Journal of International Law and Commerce* 32 (2005): 233-68 and is republished here in shortened and edited form with the permission of the *Syracuse Journal of International Law and Commerce.*

DOI: 10.1177/0002716205282054

The role of law in the process of social change is central. The great American example of law influencing social change began, of course, with the end of our Civil War, the freeing of the slaves, and continues through the establishment of segregation, the attacks upon it, desegregation, and the development of affirmative action. Another very important sequence of legal and social changes is the development and recognition of human rights in the European Union since World War II. That momentous development is worth studying from the perspective of law and social science.

In the first part of the following presentation I would like to offer some observations on those two examples of law and social change over a significant period of time. Using those two examples as illustrations I want then to reflect from a philosophical perspective on a series of concepts that I think are important in understanding the role of law in social change.

In my recent book, *A Personalist Jurisprudence, the Next Step* (Donnelly 2003), I reflected upon the interrelation between a series of concepts including the Rule of Law and its relation to legal protection of rights, the Language and Uses of Rights, Legitimacy, Primary Social Goods (a concept helpful in understanding rights), Horizons, Crossing Horizons and the use of rights to hammer on foreign horizons, or the establishment of rights across horizons, and analysis of the Point of View from which statements about rights are made. In *A Personalist Jurisprudence, the Next Step*, I discussed, among other matters, how these concepts and their interrelation can be used to understand and construct a method for judicial decision making. The same concepts can be used from the perspective or point of view of an attorney to discuss strategies for law reform. In this article, I want to offer those concepts and their interrelation from the perspective of a legal philosopher and lawyer as a possibly helpful means for analyzing the gradual establishment internationally of the rule of law accompanied by the advance of human and civil rights. These concepts may also prove helpful to social scientists as well as legal philosophers in discussing and understanding the role of law in the process of social change. Social change may also include the gradual establishment of the rule of law both within individual countries and internationally. Part of my argument is that advances in the protection of individual rights also support the developing rule of law and vice versa.

I organize that discussion around an analysis of the language and uses of rights including how rights are used in the process of social change and how the pursuit of rights relates to establishing the rule of law. What do we mean, then, by the rule of law? And how is the rule of law related to legal protection or protection by courts of individual rights? I address those questions in the second part of this article.

The third part addresses what we mean by rights. How do we discern fundamental rights and why should we recognize those rights? How do rights come to be perceived as legitimate? Primary Social Goods is a concept I have taken from John Rawls and adapted to my own understanding (Rawls 1971, 396-447).

The fourth part discusses Rights, Horizons, and Point of View Analysis. In my understanding, rights always are perceived within horizons—the limitations of human understanding and knowledge—and from a point of view. In the international sphere, one could argue that a number of controversies arise because particular rights or questions concerning the existence of rights are perceived within the horizons of different cultures. An advocate for rights may have to cross or penetrate foreign horizons to persuade persons of another culture to accept certain rights (Donnelly 2003, 254-60). The advance of rights and the rule of law may require those studying or seeking to promote law reform and social change to understand horizons and the art of crossing horizons. Because rights are always understood within a horizon and from a point of view, those promoting or studying change should strive to understand the use of rights and the language of rights as

---

Somerset v. Stewart was an important precedent that gave legitimacy to the abolition movement in the United States, England, and the British colonies.

---

tools for crossing horizons, for hammering on foreign horizons, or encouraging others to cross horizons. Rights traditionally may be understood as remedies offered by law, as conclusions drawn within a legal system, or, in more advanced theory, as reasons for decisions or reasons in the decision-making process that will trump competing reasons. From the perspective of one studying or promoting law reform, I suggest that we understand how rights are used as tools, as goals to be pursued in the law reform process, as means for achieving those goals, and as political resources. The fifth part will address the Language and Uses of Rights: Rights as Tools in the Process of Social Change.

Using the concepts developed in the previous discussion I want to reflect on what we mean by and how we use natural law and how it might contribute to understanding and advancing human rights, the rule of law, and the process of social change that may lead to their acceptance.

I comment from the perspective of a lawyer and a philosopher of law. That precisely is not the perspective of a social scientist. I would describe a social scientist as concerned with description and explanatory theory. Some explanatory theories are particularly powerful and grand. Lawyers hardly ever seek explanatory theories of the kind admired by social scientists and normally do not emphasize description as a primary task. Lawyers are concerned with decision making and persuading decision makers. Understanding law from the point of view of the decision maker is central to a lawyer's work and central to legal philosophy as practiced in the United States. To the extent that social scientists and legal philosophers provide lawyers with reflections on decision making or tools for decision making, they may be very helpful to intelligent practicing attorneys.

I take the perspective of one performing that task in the following discussion. Promoting human rights and establishing the world rule of law is a task for statesmen and lawyers as well as an academic subject to be examined from the perspective of legal philosophers and social scientists.

Law and Social Change:
Great Examples

To study the promotion of human rights and the establishment of a world rule of law, we must think about social change both worldwide and in individual countries. We must also study the role of law in social change.

Brown v. Board of Education. The legal, political, and cultural events and circumstances just prior to and following *Brown v. Board of Education of Topeka, Kansas* are a great example, studied by many social scientists, of how the interaction of law and culture results in social change.[1] Actually that sequence of legal and cultural changes began almost two centuries before that great 1954 decision of the Warren Court.

Arbitrarily, I would select 1773 and the equally great decision of King's Bench in *Somerset v. Stewart*[2] as the starting point for the falling dominos that led to the abolishment of slavery, desegregation, and affirmative action in the United States. In *Somerset*, Lord Mansfield, the chief justice, speaking for King's Bench in a habeas corpus case, freed a black slave, James Somerset, who was being held at his master's orders on a ship in the Thames for sale in Jamaica. Mansfield found the return on the writ insufficient since there were no relevant laws, cases, or statutes authorizing slavery in England. He explained that slavery was too obnoxious to be established by custom. Given the common law doctrine of precedent, Mansfield abolished slavery in England and freed fifteen or sixteen thousand slaves (Heward 1979, 144).

A short law reform campaign preceded *Somerset*, largely conducted by the London radical Granville Sharp, who had obtained the writ of habeas corpus for James Somerset from Lord Mansfield.

More significant for the study of law and social change is the gradual fall of the dominoes after *Somerset v. Stewart*. That 1773 decision before the U.S. Declaration of Independence on July 4, 1776, would be considered binding precedent in most American states. Why then did slavery not immediately fall in the United States? Mansfield's decision in *Somerset* turned on the absence of legal authorization, either statutory or case law, for slavery. A number of states, particularly in the South, had legislation regulating slavery. Nevertheless, *Somerset v. Stewart* was an important precedent that gave legitimacy to the abolition movement in the United States, England, and the British colonies.

Duncan Kennedy (1986) describes "legitimacy power" as an important element in social change through law. As our discussion proceeds we should pay some attention to the notion and uses of legitimacy power.

In England shortly after *Somerset*, Granville Sharpe began to use his newly acquired legitimacy power to attack the slave trade. Mansfield had been careful in *Somerset* to abolish slavery only in England. He distinguished it from the slave trade, which was important to the commerce of England, and did not affect it. Granville Sharpe, however, persuaded a young member of parliament (Lord Wilberforce, who ultimately became one of the great figures in the war against Napoleon) to file a bill abolishing the slave trade. That bill was filed and ignored each year for twenty years until it was finally passed and became effective in 1807, the middle of the war against Napoleon. Stopping ships to search for illegal slaves probably aided in the blockade of Napoleonic France. It has been rightly remarked that an ideal coupled with an interest is a powerful political force.

The slave trade was effectively brought to heel, if not stopped, after England and the United States agreed in the 1840s to jointly patrol the coast of Africa. At that time, England was attempting to obtain toeholds on the coast of Africa. Again, we see the power of an ideal coupled with an interest.

Between those events, the great powers of Europe agreed to the abolishment of the slave trade at the Congress of Vienna at the close of Napoleon's wars. Participation in the slave trade was thereafter added to piracy as a crime of international jurisdiction, crimes that could be prosecuted and tried by any nation. Observe the gradual social change influenced by law, which led toward the establishment of human rights and the rule of law. And note the importance of legitimacy power in that process.

The dominoes, of course, fell dramatically thereafter, first in the Caribbean and then in the American South and ultimately in Brazil. The great drama leading to the abolishment of slavery came to an end.

But then a new episode began as the American South replaced slavery with segregation through a long series of struggles culminating legally in *Plessy v. Ferguson*.[3] Following *Plessy*, a new era of law reform began, not unrelated to *Somerset v. Stewart* and the abolishment of slavery. The great law reform campaign organized by the NAACP, beginning in 1929, gradually established legitimacy power for desegregation. The work of their lawyers, however, was not the only force leading in 1954 to *Brown v. Board of Education of Topeka, Kansas*.

Arguably, the era of law that William Wiecek (1998) described as legal classicism came to an end with Franklin Roosevelt's appointments to the United States Supreme Court in the late 1930s. At the time of *Brown v. Board of Education*, many of the Roosevelt appointees were still serving on the Court. In *A Personalist Jurisprudence, the Next Step*, I describe some of the forces leading to *Brown* as follows:

> The period between 1937 and 1954 was a tumultuous time including the end of the Great Depression, the Second World War, the Holocaust, the Korean War and the beginning of the Cold War confrontation with Russia. Arguably these experiences changed our national outlook and understanding. On racial questions, the experience of Americans in the

armed forces, Truman's desegregation of the military and the shock of the Holocaust prepared our national culture for a changed position on race. Legally the demise of legal classicism and the advance of pragmatic instrumentalist thought was helpful. The great law
reform campaign conducted by lawyers for the NAACP beginning in 1929 had established
a series of useful precedent. (Donnelly 2003, 144-45)

The process of social change leading to and following from *Brown* have been the
subject of many social science studies. Controversially the *Brown* court relied on
social science studies including Gunnar Myrdal's *An American Dilemma* (1944) in
support of its decision. In contrast, the quality of the reasoning process in *Brown*
has been the subject of many competing works of legal philosophy. The quarrels
over *Brown* may be the heart of what I describe as the great modern quarrel over
method.

A legal philosopher may ponder fascinating questions such as How should Chief
Justice Warren have justified his decision in *Brown*, and is the decision justifiable?
A law reformer would find worth in examining the strategies of the NAACP and
Thurgood Marshall. A very helpful work of social science derived from the effort is
Stuart Scheingold's *The Politics of Rights* (1974). Social scientists who want to con-
tribute to the advance of human rights should follow the example of Scheingold.
Legal philosophers creating or criticizing decision making methods should strug-
gle to understand the relation between social forces and the work of decision
makers.

The Rule of Law

The English-speaking countries of the world are renowned citadels of the rule
of law. Historically, a state monopoly for the use of violence is central to the rule of
law. A state loses legitimacy if it cannot provide security for its citizens against private violence. From the time of the conquest, English kings put a strong emphasis
on the suppression and control of private violence, and people in the United States
have followed their example. In English-speaking countries, however, the rule of
law has a long-standing association with the protection of civil liberties. An interesting question is why the protection of civil liberties should be associated historically with the advance of the rule of law.

A possible answer is that in our understanding the rule of law governs those in
authority as well as members of the public. Under the rule of law, citizens should be
protected by law against their government as well as against private violence. The
courts are the traditional instrument in the English-speaking countries for securing that protection. The courts have another important role in maintaining the rule
of law. Instead of fighting in the streets, instead of resorting to private violence, disputants are encouraged to take their cases to court and abide by the result.

In *Somerset v. Stewart*, which ended slavery in England, Granville Sharp, the
London radical, served the writ of habeas corpus issued by Lord Mansfield on Captain Knowles who was holding the slave James Somerset on his ship in the Thames.

Instead of raising his sails and sailing to Jamaica, Captain Knowles appeared in court and made a response to the writ. Captain Knowles was a law-abiding ship captain (Fifoot 1936).

Because people bring their disputes to court and abide by the result, courts have power, are able to maintain the rule of law, and can advance civil liberties.

From the experience of the English-speaking countries and other parts of our world, we can develop some suggestions that are not particularly original for advancing the world rule of law.

A state loses legitimacy if it cannot provide security for its citizens against private violence.

---

1. *The Control of Private Violence:* The advance of the rule of law within a particular country depends on providing security, on effectively controlling private violence. On the world stage, the United Nations, the Security Council, or some similar institution must have the authority to authorize the international use of violence by one country against another. International violence without authorization should become illegal. International law is moving in that direction, but has not yet established central control of international violence.

2. *The Role of Courts:* Historically, the courts have two important roles in maintaining the rule of law: (i) protecting civil liberties by subjecting government officials to the rule of law and (ii) contributing to the control of private violence by encouraging disputants to bring their disputes to court and abide by the result. The two roles are not unconnected.

Encouraging the citizens of any particular country to bring their disputes to court rather than fight in the streets would be a positive contribution to the rule of law and would lay a foundation for courts to assist in the protection and advance of civil liberties.

Internationally, we are making some progress in the establishment of courts to which countries and their citizens can bring their disputes. Most remarkable is the growing power of the courts of the European Community. In Europe, the European Covenant on Human Rights, the work of the European Court of Human Rights, and the gradual inclusion of the covenant in the domestic law of the European states show dramatic progress, although progress that was made gradually.

3. Gradual progress can be made toward establishing the international rule of law in several ways. Using European developments as a model, regional courts can be established. International investment and commercial activity within countries will be advanced by growing acceptance of the rule of law and by the availability of

courts that will resolve commercial disputes. International commercial treaties, arbitration, and the availability of courts for dispute settlement gradually will accustom disputants to take their disputes to court and to abide by the results.

4. There is a close connection between the function of courts in protecting the rights of citizens against their governments and the establishment of the rule of law. The rule of law as we understand it requires that government officials be governed by law. When courts enforce the rule of law, the confidence of citizens in the courts and their willingness to bring their disputes to court should increase, thereby reducing at least the major incidents of private violence. Surely, the series of propositions I just offered can be transformed into hypotheses that can be studied using the tools of social science.

Legitimacy, Rights, and Primary Social Goods

Legitimacy power, according to Duncan Kennedy, is enhanced when a judge decides an important case that takes a significant step in law reform while offering good legal arguments in support of the decision (1986, 527-28). Changes or developments in law or legal institutions can enhance the legitimacy power of the courts or society or they can produce legitimacy costs. Ultimately, *Brown v. Board of Education* enhanced the legitimacy power and the historical reputation of the Warren Court. The decision itself is one of the great historic achievements of our court system. It has the quality that I describe as ultimate legitimacy (Donnelly 2003, 98). Nevertheless, in its immediate aftermath and over the years, the *Brown* decision produced legitimacy costs.

Legitimacy power can accumulate slowly during a sequence of law reform or over the history of an institution. A judge who renders a series of important decisions supported by good legal argument grows in legitimacy power. As an example, consider Judge Nathan Cardozo and such decisions as *MacPherson v. Buick Motor Co.*[4] and *Palsgraf v. Long Island Railroad*.[5] Consider as a second example the growing legitimacy power of the institutions of the European Union.

Various authors offer differing theories of legitimacy. *A Personalist Jurisprudence, the Next Step* (Donnelly 2003, 239), for example, compared the differing views on legitimacy of Cass Sunstein (1996) and Ronald Dworkin (1986). One can also derive insights regarding legitimacy from the now ancient quarrel between H. L. A. Hart (1958) and Lon Fuller (1958). Hart understood law as a system of rules accepted by the people and spent considerable time explaining what he meant by acceptance. Lon Fuller was more concerned with the circumstances and conditions that would enhance the acceptability of law and make it more likely that it would be acceptable. An inquiry using the tools of social science into the qualities that make law or changes in law more likely to be acceptable would seem to advance our understanding of how to promote the rule of law and the advance of human rights.

Dworkin contended that the legitimacy, and I would say the acceptability, of law is grounded "not in the hard terrain of contracts or duties of justice or obligations of fair play that might hold among strangers, where philosophers have hoped to find it, but in the more fertile ground of fraternity, community and their attendant obligations" (1986, 206). Dworkin argued that "political association, like family and friendship and other forms of association more local and intimate is itself pregnant of obligation" (1986, 206). Dworkin's understanding of legitimacy then resembles his theory of political friendship.

Political friendship as a grounding for the legitimacy and acceptability of law and society's institutions would seem to present both problems and opportunities for furthering the world rule of law. A new institution, an international court, for example, does not fit easily into the existing pattern of political friendships and interactions. It will become more acceptable, however, as human interactions slowly grow around that new institution. Witness the growth in authority and legitimacy of the European courts. Those activities may be the normal interactions of people who move from country to country. Commercial activities in our world today will be an important element of interactions that lead to political friendships.

Personalist theory offers a foundation for political friendship in the perception that persons are interrelated, that we are more fully persons when in relation with other persons. At the foundation of personalist theory is the perception of a necessary interrelationship between persons and a commitment to afford each person deep respect and concern. That perception and that commitment provide a basis for personalist acceptance of Dworkin's (1986) theory of political friendship. Political friendship as understood in view of that perception and commitment then leads to a theory of rights, obligations, and legitimacy (Donnelly 2003, 241-44).

> In personalist theory one has an obligation to cooperate in building and maintaining the reasonable institutions of the society in which he finds himself, that is because one has a duty of respect and concern for the persons with whom one inevitably is engaged in interaction. One interacts with others through language, through the circumstances of daily living, through all the ways in which one exists in modern society. One understands himself as a person through that interaction with other persons whom one perceives in the course of action as persons. (Donnelly 2003, 241)

The theory of rights, like the theory of political obligations, arises from that perception of persons acting together in society and hence growing more fully as persons. Each person under personalist theory has a right to participate in the common action of society and a right to the means necessary for that participation.

The means necessary for participation in the common action of society could be described as primary social goods. The primary social goods are those necessary or important both generally and in any particular society for participation in the common action of that society. The concept, primary social goods, is borrowed, and slightly transformed, from John Rawls's *A Theory of Justice* (1971). Rawls would define primary social goods as those necessary to pursuing any rational plan in life. In Rawls's theory, the principles of justice derived in his Original Position are those that will ensure all parties the best chance of maximizing their share of the primary social goods on lifting of the "veil of ignorance." They also offer the best chance of minimizing disastrous losses of the primary social goods.

In personalist theory—without the crutch or aid of the "original position" and the "veil of ignorance"—primary social goods are nevertheless very helpful in constructing a theory of rights. Basic rights are those designed to protect the primary social goods (Donnelly 2003, 99-103). A number of these rights would be found in our United States Constitution and some in the rest of U.S. law.

> Respect, then, for each person's right to participate in the intersubjectivity or political friendship of the common action, the life of the community becomes the basis for the primary rights. Primary rights are those which would protect against deprivation of the personal, economic, and political goods necessary to basic participation in any society's and in this particularly society's common action. (Donnelly 2003, 107-8)

The understanding of legitimacy in personalist theory is grounded in political friendship, respect and concern for each person, persons interacting in the common action, and their right to the primary social goods necessary to continue that participation. Legitimacy in personalist thought then shares a common grounding with the theories of rights and obligations.

"A society is legitimate to the extent that it strives to advance and protect everyone's and each one's share of the primary social goods" (Donnelly 2003, 241). Particular institutions and activities of society are legitimate insofar as they share or participate in society's mission of enhancing the common action, affording respect and concern for each person, and protecting and improving each person's share of the primary social goods, that is, each person's opportunity to participate in the common action of society.

o   o   o

These interrelated concepts may be helpful in understanding the advance of the rule of law and the related promotion of human rights. Social scientists must tell whether they can use these concepts, and practitioners will discover whether they are useful as a basis for refining their tools. Ultimately, the test of this pudding will be in the eating.

Some of the obstacles to the further development of the international rule of law and the advance of human rights perhaps may be captured in some further but related concepts. In the next part, I discuss the problem of horizons and the various points of view from which rights are perceived.

The Language and Uses of Rights: Rights as Tools in the Process of Social Change

A great obstacle to the advance of human rights and to the establishment in the international sphere of the rule of law is the phenomenon I refer to as *horizons*.

This is a familiar phenomenon. One regularly encounters in international human rights discourse the question of whether economic rights are more important than civil liberties or vice versa. Not surprisingly, the priority for economic rights is favored in some developing countries with strong or dictatorial central regimes, while thinkers like John Rawls, writing in democratic countries, would favor a priority for civil liberties (1971, 53). Likewise, rights considered basic and important in European and Western circles are questioned in the Middle East.

Every statement concerning rights is made within a horizon and from a point of view (Donnelly 2003, 260). I would like to begin this part of the discussion by elucidating that argument and by explaining the terms *horizon* and *point of view*.

The term *horizon* is used by philosophers such as Bernard Lonergan (1972, 235-36), Martin Heidegger (1969, 34-35), and Hans-Georg Gadamer (2004, 303-7) as a metaphor to discuss the normal human condition of having "limited knowledge and understanding" (Donnelly 2003, 83). Literally, horizon refers to the line at the edge of the sky and earth that marks the limits of our physical vision. We all know that there are mountains, valleys, cities, and lakes beyond the circular line of the horizon and hence beyond our physical vision. A valuable aspect of the metaphor is that we also know that we can cross beyond our present physical horizons and find those cities and mountains. I can leave this university, hop into my car, and drive to Skaneateles Lake. If I do, my whole view, my physical scenery, and my emotional mood will change.

Likewise, we can cross our intellectual and cultural horizons. I can leave the law school and cross the parking lot to the Maxwell School of Citizenship where I can study economics, history, or sociology, thereby changing my intellectual outlook and vision.

Both physical and intellectual horizons create and also confine vision. I can see to the edge of the horizon, to the limits of my current knowledge and interest, but not beyond. By crossing horizons physically and intellectually, I can expand my vision. Fascinatingly, however, when I cross horizons I find myself in a new horizon that also creates and confines vision. When I leave college with a degree in economics, sociology, or history and enter law school, I find new vision but gradually forget and lose interest in the social sciences.

Horizons affect our understanding of rights. A philosopher and a lawyer will discuss rights differently as will persons brought up in various cultures. Representatives from the Near East, for example, regularly tell us that our Western understanding of rights does not make sense in their cultures. A familiar phenomenon, however, is that a person returning to the East from an education in Paris or Boston may turn out to be an advocate for a more Western understanding of rights in his or her home country and culture. What Hans-Georg Gadamer (2004) called a fusion of horizons may also take place.

To understand statements regarding rights, one must recognize that every rights statement is made within a horizon and from a point of view. A district attorney talking about rights, perhaps the rights of a victim, is speaking from a different point of view and perhaps with a different meaning than a defense attorney. The judge's point of view is still different. Social scientists and some legal philosophers could talk about rights from a descriptive point of view. That very definitely is not the point of view of a law reform attorney campaigning for the establishment of new rights. That would not have been the point of view of Thurgood Marshall during the long campaign leading to *Brown v. Board of Education*.

Law reformers such as Thurgood Marshall or Granville Sharpe would not perceive rights descriptively, or as entitlements, or as conclusions to be drawn within a system of law. They would find only moderately helpful Llewellyn's Holmesian understanding of rights as predictions that a court would afford a remedy. They would rather perceive rights as goals to be pursued and great decisions such as *Somerset v. Stewart* or *Brown v. Board of Education* not only as important victories but also as resources for further pursuit of the goal of complete abolishment of slavery or of desegregation. As Stuart Scheingold pointed out, the legitimacy power of a great victory becomes a resource for the next battle in the further pursuit of rights (1974, 83).

> *[I]t helps to understand rights not simply as rules or entitlements but as tools for the accomplishment of human purposes.*

From the point of view of a judge—one concerned with action, with deciding a case—rights are not predictions of what a court will in fact do. The point of view of a judge is not a descriptive nor a predictive point of view. To H. L. A. Hart, a judge may perceive rights as conclusions to be drawn in a system of rules (1958). Or he may perceive the rights he is about to establish as an appropriate resolution in his culture of a long-standing dispute.

Both the judge and the law reform attorney should be conscious of the phenomenon of horizons. When a law reformer is addressing a judge whose horizons are narrow, he must find a way to make his arguments comprehensible within the narrow horizons of the judge. In the alternative, he must find ways to persuade the judge to cross beyond those narrow horizons to see and understand the problems of his client. Some great appellate advocates have that skill.

As Stuart Scheingold pointed out, rights are resources to be used in the political campaign for law reform (1974, 83-89). The legitimacy power of courts allows a reform campaign to rally its supporters and to attack its opponents. When arguing before a judge, a law reform attorney may use the legitimacy power of rights to hammer on the judge's narrow horizons demanding that the judge respect and pay attention to his client's rights, his client's interests, and his client's standing as a person.

Events in the wider world may provide society and courts with the vital experiences necessary to abandon or cross old horizons. Not long before the decision in *Brown v. Board of Education*, the world was challenged by the experience of World War II and the Holocaust. Shortly before that, U.S. citizens experienced the Great Depression and, after the war, Truman's desegregation of the military, the beginning of the Cold War, and the Korean War. All of these experiences, along with the NAACP's extensive law reform campaign, contributed to the new necessary change of horizons that made *Brown v. Board of Education* possible. World War II, the Holocaust, and the Cold War also were experiences that changed European horizons and contributed to the new atmosphere that allowed development of the European Union and the evolutionary advance of human rights in Europe.

A law reformer and one concerned with the advance of the rule of law and human rights should be conscious of the phenomenon of horizons, of the experiences that open the opportunity for expanding our understanding. They should seek the tools necessary for crossing foreign horizons. Among those tools are the legitimacy power of rights that can be used as resources in pursuing further goals or the goal of establishing additional, more basic or more fundamental rights.

From the perspective of a conscientious judge, consciousness of the phenomenon of horizons would be significant. Judges who recognize their horizons, their limited knowledge and understanding, and desire to decide justly or to respect all persons should accept an additional and corollary obligation to cross horizons and to develop methods for crossing horizons. Social science and social science data, perhaps because of their controversial use in *Brown v. Board of Education*, are among the tools for enabling judges to cross horizons and to recognize the impact of their decisions on those on foreign horizons. A commitment to and methods for crossing horizons are means for promoting human rights and a topic for exploration by legal philosophers and social scientists.

The process of developing and establishing rights then should be perceived and studied in relation to the problem of horizons, the possibility of crossing horizons, and the means for doing so. The problems can be studied from various points of view by lawyers, legal philosophers, and social scientists. For example, lawyers and legal philosophers should be conscious of horizons and should seek to create tools for crossing them from the point of view of the judge and the point of view of an advocate for the disadvantaged.

The advance of rights is related in turn to the advance of the rule of law and to the legitimacy of new governmental arrangements. People are encouraged to take their disputes to court to the extent that rights are secured and recognized within a horizon, to settle them peacefully, to sue government officials or entities who are subject to the rule of law rather than starting revolutions or campaigns of terrorism. A campaign seeking the establishment of new rights is a substitute for revolution. That campaign can take place within a particular country, within a regional organization such as the newly developed structures in Europe, or on a worldwide basis. The availability and regular use of the process of law reform to establish rights should contribute to the legitimacy and stability of governments and regional organizations. The regular use of law reform campaigns should contribute to strengthening and expanding the rule of law.

For that purpose, it helps to understand rights not simply as rules or entitlements but as tools for the accomplishment of human purposes. *A Personalist Jurisprudence, the Next Step*, describes a number of different uses of the language of rights (Donnelly 2003, 247-72). Rights may be perceived as remedies or predictions that a court may afford a remedy. Rights may be seen as conclusions drawn within a system of rules by way of a judicial decision, by arguments for that decision, or criticisms of it, as particularly powerful reasons that will trump competing reasons, as goals to be pursued, or as resources for pursuing those goals.

Natural Law

In the first volume of his *History of the English Speaking Peoples*, Winston Churchill, discussing Magna Carta, explained,

> If the thirteenth century magnates understood little and cared less for popular liberties or Parliamentary democracy, they had all the same laid hold of a principle which was to be of prime importance for the future development of English society and English institutions. Throughout the document it is implied that here is a law which is above the King and which even he must not break. The reaffirmation of a supreme law and its expression in a general charter is the great work of Magna Carta; and this alone justifies the respect in which men have held it. The reign of Henry II, according to the most respected authorities, initiates the rule of law. But the work as yet was incomplete: the Crown was still above the law; the legal system which Henry had created could become, as John showed, an instrument of oppression.
>
> Now for the first time the King himself is bound by the law. The root principle was destined to survive across the generations and rise paramount long after the feudal background of 1215 had faded in the past. The Charter became in the process of time an enduring witness that the power of the Crown was not absolute. (Churchill 1956-58, 256-57)

Winston Churchill sketched some major steps in this passage in the establishment of the rule of law. Most important, the institutionalization (Magna Carta) of a higher law subjected the king to the rule of law. Governments' subjectivity to the rule of law lays a strong foundation for the development of civil liberties and the advance of human rights. The institutionalization of higher law for this purpose is in the main stream of the natural law tradition.

Natural law in its many incarnations over the ages has served as a vast storehouse of resources to advance the rule of law. The Romans borrowed the notion of natural law from Greek philosophers, particularly the Stoics, and used it to mold the law necessary to govern their vast empire. As their empire grew, the Romans confronted a problem not entirely dissimilar to the current world situation. For the sake of commerce, good order, and justice, the Romans required an international law, a law of nations, a jus gentium, as they described it. That jus gentium should not be the law of a particular state including their own. Rather, they drew on the themes common to many laws to create a higher law. The labors of the great Roman juris consults in developing the jus gentium and the *jus naturale* were ultimately codified by the Emperor Justinian in his famous Codex, which has served to advance the rule of law over the ages (d'Entreves 1970).

Medieval natural law, as Churchill (1956-58) explained, influenced the Magna Carta, jump-starting the history of English civil liberties. The tradition that began with the Magna Carta and was supported by the natural rights philosophy of John Locke provided a foundation for the overthrow of the Stuart kings and their pretensions to absolutism. About the same time, the great seventeenth-century natural lawyers, Grotius and Pufendorf, were using the resources of the natural law tradition to form the foundations of modern international law, a distinct advance in establishing a world rule of law.

Thomas Jefferson in the next century drew on John Locke's natural rights theory to lay the foundation for development of the American tradition of human and civil rights in the Declaration of Independence. In turn, the American tradition made perhaps the most significant contribution to the modern worldwide advance of human rights.

The notion of a higher law is the essential contribution of the natural law tradition to the advance of the rule of law and the promotion of human rights. In the absence of positive law a jus gentium or modern international law can be developed on the foundation of that higher law. Under the authority of that higher law, kings and governments can be subjected to the rule of law and their citizens' civil and human rights can be protected against those ruling powers. That protection of citizens and the control of rulers, however, has been promoted best by the institutionalization of that higher law. To mention some instances, the institutionalization of higher law is represented by the Magna Carta; the British Bill of Rights of 1688; the American Constitution and its Bill of Rights as administered by the Supreme Court; the United Nations Declaration of Human Rights; the Covenants on Civil and Political Rights, and on Economic, Social and Cultural Rights; the European Union; the European Convention on Human Rights; and the European Court of Human Rights.

Clues can be derived from that history for advancing the rule of law and the protection of human rights in our modern world. International law could serve as the higher law that could subject otherwise unrestrained rulers to the rule of law and respect for the human rights of their citizens. There is some indication in the flow of current events that this process is beginning. It is necessary, however, to institutionalize that process probably through the United Nations and regional organizations modeled on the European Union.

The set of related concepts offered in this article and discussed above may be helpful to understanding the relation between a higher law perhaps derived from natural law, the institutions that apply that higher law, and the evolutionary development of the rule of law and the related advance of human rights. Those concepts include the rule of law, the language and uses of rights, primary social goods, legitimacy, horizons, crossing horizons, point of view analysis, and the use of rights as tools in the process of social change.

○   ○   ○

St. Paul once described what has come to be called the natural law as written in the hearts of human persons (Romans 2: 14-16, New Revised Standard Version). As a scripture scholar, Paul was drawing on a thousand years of learning in the tradition descended from Abraham that many of us hold in common. A reasonable interpretation of that could be put as follows. In the course of human interaction and experience, we gradually come to understand our fellow human beings as persons who share human feelings, desires, sufferings, and moral struggles. Out of that understanding grows respect and concern for others, for many others. That respect and concern can be contemplated philosophically, be generalized, be transformed into individual and community commitments. It can be institutionalized into the rule of law, great ideals, respect for rights, the importance of courts, and of rights litigation and reform. It is a gradual process, a process of continual development of human experience, influenced by vital and sometimes traumatic experience, by World Wars, by the abolition of slavery, by the Holocaust, by the successful establishment of regimes of rights such as the European Union. An important part of natural law as so understood is the process of social change and the role of human experience and ideals in that process of social change.

Natural law then is not a set of propositions or even ideals, important as they are to natural law, but a process of human experience by which our regard for our fellow human beings grows, is generalized into ideals and commitments, is institutionalized, and is regularly changed by crossing horizons. As we gather the experience of life, our understanding and regard for our fellow human persons deepens and broadens. I submit that this process particularly as it is represented by institutionalized social change can be studied by lawyers, legal philosophers, and social scientists.

Notes

1. *Brown v. Board of Education of Topeka, Kansas* 347 U.S. 483 (1954).
2. *Somerset v. Stewart* 98 Eng. Rep. 494 (K.B. 1772).
3. *Plessy v. Ferguson* 163 U.S. 537 (1986).
4. *MacPherson v. Buick Motor Co.* 217 N.Y. 382 (1916).
5. *Palsgraf v. Long Island Railroad* 248 N.Y. 339 (1928).

References

Churchill, Winston. 1956-58. *History of the English speaking peoples.* London: Cassell.
d'Entreves, A. P. 1970. *Natural law, an introduction to legal philosophy.* London: Hutchinson University Library.
Donnelly, Samuel. 1994. *The language and uses of rights: A biopsy of American jurisprudence in the twentieth century.* Lanham, MD: University Press of America.
———. 2003. *A personalist jurisprudence, the next step. A person centered philosophy of law for the twenty-first century.* Durham, NC: Carolina Academic Press.
Dworkin, Ronald. 1986. *Law's empire.* Cambridge, MA: Belknap.
Fifoot, C. H. S. 1936. *Lord Mansfield.* Oxford, UK: Clarendon.

Fuller, Lon. 1958. Positivism and fidelity to law—A reply to Professor Hart. *Harvard Law Review* 71:630-72.

Gadamer, Hans-Georg. 2004. *Truth and method*. Joel Weinsheimer and Donald G. Marshall, trans. New York: Continum.

Hart, H. L. A. 1958. Positivism and the separation of law and morals. *Harvard Law Review* 71:593-629.

Heidegger, Martin. 1969. *Identity and difference*. J. Stanbaugh, trans. New York: Harper & Row.

Heward, Edmund. 1979. *Lord Mansfield*. Chichester, UK: B. Rose Ltd.

Kennedy, Duncan. 1986. Freedom and constraint in adjudication, a critical phenomenology. *Journal of Legal Education* 36:518.

Lonergan, Bernard. 1972. *Method in theology*. New York: Herder and Herder.

Myrdal, Gunnar. 1944. *An American dilemma: The Negro problem and modern democracy*. New York: Harper.

Rawls, John. 1971. *A theory of justice*. Cambridge, MA: Belknap.

Scheingold, Stuart. 1974. *The politics of rights: Lawyers, public policy, and political change*. New Haven, CT: Yale University Press.

Sunstein, Cass. 1996. *Legal reasoning and political conflict*. New York: Oxford University Press.

Wiecek, William. 1998. *The lost world of classical legal thought: Law and ideology in America 1886-1937*. New York: Oxford University Press.

Can the Welfare State Survive in a Globalized Legal Order?

By
SAMUEL KRISLOV

The notion that markets lead to law and freedom is said to have originated in Adam Smith's work and is rooted in history. Both the progression and roots seem highly problematic. Neo-Smithian approaches have been refurbished by general acceptance of a contingent nature of the relation. They have also been enhanced by the failures of European Marxist economics in ways predicted with uncanny accuracy. On the other hand, neoclassical claims that democratic welfare systems were only a step away from similar failures have been refuted. Hopes that an international system might impose democracy from outside the nation-state are overly optimistic. Nationalism is rife, with a continuing outburst of ethnic secessions, and little yielding of power to supranational decision makers. The greatest success of supranational authority has rather been in creating subsidiary structures, unlikely to implement fundamental transformation but with potential for supporting such a thrust. These include expert-based operations and the network of nongovernmental organizations.

Keywords: markets; freedom; political systems; legal development; economics; politics; welfare state; globalization

The fall of Eastern European Marxism was rightly seen as epoch making, a conclusion given an exclamation point by the emergence of Chinese military-dominated capitalism. The lingering, isolated, Marxist societies survive as presumptive possibilities generally focused on faulty economics, including the inability of the

Samuel Krislov is currently a distinguished adjunct professor of public administration at American University. He has received fellowships from the Guggenheim, Rockefeller, Ford, Russell Sage, and National Science Foundations; and he has served as chairman of the National Research Council Committee on Law and Criminal Justice, as president of the Law and Society Association, and as editor of the Law and Society Review. *Among his books are* Representative Bureaucracy *(1974) and* How Nations Choose Product Standards *(1977). He was a contributor to the multivolume series* Integration through Law *edited by Cappelletti et al. (1985), and he received a lifetime achievement award from the Law and Courts section of the American Political Science Association in 1998.*

DOI: 10.1177/0002716205283131

controlled enterprises to generate any system to measure efficiency and therefore to generate either efficiency or quality. This was exasperated by the fusion of political and economic monopolies that made repression the easy road to answer critiques of the state of affairs. Pope John and Ronald Reagan added small shoves to a crumbling order that had defaulted for decades on its promises of a better and more liberated life. The analyses of writers of the Hayek Chicago School, and most especially of Hayek himself, were uncannily predictive.

Flushed with a historic triumph, many neoclassical theorists applied much the same tools of analysis to both their predicted demise of the welfare state and a kind of monotonic world resulting form globalization. In the United States, some have believed that privatization and dismantling of safety nets in place since the New Deal is not only in the offing but is well under way. David Stockman, director of the Office of Management and Budget under Reagan, mounted that attack by deliberately developing huge deficits and, in his view, making the welfare state economically unfeasible. Whether current Bush policies help create much the same situation, there is little evidence of such a design; at least superficially it comes from a mind-set, formerly regarded as a liberal one, that deficits do not matter.

The legal counterpart of this political move to roll back welfare is the effort to roll back the post-1937 constitutional order. Court of Appeals Judge Douglas Ginzberg for example has expressed nostalgia for "the Constitution in exile," and newly confirmed U.S. District Judge Mary Brown has explicitly called for such a rollback. Former Judge Bork has expressed skepticism for such projects, characterizing for example the development of incorporation of the Bill of Rights into the Fourteenth Amendment as something he would not necessarily have done but that is now too firmly based to undo.

A third strand of antiwelfare effort has centered on a form of globalization theory and a claim that competitive pressures doom welfare states. They are in this view luxury systems inhibiting relentless bare-bones pursuit of international efficiency. The less regulation, the less add-on benefits and job protection, the more prosperous the international community collectively and its component nation-states individually will be. The higher level of prosperity will, in turn, somehow provide for those dramatically disadvantaged by quick, flexible changes in job availability, and the market will ensure most quality demands and limit the pain externalities.

These arguments reached a crescendo after France and the Netherlands rejected the European Community Constitution in mid-2005.[1] This, and the virtual deadlock between the German conservative Christian Democrats and Schroeder's Social Democrats, who had a truly dismal record of economic mismanagement, were seen as nostalgia-based efforts by Western European voters to

NOTE: This article is derived from a paper on "Evolutionary Law, Markets and Freedom" delivered at the conference on Law and Democratic Development held April 16-17, 2005 at Syracuse University. A few portions of this paper are also included in an article, "Do Free Markets Produce Free Societies?" in Syracuse Journal of International Law and Commerce 33 (January 2006).

cling to a social insurance state whose day had come and gone. The stagnant economy and high unemployment rate were seen as engendered by voters' unwillingness to face social realities. In the United States, in contrast, the voters seemed to accept curtailment of pension benefits and medical plans and had attained a sluggish economy with only medium unemployment rates.

The argument that jettisoning the welfare state is an economic necessity is not without irony. In a sense, it is the "race to the bottom" argument around which the left tried to mobilize opposition to NAFTA and the Central American Free Trade Agreement (CAFTA). Many of those now pushing for elimination of regulation and social benefits made reassuring noises until these treaties were approved and hailed, for example, David Vogel's work demonstrating that in more instances than not higher standards and regulations ensued.[2]

[T]he welfare state experienced heady expansion after World War II, only to find it had overreached its ability to deliver on its promises.

But more important, there looms a simple fact: the record of development, of success and failure, is such a mixed one that it suggests caution about the efforts of economic changes, particularly relatively small ones. There is a much stronger consensus today that the International Monetary Fund (IMF) Bank and its new leader, Paul Wolfowitz, have no clearer map for investment or encouragement of aspiring economies than when the Bank began operations three-quarters of a century ago. Indeed, the main change is that the Bank and the Fund have lost some certainties and abandoned some orthodoxies.[3]

It is a quite different set of priorities that suggests future problems for the future of the Western welfare states. These are intertwined with demographics and their trends. It seems likely that there will be some global adjustments in wealth simply as some sort of regression toward the mean, that the remarkably high concentration of wealth in a small fraction of the globe will be modified. More important, the age distribution patterns within such societies and the heavy increase of the aged will require severe rethinking. But that shift and its concomitant economic complications will also shift political realities and political realignments.

The Waning of the Welfare State

Almost parallel to the rise and fall of the "evil empire," the welfare state experienced heady expansion after World War II, only to find it had overreached its ability to deliver on its promises. Its decline, though, has witnessed careful pruning, rather than collapse. While some conservatives suggest that the failures of communism, democratic socialism, and liberal welfare systems are all three of the same cloth, the survival power of truncated welfare states suggests the picture is much more complex.

The reach of democratic socialist systems has varied both in scope and time span. Sweden's preceded World War II and largely avoided nationalization.[4] Britain's was more far reaching in its nationalization of the economy. All of the West European systems had historic experience with some degree of a mixed economy. All proceeded in the 1940s and 1950s with slow expansion of welfare capitalism, most with an eye toward achieving something less than total governmental control of the economy. None of them had aspirations for total planning or the nonmarket price-fixing dilemmas of the Marxist states.

Those that nationalized industries followed the path of controlling the "commanding heights" of the economy: steel production, coal, energy, transportation, and to a lesser degree, finance. The investments in coal and steel were historic misjudgments, as those industries' crucial role of the moment was beginning to be eclipsed in part because of new Asian competition. Neither public nor private efforts have yet to stabilize these industries, though the European coal and community's program to curtail competition helped.

British nationalization of steel and coal was a particularly disastrous step, for it also presented the Labour Party, with its heavy commitment to organized labor unions, with political as well as economic headaches. Those unions were not always led by the wisest of thinkers. For example, Arthur Scargill of the miners union insisted on the proposition that all extant mines be fully kept in operation, even if the coal produced was of too low a grade to be sellable and would incur additional costs for storage. More remarkably, he called a national strike on this issue and seemed perplexed by the absence of public support. The Labour Party was whipsawed by union demands: if it agreed to them it lost middle-of-the-road voters, but continuous denial of claims threatened its base.

Labour's strategic error in investing in wasting industries and clinging to them for political and ideological reasons helped Margaret Thatcher to gain political power and undo much of the nationalization program. Denationalization of coal and steel was spectacularly successful. Privatization of local transportation and the airlines seems to have worked, but railroad privatization toted as promoting increased investment was followed by neglect and a well-publicized rise in the accident rate. By and large, the Blair years have seen no appetite to undo the significant Thatcher-Major denationalizations, a tacit concession of the inefficiencies of the efforts at socialism.

In the same vein, Thatcher only nibbled at the fringes of the welfare state acknowledging its political power. The crowning jewel, the National Health Service, was already modified under labor by copayments and other attempts to control the realities of hypochondria and misuse of free goods. The Conservatives were keen on further limits on health and other benefits. Resurgent labor invested rather more with phlegmatic results, but the Conservative Party's stance that it could do more with less has not impressed the electorate.

[G]overnment operations of nontraditional enterprises were mostly failures, and privatization largely (though often marginally) more successful, with some clear triumphs. However, privatization also had a number of failures.

Continental socialism had less to systematically divest and had the cover of the European Union as it evolved toward the free market of Europe. The privatization of energy systems and auto manufacturing has been country by country rather than systematic or EC-sponsored. Transportation, too, has slowly moved back into the private sphere with national airlines succumbing to markets created by the European Union's politically cautious but inexorable move to end government-manipulated special protections.

On any scale, the United States has eschewed much government ownership, preferring regulation in most instances. The move to privatization has been mostly to contract out to existing enterprises rather than divesting; conspicuously, the spinning out of semigovernmental enterprises—Amtrak and the post office—have left their umbilical cord uncut. Neither have they succeeding financially, paralleling the financial difficulties those essentially service agencies are experiencing throughout the world.

Similarly, the American welfare system was both belated and tentative. As Europe advanced its extensive programs, rudimentary safety nets were provided in the United States by extensive Civil War pensions, masking the underlying social problem.[5] Conspicuously, the United States is alone among major industrial relations in resisting health coverage; much of its welfare pension and other safety nets rest on corporate benefits. With tight international competition, loose financial controls, and the loss of power by labor unions, many of those are dwindling.

Nevertheless, like Britain and Scandinavia, the United States has recently curtailed its governmental programs but experienced unanticipated growth in expenditures. The Clintons's failure to rally support for universal health protection was a political disastrous blow that led the president both to move to the center and to govern only with extreme caution for the remaining six years. Led by Gore's push for "reinventing government," some nondramatic steps toward contracting out were initiated, also suggesting a watershed had been reached.

On the Continent, too, welfare protection has been cut back, though seldom threatened in principle. Some of the more extreme theories of entitlement—for addicts, systematic subsidization of alleged art, bountiful unemployment benefits—have paralleled cuts in such benefits in the private sector including curtailment of mandated benefits. This readjustment is a minimalist recognition of the limits imposed by economic realities and the consequences of grandiose efforts, like Mitterand's attempts to prevent movement of capital to allow semiautarchic semisocialism.

Because, as Peter Berger has noted,[6] none of the Western welfare states ever attempted a total socialist economy, they experienced relatively few of the problems of measurement associated with controlled administrative pricing.[7] Not only did some of those countries retain competitive enterprises, they also were subject to substitutable products and imports that permitted comparisons. Of course, state enterprises kept balance sheets—of various transparency—and posted profits and losses. The rapid disintegration of the nationalized sector represents a judgment based on these experiences. In industries such as coal and steel, the inefficiencies were inherent in the decision to acquire a wasting enterprise. But political management was also not as adept at pruning, discarding, and reformulating as private enterprise, aided by governmental pulls and shoves. (On the whole, though, Europe was probably more successful at coping with the new situation of steel than the U.S. sector, now largely in foreign hands.) Perhaps the strongest indicator of the weakness of governmental ownership was in the automobile industry. After years of taking comfortable profits, European government companies were unable to make shifts of design and quality when faced by a new era inaugurated by Japanese competition. To survive they were privatized.

In short, government operations of nontraditional enterprises were mostly failures, and privatization largely (though often marginally) more successful, with some clear triumphs. However, privatization also had a number of failures. Freemarketers have concluded that this record unequivocally supplements the conclusion from the Eastern Europe fiascos that private companies always do better, though the record is spottier than that. It strongly suggests governmental companies have considerable handicaps in areas of rapid change and creativity and over time accumulated significant inefficiencies.

The trimming of welfare benefits also came from demonstrated costs and competitive disadvantages in international trade. There was also a revulsion as these benefits encouraged grosser and grosser claims of entitlement by nonproductive segments of society rather than more socially responsible attitudes expected by welfare statists. The public in most countries supported curtailment of benefits (and sometimes classes of beneficiaries) but generally turned again to welfarist parties after a conservative cleansing. And the Danish, even under rightist coalitions, have maintained their tight system, resisting European Union powers to curtail their welfarism. (As a small country with niche markets and an effective labor force, its special situation has so far permitted this without visible pain.) In short, European welfare states have been willing to pay economic costs for perceived social benefits and social solidarity. As noted above, this is precisely what the critics of such systems claim is unrealistic and has led to bad politics, as well as economics.

[F]urther elimination of "safety nets" and lowering the sense of social solidarity can be expected, even though the very theory of globalism anticipates an increase in unforeseeable economic changes.

While the trimming of benefits is seen by free marketers as a retreat on the way to a rout, welfarists see it as a prudent regrouping. In many instances, leftish coalitions have taken the corrective steps to save the underlying system; in others, they have refrained from reversing the cuts made after losing elections by conservative governments.

From a political standpoint, this suggests that Hayek's projection of a "road to serfdom" is simply yet another "slippery slope" catastrophe theory with little behind it. Both pure welfare states and ones well into nationalization have demonstrated the political will and clear freedom to reverse any process where economically required and politically desired. Hayek argued that willy-nilly welfarists would emerge as objective Bolsheviks suppressing dissent and tightening governmental control. His sole support, beyond an appeal to inexorable logic, was a sinister statement by Harold Laski, then Hayek's colleague at the London School of Economics and one-time chairman of the Labour Party (but never an MP or government official). Laski suggested that to achieve socialism, Labour would have to extract a promise from opposition parties not to undo nationalization or else suppress parties not willing to give such a pledge. But Hayek did not note that Laski, a careless scholar who invented footnotes and events, said many contradictory things about a passage to socialism including predictions of violent revolution.[8] And he in his way was as off the mark about the future of Britain, Europe, and the United States as was Hayek (though the latter was uncanny in his judgments about what was happening behind the secrecies of Eastern Europe). The inefficient burdens of the welfare state have on the whole not adversely affected law, democracy, and freedom.

In one major respect, the welfare state has failed. Its premise was that it would be a clear enabler, creating "positive freedom" for those unable to affirm their own independence. In its objectives of diminishing poverty, expanding educational opportunity and of life-achievement standards, it has been a nonunqualified success but nonetheless has had measurable impact. At the same time, by creating a multitude of political and economic areas, it has reduced the ability of most citizens to comprehend and control the myriad of interstitial decisions swirling about.[9] This "paradox of the welfare state" grows more acute and apparent the wider the success of policies and the more people benefit from its results. Much of this is due to entrenchment of welfare professionals behind the intricacies of procedure.[10] But the successes of the welfare state are impressive, and not only its uplift of the lowly and its safety nets for the unlucky.

Far from moving people into lockstep conformity-serfdom and subservience, the welfare state has created problems for itself by its very success in complicating social differentiations. The Swedish model—which became the Scandinavian and Dutch model as well—supplemented formal elective processes with exhaustive consultation among the leading interests. When these interests were few—essentially the government acting as more-or-less honest broker between capital and labor—this process was tedious but ended with a consensual compromise. As professional service, artistic, and variegated types of business emerged with minutely different interests developed, this type of bargaining increasingly has become more difficult, to the point that it breaks down or is overtaken by events. As Schmitter has classically pointed out, the Scandinavians had created not just a welfare state, but a Protestant version of corporatism,[11] where the key "pillars" of society (as the Dutch would parse it) are directly integrated into the decision process. (Older Catholic models have had a checkered career, culminating disastrously in Fascist Italy and the clerical-fascist systems of Franco's Spain and Salazer's Portugal.) Chicago school economists could argue that this processal problem and multiplication of interests is precisely why government and welfare should be minimized. But to date it is impressive that Swedish-type welfare politics has at least superficially managed to cope with this growing social heterogeneity, as ethnic diversification entailed in EU migration policies and modern-day mobility.

Welfare state countries show little signs of marching away from freedom. To the contrary: in spite of considerable controls over personal transfers of funds and other severe regulations for taxing purposes, they manage to preserve even economic liberty at a high level. (*The 2004 Index of Economic Freedom* of the conservative Heritage Fund[12] rated Denmark as 8th, Sweden 12th, the Netherlands 19th, and Norway 28th in economic freedom among the 155 countries they rated. The United States was 10th.) Their emphasis on personal rights is even more profoundly respected throughout the world and has not been drastically altered since Hayek wrote sixty years ago. On the whole, their feet are firmly planted in an enduring tradition of personal freedoms, and they are on no road to a different road. Holland in particular has reacted to memories of the Nazi occupation with legal protections against the authorities and to further emphasize autonomous *Stichtung*, minimally regulated and easily created associations, as the bedrock of its educational religious and social society. Other European welfare states have had only minimal problems adjusting to the European Union's requirements on personal liberty, though this has required reassessment of old attitudes on cultural homogeneity and has been accompanied by racism not previously experienced. These developments are a product of modernization, not economic policies, and in sum suggest the welfare state is consonant with the Western tradition of liberty.

Asian Experience
Challenges Theorists of All Schools

With Japan's spectacular emergence as a quality producer of better as well as cheaper cars came "chicken-little" pronouncements that set the pattern. The "Little Tigers" of Korea, Singapore, Hong Kong, Formosa, and Malaysia moved into the world market. One had only to extrapolate growth at the rate then current to conclude U.S. and Europe would quickly be eclipsed. (The reasoning paralleled Henry George's jibe at Malthus: the illusion of a farmer that because day to day he adjusts to lifting a growing calf, eventually he will be able to lift a cow.) These warnings were often accompanied by warnings that the United States could preserve its patrimony only by erecting strong barriers to trade and severe constraints upon foreigners' ability to purchase American enterprises and assets. We were in danger of being engulfed by cheap foreign labor. We were relinquishing leadership in manufacturing and becoming an outlier engaged in distribution—a broker, or factor, rather than an industrial leader.

New systems of production could easily adopt the latest technology unencumbered by needs of scrapping legacy systems, writing off costs including payments to obsolete workers. With cheap labor and presumably cheap training costs, they have potentially considerable advantages including work habits (longer and more flexible hours) that permitted recouping of any need for longer training costs. These advantages are real, but only part of the picture. Offsetting them were a generally less educated and therefore less flexible labor force, the need to pay for foreign technology (either directly through licensing or through payments to foreign experts), and much heavier management and office costs, a product of cultural inflexibility including culturally based poor use of women's skills.

The emergence of those new economics seemed to provide a natural experiment in which developmental constructs and paths of progress could be mapped. Results at first seemed to follow predicted byways, but later—and sometimes more precise—studies muddied the picture. Studies based on the early years of Asian development found significant correlation between degrees of authoritarianism and developmental growth. Later studies have not found this pattern.[13] Indeed, the absence of any solid relationship has been disappointing and, as so often happens in the social sciences, led to less study of what has become an unfashionable focus. Given the small number of countries under the microscope, it is quite possible that the initial results were spurious. But the total pattern might also be real. There are initial advantages that plausibly might accrue in an authoritarian system where limited societal capital could be concentrated and targeted for significant projects with high immediate impact. Arguably, early projects of that sort are more obvious and later choices more difficult so that the authoritarian system over time will lose its original effectiveness. At that point, individual rationality will probably he superior. (Arguably, this is what happened in the Soviet Union. The totalitarian effort made it possible to move a floundering system into the ranks of industrial powers, but a successive series of predictably bad choices created a system doomed to fail.)

At any rate, it is generally assumed that an authoritarian system can nonetheless create free and/or dynamic markets. While some argue authoritarian restraints in terms of the flow of information and restrictions on personal mobility will be ultimately reflected in the growth rate, that does not seem to account for as much retardation as direct interference with the economic system itself. China seems to operate in a sphere of its own, flouting all these generalizations.

Only Korea and Taiwan have followed the idealized pattern of moving from market system to law-constrained economy to freedom, joining Japan and India as manifestations of Asian democracy and free expression. (India's ethos is quite deviant, reflecting its British colonial past. But many other colonies have generally repudiated their democratic legacy.)

What is interesting too is that these two societies are hardly the ones that would have been projected by market theorists. Their perennial favorites—Hong Kong and Singapore—remain as authoritarian as ever; indeed, they probably have slipped in recent years on any democratization index. Hong Kong, to be sure, is also a unique case, having been transferred from British domination to that of communist China. The result is that key decisions are made by external governors who felt and feel little political pressure from Hong Kongers and much more from their heartland political imperatives.

This somewhat motley result is hardly surprising for anyone with a contingency, or even probabilistic, view of history. It certainly does not falsify the marketers' projections. But it has resulted in more modest and even guarded statements about historical outcomes. So Robert Barro has interestingly suggested that "freedom" and "personal rights" are "luxury goods" emerging as a side product from personally "necessary" liberties of the marketplace. Instead of a monotonic progression, we are offered a more contingent possibility of a type recorded history seems to project. Posner has suggested an analogous development: richer countries can afford a more elaborate and nuanced, and therefore freer, machinery for social control.[14]

It is interesting that when all the dust settled, the United States emerged as a major player and the big winner from all of these processes. It has indeed transformed itself into a nation benefiting from intellectual property—industrial know-

how, skill at training and entertaining others—and the coordinator of internationalized assembly of multinationally produced parts into finished, maximally
profitable products. Its productivity has been record breaking, its affluence impressive, and its political power massive. In embracing growth and democracy for
others, it has done well for itself.

---

*The classic national state is seemingly
weaker than a half century ago, but much more
as a result of communication breakthroughs
and economic development than any external
legal imperatives.*

But like most Western societies, the United States faces a demographic challenge to its system of social safety nets. Although the United States has a relatively
conservative system of such supports—for example, no medical insurance for
millions—it has witnessed a relatively strong political revolt against benefits. The
argument that elimination of regulatory hindrances will enrich society has gone
hand in hand with an unwillingness to regard sudden or catastrophic economic
changes as beyond individuals' control and therefore partly a social responsibility.
Given the future where the contributor-beneficiary ratios will change, further
elimination of "safety nets" and lowering the sense of social solidarity can be expected, even though the very theory of globalism anticipates an increase in unforeseeable economic changes.

Globalization and Its Portents

The claims of globalization advocates at its apex amounted to yet another "end
of history" thesis. Parochialism, local boundaries, obstacles to a seamless international economy were to be swept aside and would be replaced by an ever more
prosperous world.

The predicted efficiency would be a by-product largely of two factors. There
would be an intensification of the trend toward mobility of the factors of production and coproduction of goods. Increasingly, components of a product would be
furbished or refurbished at the optimal place for its creation, and the various
subproducts brought to its final assembly point, with transportation preplanned to

be minimal. The absence of legal, and minimization of physical, barriers would permit the second factor to come into play. Economists had throughout history argued that nations should produce what they could produce at the greatest comparative efficiency. Countries had evaded the import of this axiom, by tariff barriers and other measures, which were objectively to their disadvantage and that of the world, though this reality was hidden from view. Globalization would demonstrate that axiom's truth, and its implementation would be universally beneficial.

At its worst, the competitive axiom has been treated as an injunction to the developing countries to follow their past productive history. Such upstart efforts as those of Japan and Korea would perhaps not have been undertaken in the light of economic theory, though it is possible that there really were careful projections rather than aspirations to greatness that led to the drive to break the mold. (Interestingly, the Koreans follow a clear path: expansion of textiles, then steel plates, then electronics and cars. In the later instance, they failed in their first try at Hyundai, but persevered. Still, later ambitions led to developing too many companies and producing bankruptcies that also brought down banks and other enterprises.)

Marxist and leftist theorists have seen the classical argument about sticking to comparative advantage as a way to keep disadvantaged nations in their place. This was the explanation of the phenomenon of "imperialism" suggested by, inter alia, Lenin himself. Empires were seen as extractive enterprises designed to enrich the mother country. In fact, empires (including the Soviet one) have under analysis been shown to usually represent transfer of funds to the colonies. The mother country in effect buys and pays for political status by projecting itself as an international player in both the political and economic spheres. The truth of this was demonstrated by the British, French, and Dutch decisions in the aftermath of World War II to walk away from most of their empire. They decided they could not foot the bill.

The rescue approach to "imperialism" was "dependencia" theory. It argues that modern industrialism is an ever-productive system that moves societies to further development by requiring expanding substructure (e.g., roads, methods of transportation) and superstructure (e.g., computerization, electronic tracking of goods, methods of research and retrieval). Agricultural production follows routine ruts and agricultural countries therefore fall further and further behind industrial societies. Dependent countries find themselves ever more depressed and backward, since they do not need or create ancillary supportive economic structures.[15]

This interesting, even cogent, theory has the unusual fate in the social sciences of having been proved wrong. (Most social science is dismissed by, e.g., physicists, as "not even wrong.") Data from supplier countries in Latin America, the source of "dependencia" theory, demonstrated that infrastructure and institutions do develop around market movement of commodities, in quite comparable fashion to industrial goods. Roads, banks, futures markets, insurance, and innovations are all familiar to growers and distributors and are comparable in their elaboration to industrial proliferation. The means for independencia are there, in these ancillary economic developments.

However, it does appear that many nation-suppliers of natural commodities rely upon a single crop or small number of commodities. Obviously, this leaves a country at risk in the face of price fluctuations and worldwide supply patterns. But it also exposes them to the facts of life, that over time most commodities decline in value, since productive cost generally decline with more efficient methods. In short, whether agriculturally based or industrially based, single-commodity countries should be alert to diversify or at minimum specialize or establish a brand or similar quality to gain income to offset the long-range loss of income. This is particularly imperative for countries with a growing population since equipment and capital investment are the major path to cost reduction.

[T]hose who see in the UN a potential for "a parliament of man" are generally cult-like relics of the post–world war hopes.

Such opportunities, it is argued, will be opened wide when obstacles to competitiveness are removed. As Stiglitz noted, globalization is "a closer integration of the countries and people of the world which has been brought about by the tremendous reduction of costs of transportation and communication" spurred on "by the breaking down of artificial barriers to the flow of goods services, capital, knowledge and (to a lesser extent) people."[16] Clearly, there have been enormous benefit to people throughout the world. At the same time, he noted, globalization arouses great animosity as well as praise. And countries that have followed their own predilections—again China looms as the most conspicuous example—have done as well or better than those that have followed the "guidance" of international agencies and their batteries of experts.

The assumption of these experts was that the tactics they advised and even required at the country level for international loans could be simply translated to the international trade level and would be easily absorbed, giving a great impetus to growth and prosperity. The increased mobility of the factors of production and the development of specialization of input would produce cheaper, perhaps better, goods and would reduce disparities throughout the world. In short, the worldwide expansion of the marketplace would bring a new stage of efficient production to the advantage of producers, customers, and investors.[17]

As Stiglitz summarized the critics, all of this ignores the asymmetries and timing of "this great leap forward" and ignores the effect on human experience. This is in part because, as Stiglitz suggested, the international system honors freedom of migration rather more in the breach than in the observance. Even in a relatively homogeneous society, uprooting oneself and family is harder for individuals then moving machinery or relocating ATMs. This is recognized by many corporations and governments, with steps to make human transitions easier or less costly. Such help can be carried to extremes, as suggested by our earlier example of Scargill's suggestion that to keep miners in traditional settings unusable coal should continue to be mined and then stored. But generally, societies have recognized that abrupt personal upheavals have economic and social consequences such as crime, mental illness, and neglected education. Therefore, they attempt to mitigate consequences of migrating job opportunities.

At the international level, these issues are not merely exasperated by distance or even oceans. Government and boundaries intervene, and "free trade" of persons remains much more a slogan than a reality. Even the European Community has administered its free migration policies with much less vigor than its drives against tariffs and other trade barriers. The political costs of enforcement are quite different. In the real world, it is difficult to follow the job trail across borders unless one has specialized skills or is willing to live in the shadow of illegal immigration. Generally, when jobs migrate to foreign shores, they are filled by locals, not transplants.

And jobs do migrate, when barriers to movement of capital drop as producers seek cheaper labor where they can find similar skills. (An added bonus is they can find international or national subsidies for new facilities as they abandon legacy machinery.) Such a result is defended both on the grounds that jobs transformed abroad involved substandard skills and wages, positions perhaps occupied by illegals, who can appropriately be best employed in their home country. More forthrightly, it is suggested that the distribution of jobs is both efficient (in reducing costs) and just (in reducing worldwide income disparities).

As long as the jobs in the United States were low skill, grumbling was muted. Recent revelations that computer programming and other skilled positions were being outsourced abroad raised new issues. Those with high investment in education and skills could also lose employment, and the international system is really still inflexible about migration. The ado diminished when it became evident that relatively few cases had actually occurred, but it did not answer the question raised: the capital investment in humans is much more immobile under modern conditions than most other forms of capital.

The dramatic increase in the mobility of capital in recent decades is the major background for this dilemma. The Internet permits communication of a sort that is difficult for governments to control. The French under Mitterand found their efforts to track international transfers were much weaker than, for example, Italy and Germany were able to institute in the 1930s because of ease of communications and the existence of multinational firms. Those could use communication to transfer assets in rapid fashion, say, by changing accounting methods.

A further asymmetry is the differential monitoring of international finance between nations. Some countries have reasonably sophisticated methods for monitoring international corporations, but with the growing number of nation-states that subdivide year by year, many do not. All countries, but especially the recent proliferated nations, have difficulties in dealing with the multinationals even with respect to negotiated agreements between state and the companies. These nations have trouble in trying to get producers to act in reasonably efficient ways and not transfer future costs—for example, pollution—to the locality and then fold up shop when it suits them.

Another asymmetry comes from the reality that nation-states affect international pricing through their power over import (and export) taxes and their subsidies to production and export; the fiction of free trade suggests all are working to eliminate these at the same or approximately the same rate. But of course things are much more complex. Barriers and subsidies are increased with the left hand even as the international overt autarchic policies are cut with the opened right hand.

Nations differ in their negotiating skills and in their leverage in negotiating. The larger and more diverse the market, the more indifferent that nation is to outcomes and the greater its leverage. The failure of the Cancun international agreement on agriculture in 2003 was largely due to South American efforts to eke out a small advantage. The United States was disappointed but assumed it could work out bilateral agreements with most countries on roughly the terms the industrialized countries wanted. For Africa, the collapse of an agreement was a disaster. African nations suffered without one and would have accepted even less favorable terms than had been informally negotiated.

In general, it is assumed the Western industrial countries have the upper hand in these negotiations. Most observers believe the Uruguay Round of GATT on tariff reductions benefited developed and penalized developing countries. On the other hand, early "rounds" had permitted developing nations to maintain much higher tariffs on the theory they were not major players, and not much was at stake. In general, developing nations retain higher rates.[18] Since these issues—tariffs and subsidies—are translatable into income and costs for producers, they affect the production and supply picture and therefore distort markets and calculations of efficiency.

The financial crisis following the growth led to a peculiar confluence: both IMF leaders and antiglobalizationalists suggested it was a proof of the weakness of "the Asian Miracle." As Bhagwati pointed out, the financial crisis was serious but was contained. In any event, it hardly detracts from the industrial growth that preceded it. Stiglitz went further. He suggested the IMF-Treasury policies created the crisis by insisting the Asian countries be opened up to a flood of foreign capital and then insisted on policies that cascaded the problems from country to country. The outside experts then blamed the problem on the Asians, particularly Malaysia and Korea, that refused to follow their advice but that actually recovered faster and more solidly than those that did.[19]

Both Krugman directly[20] and Rubin by listing some of the critiques and saying they had "good points" accept some of the notions of error. Indeed, Krugman is a leading naysayer. But both suggested choices were constrained and that the alternative remedies had other risks. "The committee to save the whole world"—Rubin, Greenspan, and Summers—still believes containing a fiscal crisis is always a dicey proposition and that, in the event, they succeeded, and most of what is written is crude Monday morning quarterbacking. Rubin suggested the critics had interesting points but no real alternative to what was done.[21]

In any event, the literature of the times tells again and again that the flow of events hardly conforms to the view that the economy responds to "old-time medicine" in ways most bank-employed researchers suggest are clear-cut and inevitable. A prime example is the U.S. failure to respond to the Federal Reserve Board's continual efforts to restore interest rates by tiny increases in the prime rate throughout 2005. Instead, the mortgage rates continued to decline, apparently because of an influx of foreign investment.

It would appear then that neither with the early development nor the high development end of economics are experts endowed with theories or tools to make accurate extrapolations. Architects of social policy, therefore, still have to make choices rather than succumb to predictions of inexorable results. Neither can they accept assumptions that free trade ensures a free society.

A Global Law

There remains one other claimed nemesis: the emergence of a global legal order may inhibit many forms of welfare regulation, as it does in the European community and in NAFTA and WTO protocols. Presumably, guarantees of democracy and liberty will be part and parcel of some universalistic system, to accompany promised prosperity. All in all, it is not likely to be tomorrow's headline.

It has become almost a cliché to write about an incipient international legal order. Certainly, usual international law has been supplemented radically in the past half century. But the pattern created is a peculiar patchwork that basically does not transcend the problematics of the system I studied in graduate school. To be sure, almost all incipient legal systems are peculiar patchworks, but radical developments not clearly foreseeable today would have to occur to crystallize such a transcendence.

Virtually all of "new legal order" conforms to the underlying reality of the nation-state. The exceptions are the regional structures that may permit individual legal action. Clearly, the European community, which has full-blown legal recourse, is in a drastically different realm of legalism than any of the other systems in which the states are the subjects and individuals the "objects" of international law.

The classic national state is seemingly weaker than a half century ago, but much more as a result of communication breakthroughs and economic development than any external legal imperatives. It is, indeed, much more the social connectiveness that lends itself to claims of future growth of law—behavior rather than any legal pioneering.

At the same time, the number of nation-states has grown at a surprising pace. New states vastly outnumber those of the pre–World War II world. And the increase in such actors results in increased potential for variegated behavior. For starters, North Korea, Iran, and Burma show only slight responses to international pressures of a magnitude historically effective.

The multiplication of national units raises many questions.[22] In most instances, these represent breakaways from old entities (usually federations) that have in our time been unstable: the Soviet Union, Czechoslovakia, and Yugoslavia have splintered. Bangladesh was to emerge from Pakistan and now faces possible succession. Kurds and Basques seek autonomous regions or independence. Africa has experienced the Ethiopian-Eritrean and other breakaways. And even Puerto Rico makes occasional separatist efforts.

New states often turn to regional or international structures in part to secure insurance against reincorporation. How do we measure the centripetal versus the centrifugal, push against pull? Obviously, most smaller units have less capacity for economic autonomy in a world market. But is a North Korean entity aided or handicapped in its desire for autarchy by its artificiality? Is it stronger or weaker in its cultural cohesion and its ability to withstand modern communications and the pull of its neighbors' television? Can the military impose its will in Myanmar and Thailand; the established religious order prevail in Iran; or the party in China, Cuba, and North Korea, while permitting some invasion of world culture because of the simple manageability of their society? Has Ukraine experienced an absorption into the Western mainstream or lost its way from the East? Those who see only amalgamation may turn a blind eye to an opposite and perhaps equal dynamic.

But the main tendency has been inertial. The larger, more established powers are reluctant to yield leadership to a motley grouping of nation-states. No one has been ingenious enough to formulate a decent structure to establish new law, on a basis regarded as legitimate, except with regard to wholesale violation of human rights and genocide where the example of antipiracy and antislavery law has provided analogies from the past.

The incipient legalism comes from many sources: (1) The UN proper, which is a system devised to deal with potential international conflict, but whose structure has made it almost irrelevant in most crises. (2) A set of specialized organizations run with varying degrees of oversight by the UN, most of which were inherited from the League of Nations and are a legacy from internationalist needs of a century ago. (3) A set of monetary regulatory systems, offshoots of the Bretton Woods Conference of 1944, namely, the International Monetary Fund and the World Bank. (4) The World Trade Organization, the most aggressively growing of all, which is the successor to GATT, a series of attempts to eliminate trade barriers. The WTO's emergence from the GATT cocoon in 1993 included machinery for officially hearing and deciding complaints, and this is the usually cited example of incipiency. (5) Various regional structures dealing with free trade. The European community, on paper a federal system, went from the European Coal and Steel Community, a highly limited system dealing with the glut in those products, to a structure for free trade. Other regionals like NAFTA are much more tenuous, and any scenario of direct litigation by individuals seems unlikely. (6) Other, more specialized regimes or organizations have been created by treaty or other form of nations cooperating. The most significant of these—the Organisation for Economic Co-Operation and Development—is a structure for cooperation of the big industrial powers. Its clout has made its rare forays into policy—for example, the amount of capital needed for financial institutions and nontax deductibility of bribes paid to officials as a cost of doing business—have had unexpected influence.

As even this cursory listing indicates, few of those institutions have the power to undertake supranational decision making, on one hand, or subnational enforceability, on the other. Rather, these organizations are assemblies to find consensus. Those few cases where supernational decisions are agreed to usually have grounds and machinery for opting out when national interest is deemed threatened. Their principal mode of enforcement is through the regular national, legal order, and exceptions to this are few, far between, and usually sidestepped.

Of course, in most cases, there is no right of individuals to sue. In general, the UN machinery grinds out bureaucratic results, sometimes rule based, but more usually ad hoc and exigency-specific. In the early years after World War II, there was some movement toward laying down principled decision making, but it has increasingly been bogged down by its unrealistic one-nation one-vote system and the intractable veto system. Indeed, those who see in the UN a potential for "a parliament of man" are generally cult-like relics of the post–world war hopes.

An important, perhaps pregnant exception to the rule that global law is detoured through municipal law is the War Crimes Tribunal, an offshoot of the International Court of Justice, recently established by the UN. Because its authority extends to alleged war criminals, however seized, and creates an absolute obligation of nations to turn over those accused, the United States has refused to participate.

The most promising aspect of the UN is its extraordinary opening up of the world of NGOs, a vast, interlinked web of transnational structures. These have virtually no legal power, but they constitute an international civic society of the type extolled by Putnam and whose decline is viewed by him with horror.[23] Here is a foundation, a buttress, a supplement to a legal order, if it should emerge. By itself, though, it is an unlikely matrix for world order.

Greater hopes have attached to the financial organs of internationalism, but perhaps this is based on misunderstanding. The IMF and World Bank have almost completely operated on a nonlegal expedient basis precisely because they have missions dealing with preserving funds and avoiding financial missteps for themselves and their client nations, though each of them sees its function differently. They are also dominated by specific nation-states: the United States over the Bank and "old Europe" over the Fund. Since they deal with abstruse economic issues they had seldom been visible to the public, until the IMF became a bête noire and a scapegoat for international financial domination of developing countries. Their austere, remote policy dominant experts sought to minimize accountability and symbolize not a desire for a legal order but one of policy determination by those who know best. There is much and understandable discussion in the EU of "a democracy deficit," but the Fund and Bank suffer from an autocracy-superiority-complex surplus.

In any event, it is the emergence of panels making "determinations" in the WTO that is the most lawlike aspect in the picture and has excited the spirits of global law enthusiasts. Even here, it is misleading to speak of "law."

WTO succeeded to GATT, which was a proto-organization centered around periodic meetings—"rounds"—that produced agreements resulting in tariff reductions. Violations (or alleged violations) triggered jawboning between signature nations who disagreed. A skeleton staff sometimes intervened, but even the rules to judge conflicts were a secret. WTO made a great leap forward with published rules, an established organization, and panels of experts making findings.

The determination of a violation—a forbidden subsidy, or an outlawed tariff—permits the discriminating country to get even by enacting measures that are proportional to the damage, if the offending country refuses to modify its behavior. So a good deal of lag time is inherently built into the system. Bad behavior by nation A has to occur and be perceived. Nation B tells nation A to mend its ways. They interact, often trading A's grievance on matter X for B's complaints about Y. If they are unable to agree, an official complaint may be filed and a determination made. When a complaint is upheld, negotiations usually occur again. If unsuccessful, then A may announce a set of retaliatory tariffs and B has to decide to modify its behavior, accept the countertariffs, or challenge them as excessive given the findings of the original damage. Given this process of several years' length, complaints often dissipate with changed economic or political conditions permitting a resolution.

While WTO provisions are by the arcane methods of international law rather more lawlike than the average, it is far from a juridical regime. It is analogous to a domestic order in which a tribunal decides whether Hatfields are entitled to go after McCoys, and whether they exceeded the approved quota. More important, it does not seem to free itself from national setting of rules, or from national implementation. So China continues to wink at pirating by its citizens of mostly U.S. intellectual property. Still, it must be acknowledged that incipient legal orders (and in some respects advanced ones) are far from neat.[24]

The counterweight to national power throughout these systems is not in fact an internationalist perspective or world attitudes; perhaps we are at too early a point in the process for that. Rather, it is to introduce "expert," "objective," or conversely "clearly erroneous and therefore improper" standards that limit and constrain governments from acting on perceived self-interest of the nation-state or, worse yet, of those in charge of the machinery of the nation-state.

By and large, the creation of these institutions has been an elitist below-the-radar maneuver justified largely on technical, technocratic, and nonmajoritarian principles. Politicians have been reluctant to turn to the public for support, and it has been easy to turn most European community plebiscites into xenophobic denunciations and claims of intrusion by Brussels bureaucrats. Even in countries dependent on the broader opening up of boundaries—Denmark is a classic example—voters and legislatures seek to gain only the economic fruits and to minimize the power of the community that creates those economic boons. In short, most countries continue to treat the EC as much as possible as a customs union and as little as possible as a proto-government. Paradoxically, it is usually the more recent members—who see the EC as having political benefits, such as quasi-guarantees of internal democracy—who are most cordial to the further spread of lawmaking and law enforcement.

Of course, at the international level there is even less possibility of public opinion affecting policy or being aware of organizations and functions. And there are no referenda or direct elections of international officials. The use of expert judgment and "objective" standards has been a useful instrument for justifying the lack of democratic instrumentalities. Such judgments can, in fact, tame excessive political manipulations and can limit some ruinous economic activities. International trade experts, for example, can remind OPEC nations that rapacious pricing and dwindling world supplies can boomerang quickly. As the economies of developing nations contract quickly in the face of zooming energy costs, they must lower their use of energy and may set into operation a downward spiral for the world economy and therefore lower OPEC profits in a very short order. Such professional advice may take on more bite when, for example, recommended by IMF advisers who can, for example, grant new loans or call in old ones. But expertise is worth what the decision makers perceive as its accuracy.

But there are international forms of expert opinion that have more direct influence. Policies on health or on product standards (including both industrial and agricultural goods) have implications for trade, travel, tourism, and national prestige that are not limited to decision makers or even business elites. Indeed, statements of below-par conduct regulation or conduct of business also contain the possible loss of confidence of investors and much the same consequence of events. So the most direct impact of the public is to be felt in the economic sphere, by "voting with one's purse." Only the not-unusual participation of NGOs either in informing the public or mobilizing opposition resembles normal political processes.

Perhaps the purest form of claim to objectivity and expertise is expressed in the form of standards. Standards are prescriptive specifications for products, goods, or service and can be promulgated by governments, associations, or even individuals.[25] Sometimes, the products of the leading entity in a sector become the yardstick, a standard as it were by default. Penalties for not measuring up also are varied, ranging from a right to refuse delivery, a lower price, or damages, all the way to confiscation or, when the nonconfirming product is deemed dangerous, criminal sanctions.

Standards are versatile and can be not just assurances of quality but also of indications of appropriate use pricing and safety. While the primary beneficiaries of standardization are consumers, governments or trade associations can protect society both with respect to ultimate usage and distribution but also as to the basics of a product's manufacture, assembly, or development.

Standards are presumptively generated by the nature of the product at hand. But the protean nature of standard setting permits considerable subjectivity and manipulation for gain. Governments, for example, often set standards to favor local products and discourage foreign competition. Vintners notoriously restrict the use of regional appellations, so that actually adjoining fields must sell their wine at vastly lower prices, when owners cannot invoke a high-price regional name. Depending on who sets standards, consumers can emerge as both overprotected or underprotected and with sometimes confusing information. Both counterorganizations and new-type expertise may then arise to enlighten the user, or to fight protectionism hiding as objective standards.

The most important entities in this arena are the national standard setters, institutionalized by most governments in imitation of the German and British pioneering efforts mostly at the turn of the twentieth century. In the United States and most countries, there are ancillary governmental, quasi-governmental, and private standardizers. In the United States, the system is largely "voluntary" but it is much more uniform than implied by that term since failure to meet standards has severe consequences in obtaining insurance reimbursement or in litigation if something goes wrong.

Neither predictions that the welfare state would endanger law and freedom or that globalization would make the welfare state obsolete seem verified by recent history.

Standards are especially useful in international commerce, helping bridge social differences and commercial argot and custom by providing very specific information. As boundaries are crossed, governments have maximum opportunity to bring into play protectionism disguised as health and safety. Foreign beef is "prone" to hoof-and-mouth disease, local stomachs are different from (and more sensitive than) those of other countries, local housing regimes more protection from fire, and labor conditions are different. (The Japanese have famously employed "exigencies" to minimize changes seemingly agreed on in treaties.)

So the move toward globalization has gone hand in hand with efforts to objectify standards and eliminate tax and nontax barriers to trade. The European Community is premised on tackling such issues and has been far more successful in that regard than in dealing with human rights, migration, or the creation of a European political order. (A masterful example was the resolution of the European Court in dealing with different countries' rates on wine, beer, or whiskey and favoring its homegrown products. The court decided alcoholic content was to be the measure.)

At the international level, progress is much slower since it is usually worked out, step by step, in bilateral or multilateral agreements. But the major industrial countries and the WTO have also agreed on some modalities—standards about standards so to speak. One, for example, is the insistence on performance standards over design standards—how much a crane can safely hoist, rather than created from, say, an alloy made only in the regulating country or forbidding, say, plastic parts. While performance specifications can be manipulated, it is more difficult to do so. And the general attitude implied by the differentiation is also significant.

To date, standards remain largely set by national setters or under their procedures. In the United States, for antitrust reasons as well as an aversion to government control, neither the governmental National Institute of Standards and Technology nor the ANSI, the semiprivatized official standard supervisor, do very much to develop specific standards. Rather, ANSI sets up a process and supervises authorized standard setters. These can be government agencies, like the Department of Defense, the paramount developer. With small historically based exceptions, ANSI limits itself to a supervisory role.

The International Organization for Standardization (ISO) was not a major player in the field, until it invented the ISO 9000 services, and the process of self-certification, a wildly successful program. This success of the ISO is a result of its imaginative realization that many products and services are not regulated and would benefit from an individualized validation[26] of consistency. It has little or nothing to do with ISO's international status. For virtually all standard developers and users, a national standard authorized by a leading organization, especially ANSI, maximizes access to a national market and has at least equal clout, compared to ISO, in other countries.

In a sense, the continued nationally based standards structure, the lack of true significance of any true internationalization, is something of a paradigm for globalism. The world grows closer because it acknowledges American, German, European, and Japanese models. The Aerobus with its regionalized financial and design efforts has been put forward as a counterpoise, but it is both sui generis and regional. Internalism and international law are still largely the products of the slow spread of national patterns and work their way overwhelmingly through existing national operations.

Of the structures we have examined, regional pacts seem to have the greater potential. The EC serves as an example, especially its current effort to become a true political entity. But the following is basically as true today as when Emile Noel said it to me three decades ago: "The EC has economically been successful beyond its wildest dreams, but sadly lags in its true political achievements. Perhaps that is because businesses do not usually become governments."[27] The Community lurches from crisis to crisis, backing and filling, advancing and retreating. But each stage has been cumulatively remarkable. Its political achievements are fragile, yet they are impressive by any standards. As good an index as any is the slow but steady growth of the Parliament, or alternatively the creative diminishment of the crude old veto policies instituted to placate De Gaulle.

The advantage regional trade groups have is that they start with clear objectives, usually come after a period of less formal cooperation, and are intended to resolve concrete problems. They are not intended to be diplomatic venues, which already exist. If they do not contribute to resolving trade issues, there is no reason to preserve them for other types of crises. If they do succeed, they do so with decision machines that can be used at another stage of integration.

Most of the other structures seem at this point in history to be highly limited in their capacity to develop ideas or to gain acceptance. The likelihood in my view is that the underpinnings and intertwinement of competing legal orders will continue to create conflicts resolved either through political negotiations, or by creation of odd limited agencies, but increasingly with limited decision power, like the WTO. The growing conflicts of law generated will be resolved also by convergence of domestic law systems, with the additional potential of unified regional bodies of law and administration. A primary area crying out for some mutuality is patent and copyright law. (The gap between the owners and users of intellectual property is great enough so, e.g., China essentially flouts these rights, but as the gap narrows, the Chinese will want respect for their valued achievements. In the interim, other countries will consolidate their systems.) Where systems remain divergent, efforts to facilitate understanding will multiply.

In all of this, the growth of an intellectual and social community will, of course, play a paramount role. The citing of case decisions from other countries by Justice Frankfurter was regarded as an affectation, and Justice Breyer's mention of such decisions in his opinions has been criticized by Justice Scalia as an improper legal exercise since they are in no sense precedents in American law. (In point of fact, British precedents were cited frequently in early Supreme Court opinions, including the decision that "double jeopardy" extended to cases involving other punishments than death or dismemberment. That this was the "plain meaning" of the provision at time of adoption is clear.) But ultimately, there is no gainsaying the rights of judges in the United States or in foreign countries from seeking wisdom where they find it. The facilitation of legal information, like medical information, improves the quality of decisions as well as bringing it closer in spirit to universal aspirations.

The existence of Internet communication generally makes the universe of information more global in all areas of human discourse. The organization of people with similar viewpoints in NGOs and in communication networks is the most dramatic change of a lifetime. The difficulties governments experience in curtailing that contact and isolating their citizenry is the strongest hope for globalization of the spirit and therefore for law.

Can we anticipate globalization will enhance or diminish freedom? Plausible scenarios argue either way, and for each utopia or prediction of perpetual peace there is a futopia, a "brave new world" or "1984." Given our past discussion of the highly contingent nature of the relations between the factors, we can fairly conclude that no overwhelming trend can be discerned. But on the optimistic side, it is not unreasonable to hope for more freedom in the offing.

Both big and small states have had their share of free and servile societies, Madison argued that larger states had more pluralistic tendencies that minimized domination and that a federalized system also slowed down and tempered illiberal tendencies. There is no convincing evidence for either claim. Dahl and Tufte have argued for small democratic settings an argument contrary to Madison's expectations.[28] Neuman and Riker[29] have found no greater support for liberty in federal states, though their numbers examined are small, and the Nazis' astoundingly rapid rise to totalitarian control tends to dominate any analysis, and rather obviously motivates Neuman's classic discussion.

Where then is the source of optimism? (1) The Madisonian logic has not been refuted, merely not confirmed. Common sense suggests that complex structures' sources of constraint (checks and balances in the bread sense) are sources of freedom. If historical analysis does not bear that out, the relationship may be weaker than imagined, the methods of analysis inadequate to measure it, or, by chance, the relationship did not occur. (2) For more than a century, we were inundated with predictions of the triumph of systems denying freedom. They were hailed as the "wave of the future." We can share in Fukayama's manifesto and the demonstration of history that those self-proclaimed inheritors of the future had little staying power. (3) Many of the conglomerates contain requirements and buttresses for freedom. The most conspicuous is the EC requirement that member-states maintain a democratic structure and adhere to human rights defined in part by the Strasbourg convention of Human Rights and legally cognizable in EC as well as member-state courts. As we know, many such assurances have been made by totalitarian states, and their violations have been blinked at by their supposed fellow guarantors. In the case of the EC, it is clear that member-states believe the requirements will be enforced, and some countries—Greece and Spain come quickly to mind, as well as former Soviet satellites—were as eager to join to buttress internal democracy as well as to gain economic advantage. This dimension in many ways follows the path of the United States since 1937 in using the Fourteenth Amendment as a shield against its state government encroachment on liberty.

Conclusions

Neither predictions that the welfare state would endanger law and freedom nor that globalization would make the welfare state obsolete seem verified by recent history. Clearly, there has been retrenchment, particularly in denationalization, for fundamental economic reasons. But most retrenchments have occurred as in the United States for attitudinal reasons and the sense that social benefits were overgenerous. The future will see a more fundamental challenge as demographic shifts make the funding assumptions, based on past ratios of contributors to recipient, drastically challenge not just social security, but health, care, and unemployment protection patterns generally. Change in the "safety nets" will also challenge rights and full-class citizenship of those who find themselves unsuccessful or unlucky.

Notes

1. For a typical example, see Steven Pearlstein, "European Union Bitten by Fear of Free Markets," *Washington Post*, June 22, 2005, p. D1.

2. David Vogel, *Trading Up* (Cambridge, MA: Harvard University Press, 1995).

3. This is the conclusion that emerges from a painstaking review of the literature in a 2005 Ph.D. thesis by Pablo Alonso, "Multi-polarity and Institutional Development" (School of Public Affairs, American University, Washington, DC). An even harsher verdict on prevailing macroeconomics is delivered by Robert Samuelson, "Time to Toss the Textbooks," *Washington Post*, June 22, 2005, p. A21.

4. Timothy Tilton, "Why Don't the Swedish Social Democrats Nationalize Industry," *Scandinavian Studies* 59 (1987): 142-166.

5. See Ann Shola Orloff, "The Political Origins of America's Belated Welfare State," in *The Politics of Social Policy in the United States*, ed. Margaret Weir, Ann Orloff, and Theda Skocpol (Princeton, NJ: Princeton University Press, 1988).

6. Peter Berger, in Larry Diamond and Marc Platner, eds., *Capitalism Socialism and Democracy Revisited* (Baltimore: Johns Hopkins University Press, 1993), 3.

7. See Francis Fukeyama in ibid., 95-100, for a discussion of the greater complexity facing planners under modern conditions.

8. Fredrich Hayek, *The Road to Serfdom* (Chicago: University of Chicago Press, 1944), 62. On Laski, see, e.g., A. T. Mason, *Harlan Fiske Stone: Pillar of the Law* (New York: Viking, 1956), 334-35. Note especially the evaluation by Mark de Wolfe Howe on p. 335.

9. Samuel Krislov and Robert Kvavik, "Constitutional Design and the Channeling of Social Political Goals in the Welfare State," *Scandinavian Studies* 59 (spring 1987): 167-83.

10. Anton C. Zijdenfeld, *The Waning of the Welfare State* (New Brunswick, NJ: Transaction Press, 1999), 64-67.

11. See Phillipe Schmitter and G. Lembruch, *Trends toward Corporatist Integration* (Beverly Hills, CA: Sage, 1979); and Arend Lijphart, *Democracies* (New Haven, CT: Yale University Press, 1984).

12. Marc Miles, Edwin Feulner, and Mary O'Conner, *The 2004 Index of Economic Freedom* (Washington, DC: The Heritage Foundation; and New York: Dow Jones, 2004).

13. See the introduction to Robert Applebaum and Jeffery Hendersen, eds., *States and Development in the Pacific Rim* (Newbury Park, CA: Sage, 1992), for a succinct summary of the literature.

14. For a brief discussion of Barro's and Posner's ideas, see Ethan Kapstein and Dimitri Landis, "The Pluses and Minuses of Globalization," in *Globalization, Power and Democracy*, ed. Marc Plattner and Alexander Smolar (Baltimore: Johns Hopkins University Press, 2000), 132-38. Kapstein and Landis even referred to the "Barro-Posner model."

15. Bhagwati reported that the Brazilian economist Cardoso invented "dependencia" theory, but when he became president of Brazil, he sought globalization. See Jagdish Bhagwati, *In Defense of Globalization* (New York: Oxford University Press, 2004), 9.

16. Joseph Stiglitz, *Globalization and Its Discontents* (New York: Norton, 2002), 10.

17. Richard Rosecrance has ambitiously tried to encapsulate this view in *The Rise of the Virtual State* (New York: Basic Books, 1999). In part, I think it has not caught on because the term is inapt. "Virtual industry" is closer, but in fact the industry is real enough. But it is not defined by the borders of the "producing" state.

18. Compare Stiglitz, *Globalization and Its Discontents*, 43-53, with Bhagwati, *In Defense of Globalization*, 231-33, who suggested the poorer countries were "indulged" on tariff reductions in the first rounds.

19. See Bhagwati, *In Defense of Globalization*, 77; and Stiglitz, *Globalization and Its Discontents*, 211-12.

20. Paul Krugman, *The Return of Depression Economics* (New York: Norton, 1999), 117.

21. Robert Rubin, *In an Uncertain World* (New York: Random House, 2003), esp. 253-58.

22. See, e.g., Rupert Emerson, *From Empire to Nation* (Boston: Beacon, 1962); and Ernest Gellner, *Nations and Nationalism* (Ithaca, NY: Cornell University Press, 1983).

23. Robert Putnam, *Making Democracy Work: Civic Traditions in Modern Italy* (Princeton, NJ: Princeton University Press, 1993).

24. See, e.g., Mary Tachau, *Federal Courts in the Early Republic* (Princeton, NJ: Princeton University Press, 1978).

25. For elaboration of what follows, see Samuel Krislov, *How Nations Choose Product Standards and Standards Shape Nations* (Pittsburgh, PA: Pittsburgh University Press, 1997).

26. The business-oriented cartoon *Dilbert* parodied the ISO process: if I promise to produce a useless, rotten product and reproduce it exactly each time, I can get ISO certification.

27. Samuel Krislov, "Technology Law and Politics," in *The Fundamental Interrelationship between Government and Property*, ed. Nicholas Mercuro and Warren Samuels (Greenwich, CT: JAI, 1999), 125-26.

28. See, e.g., Robert Dahl and Edward Tufte, eds., *Size and Democracy* (Stanford, CA: Stanford University Press, 1973).

29. Franz Neuman, in A. W. MacMahon, *Federalism: Mature and Emergent* (Garden City, NY: Doubleday, 1955); and William Riker, *Federalism* (Boston: Little, Brown, 1964).

Case Studies
A. Moves toward Democracy

Overcoming Apartheid: Can Truth Reconcile a Divided Nation?

By
JAMES L. GIBSON

Throughout the world, truth commissions are being constructed under the hope that discovering the "truth" about a country's conflictual past will somehow contribute to "reconciliation." Most such efforts point to South Africa's process as an exemplar of the powerful influence of truth finding. But has truth actually contributed to reconciliation in South Africa? No rigorous and systematic assessment of the truth and reconciliation process has ever been conducted. This article investigates the hypothesis that truth leads to reconciliation. Based on a survey of thirty-seven hundred South Africans in 2001, the author begins by giving both "truth" and "reconciliation" clear conceptual and operational meaning. The author reports empirical evidence that the Truth and Reconciliation Commission's "truth" is fairly widely accepted by South Africans of all races, that some degree of reconciliation characterizes South Africa today, and that the collective memory produced by the process ("truth") did indeed contribute to reconciliation. The author then considers whether other divided countries might be able to use a similar process to propel themselves toward a more peaceful and democratic future.

Keywords: democratization; collective memories; conflict resolution; intergroup conflict; political culture

Introduction

Perhaps no country in history has so directly and thoroughly confronted its past in an effort to shape its future as has South Africa. Working from the explicit assumption that understanding the past will contribute to a more peaceful and democratic future, South Africa has attempted to come to grips with its apartheid history through its truth and reconciliation process. This bold undertaking to mold the country's fate consumed much of the energy and many of the resources of South Africa during the initial days of its attempted transition to democracy.

The gargantuan task of addressing the past has been under the supervision of South Africa's Truth and Reconciliation Commission (TRC). Established in 1995, the TRC spent roughly five

DOI: 10.1177/0002716205282895

years examining and documenting atrocities committed during the struggle over apartheid. At one level, the TRC was extraordinarily successful: it held hundreds of hearings, interviewed thousands of victims of apartheid, granted amnesty to nearly a thousand human rights violators, and produced a massive multi-volume "Final Report."[1] In terms of uncovering detailed evidence of what happened under specific circumstances (as in exactly what happened to the "Cradock Four"), the TRC seems effective as well.[2] In many respects, and according to most, South Africa's truth and reconciliation process appears to have been phenomenally successful.

Indeed, the world has acknowledged the success of South Africa's experiment through the numerous attempts to replicate its truth and reconciliation process in other troubled areas of the globe. Truth commissions modeled on the South African experience have proliferated, and one of the leaders of South Africa's TRC has created a major institute in New York to assist countries in developing plans for reconciliation in the world's many festering hot spots. Perhaps the judgment that the TRC succeeded is based on nothing more than the simple (and simplistic) observation that South Africa appears to have made a successful, relatively peaceful, and quite unexpected transition from the apartheid dictatorship to a reasonably democratic and stable regime. Some surely attribute South Africa's transformation to its truth and reconciliation process. If a TRC "worked" in South Africa, perhaps it can work elsewhere.

James L. Gibson is the Sidney W. Souers Professor of Government at Washington University in St. Louis. He studies mass psychology and behavior and democratization in the United States, Europe, and Africa. His research seeks to understand why ordinary people think the way they do about political issues (especially political tolerance) and how such thinking translates into public policy and democratic reform. He has published more than one hundred refereed articles, in a wide range of national and international social-scientific journals, including all of the leading political science journals. He has also published five books, with his Overcoming Intolerance in South Africa: Experiments in Democratic Persuasion *(with Amanda Gouws) published by Cambridge University Press in 2003, and his* Overcoming Apartheid: Can Truth Reconcile a Divided Nation? *published by the Russell Sage Foundation in 2004. In addition to his continuing research on democratization in Russia, he is currently working on a new study of the problem of historical injustices and "land reconciliation" in South Africa.*

NOTE: This article was originally published as James L. Gibson, "Overcoming Apartheid: Can Truth Reconcile a Divided Nation?" *Politikon: South African Journal of Political Studies* 31, no. 2 (November 2004): 129-55. Reprinted by permission of Taylor & Francis, http://www.tandf.co.uk. This research has been supported by the Law and Social Sciences Program of the National Science Foundation (SES 9906576). Any opinions, findings, and conclusions or recommendations expressed in this material are those of the author and do not necessarily reflect the views of the National Science Foundation. The project is a collaborative effort between Amanda Gouws, Department of Political Science, the University of Stellenbosch (South Africa), and me. I am indebted to Charles Villa-Vicencio, Helen Macdonald, Paul Haupt, Nyameka Goniwe, Fanie du Toit, Erik Doxtader, and the staff of the Institute for Justice and Reconciliation (South Africa), where I am a distinguished visiting research scholar, for the many helpful discussions that have informed my understanding of the truth and reconciliation process in South Africa. Most of the research on which this article relies was conducted while I was a visiting scholar at the Russell Sage Foundation, to which I am extremely grateful. I also appreciate the research assistance of Eric Lomazoff of the Russell Sage Foundation.

South Africans themselves are not so sanguine about the process. Many complain that the TRC exacerbated racial tensions in the country by exposing the misdeeds of both the apartheid government and its agents and the liberation forces. Some vehemently reject the conjecture that "truth" can somehow lead to reconciliation, claiming instead that uncovering the details about the horrific events of the past only embitters people, making them far less likely to be willing to coexist in the new democratic regime. Indeed, based on my casual observations of the South African media, complaints and condemnations of the truth and reconciliation process seem to far outnumber laudatory assessments.

[T]here is no evidence whatsoever that the "truth" proclaimed by the South African [Truth and Reconciliation Commission] damaged reconciliation, as so many feared.

Social scientists must be more agnostic about the success of the truth and reconciliation process. Indeed, it is perhaps shocking to note how little systematic investigation has been conducted into the question of whether the truth and reconciliation process succeeded in its objectives. Many enumerate the goals of the commission itself, and document its activities. There is no surfeit of judges when it comes to evaluating the process, but no earlier research has treated the various components of the truth and reconciliation process as hypotheses subject to confirmation or disconfirmation through rigorous social science methods. To put it bluntly, we simply do not know even today whether (and to what degree) the truth and reconciliation process in South Africa succeeded in achieving any of its objectives.

Of course, assessments of "success" depend mightily on the specification of the goals of the process. Though the TRC was charged with conducting several types of activities—for example, granting amnesty to gross human rights violators (Gibson 2002)—my central, uncontroversial contention in this research is that the objective of the truth and reconciliation process was to produce reconciliation in South Africa. This may not seem like a very rigorous or helpful specification of the country's aspirations since "reconciliation" is one of the most abused and ambiguous words in the lexicon of South Africa. And others take different tacks, with some seeking to discover whether the process accurately discovered the truth of certain events (Ignatieff 1996), others assessing whether the TRC maintained fidelity to the law that created it (Jeffery 1999), and still others judging the process in terms of philosophical standards of justice—especially retributive justice (Minow 1998). But no prior investigation has squarely and systematically attacked the big question: has truth led to reconciliation in South Africa?[3]

This question is, without doubt, as important as it is complicated (or some might even say "intractable"). To begin, what is "truth"; what is "reconciliation"? Is it fanciful to think that such grand and amorphous concepts can be given any rigorous empirical meaning? For instance, how should "truth" be conceptualized and measured? Even if we can agree on a definition of "reconciliation," we must specify who must reconcile with what or whom. Given the challenges of trying to produce systematic and rigorous evidence on how well truth commissions have performed, it is perhaps not surprising that scholars have often fallen back on either ideological judgments or highly incomplete, subjective, and qualitative evaluations of the work of such commissions.

It is no longer necessary to rely exclusively on such assessments. I have recently completed a major analysis of the work of South Africa's truth and reconciliation process (Gibson 2004). That study is perhaps the first effort ever to evaluate systematically the performance of a truth and reconciliation process. Though this research does *not* purport to be the last word on the success of South Africa's TRC, it concludes on the basis of empirical evidence that the truth-finding process contributed to at least some forms of reconciliation among at least some groups. Perhaps just as important, there is no evidence whatsoever that the "truth" proclaimed by the South African TRC damaged reconciliation, as so many feared. The findings of this research will most likely be interesting and informative to those contemplating establishing a truth process as a means of bringing about some degree of reconciliation and peaceful democratic change.

An overview of the study and its findings is useful but also risky in the sense that when addressing large sociopolitical issues like whether truth leads to reconciliation, the devil is indeed often in the details. But I nevertheless will attempt in this article to summarize the study's findings on (1) whether the TRC was successful at promulgating a "truth" that now serves as a collective memory of apartheid, (2) to what degree South Africans are reconciled, (3) whether "truth" in fact has made a contribution to reconciliation, and (4) why and how (through what processes). I will also speculate about the degree to which these findings from South Africa might be generalizable to other areas of the world wracked by a state of "irreconciliation."

The Meaning of *Reconciliation*

Two themes dominate contemporary discussions of the truth and reconciliation process in South Africa. First, no one seems to know what "reconciliation" means. Hay (1998, 13), for instance, called *reconciliation* "one of the most abused words in recent history in South Africa." Indeed, some have gone so far as to claim that "of course, reconciliation is a concept that cannot be measured" (du Preez 2001, 13). Indeed, du Preez (2001) apparently felt that this assertion was so self-evidently true that it was not necessary to offer a defense of his point of view. Second, however, everyone is certain that "reconciliation" has failed, or at least has not lived up to the expectations of most South Africans. People may not be able to define and measure the concept, but they seem to think they "know it when they see it," or at least when they do not see it.

But surely "reconciliation" means *something*. Indeed, the problem with the concept may be that it has *too many* meanings, not too few. For instance, Hamber and van der Merwe (1998) claimed to have isolated five distinct ways in which reconciliation has been either implicitly or explicitly used. The problem with "reconciliation" is not that it is devoid of content; the problem is instead that reconciliation is such an intuitively accessible concept that everyone is able to imbue it with her or his own distinct understanding.

Perhaps "reconciliation" is not such a difficult and complicated concept after all. Surely, a great deal of complexity can be attached to the idea, but the concept can be distilled down to a few simple and specific elements. Reconciliation is often discussed as a relationship, as for instance between victims and perpetrators, or between beneficiaries and the exploited. To make the concept empirically manageable, I must first be clear about who is being reconciled with whom.

Discussions of reconciliation in South Africa typically refer to two distinct phenomena: dealing with the micro-truth of what happened to specific loved ones, and with the macro-truth about the nature of the struggle over apartheid. At the microlevel, discussions often focus on the reconciliation of victims and perpetrators. This is the clearest meaning of the term *reconciliation,* and it has been the subject of wide media coverage in South Africa. Stories about the most profoundly injured victims (or their families) granting forgiveness to their evil tormentors are the stuff of which soap operas are made, and they captured the fancy of the South African mass public, at least for a while.[4] When applied to victims and perpetrators, reconciliation typically means acceptance of blame, apology, and forgiveness. For many in South Africa, led by Desmond Tutu (cf. Tutu 1999), this type of reconciliation has deeply religious overtones, as in definition number three, proposed by Hamber and van der Merwe (1998), which stresses a "strong religious ideology of reconciliation," based on identifying a "humanity" common to all groups in South Africa. Central to this definition is forgiveness, although Hamber and van der Merwe assert that "this perspective runs the risk of mistakenly equating forgiveness of past enemies with reconciliation."[5]

The second meaning of the term has to do with the larger South African society, and in particular reconciliation among the races, and, closely related, between those who profited from apartheid and those who were injured by it. Markel (1999) referred to this as "the public reconciliative relationship" and asserted, "The TRC hoped to cultivate a broad-swathed public reconciliative role among and with the various racial and ethnic groups of South Africa, so that social groups would learn the skills necessary to cope with the pain experienced as a group in the past" (p. 407). This understanding of reconciliation has little to do with any specific human rights violation; rather, it involves coming to grips with—accepting responsibility and blame for—the subjugation of the black majority by the small white minority under apartheid. As Krog (1998) noted, "Reconciliation in this country is not between operators and victims, but between the beneficiaries (whites) and the exploited (blacks)." This is similar to the first definition proposed by Hamber and van der Merwe (1998)—their "non-racial ideology of reconciliation," which is basically a condition in which South Africans live together as "non-racial citizens within a harmoniously integrated social setting." It is also similar to their second definition, which emphasizes "intercommunal understanding," and calls for "bridging the divide" between various distinct and generally separate racial communities. "From this perspective the TRC is considered to be a facilitator that can improve communication and mutual tolerance of diversity" (p. 1). My concern in this research is thus with these broader sociopolitical aspects of the reconciliation of all South Africans, not just victims and perpetrators. Reconciliation may therefore be thought of as a continuum describing the relationship between those who were masters and slaves under the old apartheid system, not just those who were victims or perpetrators of gross human rights violations.

Whether one likes it or not, an explicit objective of the [Truth and Reconciliation Commission] was to produce a "collective memory" for South Africa.

In South Africa, the groups that must reconcile are the four main racial groups in the country—whites, Africans, Coloured people, and South Africans of Asian origin.[6] The root cause of the interracial alienation was colonialism; the proximate cause is of course apartheid. The harm inflicted was that of inequality. Whites treated Africans, Coloured people, and South Africans of Asian origin as if they were inferior in nearly every sense, including the political and legal domains. The key to reconciliation is therefore that South Africans of every race accept all other South Africans as equals and treat them as equal, extending dignity and respect to them. The TRC Final Report asserted that reconciliation requires the recognition that "We are all in the same boat—we simply need to understand each other better and be more respectful of each other's culture" (TRC 1998, vol. 9, 425). When people talk about reconciliation, they often mean nothing more than the races getting along better with each other—that is, a diminution of racial animosities. This may mean that people come to interact with each other more (the breakdown of barriers across races), communicate more, in turn leading to greater understanding and perhaps acceptance, resulting in the appreciation and exaltation of the value of racial diversity and multiculturalism (the "Rainbow Nation").

"Reconciliation" also takes on three additional meanings beyond interracial reconciliation. The first is simply political tolerance, the willingness of South Africans to put up with their political foes.[7] South Africans may not be required to like or agree with each other, but many expected the truth and reconciliation process to contribute to a sort of relatively peaceful coexistence. In its minimalist version, this means putting up with those who hold different or even repugnant ideas and viewpoints. In its maximalist rendition, tolerance means embracing one's former enemies, forgiving them, and perhaps even joining in political coalitions with them.

A third aspect of "reconciliation" has to do with the development of a political culture in South Africa that is respectful of the human rights of all people. The creation of a human rights culture was one of the explicit goals of the TRC. Its report asserts, "Reconciliation requires that all South Africans accept moral and political responsibility for nurturing a culture of human rights and democracy within which political and socio-economic conflicts are addressed both seriously and in a nonviolent manner" (TRC 1998, vol. 5, 435). This is similar to the fourth definition of reconciliation proposed by Hamber and van der Merwe (1998). For South Africa's nascent democracy to prosper, the political culture must be one in which the universalistic application of the rule of law—and the rejection of the arbitrary exercise of governmental authority and power—is deeply valued and respected.

Finally, it is important as well to address the *institutions* that serve as the backbone of South Africa's new democracy since democracy is both a set of formal institutions and a set of cultural values. For instance, South Africans must come to tolerate each other, to be willing to countenance the expression of displeasing political ideas. But they must also come to support institutions that have the authoritative means of enforcing political tolerance as effective public policy. Just as the truth and reconciliation process sought to encourage respect for human rights, it also implicitly sought support for the institutions charged with the protection of those human rights. If South Africans fail to extend legitimacy to the institutions of majority rule and the protection of minority rights, it would be difficult indeed to consider them reconciled with the newly implemented democratic system. To extend these institutions' legitimacy is to accept at an elemental level South Africa's new system of democratic rule, to reconcile with the reformed political dispensation in the country. Thus, reconciliation requires that all South Africans recognize the legitimacy of the political institutions created after the fall of apartheid.

Consequently, a "reconciled" South African is one who

- eschews racial stereotyping, treating people respectfully, as individuals, not as members of a racial group;
- is tolerant of those with whom he or she disagrees;
- subscribes to a set of beliefs about the universal application of human rights protections to all South African citizens; and
- recognizes the legitimacy of South Africa's political institutions and is predisposed to accept and acquiesce to their policy rulings.

Thus, in this research I investigate reconciliation between *people*, among *groups*, with basic constitutional *principles*, and with the *institutions* essential to the new South African democracy.

The Meaning of "Truth"

While reconciliation is a challenging concept to measure, one should not treat "truth" lightly, and I do not. Indeed, "truth" is likely more worrisome than "reconciliation," especially since so many of us bridle (or should bridle) at even the intimation that *"the* truth"—official truth—exists. Whether one likes it or not, an explicit objective of the TRC was to produce a "collective memory" for South Africa. This is not just a chronicle of who did what to whom; instead, it is an authoritative description and analysis of the history of the country. Was apartheid a crime against humanity? Was the criminality of apartheid due to the missteps of a few rogue individuals, or was apartheid criminal by its very ideology and institutions? These are questions for which the TRC provided unambiguous and, by its accounting, definitive answers. My goal here is not to assess the historical accuracy of these claims but rather to determine the degree to which ordinary South Africans accept the truth as promulgated by the TRC—its collective memory. When I consider the "truth leads to reconciliation" hypothesis, in every instance I am investigating the hypothesis that *those South Africans who accept the truth as documented by the TRC* are more likely to be reconciled. Truth as I use it in this research means the TRC's truth, nothing more.

Connecting Truth with Reconciliation

Some in South Africa believe that not only does truth not lead to reconciliation but instead it leads to "irreconciliation" by exacerbating tension and conflict between those who struggled for and against apartheid. The view here is that the truth process has uncovered horrific human rights abuses (see, for example, the revelations in de Kock 1998), has reawakened long dormant memories and animosities, and has generally forced all sides in the struggle over apartheid to confront each other. In short, everyone can find something to hate in the findings of the truth and reconciliation process.

Perhaps this is so. But an alternative view is that the truth and reconciliation process succeeded in getting people to rethink their views about the struggle over apartheid. As Figure 1 depicts, the truth and reconciliation process may have changed the way South Africans think about each other by creating cognitive dissonance and by mitigating cognitive dogmatism. In short, the truth and reconciliation process may have created uncertainty and doubt about the goodness and morality of one's cause. Virtually all parties in South Africa—from the African National Congress to the National Party—condemned the TRC's Final Report. And as I demonstrate below, one of the most consequential lessons of the TRC was that all sides in

FIGURE 1
PROCESSES BY WHICH "TRUTH" LEADS TO ATTITUDE CHANGE

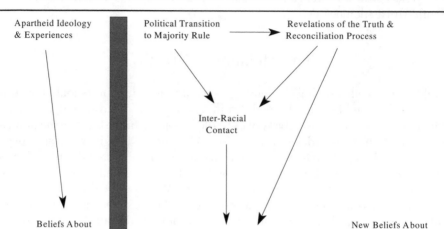

the struggle did horrible things. Truth exposed atrocities, perhaps making people less likely to reconcile. But the South African truth process also documented atrocities on all sides in the struggle over apartheid, making many South Africans less certain about the purity of their side in the struggle, and forcing people to acknowledge that the "other side" was also unfairly victimized. Sharing responsibility, blame, and victimhood evens the score ever so slightly, providing a basis for dialogue. If people are no longer dogmatically attached to a "good versus evil" view of the struggle, then perhaps a space for reconciliation is opened.

Measuring Reconciliation in Contemporary South Africa

A central contention of this project is that concepts like "truth" and "reconciliation" can be (and should be) measured and assessed using rigorous and systematic social science methods. The four components of reconciliation are

Interracial reconciliation. This refers to the attitudes South Africans hold toward those of different races. A reconciled South African is one who respects, understands, and trusts those of other races, and who rejects stereotypes about them. For purposes of economy, the questions we ask refer to a member of the "opposite race." For black South Africans, our questions refer to whites; for whites, Coloured people, and those of Asian origin, our questions refer to blacks. The questions measuring interracial reconciliation (and the other aspects of reconciliation) are reported in the appendix.

TABLE 1

SUMMARY LEVELS OF RECONCILIATION,
PERCENTAGE SOMEWHAT OR HIGHLY RECONCILED, 2001

Dimension of Reconciliation	African	White	Coloured	Asian Origin
Interracial reconciliation	37	57	72	59
Support for a human rights culture	45	77	62	54
Political tolerance	21	35	26	25
Institutional legitimacy	81	62	78	67

A South African culture of human rights: Support for the rule of law. The legislation establishing the TRC called for the development of a culture respectful of human rights in South Africa. Perhaps the "first principle" of such a culture is respect for the rule of law. In particular, a human rights culture cannot be established without a commitment to the universal application of law, and especially the unwillingness to set law aside to accomplish other objectives.

Political tolerance. Merely putting up with one's political enemies may be a minimalist definition of reconciliation, but given the crucial role of tolerance within democratic theory, achieving reconciliation through tolerance is a lofty objective. South African culture is not well known for its tolerance; building respect for political differences and willingness to debate openly all political thoughts is essential for intergroup reconciliation.

Institutional legitimacy. If South Africans fail to extend legitimacy to the institutions of majority rule and the protection of minority rights, it would be difficult indeed to consider them reconciled with the newly implemented democratic system. To extend these institutions' legitimacy is to accept at an elemental level South Africa's new system of democratic rule, to reconcile with the new political dispensation in the country. I therefore measured South Africans' attitudes toward their Parliament and their Constitutional Court.

Thus, I conceptualize a reconciled South African as one who is trustful and respectful of those of different races, who is tolerant of her or his political enemies, who is committed to protecting human rights through the rule of law, and who extends legitimacy to the political institutions of the New South Africa. How many such people are there in South Africa?

Table 1 summarizes the empirical results on the four types of reconciliation investigated in this project.[8] I report for each group the percentages for each subdimension scoring as at least somewhat reconciled.[9]

In terms of the individual components of reconciliation, none of the racial groups is very reconciled at all when it comes to political tolerance; all are at least somewhat reconciled when it comes to institutional legitimacy. Levels of reconciliation in terms of interracial attitudes and support for a human rights culture lie in between legitimacy and tolerance.

FIGURE 2
RACIAL DIFFERENCES IN OVERALL LEVELS OF RECONCILIATION

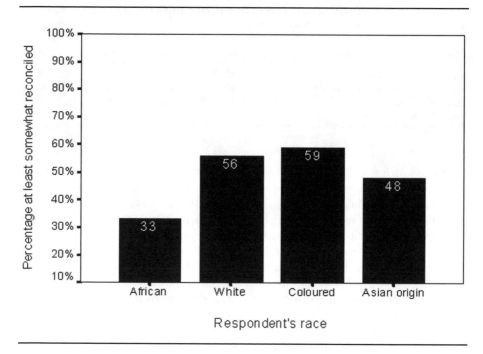

Based on a summary of these summary scores, one might draw the following conclusions about the level of reconciliation prevalent among South Africa's various racial groups: Africans—not very reconciled; Whites—somewhat reconciled; Coloured South Africans—somewhat reconciled; and South Africans of Asian origin—somewhat reconciled. That is, using a mean score summarizing *all four subdimensions* of reconciliation (data not shown), Coloured South Africans are most reconciled, followed by whites, then South Africans of Asian origin, and finally Africans. After categorizing that mean, I find the following percentages of each group are at least somewhat reconciled: 33 percent for Africans, 56 percent for whites, 59 percent for Coloured people, and 48 percent for those of Asian origin (see Figure 2). Thus, whites, Coloured people, and those of Asian origin hold similar, moderately reconciled views, but Africans are significantly less reconciled. In terms of the various ethnic/linguistic groups, the most reconciled are English-speaking Coloured people (75 percent), followed by English-speaking whites (64 percent). The least-reconciled South Africans are North Sotho speaking blacks (17 percent). Thus, enormous variability exists in levels of reconciliation across the various groups.

In South Africa as a whole, which is of course composed mainly of Africans, the data reveal that about 44 percent of the population is at least somewhat reconciled. What overall conclusions about reconciliation can be drawn from these figures?

No comparable data exist to indicate levels of reconciliation in the apartheid past. It seems entirely reasonable to assume, however, that reconciliation as defined in this research was considerably lower than 44 percent. That nearly one-half of the South African population expresses some degree of reconciliation in less than a decade after the formal demise of apartheid represents, from my perspective, an unexpectedly high level of reconciliation. Reconciliation seems to have made inroads into a sizable portion of the South African population.

Still, it would be hard to characterize South Africa as a widely reconciled society. Progress since the transition has been made, but a long road must be traversed before reconciliation predominates in South Africa.

Measuring Acceptance of the TRC's Truth

One of the objectives of the truth and reconciliation process was to create a collective memory for South Africa.[10] A collective memory is an accepted version of the truth about the country's past. By establishing a collective memory, it becomes difficult (although not impossible) for people to deny that certain activities took place. As Ignatieff (1996) has proclaimed, "All that a truth commission can achieve is to reduce the number of lies that can be circulated unchallenged in public discourse" (p. 113). The TRC's multifaceted truth is not necessarily an officially sanctioned truth, but is instead an amalgamation of ideas about the past with which all South Africans must now at least contend.

To test the hypothesis that truth contributes to reconciliation, I must develop a summary measure of the degree to which each individual recognizes the TRC's historical truth about apartheid. Thus, the respondents were asked to judge five propositions that most analysts would agree represent the findings of the TRC. The statements about apartheid I consider to be self-evidently true or untrue according to the TRC are

Apartheid was a crime against humanity. (True)
There were certainly some abuses under the old apartheid system, but the ideas behind apartheid were basically good ones. (False)
The struggle to preserve apartheid was just. (False)
Both those struggling for and those struggling against the old apartheid system did unforgivable things to people. (True)
The abuses under apartheid were largely committed by a few evil individuals, not by the state institutions themselves. (False)

These five statements are simple, widely accepted (at least throughout the world, if not in South Africa), and are interrelated, and the veracity[11] of the statements would undoubtedly not be controversial among the leaders of the truth and recon-

TABLE 2

ACCEPTANCE OF THE TRUTH AND RECONCILIATION
COMMISSION'S (TRC'S) VIEW OF SOUTH AFRICA'S PAST

	Percentage Believing the Statement to Be True			
	African	White	Coloured	Asian
Apartheid was a crime against humanity	94	73	86	89
Despite abuses, apartheid ideas were good ones	36	51	35	42
The struggle to preserve apartheid was just	39	34	24	36
Those struggling for and against apartheid did unforgivable things	76	74	66	83
Abuses of apartheid due to evil individuals, not state institutions themselves	41	43	28	47

NOTE: The positions I assert to represent the view of the TRC are as follows: true—first and fourth statements; and false—second, third, and fifth statements.

ciliation process themselves. Most important, these are all truths that the TRC discovered and proclaimed.[12]

The statement declaring apartheid a crime[13] turned out to be widely accepted among South Africans of every race, and thus constitutes an important element of a collective South African memory (see Table 2). But despite this apparent condemnation of apartheid, a significant proportion of South Africans *of every race* also believe that the *idea of apartheid* was good, even if the implementation of the ideology was not. Most likely, reactions to this statement are in reference to the "separate development" implications of apartheid, rather than to the idea that a racial hierarchy with racial subjugation is acceptable and/or desirable.[14] Apartheid is sometimes understood as a system of racial separation and the development of blacks apart from whites, a view compatible with some elements of black nationalism. For instance, the Black Consciousness Movement, under the leadership of Steve Biko (e.g., organizations such as the South African Students' Organization, Black People's Convention, Azanian People's Organization), had as its main aim the psychological liberation of black people from feelings of inferiority and the restoration of their human dignity (Sibisi 1991) and rejected interracial integration as an important goal (at least in the short term). Similarly, the Pan-Africanist Congress (PAC) has never been interested in building a multiracial South Africa, so it seems entirely plausible that PAC supporters would favor at least some form of "separate development." Thus, it seems credible that not all blacks in South Africa view apartheid as a system of unequivocal evil. In light of these ambivalent attitudes toward apartheid, it is not surprising that a substantial minority of South Africans—and fully 39 percent of black South Africans—believe that the struggle to preserve apartheid was just. Again, perhaps this indicates that people accept that each racial community has the right to a separate existence, and if so, it follows that efforts to preserve separateness are legitimate.[15]

South Africans of every race also accept what was probably one of the most important conclusions of the TRC—that those who struggled for *and* against apartheid committed horrible abuses.[16] Nonetheless, a plurality of blacks, whites, and those of Asian origin is willing to attribute the abuses *to individuals*, not to the state institutions themselves, a finding consistent with the view of many that apartheid was a good idea poorly implemented.

On the basis of the responses to these five items, I calculated an index of truth acceptance, which varies from 0—*rejecting all statements*—to 5—*accepting the veracity of each one* (i.e., the two "true" responses and the three "false" responses). Cross-race differences are statistically significant, but quite small, with $\eta = .15$. Not surprisingly, blacks are most likely to accept the veracity of these statements, whereas whites are least likely. However, the substantive differences are *not* great—the means range from 2.8 for whites to 3.2 for blacks, with a median of 3 items accepted among all four racial groups.

Thus, this survey reveals that views about the country's apartheid past are complicated. In principle, apartheid is *not* perceived as inherently evil by everyone, even if most agree that the implementation of apartheid ideas was criminal. Not surprisingly, whites are more forgiving of the failures of apartheid, but blacks, Coloured people, and South Africans of Asian origin hold unexpectedly tolerant views of the apartheid system. Generally speaking, the truth and reconciliation process succeeded at exposing human rights abuses by both sides in the struggle over apartheid—thereby contributing to a collective memory for the country.

Moreover, if reconciliation is nothing more than accepting the TRC's truth about the past, then at least some level of reconciliation has indeed taken place in South Africa. Though my analysis certainly introduces caveats, the fact that large majorities of blacks, Coloured people, and those of Asian origin accept that apartheid was a crime against humanity is a terribly important finding. Apartheid was not a noble experiment, and few in South Africa believe it was. Whether these beliefs are due to the TRC cannot be clearly established with the data at hand, but I believe and the data suggest that the TRC's revelations played some role in producing a common understanding among all South Africans of the country's apartheid past.

The Success of the Truth and Reconciliation Process in South Africa

At some level, the truth and reconciliation process clearly succeeded in South Africa. In the early 1990s, many feared a civil war would engulf the country, and political violence was widespread. Even the relatively more optimistic feared massive white flight and destabilization. And with the African National Congress (ANC) holding nearly enough power to change the constitution unilaterally and at will, some prognosticators dreaded that South Africa would go the way of the many failed democracies of Africa.

None of these things happened. It thus appears certain that something must have altered the course of the South African transition.

The central contention of this research is that the truth and reconciliation process itself contributed to at least some degree to reconciliation in South Africa. This is a strong claim, one that many skeptics (especially in South Africa) are ill prepared to accept. Let us see what the data indicate about the relationship between these two variables.

The data demonstrate that truth and reconciliation do indeed go together and are compatible with the view that the collective memory produced by the truth and reconciliation process contributes to levels of reconciliation. I reach this conclusion because I find only slight racial differences across groups in understandings about the country's apartheid past (see above) and because for blacks, whites, Coloured people, and (to a limited degree) those of Asian origin, *those who are more accepting of the TRC's truth are more likely to be reconciled*. Using the index summarizing all four subdimensions of reconciliation, the correlations between truth acceptance and reconciliation are

Africans	Truth Acceptance — .23 → Reconciliation
Whites	Truth Acceptance — .53 → Reconciliation
Coloured people	Truth Acceptance — .34 → Reconciliation
Asian origin	Truth Acceptance — .09 → Reconciliation

Thus, for most South Africans, but especially for whites, there can be little doubt from these data that truth acceptance and reconciliation are to some degree connected.

The issue of causality remains, however. It may well be that those already predisposed to reconciliation were more likely to accept the findings of the TRC and that consequently the causal flow is not as I have designated it here. With cross-sectional data, the question of causality can never be definitively answered. Statistical analysis of the causal flow (e.g., two-stage least squares) supports the view that truth caused reconciliation, and not vice versa, but causal inferences can never be more than inferences in which we have more or less confidence (Gibson 2004). At a minimum, these data entitle me to conclude that *accepting the TRC's truth does not contribute to "irreconciliation,"* as so many feared (i.e., no negative relationship exists), and that the bulk of the available statistical evidence implies that truth did indeed contribute to producing more reconciled South Africans.[17]

Conjectures about the Processes by Which Truth Leads to Reconciliation

To get some additional purchase on the processes of attitude change that may have resulted from South Africa's truth and reconciliation process, it is necessary to move beyond the available data, which, after all, are drawn from a single point in time. I begin by imagining what interracial attitudes might have been like under apartheid.

The decade of the 1980s was a period of low-scale civil war in South Africa. The ANC had launched a campaign to make the country "ungovernable" and it succeeded to a remarkable degree. The apartheid régime was forced to declare a state of emergency, and urban terrorism became fairly commonplace. This was a time of intense political conflict between the forces of apartheid and the forces of liberation.

It is easy to imagine that racial attitudes were extremely polarized as a result of the struggle. The views of white South Africans toward blacks were most likely heavily tinged by the historical racism dominating most of their lives under apartheid. Moreover, whites viewed the liberation movement as the spearhead of a communist threat, believing the ANC to be a stooge of worldwide communism. Not only were the liberation forces dominated by communists, but they were godless as well. Urban terrorism terrified whites. Some whites imagined that their black housekeepers would rise up in revolution, perhaps even poisoning their families while serving one of the daily meals. Enforced racial segregation made anything but pro forma interracial contact unlikely, and what contact took place was inevitably grounded in inequality. It is easy to suppose that most whites, even those who did not strongly support apartheid, viewed the liberation movement as a movement dominated by evil. The war against the liberation forces was according to them a "just war." Reconciliation under such circumstances was extremely unlikely.

Black attitudes toward whites were unlikely to have been any more favorable. Whites were viewed as irretrievably racist, irrevocably committed to apartheid, and willing to deal with blacks only when forced to. Apartheid was a "crime against humanity," making those who benefited from apartheid criminals themselves. Contacts with whites were rare, and often took place within the context of dehumanizing circumstances. Many black South Africans were forcibly removed from their places of living, with some being banished to the so-called Bantustans. Resentment and outrage against the white system were widespread. For many blacks, apartheid was the source of all that was wrong with South Africa. The war against the apartheid state was according to them a "just war."

If I am correct about the nature of attitudes prior to the transition, then strong impediments to reconciliation existed. Both blacks and whites most likely understood and trusted each other very little, rarely interacted, held vicious stereotypes about each other, and disliked and were highly threatened by those of other races. This is almost certainly the landscape facing the TRC when it began its efforts at creating a more reconciled South Africa.[18] Some exogenous force was necessary to open the door to a change in attitudes.

The primary process by which the TRC might induce attitude change is through the creation of cognitive dissonance. To get South Africans to change their attitudes toward those of other racial groups, it is essential that the cognitive basis of racial beliefs be shaken up. Change in racial attitudes is often difficult to achieve because exogenous forces capable of generating widespread dissonance rarely occur naturally, and most people are able to fend off a trickle of unwelcome information as it filters into their consciousness.

The truth and reconciliation process in South Africa, with its attempt to reshape the country's understanding of its apartheid past, is a force perhaps capable of getting people to rethink their attitudes. If the TRC was successful in stimulating South Africans to revaluate their understandings of race and racial conflict in South Africa, perhaps it was capable of creating enough attitudinal dissonance to provide an engine for change in racial attitudes.

How might the truth and reconciliation process have created this dissonance? Perhaps the most important lesson of the TRC was that both sides in the struggle did horrible things. Let me consider how this finding of the TRC might have affected white and black attitudes.

White people could have learned from the truth and reconciliation process that the defense of the apartheid state included many indefensible actions. Many of the revelations unearthed by the TRC involved extreme excesses in the political repression the state applied against dissidents. Whether they should have known or not, many white South Africans claim to have been shocked by these revelations, claiming to have never imagined that the state would go as far as it did to crush resistance to apartheid.[19] For instance, when asked about this, a group of white South Africans in one of our focus groups[20] had the following replies:

> Yes, all these things when they came out at the TRC, I thought, my God, where was I living? Was that in South Africa?
> It's a very good point.
> The whites, you didn't know any of that was going on. You looked on apartheid and you were comfortable because you could go to the shops and go where you liked.
> It was a very clever system.
> It was wonderful, but I didn't know these things were happening. I was shocked to learn what was going on. But that was the government we were living under.
> I remember having arguments with my father. He was saying, "don't believe everything you get told." I'm telling him, "this is happening to my friends" and he kept saying they were communists and . . .
> That's it, you see! Because that is what the justification for all this was, to us.
> It was the brainwashing.
> **Q:** So there are quite a lot of people here, let me understand this nicely, you're saying that to some or to a large extent you weren't actually aware of the atrocities until you saw . . .
> I think we were aware of people being separated, separate toilets, buses, you know this.
> The superficial things.
> But, in my opinion . . . I can remember growing up, hearing drums on the farm, having a wonderful time and to me, that was some of their choice.
> They were happy living in these . . .

> Yes, they were happy. We were ignorant in a sense of knowing what actually really went on.

Perhaps some whites, even those who still cannot accept that apartheid was a crime against humanity, have come to view the implementation of apartheid, or at least its defense, as criminal. At a minimum, it seems quite unlikely that the defenders of apartheid were as heroic and legitimate after the revelations of the truth and reconciliation process. The "just war" in defense of apartheid seems less just, after the exposés of the TRC.

White South Africans have also learned that liberation does not lead to communism. The TRC did not have to teach whites this lesson; history was sufficient. With the breakdown of the worldwide communist movement, with the moderation of both the Mandela and Mbeki governments, few whites today would equate ANC rule with the rule of godless communists.

Whites cannot have helped but be impressed by the magnanimity and graciousness of Nelson Mandela during the early days of the transition. Mandela's continuous pleas for tolerance and reconciliation—not to mention his well-publicized donning of a rugby shirt (the sport of choice among whites)—have undoubtedly contributed to more benign racial attitudes among whites.

Whites may also have come to accept some of the guilt and blame for the benefits they enjoyed under apartheid and for the costs the system imposed on the vast majority of South Africans. Although some whites may have been unaware of the atrocities committed by their state against the liberation forces, no whites could claim to be unaware of the enormous subsidy apartheid provided for their standard of living.

Thus, whites attentive to the truth and reconciliation process basically learned that their side was less than noble in creating and defending apartheid and that the opposition was perhaps less radically evil in its efforts to create a new system in South Africa.

The truth and reconciliation process may have contributed as well to attitude change among blacks; although because the revelations of the process were often not new news to blacks, attitude change may not have been as radical or as widespread.[21] Prior to the TRC, blacks in South Africa were entirely aware of the evil of apartheid, and the TRC did little to dispel this knowledge. But the truth and reconciliation process may have also taught blacks that horrible things were done— against blacks and against whites—in the name of liberation. In many respects, the campaign of ungovernability in the 1980s turned blacks against blacks, with great pressures toward conformity (reinforced by the horrific crime of "necklacing," wherein a tire is put around the victim's neck and set alight), and with some degree of gangsterism occurring under the guise of the struggle (Marks 2001; Gobodo-Madikizela 2003, 147). We put the following question to the subjects in one of our African focus groups:

Q: (Reads second statement: Those struggling for and against apartheid did terrible things to others.) What do you think of that?

It's very true, both sides have blood on their hands.

Even the so-called liberators had very inhumane methods that they used when they wanted to put through a message—in camps abroad and within the country. A lot of people were hurt in the townships; if you were successful you were accused of selling out.

We as blacks don't empower our people; whites lift each other up. When we blacks get to the top, we forget our own.

Q: Anyone else?

It's true, both sides did bad things.

Q: You only mention the liberation movements, why not the white régime?

That is obvious, with them we don't even need to mention it because we know exactly what happened.

Q: But was it justified for both camps to do what they did?

Not at all.

But in those days there was no time to think about whether the actions were justified or not.

Q: So both sides did wrong?

Yes.

Two wrongs don't make a right.

Moreover, the truth and reconciliation process was important for blacks because it often confirmed what many had regarded as "disinformation" created by the apartheid regime. In the 1980s, one never knew what to believe. Some Africans were also no doubt moved by revelations of terrorism directed against innocent white civilians. Many black South Africans most likely came away from the truth and reconciliation process believing that the struggle against apartheid was indeed a "just war" but many unjust actions were taken in the name of liberation.

Moreover, black South Africans have surely learned that apartheid is not the sole source of the myriad problems facing blacks. Perhaps it is true that apartheid caused poverty that in turn causes AIDS (as President Mbeki argues), but few in South Africa accept this linkage today. The end of apartheid did little to offer immediate relief to the millions of South Africans living in abject poverty.

Thus, one can imagine that the possibility of reconciliation with whites was opened by encouraging Africans to rethink the view that apartheid was a system of infinite evil that was brought down by a movement of ultimate good.

Furthermore, with the fall of the forced segregation of apartheid has come at least some increase in interracial interactions within South Africa. One must be careful not to overstate the point, but whites encountering blacks in situations of social equality was very rare before 1994 and is less rare since 1994. Not only has the frequency of intergroup contact surely increased since the transition, but so too has the quality of the interaction, especially in terms of formal equality (and to a lesser degree, power). The opportunity for blacks and whites to get to know each other has blossomed since the transition (even if taking advantage of the opportunity has been unevenly distributed). This likely contributes to greater possibilities for reconciliation.

Thus, the effect of the truth and reconciliation process may have been to get people to question their beliefs about good and evil in the past and present in South Africa. As the commission proclaimed,

> One can say that the information in the hands of the Commission made it impossible to claim, for example, that: the practice of torture by the state security forces was not systematic and widespread; that only a few "rotten eggs" or "bad apples" committed gross violations of human rights; that the state was not directly and indirectly involved in "black-on-black" violence; that the chemical and biological warfare programme was only of a defensive nature; that slogans by sections of the liberation movement did not contribute to killings of "settlers" or farmers; and that the accounts of gross human rights violations in the African National Congress (ANC) camps were the consequence of state disinformation. Thus, disinformation about the past that had been accepted as truth by some members of society lost much of its credibility. (TRC 1998, vol. 1, 111-12)

If one accepted the positions of the TRC, one might have come to see the struggle over apartheid as one of pretty good against pretty bad, not as absolute good versus infinite evil. It is hard to reconcile with infinite evil; it is perhaps easier to reconcile with bad that is not entirely evil (especially if there is some degree of repentance). Truth may have opened the door to reconciliation by encouraging people to abandon their views that South Africa is made of people of worldviews so distant that they are unreconcilable. The revelations of the truth and reconciliation process may have encouraged self-reflection and self-criticism, resulting in more moderate views of the adversaries in the struggle. As Gobodo-Madikizela (2003, 119) asserted, to demonize one's enemies as monsters is too easy—it lets them off too easily; further, "to dismiss perpetrators simply as evildoers and monsters shuts the door to the kind of dialogue that leads to an enduring peace" (p. 125). Continuing, she argued,

> Daring, on the other hand, to look the enemy in the eye and allow oneself to read signs of pain and cues of contrition or regret where one might almost have preferred to continue seeing only hatred is the one possibility we have for steering individuals and societies toward replacing long-standing stalemates out of a nation's past with genuine engagement. Hope is where transformation begins; without it, a society cannot take its first steps toward reconstructing its self-identity as a society of tolerance and coexistence. (pp. 125-26)

In general, strong impediments exist to new information generating attitude change. However, the information provided by the truth and reconciliation process had several attributes rendering it likely to be influential. First, information was widely accessible. I mean this not only in terms of the quantity of information available—which by all accounts was absolutely overwhelming—but also in terms of the type of information broadcast. The South African media focused overwhelmingly on the human interest side of the TRC's activities, in contrast to the broader ideological and intellectual goals in which the TRC was also interested. South Africans learned of the suffering of ordinary people through the TRC. What they learned was often extremely graphic—as in Policeman Benzein's demonstration of his notorious "wet bag" method of torture, broadcast widely throughout

South Africa. It was the type of fare often addictive to ordinary people, and few in South Africa could have escaped exposure to the reports of the activities of the truth and reconciliation process.

The information typically had no conspicuous ideological content; no obvious message was being sold. Consequently, reports on the TRC did not necessarily raise the sort of defensive alarms that often make new information impotent in terms of bringing about attitude change. This flows in part from the human interest dimensions of the reports, but also in part from the conscious desire on the part of the TRC to reach all segments of society. Surely, the truth and reconciliation process was used by some to launch ideological attacks on either the apartheid system or the liberation movement, but much of what the TRC put before the South African people was simple and subtle; it had to do with bad guys hurting good guys.[22] Without an obvious and explicit ideological veneer, many of the messages and stories of the TRC were attractive and palatable to South Africans of many different ideological persuasions.

Allowing people to come forward and tell their stories—and allowing South Africans to hear these stories, in all their gory and human detail—had a tremendous effect on how people reacted to the truth and reconciliation process.

The information presented to South Africans by the TRC was also typically unrebutted, in part because miscreants were coming before the TRC to admit their crimes and to be awarded amnesty. Certainly, conflict was occasionally involved (e.g., some victims challenged the motives of the perpetrators, arguing for instance that they were economic, not political, and therefore not covered by the amnesty legislation). But generally, the intense denials that often cloud political controversies were limited in the case of the TRC.

Thus, many of the factors generally contributing to persuasion in fact reinforce the possibility that the TRC might have created attitude change. The information was salient and interesting, not threatening, thereby avoiding defense mechanisms, subtle in its messages, and largely not greeted by counterarguments. These are just the conditions likely to give rise to social persuasion.

The Generalizability of the Findings

I do not argue on the basis of this analysis that truth inevitably leads to reconciliation. The most puissant characteristic of the collective memory created by South Africa's TRC was its willingness to attribute blame to all parties in the struggle over apartheid. Because all sides did horrible things during the struggle, all sides are compromised to some degree, and legitimacy adheres to the complaints of one's enemies about abuses. Once one concedes that the other side has legitimate grievances, it becomes easier to accept their claims, and ultimately to accept the new political dispensation in South Africa.

A different truth process might well have led to an entirely different outcome. A truth process pointing to unilateral blame is not one likely to produce reconciliation. Discussing truth and reconciliation attempts in other countries, Gobodo-Madikizela (2003) asserted,

> Their tendency to focus only on perpetrators on one side of a political conflict may, however, disrupt whatever fragile unity might be forged by two sides previously at war with each other. This could then fuel the anger of one side, which may feel that the law is biased against it as the "oppressor" group, when in fact this is often a record of human rights crimes committed by the oppressed group as well. The issue is not a simple one, for in recognizing that both sides produced victims, one may seem to be applying the same moral standards to the actions of the oppressor and those of the group that was fighting to end its oppression. But in societies trying to break the cycle of hatred and revenge, it is important first to acknowledge, as did the TRC, that human rights abuses were committed by both sides, and then to find an effective way of moving society forward. (p. 171)

Obviously, the truth that can be produced by a truth and reconciliation process is constrained to some degree by reality; not any collective memory can be fabricated out of any given set of historical circumstances. But truth commissions can seek to act impartially, allocating blame wherever it may lie, or truth commissions can engage in a form of "victor's justice" in which the victors are held to lower human rights standards than the vanquished. The South African TRC sought the path of impartiality (dubbed "poisonous even-handedness" by its critics), choosing to cast the net of blame widely. It is unclear that the circumstances providing the TRC such authority, and that motivated the leaders of the TRC to place reconciliation as their consummate goal, can be reproduced elsewhere.[23]

To the extent that truth processes involve the granting of amnesty, they begin with a debilitating "justice deficit." This deficit is created by exonerating guilty people, a particularly bitter pill for victors to swallow. In the South African case, this problem was exacerbated by revelations during the truth and reconciliation process that the apartheid state engaged in far more barbarous and far-flung (and illegal) human rights abuses than even most blacks imagined. For many who thought they had won the war, losing the peace embittered.

My research suggests that perhaps another effective but idiosyncratic element of South Africa's truth and reconciliation process was its emphasis on non-retributive forms of justice. Even despite granting amnesty to gross human violators, the truth and reconciliation process in South Africa generated justice that appeared to satisfy—the "justice deficit" was overcome. The justice was in part distributive (but in the view of many, a too small part), but was also procedural and restorative. Allowing people to come forward and tell their stories—and allowing South Africans to hear these stories, in all their gory and human detail—had a tremendous effect on how people reacted to the truth and reconciliation process. And undoubtedly some perpetrators expressed heartfelt remorse, apologizing for their actions in terms that were widely understood to be sincere. The truth and reconciliation process contemplated that distributive justice (compensation) might ameliorate the pain of failing to receive retributive justice. But few who designed and participated in the process anticipated that procedural and restorative justice could have such salutary consequences. Other truth processes have most likely foundered on their inability to generate compensatory forms of justice capable of mollifying citizens and getting them to accept the injustices forced on them by the transitional process.

To the extent that reconciliation generates
pressures toward consensus . . . reconciliation
does not serve democracy.

South Africa's truth process had, I believe, other characteristics that contributed to its success. Because the process was open, humanized, and procedurally fair, the TRC was able to penetrate the consciousness of virtually all segments of the South African populace with its message. Furthermore, it seems likely that the lack of legalistic proceedings made the hearings more accessible to ordinary people. Though sometimes forced to adopt fair proceedings by litigation, it would be difficult to observe the TRC's process and conclude that victims, witnesses, and perpetrators were treated unfairly (even if there were some complaints about the relative amount of attention given to abuses by the various sides in the struggle). The TRC likely succeeded in part because its processes were transparent and fair.

Finally, the roles of Tutu and Mandela were no doubt instrumental in getting people to accept the TRC's collective memory and therefore to get on with reconciliation. Tutu's message of forgiveness, though irritating to many, set a compelling frame of reference for understanding the atrocities uncovered. Mandela's constant and insistent calls for reconciliation, coupled with his willingness to accept the findings of the TRC (even when the ANC did not), were surely persuasive for many South Africans. The two giants of the antiapartheid struggle defused and delegitimized much of the potential criticism of the truth and reconciliation process.

The TRC did not engage in a "witch hunt," no matter what the allegations of some extreme segments of the white Afrikaans-speaking population. Because it did not, its findings and conclusions were not widely rejected, providing little justification to most South Africans for repudiating the collective memory out of hand. Whether this process can be replicated in other parts of the globe is entirely unclear, and certainly unanswered by this research.

Reconciliation and Consolidating South Africa's Democratic Transition

In the end, this research has actually proven little about processes of democratization. I posit that reconciliation contributes to the consolidation of democratic change, but I certainly have not established that connection empirically. No cross-sectional study can provide such proof. Nor have I the hubris to suggest or imply that the future of South African democracy can be foretold simply from the results of a survey of the attitudes and views of ordinary citizens. Whether democratic reform gets consolidated depends on way too many other knotty factors.

Indeed, I must acknowledge that the individual-level reconciliation I analyze in this article ignores macro-level processes. For instance, the intolerance of citizens may be neutralized by strong (and legitimate) political institutions capable of serving as guardians of democracy. Agreements among political elites may foreclose opportunities for interracial coalitions irrespective of the desires of ordinary citizens. South African democracy depends upon more than the degree to which each South African is reconciled, even if such micro-reconciliation is an important determinant of the likelihood of consolidating South Africa's democratic transition.

How much reconciliation is necessary for the consolidation of democratic reform in South Africa? This question is difficult if not impossible to answer with any degree of certitude. I can, however, sketch the outlines of a theory specifying how reconciliation both helps and hinders the practice of democratic politics.

Some contend that democracies require that people form political allegiances based on *interests*, not identities. To the extent that group boundaries are rigidly established and group members perceive themselves as having little in common with people of other groups, multigroup interest-based coalitions are difficult to assemble. From this perspective, irreconciliation clearly undermines the formation of like-minded coalitions, which are essential to democracy.

Reconciliation contributes to democracy by breaking down the walls built around racial groups, making interracial cooperation possible. To the extent South Africans view those of other races with suspicion, it is unlikely that such cooperation will emerge. Perhaps one hopeful scenario is that tolerance of different groups will lead to a recognition of a certain degree of commonality of interests, which in turn will contribute to the respect and understanding that facilitates political coalitions. It is perhaps too soon to predict that truly multiracial political movements will form in South Africa—and, ironically, the most likely such candidate today is for the nascent coalition of Afrikaans-speaking whites and Coloured people to consolidate—but without some degree of interracial accommodation, I confidently predict that the South African experiment in democratic change will founder.

I must acknowledge at least one pathway through which reconciliation might *undermine* the consolidation of democratic change, rather than contribute to it. Democracies thrive on conflict; they are at their best when citizens and groups disagree with one another, when pluralism prevails. To the extent that reconciliation generates pressures toward consensus, pressures that delegitimize difference and differing points of view, then reconciliation does not serve democracy. In a democracy, people do not have to agree with one another; they do not even have to respect the views of others. Instead, they must agree to disagree, they must accept a set of institutional and cultural norms that allow all competitors to enter the marketplace of ideas. If reconciliation means treating strong political differences and animosities as somehow illegitimate, then reconciliation will not have served South Africa's democratic transition.[24]

In the end, South Africa is an African nation, a breed of states not notable for their success at democratic governance. The threats to successful democratization are numerous and formidable (as in the pressing need for economic equality and wealth redistribution). But if South Africans can come to accept those of other races, or at least to put up with their political foes—within a context of a culture in which support for human rights is widespread and where political institutions are empowered with the legitimacy necessary to protect those human rights—then perhaps apartheid can at last be overcome and democracy will prevail in the land once dominated by apartheid.

Appendix
Measures of Reconciliation

Interracial reconciliation:

I find it difficult to understand the customs and ways of [the opposite racial group].
It is hard to imagine ever being friends with a [the opposite racial group].
More than most groups, [the opposite racial group] are likely to engage in crime.
[The opposite racial group] are untrustworthy.
[The opposite racial group] are selfish, and only look after the interests of their group.
I feel uncomfortable when I am around a group of [the opposite racial group].
I often don't believe what [the opposite racial group] say to me.
South Africa would be a better place if there were no [the opposite racial group] in the country.

I could never imagine being part of a political party made up mainly of [the opposite racial group].

Support for human rights:

Sometimes it might be better to ignore the law and solve problems immediately rather than wait for a legal solution. (Disagree)
It's alright to get around the law as long as you don't actually break it. (Disagree)
In times of emergency, the government ought to be able to suspend law in order to solve pressing social problems. (Disagree)
It is not necessary to obey the laws of a government that I did not vote for. (Disagree)

Political tolerance:

We measured political intolerance by asking the respondents whether their hated political foes should be allowed to engage in certain types of political activity. The following questions were asked with regard to the group in South African politics the respondent disliked the most and another group highly disliked by the respondent (based on the "least-liked" measurement technology developed by Sullivan, Piereson, and Marcus 1982):

Members of the [THE DISLIKED GROUP] should be prohibited from standing as a candidate for an elected position.
Members of the [THE DISLIKED GROUP] should be allowed to hold street demonstrations in your community.
[THE DISLIKED GROUP] should be officially banned in your community.

Thus, for many respondents the first question called for agreement or disagreement with the statement that "Members of PAGAD [People Against Gangsterism and Drugs] should be prohibited from standing as a candidate for an elected position."

Institutional Legitimacy:

If the [the institution] started making a lot of decisions that most people disagree with, it might be better to do away with [the institution] altogether.
The right of the South African Constitutional Court to decide certain types of controversial issues should be done away with.
The [institution] can usually be trusted to make decisions that are right for the country as a whole.
The [institution] treats all groups who come before it—black, white, Coloured, and Asian—the same.

Notes

1. In the middle of 2001, President Thabo Mbeki charged the Truth and Reconciliation Commission (TRC) with producing a codicil to the original report. The sixth volume had not yet appeared as of early 2003), mainly due to litigation by the Inkatha Freedom Party (IFP).

2. But see Jeffery (1999), who complains about numerous inaccuracies and bias in the TRC's history of several incidents.

3. For a most important and useful collection of essays about the TRC, see Villa-Vicencio and Verwoerd (2000).

4. See the widely popular and much discussed Krog (1998); see also Orr (2000). Amy Biehl's father is one of the most poignant examples. A statement by Biehl's parents is included in the decision granting amnesty to her killers. See Amnesty Decision: Vusumzi Samuel Ntamo (4734/97); Ntombeki Ambrose Peni (5188/97); Mzikhona Eazi Nofemela (5282/97); Mongesi Christopher Manqina (0669/96) available on the TRC Web site: www.truth.org.za.

5. See Wilson (2001) for a critique of the TRC for injecting religious overtones into its work.

6. For a more detailed consideration of race in South Africa, see Gibson and Gouws (2003). In general, I accept the racial categories as identified by the editor of a special issue of *Daedalus* focused on South Africa: "Many of the authors in this issue observe the South African convention of dividing the country's population into four racial categories: white (of European descent), coloured (of mixed ancestry), Indian (forebears from the Indian subcontinent), and African. The official nomenclature for 'Africans' has itself varied over the years, changing from 'native' to 'Bantu' in the middle of the apartheid era, and then changing again to 'black' or, today, 'African/black.' All of these terms appear in the essays that follow" (Graubard 2001, viii). Note as well that Desmond Tutu felt obliged to offer a similar caveat about race in South Africa in the Final Report of the TRC. Though these racial categories were employed by the apartheid régime to divide and control the population, these are nonetheless labels South Africans use to refer to themselves (see, for example, Gibson and Gouws 2003). I use the term "Coloured" to signify that this is a distinctly South African construction of race, and "Asian origin" to refer to South Africans drawn from the Indian Subcontinent.

7. For a major study of political tolerance in South Africa, see Gibson and Gouws (2003).

8. This analysis is based on a representative survey of the South African mass public conducted in 2000/2001. A total of 3,727 face-to-face interviews were completed. The average interview lasted eighty-four minutes. The overall response rate for the survey was approximately 87 percent. Nearly all of the respondents were interviewed by an interviewer of their own race. Interviews were conducted in the respondent's language of choice, with a large plurality of the interviews being done in English (45 percent). The questionnaire was first prepared in English and then translated into Afrikaans, Zulu, Xhosa, North Sotho, South Sotho, Tswana, and Tsonga. The sample included representative oversamples of whites, Coloured people, and those of Asian origin. The vast majority of respondents were interviewed by an interviewer of their own race.

9. My assessments of Table 1 are based on the following judgments of the average group scores on each of the subdimensions: 1.0-1.9, not at all reconciled; 2.0-2.9, not very reconciled; 3.0-3.9, somewhat reconciled; and 4.0-5.0, highly reconciled.

10. A substantial empirical literature on collective memories exists. See for examples Schuman and Corning (2000), Jennings (1996), and Schuman and Scott (1989).

11. I use the term *accepting the veracity* to indicate accepting that the statement is either true or false, depending upon the coding scheme reported in the text.

12. See Gibson (2004) for a detailed justification of this claim.

13. In 1970, Resolution 2671 of the General Assembly of the United Nations declared that the policies of apartheid were contrary to the charter of the UN and constituted a crime against humanity. According to Vestergaard (2001, 25), the truth and reconciliation process "has been central to the creation of the new South Africa, as it affirms one of its fundamental premises—that apartheid was a 'crime against humanity.' "

14. H. F. Verwoerd, the principal architect of modern apartheid, propounded the ideology of "separate development." Defending the viewpoint in the 1960s, Prime Minister John Vorster spoke of "recognising [sic] the right of existence of distinct nations and colour groups" and of "providing each with opportunities to develop according to their ability and with the maintenance of their identity" (quoted in Giliomee and Schlemmer 1989, 64, citing *Die Burger*, May 18, 1968). Note that the ANC has always explicitly rejected the ideology of separate development.

15. As repugnant as apartheid was, research has consistently shown that not all South Africans reject the apartheid system. For instance, based on a survey conducted in 1996, Gibson and Gouws (2003, 198) showed that about one-fourth of black South Africans claimed to have lived better under apartheid than at the time of the survey. Two lessons seem appropriate: repressive political systems do not repress every single citizen, and citizens reach varying compromises and accommodations with such systems.

16. Desmond Tutu asserted in the Final Report that "We believe we have provided enough of the truth about our past for there to be a consensus about it. There is consensus that atrocious things were done on all sides" (TRC 1998, vol. 1, 18).

17. Complex issues of causality are involved in these relationships that are too complicated to address in this article. (For a complete statistical analysis of the causality issue, see Gibson 2004.) The conclusion of that analysis is that truth largely causes reconciliation, not vice versa.

18. The intense antipathy focused *within* the black community in South Africa should not be overlooked. Most of the political violence in South Africa in recent times has been black-on-black violence, even if the root cause of such violence can be found in the instigations of the apartheid state.

19. Pumla Gobodo-Madikizela, a member of the Human Rights Violations Committee of the TRC, concludes that it is plausible that whites did not know of many of the reprehensible activities of the apartheid government. (See Gobodo-Madikizela 2003, 26, 109.) She referred to this as an "apartheid of the mind."

20. During June 2000, six focus groups were held, two each in Cape Town, Durban, and Johannesburg. Focus group participants, who of course could not constitute a representative sample of any population, were recruited by the survey firm staff and were paid to participate in the discussions.

21. Because the information produced by the TRC was in part redundant, the effect of truth on reconciliation is likely weaker among blacks than among whites. This probably accounts for the weaker correlation coefficient between truth and reconciliation I reported above for black South Africans.

22. As Iyengar and Simon (2000, 156) observed, the image of President Ford attempting to eat a tamale without first shucking it was a very clear signal to Hispanics in the United States of the insensitivity of the president to this constituency. Subtle messages are often more effective at social persuasion than more explicit appeals to attitude change.

23. It is beyond the scope of this analysis to assess the macro-level factors that allowed the TRC to act impartially. Perhaps the fact that South Africa's transition was brokered, based on a political and military stalemate, has something to do with how the TRC functioned. Perhaps it is important as well that all sides in the struggle had to live together after the transition; partition of the country was viewed by nearly everyone as unacceptable (just as federalism was viewed by most as desirable). For an excellent macro-level analysis of truth commissions, see Hayner (2002).

24. See Marx (2002) for an explication of this point. Marx is particularly concerned about the ways in which the African concept *"ubuntu"*—from the Xhosa expression *Umuntu ngumuntu ngabanye bantu* (People are people through other people)—and traditional African collectivism foster conformity and undermine the legitimacy of political conflict. The truth and reconciliation process, and Archbishop Tutu in particular, often referred to ubuntu as essential to the process of reconciliation.

References

de Kock, Eugene. 1998. *A long night's damage: Working for the apartheid state.* Saxonwold, South Africa: Contra Press.

du Preez, Max. 2001. Too many truths to tell. *The Sunday Independent*, Johannesburg, South Africa, June 24.

Gibson, James L. 2002. Truth, justice, and reconciliation: Judging the fairness of amnesty in South Africa. *American Journal of Political Science* 46 (3): 540-56.

———. 2004. *Overcoming apartheid: Can truth reconcile a divided nation?* Cape Town, South Africa: HSRC Press.

Gibson, James L., and Amanda Gouws. 2003. *Overcoming intolerance in South Africa: Experiments in democratic persuasion.* New York: Cambridge University Press.

Giliomee, Herman, and Lawrence Schlemmer. 1989. *From apartheid to nation-building: Contemporary South African debates.* Cape Town, South Africa: Oxford University Press.

Gobodo-Madikizela, Pumla. 2003. *A human being died that night: A South African story of forgiveness*. Boston: Houghton Mifflin.

Graubard, Stephen R. 2001. Preface to the issue "Why South Africa matters." *Daedalus* 130 (1): v-viii.

Hamber, Brandon, and Hugo van der Merwe. 1998. What is this thing called reconciliation? Paper presented at the Goedgedacht Forum "After the Truth and Reconciliation Commission," Goedgedacht Farm, Cape Town, South Africa, March 28, www.reconciliation.org.za.

Hay, Mark. 1998. *Ukubuyisana: Reconciliation in South Africa*. Pietermaritzburg, South Africa: Cluster Publications.

Hayner, Priscilla B. 2002. *Unspeakable truths: Facing the challenge of truth commissions*. New York: Routledge.

Ignatieff, Michael. 1996. Articles of faith. *Index on Censorship* 25 (5): 110-22.

Iyengar, Shanto, and Adam F. Simon. 2000. New perspectives and evidence on political communication and campaign effects. *Annual Review of Psychology* 51:149-69.

Jeffery, Anthea. 1999. *The truth about the Truth Commission*. Johannesburg: South African Institute of Race Relations.

Jennings, M. Kent. 1996. Political knowledge across time and generations. *Public Opinion Quarterly* 60 (2): 228-52.

Krog, Antjie. 1998. *Country of my skull*. Johannesburg, South Africa: Random House.

Markel, Dan. 1999. The justice of amnesty? Towards a theory of retributivism in recovering states. *University of Toronto Law Journal* 49:389-445.

Marks, Monique. 2001. *Young warriors: Youth politics, identity and violence in South Africa*. Johannesburg, South Africa: Witwatersrand University Press.

Marx, Christoph. 2002. Ubu and Ubuntu: On the dialectics of apartheid and nation building. *Politikon* 29 (1): 49-69.

Minow, Martha. 1998. *Between vengeance and forgiveness: Facing history after genocide and mass violence*. Boston: Beacon.

Orr, Wendy. 2000. *From Biko to Basson: Wendy Orr's search for the soul of South Africa as a commissioner of the TRC*. Saxonwold, South Africa: Contra Press.

Schuman, Howard, and Amy D. Corning. 2000. Collective knowledge of public events: The Soviet era from the great purge to glasnost. *American Journal of Sociology* 105 (4): 913-56.

Schuman, Howard, and Jacqueline Scott. 1989. Generations and collective memories. *American Sociological Review* 54 (3): 359-81.

Sibisi, C. D. T. 1991. The psychology of liberation. In *Bounds of possibility: The legacy of Steve Biko and black consciousness*, ed. N. Barney Pityana, Mamphela Ramphele, Malusi Mpumlwana, and Lindy Wilson, 130-36. Cape Town, South Africa: David Philip.

Sullivan, John L., James E. Piereson, and George E. Marcus. 1982. *Political tolerance and American democracy*. Chicago: University of Chicago Press.

Truth and Reconciliation Commission (TRC). 1998. *Truth and Reconciliation Commission of South Africa report*. Cape Town, South Africa: Juta.

Tutu, Desmond Mpilo. 1999. *No future without forgiveness*. New York: Doubleday.

Vestergaard, Mads. 2001. Who's got the map? The negotiation of Afrikaner identities in post-apartheid South Africa. *Dædalus: Journal of the American Academy of Arts and Sciences* 130 (1): 19-44.

Villa-Vicencio, Charles, and Wilhelm Verwoerd. 2000. *Looking back reaching forward: Reflections on the Truth and Reconciliation Commission of South Africa*. Cape Town, South Africa: Cape Town University Press.

Wilson, Richard A. 2001. *The politics of truth and reconciliation in South Africa: Legitimizing the post-apartheid states*. New York: Cambridge University Press.

The Federal Constitutional Court: Guardian of German Democracy

By
DONALD P. KOMMERS

Germany's Federal Constitutional Court rivals the Supreme Court of the United States in protecting political democracy. Its jurisprudence of democracy has shaped the course and character of German politics while upholding the rule of law and defending the constitutionally prescribed "free democratic basic order." In furtherance of these objectives, the Constitutional Court has invalidated regulations limiting the rights of minor parties and constitutionalizing measures designed to stabilize Germany's system of parliamentary government. These purposes have been served by constitutional decisions on voting rights, public funding of election campaigns, dissolution of Parliament, and proportional representation, including the limiting 5 percent clause. These decisions, along with a discussion of the *Hessian Election Review Case*—a reminder of *Bush v. Gore*—are calculated to make political representation both responsive and responsible and to anchor the political system firmly in the democratic values at the heart of the Basic Law.

Keywords: Germany; party finance; democracy; representation; voting rights; parliament

T his article focuses on the constitutionalism of democracy in Germany. The Basic Law, Germany's constitution, defines the nature of this democracy in abundant detail. It provides for its organization and procedures and imposes substantive limits on its exercise. The constitution also empowers Germany's Federal Constitutional Court (FCC) to monitor the process of democracy and to keep it tethered to constitutional values. Over the course of the past fifty years, the court has produced a significant body of constitutional case law on the meaning and

Donald P. Kommers is the Joseph and Elizabeth Robbie Professor of Political Science and concurrent professor of law at the University of Notre Dame. He has written widely on American and comparative constitutional law and is the author of The Constitutional Jurisprudence of the Federal Republic of Germany *(2nd ed. 1997), among other books, and coauthor of* American Constitutional Law: Essays, Cases, and Comparative Notes *(2004). His numerous awards and fellowships include an honorary doctor of laws degree he recently received from Germany's Heidelberg University.*

DOI: 10.1177/0002716205283080

limits of democracy. In doing so, the FCC has played a major role in shaping the character and course of German politics. Its decisions, and the willingness of Germany's political class to abide by its rulings, are partly responsible for transforming what was once an underdeveloped political culture into one of the world's most advanced and influential parliamentary democracies, one unmistakably governed by the rule of law.

Some preliminary remarks about the Basic Law and judicial review in Germany will place the FCC's decisional law on democracy in a more helpful context. Accordingly, this article begins with a glance at Germany's constitutionally prescribed structure of democracy and popular sovereignty. It continues with a brief discussion of the FCC's jurisdiction and its role in the nation's constitutional order and then considers selected constitutional cases on democracy likely to interest American readers. This short treatment is more descriptive than analytical. It is mainly an overview of the FCC's most important decisions on election law, political parties, and parliamentary democracy. Along the way, and where relevant, it may be useful to draw attention to the equivalent jurisprudence of the United States Supreme Court.

Democracy and the Basic Law

The Basic Law of the Federal Republic of Germany, adopted in 1949 in the aftermath of Germany's defeat in the Second World War, has evolved into one of the world's most influential constitutions. This is certainly the case if influence can be measured by the frequency with which the Basic Law's provisions—and institutions—have been copied or adopted by constitution makers around the globe (Kokott 1999). Most influential among these provisions are those dealing with Germany's parliamentary system of government, particularly the Basic Law's decrees on political parties and its internal order of democracy, together with its creation of a constitutional court authorized to review and decide controversies arising under these provisions. The following summary is confined mainly to those clauses and paragraphs prominently featured in the constitutional cases discussed later in this article.

Let us begin with Article 20, paragraph 1, of the Basic Law, which defines the Federal Republic of Germany as a "*democratic* and social federal state" (emphasis added). Paragraph 2 reinforces this concept by declaring that "all state authority emanates from the people." The next sentence, however, emphasizes the *representative* character of the governing process, for the authority emanating from the people "shall be exercised by . . . means of elections and voting and by specific legislative, executive, and judicial organs," a system of representation, as the FCC has frequently observed, that disallows all popular initiatives, plebiscites, or referenda at the national level.[1] In addition, Article 38, paragraph 1, provides that members of Parliament (the Bundestag) "shall be elected in general, direct, free, equal, and secret elections" and then stipulates that they "shall be representatives of the whole people, not bound by orders or instructions, and responsible only to their conscience." Yet the Basic Law establishes political parties as major agencies of political representation. Their function, according to Article 21, paragraph 1, is to "participate in the formation of the political will of the people," for which reason the FCC has characterized Germany as a "party state" *(Parteienstaat)*, one in which political parties enjoy constitutional status, allowing them to adjudicate their rights as primary agents of electoral politics (1 BVerfGE 208, 225: 1952).[2]

[T]he FCC [Federal Constitutional Court] has evolved into one of Germany's most important policy-making institutions, a remarkable development in view of the nation's long tradition of executive predominance in constitutional matters.

As for electoral politics, it is important to note that members of the Bundestag are elected for four years, a constitutional mandate that imposes severe limits on the power to vote a chancellor out of office or to dissolve Parliament before the expiration of the normal four-year election cycle. Under the so-called "constructive vote of no confidence," set forth in Article 67, the Bundestag may remove a chancellor in a no confidence vote only by electing his successor simultaneously by a majority of its members. A new federal election is permitted ahead of schedule, however, only when the chancellor himself initiates procedures specified by Article 68. First, he must formally move for a vote of confidence in the Bundestag; second, the Bundestag by a majority of its members must vote against him; third, the chancellor must then petition the federal president to dissolve the Bundestag; fourth, the president must agree to do so and arrange for new elections to be held within sixty days. Finally, as noted later in the article, each of these procedures is subject to review in the FCC.

The electoral system as such, which the Basic Law empowers Parliament to determine, is another distinctive feature of German democracy. From the outset— since 1949—the system, often called "personalized" or "modified" proportional representation (PR) (Sartori 1997), has combined single-member districts with PR. Federal law now provides for 598 members of the Bundestag, one half of whom are elected in single-member districts in which a plurality of votes is sufficient to win; the other half is elected by PR. Accordingly, voters receive two ballots. On the first, they record their choice of a district representative; on the second, they vote for a closed list of party candidates. The outcome of the list ballot determines the total number of parliamentary seats allocated to each party. If, for example, party A wins 38 percent of the national vote, it receives that percentage of parliamentary seats. If the total number of district representatives equals less than 38 percent of party A's parliamentary membership, the remaining representatives are drawn from the list ballots until the prescribed percentage is reached. But if party A wins no district seats, all of its members are drawn from party lists.

This system, however, is skewed in two ways. First, if a major party wins more district seats than it would be entitled to under strict PR, it keeps these surplus or "overhang" seats (*Überhangsmandate*), as they are called. Second, under the law's famous "barrier clause" (*Sperrklausel*), a party receiving less than 5 percent of the national vote is excluded altogether from parliamentary representation unless it wins at least three district seats, in which case it is entitled to representation proportionate to its total national vote even though that vote is less than 5 percent. The idea behind this electoral arrangement is that a party capable of winning three district seats—a difficult achievement—has sufficient popular support to warrant full representation under PR. But if the party wins one or two district seats—and no more—and falls below the 5 percent requirement, it retains only these seats with no additional ones under PR.

The Basic Law, finally, contains numerous references to the "free democratic basic order" whose defense—like that of the principle of human dignity set forth in Article 1—the state is duty-bound to protect. As deployed in the Basic Law, these terms limit the boundaries of freedom for they do not protect the enemies of democracy. For example, guaranteed rights such as freedom of expression or the right to associate can be forfeited if used to combat democracy (Article 18). Most important for present purposes is Article 21, paragraph 2, which declares "unconstitutional" those political parties seeking to undermine or abolish the free democratic basic order. As with the forfeiture of basic rights, only the FCC may rule on the question of a party's constitutionality. Early on, in the famous *Communist Party Case*, the FCC seized upon these and related provisions to describe the German polity as a "militant democracy" (5 BVerfGE 85, 139: 1956).

The Federal Constitutional Court

The Basic Law re-created many of the political structures established by the Weimar Constitution of 1919 but eliminated those crippling defects that weakened Weimar's democracy and facilitated Hitler's rise to power. Several of the Basic Law's innovations have helped to stabilize Germany's political system. These include the elevated status of the chancellor as the nation's political leader, the correspondingly diminished power of the president, the constructive vote of no confidence, the 5 percent *Sperrklausel*, and the difficulty of dissolving Parliament and holding new elections ahead of schedule (Conradt 2001). Each has contributed to the durability of Germany's postwar democracy. But the most striking innovation of all was the creation of a constitutional court empowered to enforce guaranteed rights and to decide other controversies arising under the Basic Law.[3]

Established in 1951 after months of parliamentary negotiations (Kommers 1976; Schlaich and Korioth 2001), the FCC has evolved into one of Germany's most important policy-making institutions, a remarkable development in view of the nation's long tradition of executive predominance in constitutional matters. Organizationally, the FCC consists of two senates, each staffed by eight justices elected by the legislative branch of the national government for nonrenewable terms of twelve years.[4] The two senates exercise mutually exclusive jurisdiction that, taken together, extends to virtually all issues concerning the German nation— from abortion policy to military and international affairs—even to pedestrian disputes over the validity of rules pertaining to the correct usage of the German language (98 BVerfGE 218: 1998). As a specialized court of constitutional review, the FCC is the only tribunal in Germany empowered to declare statutes and other governmental actions unconstitutional.

The Basic Law lists sixteen categories of constitutional disputes over which the FCC has jurisdiction. The most important of these for present purposes are federal-state and separation of powers conflicts, abstract and concrete judicial review proceedings, and constitutional complaints. Apart from constitutional complaints, only governments and specified public officials have standing to petition the FCC to resolve constitutional disputes. These "officials" include candidates for public office and individual members of Parliament seeking to vindicate their electoral or representational rights. Political parties may also petition the FCC in defense of their corporate rights in and out of Parliament. Ordinary citizens may file constitutional complaints but only after they have exhausted all other legal remedies. Characteristically, in ordinary litigation before the regular courts, the conflicting parties have no standing to raise constitutional issues. In regular or concrete judicial review proceedings, only judges may place questions before the FCC and then only if they *seriously* doubt the constitutionality of the law or laws they are called upon to enforce or interpret. But the FCC is not limited to reviewing "cases and controversies" in the American understanding of these terms. At the request of the federal or a state government or one-third of the Bundestag's members, the FCC may resolve—in an abstract judicial review proceeding—mere *doubts* about the constitutionality of an enacted law or the compatibility between federal and state law. A major function of the FCC, as *the* guardian of the Basic Law, is precisely to resolve such doubts when raised by major political officials or state actors in managing the course of the nation's public life. For the German public mind, this is what it means to be governed by law, in this instance by the law of the constitution.

A glimpse at the court's workload is enough to give us a sense of the importance of judicial review in German life and law. In its fifty-three years, down to 2005, the FCC has decided some 150,000 cases, 144,000 of which have been constitutional complaints filed by individual citizens (*Bundesverfassungsgericht* 2004). The main body of its jurisprudence is to be found in 113 volumes (to date) of official reports consisting of some 2,700 full opinions. This vast body of constitutional law is fully comparable, in significance and sophistication, to the decisional law of the U.S.

Supreme Court, except that numerous disputes decided by the Constitutional Court would be regarded as nonjusticiable in American courts. As underscored by the frequency with which the FCC decides cases involving foreign and military affairs, there is no equivalent in Germany to the American political question doctrine, although in many such cases the court applies a presumption of constitutionality (Franck 1992).

The Jurisprudence of Parliamentary Democracy

The law of democracy in Germany represents a vast jurisprudence. A trip through this body of law would show that the FCC has decided controversies touching almost every phase of electoral and parliamentary politics, including the role, status, and funding of political parties. Nearly all these decisions pertain to the quantity, quality, or equality of political representation (Jesse 1985; Currie 1994, 104-16). In a series of cases over the years, the FCC has handed down decisions *ordering* higher salaries for legislative representatives (40 BVerfGE 296: 1975); *invalidating* laws unduly restricting political parties from gaining access to the ballot (3 BVerfGE 19: 1953; 5 BVerfGE 77: 1956; 12 BVerfGE 10: 1960); *forbidding* political parties from changing the order in which candidates appear on party list ballots (7 BVerfGE 77: 1957); *limiting* the conditions under which a minor parliamentary party can be excluded from representation on a legislative committee (70 BVerfGE 324: 1986; 80 BVerfGE 188: 1989); *barring* Parliament from excluding a representative from a legislative committee merely because he or she is not a member of a political party (84 BVerfGE 304: 1991); and *vindicating* the rights of parliamentary minorities to establish investigative committees to hear evidence of illegal or improper conduct by a ruling governmental majority, largely on the theory that in modern parliamentary democracies separation of powers manifests itself most effectively not in the checks and balances among branches of government but in the duty of opposition parties to confront and publicize the misdeeds of the ruling majority (49 BVerfGE 70: 1978).

The remaining cases discussed in this article focus on constitutional policies characteristic of Germany's parliamentary system. They are important because they implicate efforts to stabilize party government, to make political representation responsive and responsible, and to anchor the system more generally in the democratic values at the heart of the Basic Law. The following pages cover five sets of constitutional cases that are likely to fascinate readers not only for their intrinsic merit but also for their contrast with American constitutional perspectives and procedures. The first category deals with PR and the 5 percent clause (*Sperrklausel*); the second focuses on voting rights and their relationship to Germany's PR system; the third describes constitutional policies related to the public funding of political parties; the fourth shifts attention to a recent election case vaguely reminiscent of *Bush v. Gore* (531 U.S. 98 [2000]; and the fifth highlights the limits the Basic Law places on the power to dissolve Parliament.

PR and the Sperrklausel

As noted, Germany's electoral system combines PR with single-member districts (Kitzinger 1960). German law, however, qualifies PR by requiring a party to garner at least 5 percent of the vote to enter the national Parliament. This personalized PR system prevails in thirteen of Germany's sixteen *Länder*. A simple PR system prevails in Bremen, Hamburg, and Saarland, but these states have also adopted

---

In numerous decisions over the years . . . the FCC has imposed severe limits on the scope and allocation of public funding, virtually micromanaging the field of party finance.

---

the 5 percent clause (Gunlicks 2003). Like the U.S. Supreme Court, the FCC has ruled that single-member legislative districts are to be approximately equal in population (16 BVerfGE 130: 1963), but the addition of PR in its view makes the electoral system as a whole both equal *and* fair. Finally, in the interest of *effective* governance, the FCC has approved the use of the 5 percent clause (6 BVerfGE 84: 1957), although in one of its earliest decisions it ruled that only a compelling reason would justify a threshold requirement beyond what it called the "common German value of five percent" (1 BVerfGE 208: 1952).

In 1990, however, the court struck down the application of the 5 percent rule to the first all-German election following reunification (82 BVerfGE 322: 1990). Calculated to advance a constitutionalism of reconciliation and inclusion, this unanimous decision illustrates the protection the FCC customarily affords to minor parties. In short, the court sought to ensure that certain political parties in the eastern states, notably the previously dominant Communist Party—now called the Party of Democratic Socialism (PDS)—would have a fighting chance to enter the new, all-German Parliament.[5] The FCC reiterated its view that the 5 percent threshold is "constitutionally unobjectionable" as a general principle, but special circumstances may dictate a modification of the rule if the "political will of the electorate" is to be realized. Accordingly, and on the FCC's recommendation, the Bundestag provided that the 5 percent clause should apply separately in east and west, thus enabling the eastern Green Party and PDS to win parliamentary representation. The rule would apply only to the 1990 election, giving the eastern parties a chance to establish themselves nationally. The FCC made clear that Germany could revert to its established electoral system in subsequent federal elections.

In recent years, minor parties have mounted additional challenges to the 5 percent rule. They have also questioned the constitutionality of overhang seats, alleging that they violate the principle of proportional representation. The practice of awarding surplus seats to the major parties met its severest test in the *Overhang Mandate Case* (95 BVerfGE 335: 1997), an abstract judicial review petition filed by Lower-Saxony. In a four-to-four decision, the FCC's Second Senate upheld the validity of surplus mandates because the electoral system as a whole fostered a personal relationship between voters and their elected representatives. (It takes a majority of the justices to nullify a law.) The dissenting justices argued that surplus seats violated the principle of equality under PR, requiring a change in federal law. In a related case, decided on the same day, the FCC sustained a decision of the Bundestag to award the PDS the four district seats it had won in East Berlin, along with the twenty-six seats it was entitled to under PR, a number equal to 4.4 percent of the national vote it received in 1994. By vindicating the rule that such a party should be entitled to proportional representation even though it fails to meet the standard 5 percent requirement, the FCC felt that it was promoting equality among the parties (95 BVerfGE 408: 1997).

Voting rights and democracy

As noted in the previous section, the FCC has not only enforced the principle of direct, free, and equal suffrage, but also that of fair and effective representation. The court has emphasized the importance of the *personalized* nature of the electoral system, meaning that when citizens vote they cast their ballots for particular candidates running in single-member districts and for the order in which candidates appear on party lists (Kommers 1997, 181-97). A distinguishing feature of these decisions is the direct link the FCC has sought to establish between the people, voting, and public policy. As Article 20, paragraph 2, of the Basic Law declares, "All state authority is derived from the people" and exercised by them "through elections" and through "specific legislative . . . bodies." The FCC has made clear that the "people" in this instance refers to Germans and that any attempt to break the link in the chain between the will of Germans and their representatives offends the principle of democracy as laid down in the Basic Law.

The principle of democracy was implicated most notably in the celebrated *Maastricht Treaty Case* (89 BVerfGE 155: 1993). *Maastricht* was a surprise procedurally because the FCC accepted it as justiciable in the form of individual constitutional complaints under the right-to-vote provisions of Article 38. In their complaints, voters alleged that by transferring certain legislative powers to the European Union without the consent of Parliament, the government would invade their rights as voters and undermine the principles of both democracy and popular sovereignty. Although the FCC found the treaty compatible with the Basic Law, it warned the government that the EU threatened to break the chain of legitimation between voters and their representatives. In a highly controversial opinion, and a unanimous one at that, the FCC suggested that the transfer of authority to the EU in the face of its "democratic deficit" would diminish the voting rights of the people—the German people—and the authority of the elected parliament responsible to them for the powers it exercises. The court's decision produced shockwaves throughout Germany and Europe. Despite holding that the national Parliament retained sufficient control over its powers to satisfy the principle of democracy, the court faulted the EU for its lack of democratic representation, suggesting along the way that the legitimacy of EU policy will depend on maintaining the link between German voters, their national parliament, and the European Parliament (Pernice 1993; Kokott 1994; Meeson 1994; Foster 1994).[6]

Three years before *Maastricht*, the court had ruled that the concept of "the people" for the purpose of voting included only German citizens and not foreign residents working in Germany. Schleswig-Holstein and Hamburg had permitted foreign residents to vote in local elections. The FCC nullified the laws of both *Länder*. Voters, the court said, must be citizens unified by their common membership in and allegiance to the "body politic" (83 BVerfGE 37: 1990; 83 BVerfGE 60: 1990). Two years later, however, the Maastricht Treaty extended the franchise to all European citizens residing in a member state. It was clear that a constitutional amendment would be necessary to validate the treaty provision. Accordingly, in December 1992, the Basic Law was amended to grant the nationals of member states the right to vote in local *Land* elections (Article 28 [1]), effectively nullifying the FCC's foreign voting decisions.

In the *Official Propaganda Case*, finally, the FCC refined its conception of representative democracy. During the 1976 federal election campaign, the Social Democratic–controlled government had distributed millions of informational leaflets and brochures, including the text of various laws and treaties, describing the records of and benefits conferred by federal ministries. The Christian Democratic Union (CDU) petitioned the FCC to ban this practice. In response, the court ruled that the practice violated not only the principle of parliamentary democracy under Article 20, but also the equality of political parties under Article 21 and the principle of free and equal elections under Article 38. State agencies, said the court, may not take sides during an election campaign. The Basic Law provides "for a free and open process of forming the popular will" just as voters and parties must be left free "to form and utter their opinions fully and openly." Similarly, noted the court, political parties must begin their election campaigns at the same starting line if there is to be a free and equal process of forming, in the words of the Basic Law, "the political will of the people." Political scientists might well question a theory of democracy that posits, empirically, a direct relationship between voting and the people's will, but it is one to which the FCC has faithfully adhered.

Public funding of political parties

A distinctive feature of German constitutionalism is the formal recognition of political parties as "quasi-constitutional organs." In fact, as noted earlier in this article, Germany is officially known as a "party state" (Leibholz 1973, 68-94), one described by Michaela Richter (1995, 37) as "a unique synthesis of Western parliamentarism and the German state tradition." The parliamentary tradition finds its embodiment in the principle of popular sovereignty and the formal institutions of democracy. The state tradition, on the other hand, is manifest in the Basic Law's formal recognition of political parties as agencies engaged in the process of "will formation" and in their status—one the FCC has conferred by interpretation— as "integral units of the constitutional state" (1 BVerfGE 208, 225: 1952). Already in 1954, the FCC ruled that in their capacity as constitutional organs of the state, political parties may defend their institutional rights before the court in an *Organstreit* (interbranch conflict) proceeding (4 BVerfGE 27: 1954), empowering parties to challenge an infringement of their electoral rights much as a branch of government would seek to vindicate its rights under the principle of separation of powers.

Like the U.S. Supreme Court, the Constitutional Court has played a major role in the field of party finance, but with results emphasizing equality of party competition over arguments rooted in free speech rights, as in the United States. In an early case, the court invalidated tax provisions allowing individuals and corporations to deduct their contributions to political parties for discriminating against those parties—the Social Democratic Party (SPD) in particular—disfavored by wealthy persons and the German business community. (A year earlier, the court had nullified a law disallowing tax deductions for contributions to political parties unless the latter elected at least one representative to the national or a state parliament [6 BverfGE 273: 1957].) In this case, the court took the unusual step of recommending, in the interest of fair and equal elections, the public financing of election campaigns. Parliament obliged, its enthusiasm for state financing fully matching the generosity of its appropriations. By the late 1980s, total party income had reached DM 608.5 million, 36 percent of which consisted of public subsidies; by 1994, public subsidies accounted for 40 percent (DM 352 million) of the total party income of the parties (Nassmacher 2001, 96).

In numerous decisions over the years, however, the FCC has imposed severe limits on the scope and allocation of public funding, virtually micromanaging the field of party finance. An inaugural party finance law was invalidated by the court because it covered party activities well beyond campaign expenditures (20 BVerfGE 56: 1966). This decision sought to reconcile the tension between Articles 21 and 38. Under the first, parties are charged with competing for an electoral mandate, but under the second, representatives are declared to be independent and not bound by instructions. To allow financing unrelated to elections, said the court, would give political parties a monopoly over the formation of public opinion. Between elections, parties are fully entitled to raise money on their own, but they do so as private entities. They assume the character of constitutional organs only in their capacity as *electoral* organizations. Accordingly, public funding must be limited, constitutionally, to legitimate *campaign* expenses.

In subsequent decisions, the court has monitored laws relating to the disclosure of party contributions, tax-deductible donations to the parties, and the formulae for allocating public funds among the parties, imposing standards and limits on each of these measures, all in the interest of establishing a level playing field for political parties competing for a proportionate share of the national vote

(Kommers 1997, 200-215). In one decision, the FCC lowered the publicity threshold for contributions from the legislatively established figure of DM 40,000 to DM 20,000. As for public subsidies, the FCC disallowed legislation denying public funding even to independent candidates and, in the same opinion, struck the denial of funds to parties unrepresented in Parliament as well as to those receiving

---

[W]hile the court has limited the right of foreign residents to vote in local and municipal elections, it has otherwise sought to root Parliament's law-making powers in elections and the exercise of the franchise.

---

less than 2.5 percent of the popular vote (41 BVerfGE 399: 1976). In fact, the court proceeded to order Parliament to lower the 2.5 figure to 0.5 percent, a rule seemingly undercutting the logic behind the FCC's approval of the 5 percent clause. By 1992, however, the court concluded that it was no longer reasonable or practicable to distinguish between campaign costs and other political party expenditures (85 BVerfGE 164: 1992). From now on, ruled the court, state funding could not exceed the total amount raised by the parties themselves and, in a parting shot, admonished the Bundestag to change the law accordingly by January 1993 (Gunlicks 1994).

Hessian Election Review Case

The *Hessian Election Review Case* (103 BVerfGE 111: 2001) arose out of a party finance scandal in Hesse, one of Germany's most populous states. It warrants attention not only for the issues it raises but also for the affinity it bears to *Bush v. Gore* (531 U.S. 98 [2000]), the controversial case that decided the American presidential election of 2000 (Gillman 2001). *Bush* was controversial because many legal scholars, including four dissenting justices on the Supreme Court, thought the case failed to present a substantial federal question and should have been decided at the state level. Others advanced the view that *Bush* presented a "political question" unfit for judicial resolution (Chemerinsky 2001). *Hessian Election*, on the other hand, like most cases coming before the FCC, stands for the proposition that *any* case arising under the Basic Law and properly before the court is fully justiciable. *Bush* presents precisely the kind of issue—were such a case to arise in

Germany—that the FCC would feel obliged to resolve. The idea that certain constitutional issues, although legitimately before the FCC, should be dismissed because of their political character would offend the German sense of constitutional justice and the rule of law.

The facts of *Hessian Election*, though complex, can be summarized briefly. Christian Democrats, having narrowly won the 1999 Hessian state election, formed a coalition government with Liberal Democrats, thus relegating Social Democrats and the Alliance 90–Greens to the role of opposition, a rarity in this largely SPD state. It was discovered later, however, that the CDU campaign had been financed by illegal campaign funds stashed away in a Swiss bank account, whereupon, relying on state law, Social Democrats sought to nullify the election. State law provided for an Election Review Court (*Wahlprüfungsgericht*) composed of both judges and legislators. Its jurisdiction included the power to void an election resulting from a breach of "public morality," a decision state law defined as final. But when the review court opened its inquiry at the request of the SPD, the new coalition government immediately challenged the proceeding before the FCC in an abstract judicial review petition, arguing that the inquiry conflicted with the constitutional principles of popular democracy, the rule of law, and separation of powers (103 BVerfGE 111, 113-23: 2001). Three principal rulings emerged from the FCC's decision. First, the court found that the establishment of an election review court was fully authorized by Article 28 of the Basic Law, requiring all *Land* governments to conform to "the principle of a . . . democratic . . . state governed by the rule of law." Second, the court sustained the validity of statutory provisions providing for the nullification of an election tainted by bad morals. But the court narrowly construed the meaning of "public morality," declaring that the offensive conduct must influence the election and *significantly* affect its outcome. "Declaring an election invalid," said the court, "requires electoral irregularities of such magnitude that keeping the elected people's representatives in office would appear intolerable" (author's translation). The FCC went on to hold that no such breach occurred in the Hessian election. Third, the FCC ruled that the Election Review Court contravened Article 92 of the Basic Law, which vests judicial power in "judges." Because the review court included legislators, said the FCC, it offended the principle of separated powers. Also declared unconstitutional was the inability to appeal the election court's decisions to a higher court. The rule of law, said the FCC, requires that its decisions be subject to appellate review. One month later, finally, Hesse's Election Review Court decided that the CDU's use of illegal funds, however regrettable, did not violate "public morality" as defined by the FCC, and thus could not be said to have unlawfully influenced the outcome of the state election (Miller 2004).

Without appearing to digress too far from the jurisprudence of democracy itself, one might point out important differences between certain German and American judicial practices. First, *Hessian Election* was a unanimous decision despite its partisan nature and the even split on the Second Sensate between justices nominated by the CDU and those nominated by the SPD. *Bush v. Gore*, by contrast, was a split decision, with the court's five "conservative" justices deciding in favor of Bush.

Interestingly, German legal scholars known to the author have expressed surprise and even disdain for the frequency of five-to-four decisions on the Supreme Court—not to mention the multiplicity of concurring and dissenting opinions found in numerous other cases—a practice they have a hard time reconciling with clear rules of law. On the other hand, abstract judicial review is a practice that would find little support among American lawyers and judges. Confining federal judicial power to concrete "cases and controversies" is, of course, deeply embedded in the common law tradition and American legal culture (Ripple 1984). It is also the product of the Supreme Court's respect for the legitimate roles of Congress and the executive in the American system of government. In Germany, by contrast, abstract and concrete review cases are not designed to vindicate an individual's claim to a constitutional right or even that of the official party petitioning for review, but rather to vindicate the public's interest in constitutional government and the validity of law. At stake is the constitutional order itself as well as the integrity of the legal order as a whole (Kommers 1997, 42-48).

Dissolving Parliament

This article goes to press just as the FCC has sustained the decision of the federal president to dissolve Parliament and to hold a national election—on September 18, 2005—a full year in advance of the regularly scheduled election. The controversy surrounding this case might also remind Americans of *Bush v. Gore*, for the questions it presents are as much political as constitutional, and they touch the heart of Germany's parliamentary democracy. The controversy began with Chancellor Schröder's recent plan to dissolve the Bundestag and hold a new federal election ahead of time, a plan motivated by a string of local election defeats that left the Social Democratic–Green coalition in charge of only four of Germany's sixteen states (*Länder*), compared to the eleven it controlled in 1998. A fresh election, it was hoped, would produce a new governing mandate the chancellor desperately wanted and needed. The chancellor, however, was not only taking a calculated political risk; he was also betting on the strategy's constitutionality. As noted earlier, Parliament can be dissolved under Article 68 only when the chancellor initiates a vote of no confidence, loses, and then requests the president to dissolve the Bundestag in the *hope* that he will do so. These procedures should be distinguished from the constructive vote of no confidence permitted by Article 67, pursuant to which the Bundestag itself may remove a chancellor but only by simultaneously electing his successor by a majority of its members. If confidence is withheld and the Bundestag fails to elect a new leader, the chancellor remains in office at the head of a minority government.

Article 67, like Article 68, was a master stroke of constitutional engineering, for it has helped to stabilize Germany's political system. Since the Bundestag cannot dissolve itself, its members—that is, members of the governing parties—are ill disposed to turn themselves out of a ruling coalition unless they are confident of rejoining the government under a new chancellor. It is unsurprising, therefore, that the Bundestag has invoked Article 67 only twice in the Federal Republic's history, first in 1972 when Willy Brandt barely held off a Christian Democratic challenge to his leadership and then again in 1982 when the Bundestag chose Helmut Kohl to replace Helmut Schmidt as chancellor following the Free Democratic Party's decision to withdraw from the latter's coalition and shift its support to Christian Democrats. Schröder's initiative under Article 68, however, is the third time in Germany's postwar history that a chancellor has resorted to its procedures. Both Brandt and Kohl sought early elections shortly after their just-mentioned victories in the Bundestag in 1972 and 1982, respectively. In these two situations, the strategy worked. The ensuing elections produced substantial parliamentary majorities for both chancellors.

Counting on, or hoping for, a similar result, Chancellor Schröder initiated his no confidence vote on July 1, 2005, and lost as planned, permitting him to petition the federal president for an order to dissolve the Bundestag. Had President Horst Köhler concluded that the chancellor had *contrived* to lose a vote of confidence, he might have disallowed the request on the ground that the chancellor actually commanded the support of a parliamentary majority. But on July 22, President Köhler—formerly a member of the CDU (the opposition party)—accepted Schröder's argument that he could no longer govern effectively, remarking that "the well-being of the people is best served by new elections." Shortly thereafter, two members of the Bundestag, from the SPD and the Greens, respectively, filed an *Organstreit* proceeding challenging the validity of the president's action,[7] arguing that the order of dissolution in the face of actual majority support for the government violated their electoral mandates, ones coextensive with the prescribed four-year terms for which they were elected in 2002.

The judicial petition was not unprecedented, for the FCC decided a similar complaint when members of the Bundestag contested the validity of new elections ordered by the federal president in 1983 at the request of Chancellor Kohl. A full month prior to the newly scheduled election, and over the reservations of several constitutional scholars, the FCC, in a six-to-three opinion, backed the president, asserting that the decision to dissolve Parliament was within his discretionary authority (62 BVerfGE 1: 1983). In the course of its opinion, the FCC distinguished between the "formal" and "material" conditions for dissolving Parliament under Article 68. The formal requirements, as already noted, are four, involving, respectively, the chancellor's call for a vote of confidence, the Bundestag's "no" vote, the chancellor's request to the president, and the president's acceptance of the request. The material condition added by the court requires a "situation of instability" *(eine Lage der Instabilität)* that would in fact undermine the ability of the ruling coalition to govern effectively.

Accordingly, the FCC made clear each of the decision makers along the way—chancellor, Bundestag, and president—is duty-bound to consider the Basic Law's sharp limits on the power of dissolution. Each is required, independently and conscientiously, to decide whether the political divisions in the Bundestag had seriously impaired the ruling coalition's capacity to govern. Yet the FCC emphasized the political nature of each judgment, thus blurring the line between constitutional law and politics. Although the FCC stood ready to render its own judgment on the merits of any proposal for dissolution, the justices in the majority held that the president in particular should allow the chancellor a certain political leeway (*Spielraum*) in determining whether he is faced with a "situation of instability" that would justify new elections.

Initially, it was unclear whether Schröder's Article 68 gambit would succeed in the light of the FCC's 1983 decision. Yet the chancellor's reasoning seemed as compelling as Kohl's in 1983. First, Schröder had a scant 13-vote majority in the Bundestag (out of 603 members); second, he seemed reasonably convinced that opposition on certain issues from the Greens—the SPD's coalition partner—and from the left wing of his own party threatened his leadership; third, he had reason to feel that he had been weakened politically, in and out of Parliament, by the devastating results of recent *Land* elections; fourth, and relatedly, he was faced with a CDU-dominated Bundesrat that could thwart 60 percent of his legislative program; finally, opinion polls show that the SPD-led government was at one of its lowest ebbs in popular support. Taken together, these factors added up to a strong argument for resorting to Article 68.

But were these reasons *constitutionally* sufficient to proceed with new elections? The legal objections were substantial. For one thing, as former Constitutional Court Justice Dieter Grimm (2005) suggested, Schröder was not "weary of office" *(amtsmüde)*. He might have resigned but told the world that he would not do so. For another, he may not have been faced with a *real* parliamentary crisis. In short, a "situation of instability" may not have existed because, arguably, he still commanded a majority in the *Bundestag*. According to prevailing constitutional opinion, it is not the margin of a chancellor's parliamentary majority that is crucial but rather its stability (von Münch and Kunig 2001, 1172-75), and Schröder had not in fact lost his majority. In addition, the public's low opinion of a duly elected government has no constitutional relevance. Equally irrelevant is the nature of the relationship between the Bundestag and the Bundesrat. The relationship that counts is that between the Bundestag and the federal government. Article 68 may be invoked only when this relationship reaches the point of instability. The betting in this instance, however, was that the court would follow its 1983 precedent and validate the president's decision to dissolve Parliament and hold new elections.

This is precisely what happened. On August 25, 2005, the FCC once again held that the requirements of Article 68 had been fulfilled (*Dissolution Case II*; see www.bverfg.de/entscheidungen/es20050825_2bve000405.html). The court reemphasized its view that the Basic Law provides for no general power to dissolve Parliament. The majority was emphatic in saying that the president may not grant a chancellor's request for dissolution merely because he would wish to expand his parliamentary majority. In assessing the validity of the request, the president must be persuaded that the chancellor in fact is faced with a situation of instability in parliament. But again, the court felt, as it did in 1983, that this was largely a political question requiring a measurable degree of deference to the three political organs, namely, chancellor, Bundestag, and president. The deference was anything but total, however. Citing serious conflicts within the governing coalition—with some members of Schröder's own party calling for his resignation—and the chancellor's sincere doubts that he could govern effectively under these circumstances, not to mention the president's own careful evaluation of the chancellor's position, the court concluded that the president had not abused his discretion in approving Parliament's dissolution and calling for new elections.[8] *Dissolution II*, with its interplay between law and politics, was as fascinating a spectacle for Germans as was *Bush v. Gore* for Americans.

Concluding Remarks

As this article has shown, the FCC is an important custodian of political democracy in Germany. It has protected the rights of parliamentarians and promoted equality of opportunity among competing political parties while guarding the integrity of elections and insisting on relatively equal population in single-member constituencies. It has also defended the principle of fair and equal representation exemplified in the nation's celebrated system of personalized or modified PR. And while the court has limited the right of foreign residents to vote in local and municipal elections, it has otherwise sought to root Parliament's law-making powers in elections and the exercise of the franchise. In addition, the FCC has vigilantly shielded minor parties against discriminatory legislation, particularly with respect to the allocation of state subsidies and requirements for gaining access to the ballot. At the same time, with the single exception of the first all-German election in 1990, the FCC has sustained the 5 percent rule at state and national levels in the interest of overall political stability. Finally, by exercising its authority to pass sentence on the validity of elections and the dissolution of parliament, the court has consolidated its reputation in Germany as the ultimate guardian of both democracy and the rule of law.

Notes

1. The sole exception are the referenda required when adjoining states (*Länder*) seek to change their boundaries or merge into a single state (*Land*). Article 29 of the Basic Law requires a referendum in the affected territories and the approval of two-thirds of those voting. Any general reorganization of the states must be approved in a national referendum.

2. The parenthetical reference contains the standard citation to German constitutional case law. The Federal Constitutional Court's (FCC's) decisions appear in a set of official reports known as *Entscheidungen des Bundesverfassungsgerichts* (Decisions of the Federal Constitutional Court) and are published by J.C.B. Mohr (Paul Siebeck), Tübingen, Germany. The citation format includes, in the sequence noted, the volume number, abbreviation of the court (BVerfGE), first page of the decision, the page of the particular reference (sometimes omitted), and the year of the case.

3. Germany was one of the first countries to establish a constitutional court after World War II. The following years witnessed an explosion of constitutional (or judicial) review around the world. The singularity of this phenomenon cannot be exaggerated. It is arguably the major political development of our time, and no less revolutionary. Consider: popular democracies have transformed themselves into juridical democracies, judicial has replaced parliamentary supremacy, elected representatives have relinquished power to unelected judges, and countermajoritarian institutions have been empowered to veto majoritarian policies. In short, what was once a unique aspect of American constitutionalism has evolved into a universal feature of

the rule of law around the world. In contrast to the American experience, however, judicial review has been most often lodged, as in Germany, in a specialized constitutional court organized apart from and independent of the regular judiciary.

4. These panels are known as the First and Second Senates. The Bundestag elects one-half of the justices of each senate, the Bundesrat (the upper house of Parliament in which the *Länder* [states] are represented) the other half. The twelve-year limited term of office applies only to the justices of the Constitutional Court. They are required to retire, however, at the age of sixty-eight whether or not they have served the full term. All other German judges must retire when they reach sixty-five years of age.

5. The special arrangement for this first all-German election represented a compromise between West Germany's electoral system and East Germany's system of pure proportional representation. East German leaders objected to the 5 percent clause because the political reform groups that had played so critical a role in the nation's peaceful revolution would be unlikely to win 5 percent of the national vote. The two sides eventually worked out a "piggyback" arrangement that would permit smaller parties in the east to field candidates in alliance with other, larger parties in the west. This plan, however, favored some small parties at the expense of others. For example, the strength of Bavaria's Christian Social Union (CSU) would carry its sister party, East Germany's German Social Union (GSU), into the Bundestag, whereas the old Communist Party, now dressed up as the Party of Democratic Socialism (PDS), was unlikely to find a willing partner in the west to help it win 5 percent of the national vote. The PDS, along with the Greens and far-right Republicans, petitioned the FCC to strike down the arrangement.

6. This concept of democratic legitimacy has also played a crucial role in cases implicating separation of powers. An example is the FCC's treatment of the nondelegation doctrine. Taking seriously the Basic Law's command that statutes define the "content, purpose, and scope" of delegated authority, the court has struck down numerous grants of authority to administrative officials. The U.S. Supreme Court, by contrast, would not touch cases such as these. In still another case, which the Supreme Court would have regarded as nonjusticiable, the court declared that parliamentary approval would be required for the further deployment of German troops in Somalia (89 BVerfGE 38: 1993).

7. An *Organstreit* proceeding is usually initiated by one organ—or branch—of government against another. A constituent unit or member of an organ of government, however, has standing before the FCC if his or her rights as an agent of the political organ have been violated. In this case, members of the Bundestag—the relevant political organ—were able to argue that the premature dissolution of Parliament infringed on their constitutional right to a four-year term of office.

8. *Dissolution II* included two dissenting opinions. Justice Gertrude Lübbe-Wolff wanted to dispense with the court's "material conditions" requirement, whereas Justice Hans-Joachim Jentch opined that the requirement was not satisfied. Both thought that the dissolution was fabricated in "clear violation" of the will of the Basic Law's framers.

References

Bundesverfassungsgericht. 2004. Statistical overview of proceedings. http://www.bverfg.de/cgi-bin/link .pl?entscheidungen (accessed July 7, 2005).

Chemerinsky, E. 2001. *Bush v. Gore* was not justiciable. *Notre Dame Law Review* 76:1093-1112.

Conradt, D. P. 2001. *The German polity*. 7th ed. New York: Longman.

Currie, D. 1994. *The constitution of the Federal Republic of Germany*. Chicago: University of Chicago Press.

Foster, N. G. 1994. The German constitution and E.C. membership. *Public Law*, pp. 392-408.

Franck, T. M. 1992. *Political questions, judicial answers*. Princeton, NJ: Princeton University Press.

Gillman, H. 2001. *The votes that counted: How the Court decided the 2000 presidential election*. Chicago: University of Chicago Press.

Grimm, D. 2005. Schröder's Weg ist ungangbar. *Frankfurter Allgemeine Zeitung*, June 8, p. 39.

Gunlicks, A. 1994. The New German party finance law. *German Politics* 4:101-21.

———. 2003. *The Länder and German federalism*. Manchester, UK: Manchester University Press.

Jesse, E. 1985. *Wahlrecht zwischen Kontinuität und Reform*. Düsseldorf, Germany: Droste.

Kitzinger, U. W. 1960. *German electoral politics*. Oxford: Clarendon.

Kokott, J. 1994. Deutschland im Rahmen der Europäischen Union—zum Vertrag von Maastricht. *Archiv des Öffenlichen Rechts* 119:207-37.

———. 1999. From reception and transplantation to convergence of constitutional models in the age of globalization—With special reference to the German Basic Law. In *Constitutionalism, universalism and democracy—A comparative analysis*, ed. Christian Starck, 71-134. Baden-Baden, Germany: Nomos.

Kommers, D. 1976. *Judicial politics in Germany: A study of the Federal Constitutional Court.* Beverly Hills, CA: Sage.

———. 1997. *The constitutional jurisprudence of the Federal Republic of Germany.* 2nd ed. Durham, NC: Duke University Press.

Leibholz, G. 1973. Der moderne Parteienstaat. In *Verfassungsstaat—Verfassungsrecht.* Stuttgart, Germany: Kohlhammer.

Meeson, K. M. 1994. Hedging European integration: The Maastricht judgment of the Federal Constitutional Court. *Fordham International Law Journal* 17:511-30.

Miller, R. 2004. Lords of democracy: The judicialization of "pure politics" in the United States and Germany. *Washington and Lee Law Review* 61:587-662.

Nassmacher, K.-H. 2001. Political finance in West Central Europe. In *Foundations of democracy*, ed. Karl-Heinz Nassmacher, 92-111. Baden-Baden, Germany: Nomos.

Pernice, I. 1993. Maastricht, Staat, und Demokratie. *Verwaltung* 26:449.

Richter, M. 1995. The Basic Law and the democratic party state: Constitutional theory and political practice. In *Cornerstone of democracy: The West German Grundgesetz, 1949-89*. Washington, DC: German Historical Institute.

Ripple, K. 1984. *Constitutional litigation.* Charlottesville, VA: The Michie Company.

Sartori, G. 1997. *Comparative constitutional engineering.* 2nd ed. New York: New York University Press.

Schlaich, K., and S. Korioth. 2001. *Das Bundesverfassungsgerichts.* 5th ed. Munich, Germany: C.H. Beck.

von Münch, I., and P. Kunig. 2001. *Grundgesetz Kommentar.* 5th ed. Munich, Germany: C.H. Beck.

Religion, Constitutional Courts, and Democracy in Former Communist Countries

By
JAMES T. RICHARDSON

This article offers two main arguments, both of which have important corollaries. First, the author argues that religion, and a specific form of religion, played a major role in the downfall of communism and the Soviet Union. A corollary is that religious motivations furnished important impetus to the development of democracy in former communist countries (FCC). Second, the author argues that courts, and more specifically constitutional courts in FCC, played a major role in promoting democracy in those nations. A corollary to that assertion is that constitution courts in most FCC have demonstrated considerable respect for and promotion of the role of religion in FCC. These assertions and their corollaries are discussed in light of scholarly studies on the place of religion in the modern constitutionalism movement in former colonial and communist countries.

Keywords: religion; constitutional courts; democracy; former communist countries; Hungary; Russia; Catholic Church

This article makes two key arguments and attempts to combine them in a way that demonstrates the importance of religious motivations to the development of democracies in former communist countries (FCC). One argument concerns the role played by religion in

James T. Richardson, J.D., Ph.D., professor of sociology and judicial studies at the University of Nevada, Reno, is director of the Grant Sawyer Center for Justice Studies and the Judicial Studies graduate degree program for trial judges at the University. He has been a Fulbright fellow and a foundation professor at the University of Nevada, Reno, and served as president of the American Association of University Professors from 1998 to 2000. He has published more than two hundred articles and chapters, mainly on various aspects of new religions and the law/religion relationship. His latest book is Regulating Religion: Case Studies from around the Globe (Kluwer, 2004). In fall 2004, he was invited to present a paper at the first-ever conference on law and religion to be held in the People's Republic of China, sponsored by the Chinese Academy of Social Sciences.

NOTE: Presented at the Syracuse conference "On Law and Democratic Development," in honor of Richard D. Schwartz, retiring professor, Syracuse University of Law, Syracuse, New York, April 15-18, 2005.

DOI: 10.1177/0002716205281634

undermining communist governments that made up the Former Soviet Union (FSU) and its satellite countries in Eastern and Central Europe. A corollary to this first argument is that religious motivations have also given major impetus to burgeoning democratic movements within these nations as they struggle to redefine themselves after the fall of communism.

Another major argument is that courts, and more specifically constitutional courts, have played and are playing an important role in promoting democratic impulses in some FCC, as these new judicial institutions have both promoted and interpreted governing legal documents that embody democratic ideals. An important corollary to this second point is that constitutional courts in at least some FCC are, through their rulings, defining an important role for religion and religious institutions in the development of the new societies. Constitutional courts are stating in sometimes strong terms that religion has a place in the public square and that societies benefit in many ways when this is the case.

Religion and the Fall of Communism

Many different factors played roles in the downfall of communism. Some authorities claim, in now brilliant hindsight, that it was obvious the socialist economic system was not functioning as advertised and that the economic system was collapsing from within. A variation of this materialist explanation is that the unrelenting global spread of Western capitalism eventually ground under the inferior socialist systems of the communist world. On a more idealist plane, some assert that Western ideals won the day by eventually winning the hearts and minds of many behind the Iron Curtain, through modern means of communication and because they happened to be morally right. Others would proffer "great man" theories of history and give major credit to Mikhail Gorbachev or others as key people who changed the world and gave impetus to the democratic impulse behind the Iron Curtain.

Plainly, religion did play a major role in the demise of communism, although few would be foolish enough to offer religion as a monocausal explanation. My view is that religion, and a specific kind of religion, played a *catalytic* role in the downfall of communism. Given the recent death of Pope John Paul II, with all the discussion of the impact that his papacy has had on the world, few will be surprised that I might assert that the Catholic Church, led by the former archbishop of Krakow who was named pope at a key time in world history, contributed to the downfall of communism in a significant way.

Sociologists do not usually propound great man theories of history, so I must take care in explaining my position. Karol Wojtyla was a quite remarkable man who certainly tempts even a secular sociologist toward such theories. One must, however, view Pope John Paul II as a *representative of his Church*, albeit a very unusual one (the first non-Italian pope in 455 years) chosen in a very unusual circumstance (his predecessor whom Cardinal Wojtyla helped elect served as pope only thirty-three days). Cardinal Wojtyla was chosen as pope because of his remarkable personal attributes and experiences, which included living under the Nazi regime during World War II and then under communism for most of his adult life until he was chosen as pope.

Karol Wojtyla was known as a strong defender of his faith and of the Polish nation against communism. He also had apparently made his mark during Vatican II, a conclave in which he represented the Polish Catholic Church. Especially effective were his expositions in defense of human freedom, a subject on which he had great relevant personal experience. In a time of crisis, with the unexpected death of the new pope, the College of Cardinals took a risk and chose someone who had developed an impressive record while serving the church in a communist country. And the rest, they say, is history.

[R]eligion, and a specific kind of religion, played a catalytic role in the downfall of communism.

The historical context included a weakening Soviet Union, which was having trouble holding on to its territories. Those territories included Poland, a nation that was nearly totally Catholic (about 95 percent). The moral and political strength of the church grew under communism, as the church served successfully as the sometimes not so loyal opposition. Karol Wojtyla was the second best known and loved Catholic in all of Poland (second only to Cardinal Wyszynski, who spent three years in prison for his refusal to accommodate the communists). The selection of Wojtyla as pope immediately gave hope to all behind the Iron Curtain, Catholic or not. The new pope immediately started talking about human freedom, encouraging those around the world but especially those under communist rule to hold fast and to fight for their rights.

One of the new pope's first international visits was to Poland, despite the strong efforts of communist authorities there to stop him. Seventeen million people attended services held by him, and most other Poles watched on television or listened on the radio. Poland would never be the same after the pope's first visit there. If ever the domino theory might apply, it seems Eastern and Central Europe was that place, and the decade after the selection of Karol Wojtyla as pope was the time. The uprisings in Poland in the 1980s and the inability or unwillingness of the Soviets to suppress them contributed directly to oppositional developments in other satellite countries of the Soviet Union.

Some of those other uprisings involved religious motivations of the citizenry, in places such as Hungary, but I do not claim such motivations as a primary cause for developments in other countries. However, I do assert that what happened in Poland was very important to developments in other satellite countries and that the Polish case involved religion and religious motivations to a remarkable degree.

Now, I will examine the corollary idea that religious motivations were a crucial underpinning for the development of democracy in the FCC.

Religion and the Rise of Democracy

The spread of representative, constitutional democracies in FCC is one of the most astounding developments of the past century—one that few people predicted or expected. And yet it happened, and it did so in an unbelievably short period of time and with very little bloodshed. Obviously, new leaders in FCC could follow models outside the Soviet bloc as the power of the Soviet Union declined and Soviet leaders chose not to call in the tanks. The impact of important international documents such as the European Convention on Human and Civil Rights and other similarly motivated international statements was apparent; the very language of those documents appears in some new constitutions promulgated in FCC.

It may be less apparent that religious motivations played a key role in the development of these new constitutional democracies, but that seems the case. One piece of evidence that religion was important to those who crafted these new constitutions is that religion is mentioned in virtually all of them and is often given a place of prominence, as religious freedom is enshrined in those constitutions. However, a historical and cultural background led up to this prominence and is worth reciting briefly.

The example of what is defined as the first experiment with democracy in ancient Athens is, of course, significant, although that impulse died out for centuries before being revived in Western Europe. Scholars have argued that the strong emphasis placed on the worth and dignity of the individual person within the Christian religious tradition and its various major subgroupings is a key element in the development of the democratic impulse. Also, the strong belief that evolved in Western Christendom that there was a higher law above that of kings and other potentates was crucial and led some of those kings and potentates to seek support and approval from at least some subsets of their subjects.

In terms of what has happened most recently in FCC, however, the impact of Vatican II should not be underemphasized, especially since Karol Wojtyla was an active participant in those proceedings. A number of the FCC had a strong Catholic contingent within them, and in those the impact was quite direct. Vatican II was attended to by people around the globe, both Catholic and non-Catholic. Citizens in FCC and others heard and saw Vatican II make a strong statement about the value of freedom of all kinds, with religious freedom taking a leading role. This freedom was to serve as a basis for "both the sacred dignity of the human person and for inalienable rights to human autonomy and self determination" (Casanova 1994, 105). Jose Casanova adds in his chapter on Poland (1994, 105),

Only after the Catholic church officially and unequivocally embraced the principle of religious freedom and freedom of conscience at Vatican II could it develop a normative position (in favor of democracy). . . . The assumption of the modern doctrine of human rights entails . . . not only the acceptance of democracy as a legitimate "form" of government, but the recognition that modern democracy is not only a "form" of government but also a type of polity based on the universalistic principles of individual freedom and individual rights.

Thus, it seems reasonable to assume a strong role played by religious motivations in giving impetus to the democratic movement within FCC.

The Role of the Constitutional Courts

There has been a definite trend in recent years toward the adoption of constitutions by newly forming governments. The newer constitutions developed over the past century have, especially in more recent decades, demonstrated "the global influence of democratization, human rights ideology, and economic neoliberalism" (Go 2003, 71). The FCC have been no exception to this trend, and all have, to varying degrees, enshrined constitutions that embody these general values and movements.

> *One piece of evidence that religion was important to those who crafted these new constitutions is that religion is mentioned in virtually all of them and is often given a place of prominence, as religious freedom is enshrined in those constitutions.*

The modern tendency to adopt constitutions has contributed directly to the establishment of constitutional courts to interpret and enforce those constitutions. The modern constitutional court movement began in 1920 in Austria and was followed by three waves of constitutional court development, first in Germany and Italy post-WWII; then in Spain and Portugal post-Franco; and more recently in FCC, where such courts were even encouraged by the Council of Europe as a way to better ensure the development of a working democracy in those countries. Such courts have been established by all FCC, with differing degrees of success and influence. Arjomand (2003, 11) says of the constitutional court movement,

> The abuse of "legality" by Communism and Fascism necessitated a new, amplified, rights-based conception of the rule of law, which includes justiciable human rights substantively, and specifies mechanisms and institutional devices for safeguarding the rule of law—most notably the constitutional courts. . . . The key to the role of the constitutional court as the instrument of the new constitutionalism is the idea of the transition to democracy . . .

In some of the FCC, constitutional courts have become quite strong and have enjoyed considerable popular support, with perhaps Hungary being the best example of this interesting phenomenon. Kim Lane Scheppele (2003) even referred to the constitutional court in Hungary as a "courtocracy" and said, "The Hungarian Constitutional Court, through the 1990s, practically ran Hungary. . . . [I]t was the strongest body of state throughout the 1990s" (p. 222). Other FCC that have seen strong and relatively stable constitutional courts develop include Poland, Slovenia, and Estonia.

In other FCC, such courts have run afoul of political forces and either have had their powers curtailed or never were able to develop much authority. FCC whose constitutional courts never achieved much authority include Ukraine, Azerbaijan, and Belarus. Russia is an example of a constitutional court that was significantly involved initially, then encountered severe political difficulties, was disbanded by President Yeltsin in 1993, and finally was brought back "under new management" more than a year later (Scheppele 2002, 263). The Russian constitutional court has gradually regained some power, in part through creative procedural practices, but mainly because "it has moved away from a heavy emphasis on separation of powers cases toward more cases elaborating the rights of individual citizens" (Scheppele 2003, 228).

Constitutional courts in societies such as Hungary where they can function somewhat independently have proven to be immensely popular. In Hungary at one point in the 1990s, the approval rating for the constitutional court was 90 percent (Scheppele 2003, 233). In Russia, the "new" constitutional court demonstrates its popularity through the submission of fifteen thousand petitions per year to the court from individual Russian citizens (Scheppele 2003, 234). This level of support for constitutional courts may seem ironic, given that the judges are not popularly elected, but apparently "citizens see in these courts a real hope for the recognition of human rights and the rule of law" (Scheppele 2003, 221).

In short, constitutional courts seem to be viewed, in societies where conditions allow them to function, as bastions of human freedom and democratic values. The courts, according to Scheppele (2003, 233), can force politicians to honor commitments made to implement human rights and freedoms, thus serving as an important check and balance to postcommunist governments that might adopt different policies. Scholarly research has found mounting evidence that under certain conditions constitutional courts can and have become the primary vehicles of democratic values in FCC. Andras Sajo (1999), a Hungarian scholar, said that constitutional courts are "the guarantors of the basic consensus on which democracy is founded" (p. 242).

Constitutional Courts and Religion

Arjomand (2003, 13) said, "The emergence of constitutional courts as guardians of the new constitutional orders is largely due to their being instruments of unconditional enforcement of individual rights." The prominent role for the constitutional courts might be viewed as in part a reaction to the suppression of individual liberties during the time of communist domination. And it would seem reasonable to assume that constitutional courts, whose major role is to enforce human and civil rights, would render decisions supportive of religion occupying a prominent place in the societies of FCC.

Constitutional courts . . . have proven to be immensely popular. . . . [They] seem to be viewed, in societies where conditions allow them to function, as bastions of human freedom and democratic values.

Arjomand (2003, 15) pointed out, "It is interesting to note that the number of constitutions with religious provisions increases sharply in the 1990s. The need for constitutional reaffirmation of particularistic religious identity has evidently not subsided in the era of globalization." (Also see Go [2003] on the prominence of religion in newer constitutions.) FCC are no exception to this pattern, which means that constitutional courts in this region have had to take on a major role of defining the place of religion in these post-communist societies.

Arjomand (2003) also noted that religious provisions in many postcolonial constitutions had as their goal the assertion of ethic identity in opposition to the colonial past of these nations. In such instances, he warned of a possibility that this reassertion can undermine the rule of law, and he cited Iran as a case in point. When this happens, democratic principles may suffer. However, Arjomand then went on to say,

> In sharp contrast to the construction of national and religious identity (in former colonies), the rhetoric of rule of law has played a central role in the constitutional redefinition of post-Communist political community.
>
> In contrast to the presumed moral worth of nativism against the colonial rulers, the task in the era of new constitutionalism is the moral definition of democratic political community. In the context of the human rights revolution, the main focus of the moral redefini-

tion of the new democracies in contrast to the totalitarian regimes they replace is the latter's violation of human rights. (P. 16)

This sharp contrast posited between constitutionalism in postcolonial and FCC countries provoked Marat Shterin and me to examine the situation, using Russia and Hungary as examples, with a focus on how the constitutional courts in these two societies dealt with religion (Richardson and Shterin 2004). We were not convinced that all FCC could be so easily assumed to deal with religion in such a high-sounding manner. This conviction on our part derived from our studies of how minority faiths have been treated in Russia since the fall of the Soviet Union (Shterin and Richardson 1998, 2000, 2002; Richardson, Krylova, and Shterin 2004) and from my own work dealing with religion in postcommunist Hungary (Richardson 1995b).

Our comparison revealed that, indeed, religion was being treated differently in these two postcommunist societies. In Hungary, the court system in general and the constitutional court in particular were very solicitous of the role of religion in Hungarian society. In a number of decisions, the court supported a major public role for religion, and the court also acted in ways that afforded a modicum of protection for minority faiths. In part, this treatment of religion can be understood given the long-term pluralistic history of Hungary, which is reflected in provisions of the Hungarian constitution and in statutes. But the court played a role in promoting and defending religion as deserving of a prominent place in the public square of Hungary.

In Russia, the picture was mixed, a finding reflective of the dominant role played over the centuries by the Russian Orthodox Church (ROC). Whereas the ROC was strongly in favor of more religious freedom as communism was toppling, it turned out that the religious freedom promoted by the ROC was organizational only (not individual) and to be limited as much as possible to the ROC itself. Others need not apply, including individuals with different religious ideas. A coalition was formed between the ROC and more conservative and nationalistic politicians, many of them former communists. This coalition finally forced, in 1997, major changes in the quite liberal laws governing religion that had been promulgated in the early 1990s. Thus, the overall picture in Russia seemed more like postcolonial societies that Arjomand (2003) had written about, where ethnic identity was reasserted via promotion of the formerly dominant religion.

The picture in Russia is not to be likened to Iran, however, as significant countervailing forces are operating. Russia is a society of great tensions, with many political leaders and citizens wanting to be a part of the Western world, while others want Russia to remain Russian, a nation where the ROC defines and pervades all aspects of life. Those with the first view have tied Russia's future to Europe, and these political forces have succeeded in having Russia join the Council of Europe. This means that Russia must come under the sway of major European institutions, such as the European Court of Human Rights, which enforces European views of individual rights, including religious freedom for individuals and groups (Richardson 1995a).

Russia also has a modern constitution, and it has a constitutional court, even if that court encountered severe difficulties early in its history, as already noted. (A recent obvious trend toward a strong presidency model could denigrate the role of the courts as well; see Fogelklou [2003]). Although the Russian Constitutional Court has taken a more cautious and politically sensitive role since its reestablishment in 1995, it has nonetheless exerted itself on occasion in the area of religion. This is in line with its move toward more attention to individual rights already mentioned. In all but one of these cases, all of which involved challenges to rigorous reregistration rules included in the 1997 law, the court has overruled the sentiment of the Duma to exclude nontraditional faiths. Thus Jehovah's Witnesses, an evangelical Protestant group, and the Society of Jesus have been allowed through court decisions since 2000 to reregister even though they did not meet the letter of the new law. Only Scientology's request to reregister was refused, in a decision that clearly did take public sentiment into account. Therefore, it seems safe to say that even within the context of a Russia dominated by the ROC and a strong presidency, the constitutional court has made some difference in terms of support for basic human rights such as religious freedom.

Recently, I have developed a data set on two other FCC, Poland and Slovenia, both of which are thought to have strong constitutional courts (Scheppele 2003). I have yet to examine the cases in detail, but a cursory review indicates a similar pattern, with these courts affirming a significant role for religion in these postcommunist societies. I am planning to build a data set of all constitutional court cases dealing with religion for other FCC to examine any discernible patterns. Such data will allow a more rigorous test of the claim that constitutional courts in FCC are indeed affording protection for religion playing a significant role in those societies. And in so doing, those courts are affirming the spread of democratic ideals that include human and civil rights for all citizens.

References

Arjomand, Said Amir. 2003. Law, political reconstruction, and constitutional politics. *International Sociology* 18:7-32.

Casanova, Jose. 1994. *Public religions in the modern world.* Chicago: University of Chicago Press.

Fogelklou, Anders. 2003. Constitutionalism and the presidency in the Russian Federation. *International Sociology* 18:181-98.

Go, Julian. 2003. A globalizing constitutionalism: Views from the postcolony 1945-2000. *International Sociology* 18:71-95.

Richardson, James T. 1995a. Minority religions, religious freedom, and the Pan-European political and judicial institutions. *Journal of Church and State* 37:39-60.

———. 1995b. New religions and religious freedom in Eastern and Central Europe: A sociological analysis. In *New religious phenomena in Central and Eastern Europe,* ed. I. Borowik and G. Babinski, 257-82. Krakow, Poland: Nomos.

Richardson, James, Galina Krylova, and Marat Shterin. 2004. Legal regulation of religion in Russia. In *Regulating religion: Case studies from around the globe,* ed. James Richardson, 247-59. New York: Kluwer Academic.

Richardson, James T., and Marat Shterin. 2004. Constitutional courts in former communist societies: How do they treat religion? Presented at annual meeting of American Academy of Religion, San Antonio, TX.

Sajo, Andras. 1999. *Limited government: An introduction to constitutionalism*. Budapest, Hungary: Central
    European University Press.
Scheppele, Kim Lane. 2002. Declarations of independence: Judicial responses to political pressure. In *Judi-
    cial independence at the crossroads*, ed. Stephen Burbank and Barry Friedman, 227-79. Thousand Oaks,
    CA: Sage.
————. 2003. Constitutional negotiations: Political contexts of judicial activism on post-Soviet Europe.
    International Sociology 18:219-38.
Shterin, Marat, and James T. Richardson. 1998. Local laws on religion in Russia: Precursors of Russia's
    national law. *Journal of Church and State* 40:319-42.
————. 2000. Effects of the Western anti-cult movement on development of laws concerning religion in
    post-communist Russia. *Journal of Church and State* 42:247-71.
————. 2002. The Yakunin vs. Dworkin trial and the emerging religious pluralism in Russia. *Religion in East-
    ern Europe* 22 (1): 1-38.

Case Studies
B. Transitions and
Problem Cases

Transitions to Constitutional Democracies: The German Democratic Republic

By
INGA MARKOVITS

All law reform must look for local precedents to build on. Does this claim also apply to formerly totalitarian states? Building on her research on East German legal history, the author asks whether there might be some generally applicable reasons explaining why in the German Democratic Republic the first tender shoots of a rule of law appeared *before* the collapse of socialism. She finds an inverse relationship between political and legal faith: as one declines, the other rises, and vice versa. The waning of utopian hopes tends to be compensated for by an increased interest in law and rights and by the growing professionalism of a disenchanted legal class. The author believes that not only is the "prerogative state" a constant threat to the "normative state," but that, vice versa, the practice of legality, even the legality of totalitarian state, can threaten and undermine the effectiveness of autocratic rule.

Keywords: GDR; socialism; capitalism; rule of law; trial courts; law reform

To the former German Democratic Republic (GDR), the rule of law came literally overnight: on Reunification Day, October 3, 1990. To researchers who speculate about the conditions under which the respect for law and democratic rule might spread around the globe, this singular event is not particularly helpful. No other country currently struggling to cast off the legacies of autocracy and lawlessness is in the same position as the former GDR, which could adopt a sister country's legal system in one fell

Inga Markovits teaches comparative law and family law at the University of Texas at Austin, where she holds the Friends of Jamail Regents' Chair in Law. She is particularly interested in East European law and legal history and has done most of her fieldwork and her writing on East German law both before and after the collapse of socialism. Her Imperfect Justice *(Oxford University Press, 1995) traces the changeover from socialist to capitalist law in the course of Germany's reunification. Markovits is currently completing a local history of the rise and fall of socialist law in one East German town, based on the extensive records of the town's trial court and on interviews with judges, lawyers, and laypeople who were involved with or affected by its work.*

DOI: 10.1177/0002716205282408

swoop, like an entire wardrobe off the rack. Instead, reform must come gradually even to those countries whose resolve to achieve a rule of law was sparked by such a cataclysmic event as the collapse of socialism.

Nevertheless, I think that speculations about an evolution toward a world rule of law can learn from the East German example. Not from the now-defunct GDR, but from its experiences before that date, even before 1985, the year of Gorbachev's ascendance in the Soviet Union, which is usually perceived to mark the beginning of the end of socialism. My claim is that the rule of law grew its first shoots long before anyone would think of calling what looked like ordinary greenery by such a noble name. In the GDR, respect for law rose gradually over forty years of socialism in the face of (and sometimes even helped along by) a political system that originally despised the *Rechtsstaat*. It was a growth in fits and starts, often ambiguous, never really secure, and possibly more significant in the eyes of the beholder than of the powers whom law is supposed to rein in. But a close look, in a concrete case, at what specifically it was that increased the significance of law may help us speculate about the general conditions for a global spread of the rule of law.

I will try to substantiate my claim with evidence from a study that has occupied me for some time: the local history of one East German trial court, located in a medium-size town of sixty thousand inhabitants and housed in a Renaissance manor house too big for the court's limited staff and means to be kept in good repair but big enough to store all of the court's paper output and so to allow not only its trial records but also most of its other files to be preserved throughout the four decades of socialist rule. I discovered the court just in time before it found the funds to pay a hauling company to dispose of its accumulated paper on some garbage heap of history.

Using this court's judicial output, its nonjudicial records (such as correspondence with higher courts or state authorities, personnel files, arrest warrants, ledgers of all sorts, citizens' petitions and complaints, judges' notebooks from briefings, etc.), other archival sources, and interviews with the court's staff and its clients, I am currently working on a book that tries to reconstruct a grassroots picture of the rise and fall of socialist law in East Germany. The courthouse and the town that it once served (which I have called Lüritz) are good places to look for how and where the seeds of law reform and the respect for rights might grow on hostile soil (Markovits 2002).

Looking for change not at the top of a judicial hierarchy but at the ground level of ordinary daily life will allow me to bypass ideological claims about the sins and virtues of socialist legality and look instead at the successes and failures that really happened. But the method raises problems for the task at hand: a summary of East Germany's progression toward a rule of law. A bottom-up history is not structured by the important events at the center of political power (Party Congresses, new codes, Supreme Court decisions, etc.) but, like a mosaic, is composed of many tiny bits of evidence that the researcher has to collect and then arrange into a picture that hopefully will show not only the colors of daily life but also the contours of overall developments. Such a history's persuasiveness, if any, lies in the close observation and the vivid description of details. I need time and space to paint my picture, which I do not have on this occasion.

I therefore will, instead, simply assert the main lines of a book chapter that I have just completed called "The Party." It describes the changing relationship, over time, between the Lüritz court and the political authorities in their varying, primarily local, incarnations. I will try, occasionally, to give life to my assertions by illustrating them with specific examples. Maybe this method will provide us with some fodder for our speculations about the spreading of the rule of law.

The judges in [East Germany's] early years were barely trained "people's judges" with no more than grade school education, and they usually went along with orders from Party authorities.

The Party appeared as a visible and named actor in the court's proceedings only in the early years of the GDR. In the late 1940s and early 1950s, Party authorities occasionally told the court, in writing, how it should decide a specific case. The judges in those early years were barely trained "people's judges" with no more than grade school education, and they usually went along with orders from Party authorities. "This is no occasion to stumble over provisions of the Civil Code," a judge wrote in 1952 and sided with a plaintiff who had been supported by the Party. Not only the Communist Party interfered with the court's decisions. I find letters from local mayors in the files, throwing their weight about; from other political parties; from local big wigs. One has the impression of a legal landscape that has not yet been divided into individual properties, where the absence of rules and fences encourages more energetic and ruthless players to trespass on others.

By the mid-1950s, that began to change. The Party was still visible in the Lüritz court's case law, but only in the background, cited as an authority but not as a quasi-participant in the proceedings. "Our view of the issues in this case is shared by the District Party Organization," a plaintiff or defendant might write in his brief, and the assertion might carry weight. But in judicial matters, the Party and the court no longer wanted to be encountered arm in arm. When in 1958 the Party cell of a defendant wrote a letter to the court threatening direct intervention ("if the questioning of witnesses will not produce the needed evidence, our Party Organization will set matters straight"), someone in the courthouse underlined the sentence with red ink, and the defendant lost his case. By 1958, even the comrades knew that their intervention was not considered to be in good taste. "Despite the fact that you seem to object to our concern . . . ," the Party secretary's letter to the court begins, and it ends with the request to keep "the content of our letter strictly confidential." By the late 1950s, the training of East German judges had improved; their self-confidence had risen; the roles of different state authorities had become more clearly defined; and the Party was better at controlling and directing its own cadres. The East German Constitutions of both 1949 (Verfassung der DDR 1949 Article 127) and 1968 (Verfassung der DDR 1968 Article 96) assert the judges' "independence" and claim that they are "subject only to the law." From then on, "judicial independence" becomes a catchword for the Party and the administration to fend off requests to intervene in disputes before the court. In 1966, for instance, the city's housing office rejected a citizen's complaint concerning an eviction suit with the explanation that it could not, unfortunately, intervene in a case sub judice. In later years, I find occasional complaints in the briefs of plaintiffs or defendants that the Party had been no help to them in conducting their case. The Ministry of Justice and superior courts tended to reject such complaints by pointing to the "independence of judges."

The Party's apparent reluctance to intervene in ongoing judicial proceedings seems confirmed by the records of the Party's District Bureau, which, under the chairmanship of the First Secretary, convened the members of the district leadership in monthly "Secretariat Meetings." In the early 1950s, the District Secretariat seemed perfectly willing to interfere with the daily work of the local court. In a meeting of April 1953 (shortly after Stalin's death) for instance, the Secretariat invited both Judge D. and Prosecutor W. to criticize them for excessively harsh penalties for "economic crimes" committed by local farmers and to "concretely inform the Comrades of the Party's policies on these issues." The prosecutor was told to "undertake measures" to quash a particularly punitive sentence. "Concrete" is the key word here. Only in the early years do I find instances of Party intervention into a specific case before the court. The Secretariat's concern about the ideological climate at the courthouse continued beyond the 1950s. In the 1960s, it undertook several inspections to investigate and combat what it called "ideological complacency" among the judges. But specific court decisions were no longer on the agenda. After the mid-1960s, I cannot find any instance of judges being called before the Secretariat to explain their behavior. Only occasionally were they present at the meetings at all, and even then only for short periods of time to address practical issues, such as an upcoming judicial election. The disappearance of specific court decisions from the District Secretariat's list of monthly topics is mirrored at the national level. While in the 1950s, the Politbureau in Berlin discussed about ten specific criminal cases per year, that number dropped to two in 1963, and, with a single exception (one case discussed in 1971) to zero from then on (Rottleuthner 1994, 40).

All this, of course, does not mean that the courts *were* independent from the Party. East German citizens never believed they were. In all the records, from the earliest to the most recent, I have encountered citizens appealing to ideology and

Party connections to advance their cases in court. In the early years, those appeals were politically more inventive and more undisguised than in later decades: brief writers (most people wrote their own briefs in the early years) might bolster their credibility by proclaiming their commitment to world peace or, in a divorce suit, might try to strengthen their case by accusing the other side of being active in church. In later years, people more often would clothe their political protestations in economic terms ("to do good work, one needs a good apartment"). Boastful references to a writer's Party membership were more frequent in the 1950s than in the 1980s. But at all times citizens might use their Party connections with amazing cheek. A letter to the court's director in 1971 in support of a suit brought by the letter writer's son, for instance, mentions the father's conversations with "Comrade B." (the prosecutor), "Comrade L." (another judge), and "Comrade K." (the First Party Secretary of the district), "who always has an open ear for one's troubles." As recently as 1988, a party to a dispute between neighbors over the height of a hedge between their gardens tried to blackmail the Court of Appeals into reopening the case by threatening that otherwise "he would have to put his trust in the central authorities"—in other words, submit a complaint to the Central Committee. (When the complaint arrived, the Central Committee passed it back to be decided by the Court of Appeals.)

Were citizens right to believe that the Party, if properly persuaded, would pull the necessary strings to help their case? One thing these efforts at corruption show is that the Party did not even *need* to interfere in a specific court case. After the awkward meddling of the early years, it could successfully withdraw from the actual courtroom because, by then, enough other opportunities existed to push a case in the desired direction. As the 1971 letter I just cited shows, everyone with a professional role in the judicial process was a Party member: judges, prosecutors, most attorneys. So were all the administrators in town. There was a Basic Party Organization at each courthouse, whose secretary, always a prosecutor (not a judge—the system liked to keep its judges at a greater distance from the Party), would meet once a week at the so-called "Secretaries' Round" with the First Party Secretary of the district, the local prince, to discuss current issues. Again, once a month, the court's director would meet with the senior prosecutor, the chief of police, and the local head of the Stasi at so-called "security conferences" to discuss public safety issues in the district such as crimes, fires, fugitives, "parasitism," "hooliganism," and the like. At these meetings, the First Secretary was represented by his "Security Officer" (also a member of the District Bureau), who could spell out how the Party wanted to approach a particular issue. And there were many other official occasions when Party members met and when the Party leadership could tell the court's director or a judge how to proceed in an individual case.

Besides the formal occasions, there were the informal meetings. For example, the director of the Lüritz courthouse and the head of the city's "Interior Department" (responsible for legal decisions affecting "parasites," people applying for exit visas and the like) regularly played cards together. The prosecutor's office was housed in the same building as the Party District Bureau (today a Savings and Loan), and people must have met and chatted on the staircase. They attended the same concerts and birthday parties. All Party members addressed each other with the familial "*Du*," and the rejection of a particular suggestion among friends and comrades could also mean a personal slight. "You could pull five times as many strings under socialism as under capitalism," an East German attorney once told me. There always were numerous occasions, and addressees, to ask for help. If necessary for emphasis, veiled political warnings might be added to one's request.

But did the Party *tell* the judges how to decide? I asked the man who for twenty-eight years reigned as First Party Secretary in the district—under socialism, the local prince. "I wasn't very interested in the court," he said (a claim confirmed by several judges critical of his reign). The Party and the court interacted only "if one or the other side initiated the contact." He gave me an example: a fraud case, in which a number of high Party functionaries had used the Byzantine accounting methods of a socialist economy to enrich themselves considerably. The Court of Appeals had sent an investigating judge to get to the bottom of the case. But the First Secretary decided instead to use Party mechanisms to clean the Augean stables: the culprits were disciplined in Party proceedings, several people lost their jobs, and the main offender was expelled from the Party. The investigating judge went home without the issue ever having reached a courtroom. The way the First Secretary talked about the case suggests that there were rules governing the characterization of an issue either as a matter for the Party *or* the court. Party issues were preferably *not* decided by the judiciary. The contacts between the Party and the court usually dealt with matters of jurisdiction: will you take care of this case or shall we?

The Lüritz court files seem to confirm this division of functions between the Party and the court. In 1977, for instance, the court's director wrote the city's housing office to inquire whether the defendant in an eviction suit would soon be offered another apartment. "If not, I will be forced to continue with the eviction case currently before the court that was suspended after our discussion with Comrade L. from the District Party Bureau." Under GDR law, it was almost impossible to evict a tenant. In this case, the Party obviously wanted an eviction to occur because it wanted to assign the tenant's apartment to another person. But the Party had *not* told the judge simply to evict the current tenant—that would have been against the law. Instead, Party and court had agreed to *delay* the judicial decision of the case until the Party found acceptable replacement housing for the current occupant. After the judge's threat, accommodation was soon found: a note by the displaced original tenant declared the new flat to be "satisfactory." In the end, the Party got what it wanted. But the judge had *not* been willing to delay the case forever. Had the Party not been able to locate a replacement flat, the court would have proceeded with, and probably dismissed, the eviction suit. The court was willing to give the Party a chance to find what was called "a political solution." But it was neither willing, nor apparently expected, to break the law.

There are many cases in the court files that I suspect were resolved by way of similar "political solutions." Here are the symptoms: a suit is brought, then suddenly suspended for a number of months, after which the case is dropped, usually by way of a withdrawal of the original suit. In many instances, the explanation for the interruption may be innocent: the parties may have used the time to negotiate an out-of-court settlement. But in many instances, the delay was initiated not by the parties (because they wanted to cut risks and costs) nor by the judge (because she or he wanted to minimize time and efforts). Instead, the interruption very likely was initiated by state or Party functionaries seeking a solution to a dispute that would advance state interests or preserve state authority. I can tell by the issues in controversy in these cases, usually matters with some political overtones: suits by which so-called "applicants" (people who had applied for an exit visa to the West) challenged their dismissal from a job, for instance, or "group actions" by a number of workers who collectively claimed higher benefits or bonuses (to socialist authorities, a suspicious type of lawsuit because it reeked of class struggle and insurrection and because the plaintiffs in these cases were often so bitter and disappointed that it was very difficult to placate them). The "weekly reports" that each local court in the GDR had to send, by way of the Court of Appeals, to the Ministry of Justice and the Supreme Court (now in the Federal Archives in Berlin) are full of reports of trials suspended so that the search for a "political solution" could proceed. Often, such suspensions were also used to elicit guidance from the Ministry of Justice or the Supreme Court on how to deal with a particularly touchy case.

The search for a "political solution" did not necessarily mean that the parties to such a suit would get less than they were entitled to under the law. Some "political solutions" were relatively generous (especially in labor disputes), some stingy (especially in cases involving "applicants," who usually were talked into withdrawing their complaints). But in all cases, the parties were manipulated and deprived of the autonomy-enhancing functions of litigation. I assume that most did not even know *why* their cases did not proceed. A prospective emigrant, contesting his dismissal in a 1987 suit, for instance, formally complained to the Court of Appeals about the District Court's "dragging its feet" in dealing with his case. He did not know that the Court of Appeals itself had considered the issue; that, legally speaking, it agreed with the plaintiff's viewpoint; but that it had been difficult and time-consuming to arrange a "political solution" to resolve the problem out of court. Months after the initiation of the suit, the Court of Appeals thus reported to the Ministry of Justice, "We have contacted both the Regional Government Council and the Regional Party Bureau in an attempt to terminate this case without oral argument and without a formal judgment. Since the plaintiff's labor contract was not lawfully dissolved, the resumption of the trial necessarily will have to lead to his continued employment." "Political solutions" were intended to remove a dispute from the realm of law into the realm of Party politics. But they also were intended to keep the courtroom clean of violations of the law. With constitutional and administrative law issues already outside the realm of courts (under GDR law, you could not sue the state in its sovereign capacity), the search for "political solutions" thus resulted, in fact, in removing most politically touchy issues from the authority of the judiciary. With the dockets thus sanitized, the system could, indeed, preserve a locally limited kind of judicial independence in the courtroom.

East German judges thus lived in two worlds. As jurists, they were to apply, as religiously as possible, the letter of the law within the courtroom (since the law, after all, was created with the blessings of the Party, socialist judges tended to be positivists). As Party members, they were to do their best, outside the courtroom, to realize the policy goals of the Party. The system could function without frictions only if judges internalized the political convictions underlying Party politics—if the right hand knew, and approved of, what the left was doing. Hence the enormous importance of the ideological education and indoctrination of East German judges. Westerners usually think of the Communist Party as a spider, surveying and controlling its net and shooting out of its hiding place whenever a victim has been caught. But the Party did not want to be a spider. A better image to capture the self-perception of the Party is that of Pope: as the faithful turn their eyes to Rome or Mecca to receive their guidance, the Party wanted its members to look to Berlin for all their answers to important questions. "Spider" and "Pope" resemble each other in their occupying and controlling the center points of their respective realms: all roads, all finely spun threads lead back to them. But unlike the spider's, the Pope's authority is based on moral claims. The civic religion of socialism had to be taught.

Both for their legal and their moral education, East German judges, at all times, were taken firmly and authoritatively by the hand. But the teachers, and the methods of indoctrination, changed over time. In the early years of the GDR, when almost all East German judges were so-called "people's judges" (laypeople who in crash courses had been taught a mixture of law and ideology), their education was controlled by several instructors: the Ministry of Justice, which regularly sent inspectors to supervise and check the work of local trial courts; the appellate courts, who reviewed their decisions and who coordinated and directed the continued legal and ideological education of the judiciary; and the Party, which, by way of local Party authorities, checked up on the ideological climate at the courthouse.

The records of the District Party Bureau suggest that, by the 1970s, the local Party officials disengaged from the task of supervising the political commitment of their judges. The agitprop enthusiasm of earlier years seems to have petered out. The results had not been encouraging. Two Party inspections in the 1950s and 1960s had revealed a decided lack of political engagement among Lüritz's local judges. Apparently, up to 1964, the Party organization at the courthouse had discussed "only professional issues" at its monthly meetings. Faced with reproaches for "bourgeois objectivity," "left-over habits of thought," and "ideological calm" within their collective, the judges had excused their political abstinence by claiming that "they daily served the Party through their professional work." In 1965, a meeting at the District Party Bureau, at which the Party secretaries of the courthouse group, the prosecutor's office, and the notary's office were given a severe talking-to, seemed to signal increased political pressures on the judiciary.

What happened instead might be called "relaxation through routine." In 1965, the Party secretary at the courthouse had been accused of informing the district leadership only spontaneously and orally of what went on among the judges. Subsequently, he was told to produce written reports. They allowed the writer, in the peace of his own desk, to compose narratives that always seemed to follow the same pattern: a description of how warmly the judges supported the current Party policies, followed by the admission of a few minor mistakes, and ending with the assur-

ance that, in the future, everyone would do an even better job. Lord knows what
the judges really thought. The minutes of a meeting at the District Bureau of September 1968, for instance, suggest that there had been lively and sympathetic discussions at the courthouse of the recent developments in Prague. This faux pas was
corrected by a new meeting of the Party organization at the court at which "all comrades welcome the intervention of the five socialist countries" and promised "to
intensify political conversations" among them. The Party then had it in writing.
Such reports were submitted to the District Party Bureau, which accepted them
and added them to the files. I can find no other evidence of active Party meddling
with the court's work; in fact, by the mid-1970s, with one exception, I can find no
mention of the court at all in the records of the monthly leadership meetings.

The exception concerns the firing of Judge S. in 1982 (only very discretely
alluded to in the Party records), whose stepson had been sent some wristwatches
by a West German aunt, which he had sold on the black market. As I learned from
interviews, the District Party Secretary had not wanted to dismiss Judge S. for his
son's offense. The decision came from the Ministry of Justice in Berlin, by way of
the Court of Appeals. By 1982, ideological orthodoxy was enforced by the ministerial bureaucracy rather than the Party. It was almost impossible in the GDR for a
judge to lose his job for reasons of incompetence. But in the forty years of the
GDR's existence, three judges from the Lüritz court lost their jobs for political reasons—all three, incidentally, not because of their own political disloyalty but
because a child of theirs had gotten entangled with the capitalist class enemy. In all
three cases, the judge's fall was cushioned by the local Party leadership (two judges
got new jobs as in-house counsel of important local agencies) or by the judicial
bureaucracy itself (one judge, whose son had drowned while trying to flee the
country, was assigned a new job as director of a larger court in another town). The
Party took care of its judges also when they stumbled. But its *direct institutional
interference* with their work (as distinct from the haphazard attempts by individual
Party members to pull strings) no longer seems to have been much of a threat. As I
learned from the judges' desk diaries (found among the records), by the mid-1980s
even the monthly "Marxism-Leninism seminars" of the courthouse Party group no
longer dealt with Party politics at all. "ML/lay assessors training," the diaries might
say, or "ML/communal services." In translation: instead of ideology, the judges
began to use the hour to discuss practical problems (an interpretation confirmed
by the court's director). The Lüritz judges had returned to the stage that the Party
already had criticized in 1964: talking "only about professional issues" at their
meetings.

As the Party moved out of the business of directly indoctrinating the judiciary,
the Ministry of Justice and the GDR Supreme Court (all, of course, staffed with
Party members) took over. Since the beginnings of the GDR, the Ministry of Justice had kept a close eye on the lower courts—a supervision particularly necessary
in the early years, when professionally barely trained "people's judges" could be
trusted to get neither the law right, nor the Party line. In the 1950s and 1960s, a
variety of methods, often overlapping, were used to control the courts: investigations by inspectors, sent either from the Ministry in Berlin or from the Ministry's

regional offices, to check up on every aspect of a court's daily work; so-called "revisions," by which delegates from the regional Appellate Court would review and criticize a court's recent case law; and "consultations," by which a lower court might elicit a superior court's advice on how to deal with a specific problem. To ensure the continuing political education of the judges, the Ministry of Justice sent around lists of topics to be studied and discussed in monthly meetings at the courthouse and lengthy position papers to be read by every judge. The themes suggested for collective study changed over time and moved from cold war propaganda ("Violations of Legality in the Federal Republic"—1957) to largely economic topics ("Increasing the Effectiveness of Labor"—1984).

The civic religion of socialism had to be taught.

The Ministry's expectations of how religiously and how carefully judges would read the many sermons crossing their desks changed as well. The position papers that the Party sent around for careful study, now in my files, tend to be smooth and spotless and do not look as if they passed through many hands. Occasional underlinings on the opening pages of a document usually fizzle out as the convoluted and endless text wears on. The senders of these missives must themselves have doubted their pupils' attention span. Initially, the Party organization at the court had to report back, in writing, on the effectiveness of its monthly seminars. In the 1970s, the Ministry of Justice introduced questionnaires by which the leader of a political discussion group at the courthouse could summarize the impact of the exercise in spaces left blank under specific headings: "major points of discussion," "problems," "preparations for the meeting," "conclusions." A "conclusion" from March 1979: "The current format of the political education sessions for judges can be maintained." But as the years wore on, the entries became increasingly laconic. The "conclusions" of a meeting in January 1980: "none." In November 1981: "none." In November 1982: "as usual." From the meetings' lists of participants, I can see that by the late 1980s about a third of the members tended to be absent, often "repeatedly" and "without excuse."

All this, of course, does *not* mean that East German judges were political dissidents. Far from it. But it suggests that (with the possible exception of the early "people's judges") they liked the law better than the Party. "*Juristen—böse Christen*," Martin Luther said—"lawyers make bad Christians," because they are too finicky, too argumentative, too ready to make excuses. For the same reasons, lawyers were unlikely to be reliable socialists. And the Party became increasingly aware of it. Two documents found in the Lüritz court's archives reveal the Party's move from trust toward distrust of its jurists or, if you want, the Party's changeover from the role of

"Pope" (relying on its judges' ideological commitment to help create a new society) to that of "spider" (eyeing suspiciously unreliable subjects who might try to get away).

Both documents were drawn up by the Ministry of Justice and contain lists of the desirable characteristics of future judges, sent—for recruitment purposes—to local trial courts whose task it was to round up high school students interested in (and politically suitable for) the study of law. The first list, from 1969, begins with the candidates' "attitudes toward work": performance, commitment, independence, reliability, a realistic assessment of one's own abilities, and so on. These criteria are followed by "the political behavior and ideological attitudes" of a candidate, not defined as political orthodoxy, however, but quite pragmatically as a yardstick to assess his usefulness as a contributor to a new society: "readiness to carry out social tasks," "openness toward innovation," "leadership abilities and methods," and the like. Leaving aside the question whether this new society could, indeed, be built, the list reflects the priorities of a reasonable and praxis-oriented administration of justice. The 1969 text does not mention the Federal Republic.

The second document proclaiming "Criteria for Evaluating Legal Cadres" dates from 1988. The first position on its list of desirable qualities of judges is now held by the "ideological attitude and development" of a candidate, more specifically, his "relationship with the SED" (East Germany's Communist Party), his "readiness to carry out Party resolutions," and his "ideological commitment to the policy of opposition toward the imperialist Federal Republic." Then follows "aspects of socialist work ethics," defined not as a candidate's ability to get the job done but as his likely political loyalty reflected in behavior such as "state discipline" or "security concerns and watchfulness." Only when I reach item four on the long list and, even there, only at the end of a long paragraph, do I find the qualities that judges need to do proficient and timely work such as "labor efficiency" or "knowledge and experience." By 1988, the Party no longer seems to hope for true believers. The loyalty it hopes for is based not on a candidate's moral convictions and engagement but on his political correctness. Like a lover who knows that he has long lost his lady's affection, the Party, in 1988, asks only for reticence toward other suitors. A socialist judge may not flirt with the West.

East German legal developments in the 1970s and 1980s reflect both the dwindling of utopian hopes and the entrenchment of professionalism. On one hand, the loss of political faith required a tight and efficient supervision of the judiciary. After employing, initially, multiple controlling institutions (such as the Ministry of Justice, the Ministry's regional offices, and the appellate courts), which often duplicated their inspections, the administration, by the 1970s, had settled down to an efficient and streamlined system by which the lower courts were supervised and guided by the appellate courts, which, in turn, were supervised by the Supreme Court and the Ministry of Justice. A nationwide reporting system, by which each court, every week, had to inform its superior court of significant, unusual, or in any way potentially troublesome occurrences within its jurisdiction allowed the authorities in Berlin to react quickly to difficulties. If the Lüritz trial court had to decide a particularly important or politically tricky issue, the Court of Appeals (already informed, by way of the "weekly reports," of the impending problem) would "take control" of the case: request the files; if necessary, itself enlist advice from central authorities in Berlin; consult with the presiding local judge; and, in serious cases, delegate an appellate judge to assist with and supervise the local trial. As far as I can tell, the superior courts' legal advice would stay within the parameters of the positive law. If a politically desirable outcome could not be found within its boundaries, appellate courts might advise, and local courts would accept their suggestion, to suspend the case in order to search for a "political solution" to the problem. Advice from above that stayed *within* the parameters of the written law (a harsher rather than milder penalty for an offense, or vice versa, that stayed within the statutory margins, for instance) was usually accepted by the deciding judge. As far as I can tell, plainly *illegal* instructions usually were not given. The amount of independence left to the individual judge was very small and, moreover, was dependent upon what one East German judge once described to me as the "broad back of his court director." And, of course, his own. That is one side of the story—the one affected by the loss of ideological hopes, the growing suspicions of the Party, and its resulting paranoia and need for control.

The other side of the story reflects the growing professionalism of the East German judiciary. Together with the increasing political nervousness of the 1980s, I find unexpected rule-of-law tendencies in the court files: demands for more respect for defense attorneys, for example; bolder litigation strategies by those attorneys; complaints about shoddy evidence in criminal proceedings; warnings against the too compliant issuing of arrest warrants by the local courts. Like the demands for more control, the demands for the East German legal system to become more open come from above: primarily from the Supreme Court and the Ministry of Justice, whose staffs were better trained and better acquainted with Western legal developments than my grassroots judges. In judicial conferences and training sessions of all sorts, Supreme Court judges and senior officials from the Ministry of Justice admonished trial judges to display more judicial independence, to occasionally reject a prosecutor's application for an arrest warrant, to probe the evidence in criminal trials more carefully, to mistrust confessions of defendants, and to respect individual rights. "Citizens judge a legal system by the protection of their personal rights," the director of the Lüritz local court wrote at a judges' conference in 1986 into the notebook that she kept for such occasions. Or, two years later at a similar meeting focusing on the too trigger-happy issuing of arrest warrants in the GDR: "needed: a better balancing of the security requirements of society and the invasion of a defendant's personal rights."

True to the hierarchical and commandeering character of the East German legal system, the reformers tried to teach lower courts about the need for more judicial independence by way of guidance from above: local judges were *told* to be more independent. "Court has to assess prosecution's brief under own authority," the Lüritz court director wrote into her notebook in the fall of 1983. "Establish objective truth. Essential: judges' growing responsibility for their own decisions." And a year later, at a meeting of trial judges with the director of the Court of Appeals: "Personal responsibility of judge must be strengthened." The remark is followed by a sentence suggesting that it is the trial judge's own fault if he or she is not more independent: "Main criticism: that central directives are not carried out within judges' own areas of work." How East German judges were to combine greater judicial independence with the more faithful compliance with orders from above is difficult to fathom. "Execution of central decisions at the heart of our work. Individual assessment needed," Lüritz's court director noted in 1984. In 1986: "Independence of judge constitutionally required. Case law subject to primacy of politics." In 1988: "Unity of democratic centralism, individual responsibility, and judicial independence." "Important," the judge noted in the margins of her copy book.

The quotes show how confused the relationship between the Party and the court had become in the last years of socialism. The Party wanted to control but not to steer. The Supreme Court and the Ministry of Justice wanted legal change but not the responsibility for legal change. Local judges wanted to steer the right course between conflicting orders. Here, to conclude my story, is a case that reveals how, in this general confusion of values, the Party could no longer function in the role of "Pope" but, like a "spider," could intervene only to preserve its own interests.

In November 1988, the local prosecutor brought a case for "economic subversion" against Herr N., the manager of a huge chicken-breeding farm that produced about one-third of all so-called "broilers" consumed in the GDR. In the GDR, too, poultry was produced in quasi-assembly-line fashion. Herr N.'s enterprise handled the first phase of production: breeding the fertilized eggs and raising the newborn chicks for the first week of their lives. The chickens were then transferred to other cooperating chicken farms where they were fattened and eventually slaughtered.

In the fall of 1988, an overproduction of chicken had flooded the GDR market (such as it was). The enterprises that Herr N.'s farm usually supplied with week-old chickens had cancelled orders totaling five hundred thousand birds. The State Planning Agency responsible for coordinating the chicken production in the region had not managed to readjust the many misalignments of the production and distribution process. When in October 1988 one of Herr N.'s major purchasers withdrew an order for forty thousand newborn chicks and functionaries from the State Planning Agency could not be reached (the fax machine had broken down again), Herr N. decided to act on his own. He ordered the removal of sixty thousand fertilized eggs from the breeding ovens as well as the killing of forty thousand newly hatched birds. They were buried in a nearby forest where hikers discovered the mass grave and informed the local newspaper. At that time—the fall of 1988—the story was actually printed. That is how the local prosecutor and, soon after, First Party Secretary Erich Honecker in Berlin learned of the affair. At a session of the Central Committee, Honecker railed against the unsocialist practice of destroying foodstuff for which there was no demand. "This is unacceptable; it was legitimate for the prosecutor to intervene," the GDR's highest Party boss said at the meeting (Honecker 1988, 55).

That meant that Herr N. had to be convicted at his trial. Nobody in town—in fact, nobody in the region—wanted to see Herr N. punished: not the judges, not the prosecutors, not the district and regional First Secretaries. But the Court of Appeals, under pressure from higher up, sent an appellate judge to supervise the trial. To make sure that the result would conform to Party wishes, the delegate from the Court of Appeals had been told by his court's director to write the judgment himself. The Lüritz court director was furious at the suggestion. She gave Herr N. a suspended prison sentence of six months for "economic subversion," with a probation period of one year, the shortest term permissible under the law, and she insisted on writing the decision herself. After a fierce debate in the court director's office (which I learned about from another judge who had been present), the local and the appellate judge agreed on a compromise: *she* would write the decision, but he would tell his superior judge that it was *he* who had composed the judgment. It was not a fight about substance: everyone agreed to let Herr N. off with the mildest sentence possible. It was a fight over how to placate the "spider" in whose moral authority no one believed.

As political faith wanes, belief in law
is likely to take its place.

More than ten years later, I asked Herr N. whether he thought that the court had committed an injustice. "The court!" Herr N. said, contemptuously, "I never needed the court to obtain justice!" He had been an important man in the days of socialism and could rely on "political solutions," if necessary. It was the Party that he felt betrayed by, not the court. But it was a court, a capitalist court, that in a rehabilitation procedure in November 1990 quashed his conviction.

Is there anything to be learned from my story for the purposes of our topic? Here are a few suggestions:

1. An inverse relationship seems to exist between political and legal faith. The higher the political faith of a particular era, the lower its perceived need for law. As political faith wanes, belief in law is likely to take its place. That makes sense: if one knows the right answers in advance, one no longer has to search for them and therefore can do without procedures governing that search. With the loss of substantive faith, it becomes necessary to choose between competing strategies and outcomes. Collective consensus on welfare is pushed out by the individual pursuit of rights. In Poland, for instance, protests over unaffordable meat prices led to the creation of the High Administrative Court and the Constitutional Tribunal (Brzezinski and Garlicki 1995, 19-26).

2. The higher someone's legal sophistication, the more likely he or she is to be sympathetic toward law reform. Legal change in the GDR was suggested and pushed from above by legal elites (Supreme Court judges, high ministerial officials, academics) upon usually more compliant local courts. This assertion is tricky because legal elites, while on one hand eager for reform, also tend to occupy desirable positions, which makes them more reluctant to stick their necks out. Nevertheless, high court judges and academics in several East European countries advocated reform *before* the collapse of socialism. In the Soviet Union, for instance, already in the early 1980s, the USSR and the RSFSR Supreme Courts pushed for the "more thorough, complete and objective" work of trial courts and for a more extensive use of noncustodial sentences (Foglesong 1997, 294, 303). An effective way of bolstering a country's rule-of-law proclivities would be to help it to produce sophisticated lawyers.

3. In *Dual State*, Ernst Fraenkel (1941) described the "normative state" as a better-mannered helpmate of the "prerogative state": by keeping ordinary daily life afloat, while *not* excluding political interference with its rules, if necessary, the "normative state" allows the "prerogative state" to function. I think this picture is too bleak. Fraenkel wrote about the Nazi state, which existed for only twelve years, during which the "prerogative state" descended into murderous terror. Developments under socialism suggest that not only is the "prerogative state" a constant threat to the "normative state" but that the opposite might be true as well: the "normative state" constantly undermines and threatens the "prerogative state." The rule of law seems at least partially divisible. It would make sense to strengthen the legal systems even of totalitarian countries in the hope that expectations of law could help to delegitimize and push back practices of injustice.

References

Brzezinski, Mark F., and Leszek Garlicki. 1995. Judicial review in post-communist Poland: The emergence of a *Rechtsstaat*? *Stanford Journal of International Law* 31:13-59.

Foglesong, Todd. 1997. The reform of criminal justice and evolution of judicial independence in late Soviet Russia. In *Reforming justice in Russia, 1864-1996*, ed. Peter H. Solomon Jr. Armork, NY: M.E. Sharpe.

Fraenkel, Ernst. 1941. *The dual state. A contribution to the theory of dictatorship*. New York: Oxford University Press.

Honecker, Erich. 1988. *Mit dem Blick auf den VII. Parteitag die Aufgaben der Gegenwart lösen*. Aus dem Bericht des Politbüros an das Zentralkomitee der SED. Berlin: Staatsverlag.

Markovits, Inga. 2002. Justice in Lüritz. *American Journal of Comparative Law* 50:818-74.

Rottleuthner, Hubert. 1994. Zur Steuerung der Justiz in der DDR. In *Steuerung der Justiz in der DDR*, ed. Hubert Rottleuthner. Köln, Germany: Bundesanzeiger.

Verfassung der DDR. 1949. Constitution of the GDR of October 7, 1949, *Gesetzblatt der DDR* 5.

Verfassung der DDR. 1968. Constitution of the GDR of April 6, 1968 in the version of October 7, 1974, *Gesetzblatt der DDR* I 425.

Sudan: A Nation in Turbulent Search of Itself

Sudan has been intermittently at war with itself since independence on June 1, 1956, with only ten years of precarious peace between 1972 and 1983. At the heart of the conflict is a crisis of national identity. Those who have been in control of the country define themselves as Arabs and also Muslims, and identify more with the Middle East than with black Africa, though they are essentially Arab-Africans. Their physical features are similar to other African groups in the region, and their cultures and even Islamic practices are an amalgam of Arab and Islamic culture with indigenous belief systems and cultures. The outcome of Sudan's struggles is difficult to predict. Three questions are worth probing: What is the conflict about? To what extent does the comprehensive peace agreement address the root causes of the conflict? What are the prospects for a truly comprehensive and lasting peace in the Sudan?

Keywords: Sudan; Arabization; Islamization; slavery; genocide; civil war

By
FRANCIS M. DENG

Overview of the Issues

Sudan is a country in painful search of itself, afflicted by a wave of regional conflicts that are rooted in an acute crisis of national identity. Initially, civil war pitted the North against the South but has recently extended to regions of the North, the latest being Darfur. These proliferating conflicts are the result of a long historical process in which three factors—Arabization, Islamization, and slavery—played a pivotal role in shaping the identities now in conflict. While Arabization was the first to take root, Islamization accentuated the process and became a deter-

Francis M. Deng is director of the Center for Displacement Studies at the School of Advanced International Studies (SAIS) and research professor of international law, politics, and society at Johns Hopkins University. He serves as representative of the UN secretary-general on internally displaced persons and is a nonresident senior fellow at the Brookings Institution. He served as the ambassador of Sudan to Canada, the Scandinavian countries, and the United States as well as Sudan's minister of state for Foreign Affairs.

DOI: 10.1177/0002716205283021

mining factor in categorizing the races into slave masters and enslaveable groups. The normative framework provided that a person who was a Muslim, Arabic-speaking, culturally Arabized, and could claim Arab descent was elevated to a position of respect and dignity, while in sharp contrast, a non-Muslim black African was deemed inferior, a heathen, and a legitimate target of enslavement.[1]

By the nineteenth century, this historical process had crystallized into a division between the North, two-thirds of the country in land and population, becoming identified as Arab-Islamic, and the Southern third considered indigenously African in racial, cultural, and religious terms, with Christianity as a novelty associated with colonial intervention. Some regions in the North, in fact the majority, adopted Islam and to varying degrees became Arabic speaking, but remained otherwise indigenously African. Any yet, they became widely identified as part of the Arab-Islamic mold.[2]

The British-dominated Anglo-Egyptian Condominium administration governed the country as two distinct entities, with the North advancing politically and economically, while the South remained isolated and undeveloped. At independence, this dualistic administration was reversed into a unitary system in which the North dominated and began to implement a policy of Arabization and Islamization in the South. By then, not only had the South consolidated a legacy of resistance to slavery, Arabization, and Islamization, but the separatist colonial policy and the influence of Christianity and elements of Western culture had reinforced a distinct Southern identity. This resulted in the formation of two antagonistic identities with two contrasting visions for the nation—an Arab-Islamic vision and a secular black African vision. These two visions are now in a zero-sum conflict of identities that is confronting the nation with critical choices, ranging from restructuring a framework for equitable national integration instead of assimilation, to coexistence within a framework of unity in diversity, to outright partition of the country.[3]

Although Islamic fundamentalism has become the most divisive factor, it should be noted that originally, Islam in the Sudan was promoted by leading Sufi orders whose distinguishing feature was the degree to which they accommodated pre-Islamic practices, allowing the syncretism of traditional African religious beliefs with Muslim rituals. Although Islamic values and institutions eventually prevailed over preexisting practices, the latter continued to enhance the former. Islam became identified with the local community and adopted many uniquely Sudanese characteristics.

This aspect is important because it reflects a more tolerant and accommodating version of Islam than today's politicized and intolerant use of Islam by Arabized Muslim leaders at the center. Even among the modern Islamists, there are profound differences between the religious sects with roots in Sufism and the more contemporary Islamic movements that claim to represent a "rivalist" vision of Islam. In each of these sects, interpretation of the doctrine also differs significantly. Nevertheless, until the recent developments that have begun to bridge the North-South divide, what used to be known as the "Southern Problem" unified the North under the banner of the Arab-Islamic vision, which they sought to impose on the South.

The political developments and the challenges of peace and unity in the country pose a series of interlinked questions: What role has religion, specifically Islam, played in shaping the conflicting identities? To what extent do the proliferating regional conflicts represent a credible challenge to the Arab-Islamic establishment that has dominated the country since independence? What are the prospects for a more inclusive and equitably integrative national identity framework? More specifically, to what extent will the Arab-Islamic–oriented center cooperate in the process of national restructuring and reconstruction or resist the change in defense of the status quo? And what would be the likely outcome of such a resistance to a fundamental reform?

These questions are critical to the prospects of the Sudan remaining united or disintegrating along racial, ethnic, or religious lines. These alternative developments could have far-reaching implications to the wider regions, extending northward into the Middle East and southward into sub-Saharan Africa, with racial, cultural, or religious linkages into the even wider international identity configurations. Indeed, the significance of the Sudan, geographically the largest country in Africa, neighboring nine countries, with Saudi Arabia as a tenth neighbor across the Red Sea, lies in its geopolitical location as a microcosm of Africa and a crossroads between the Middle East and the continent. The country has the potential of being either a conciliator among its neighbors or a point of confrontation, with ripple effects extending far beyond the immediate regional context.

Contextualizing the Crisis

Sudan is a theater of proliferating conflicts that have at their roots seeming incompatibilities of racial, ethnic, cultural, and religious identities. The country has widely been perceived as an African-Arab dualism, which is clearly an oversimplification. While there are those of mixed Arab-African descent, the overwhelming majority in the North, especially in the Nuba Mountains, Southern Blue Nile, and Darfur, though Muslim, are black and indistinguishable from the people of the South. The Beja in the East are also indigenous. Even the Nubians in the extreme North have retained their indigenous languages and pride in their Nubian identity and heritage.[4]

It must be emphasized that it is not mere differences that cause conflicts, but the implications for the shaping and sharing of power, wealth, services, development opportunities, and the overall enjoyment of the rights of citizenship. By this yardstick, the South clearly found itself at independence the most marginalized and discriminated region in the country. As a result, the first conflict, which pitted the North against the South, erupted in 1955, only eight months before independence on the 1st of January 1956. The conflict was halted in 1972 by a peace agreement that granted the South regional autonomy, and was resumed in 1983, when the government unilaterally abrogated that agreement. While the first war was separatist, the declared objective of the second, championed by the Sudan People's

Liberation Movement and Army (SPLM/A), was to restructure the country into a New Sudan that would be free from any discrimination due to race, ethnicity, religion, culture, or gender.

This recasting of the issues in the conflict began to gain support in the North, especially in the non-Arab regions. The Nuba of Southern Kordofan and the Ingassana or Funj of Southern Blue Nile were the first to join the SPLM/A in the struggle for equality. In 1991, a group of Darfurians staged a rebellion that was ruthlessly crushed. Twelve years later, two non-Arab movements in Darfur, the Justice and Equality Movement (JEM), and Sudan Liberation Movement and Army (SLM/A), staged a second and more debilitating rebellion, triggering a horrendous counterinsurgency by the government and allied Arab militia known as the Janjaweed. Elsewhere, the Beja are reportedly restless, and it is feared that a conflict could erupt there any time. The Nubians in the extreme North are reported to have organized two movements: Kush Movement for Democracy and Constitution and Sudan Liberation Movement for South and North Dongola.[5]

It should be emphasized that what is currently happening in Darfur has been happening in the South and the bordering areas of the Nuba Mountains and Southern Blue Nile. Particularly affected has been the area of Abyei, which, though inhabited by the Ngok Dinka, who are racially and culturally part and parcel of the African South, has been administered in the Northern Province and later the region of Southern Kordofan. The government-backed Marahleen, the local version of Darfur's Janjaweed, devastated the Ngok Dinka, burning villages, killing at random, looting, and abducting women and children into modern-day slavery.[6] As a result, the Abyei area became depopulated as masses fled north and south to escape the carnage.[7]

The economic factors involved in the Darfur crisis and the mirror situation in the South and the neighboring areas are also similar: the clash between Arab herders seeking to graze and water their animals further South, under the pressure of increasing desertification, and black African farmers protecting their crops and land against this encroachment. Traditionally, these competing interests were regulated and conflicts were managed and resolved by traditional leaders in accordance with intertribal conventions and customs. With traditional leaders and the normative principles for intertribal cooperation increasingly weakened, both by the adverse attitude of the initially leftist dictatorship of Jaafar Nimeiri (1969-1985) toward native administration and by the pressures of the war, these methods have been fundamentally undermined and severely weakened.

Peace and Its Long-Term Implications

The irony is that regional conflicts are erupting in the North at a time when the war in the South was coming to an end as a result of a peace process brokered by the subregional organization, the Inter-Governmental Authority on Development (IGAD), with strong backing from the international community, in particular the troika of the United States, Norway, and the United Kingdom. A framework agreed upon by the parties in the Kenyan town of Naivasha on July 20, 2002, followed by a series of protocols, has charted a path toward peace in the South, Abyei, the Nuba Mountains, and Southern Blue Nile. The protocols also stipulate principles for inclusivity and for addressing the grievances of other marginalized areas, such as Darfur and the Beja region. The peace process culminated in a comprehensive agreement that was signed by the parties on January 9, 2005, in the Kenyan Capital, Nairobi.[8]

What is unfolding in the Sudan today is challenging the prevailing myths of identity and revealing the complexities of the country's racial, ethnic, cultural, and religious configuration.

What is unfolding in the Sudan today is challenging the prevailing myths of identity and revealing the complexities of the country's racial, ethnic, cultural, and religious configuration. With the South having resisted Arab domination, asserted an African identity, and demanded equality, other non-Arab groups are awakening to the call. This mounting pressure is challenging the Arab-dominated center to respond creatively and constructively or risk eventual overthrow by the convergence of rebellious regional forces, with even greater devastation to the country in the meantime.

In addition to the questions posed earlier in connection with the issues of the historical evolution of conflictual identities and the prospects for the resolution of the conflicts, the peace agreement concluded on January 9 poses additional questions that need to be addressed: Given the international pressure on the parties, to what extent will the peace agreement be a genuine resolution of the identity crisis or a pragmatic response to the pressure, which could mean continuing the conflict by other means? Considering the fact that the SPLM/A is primarily a military organization for armed struggle, what are the prospects of its making a constructive shift to a peacetime civilian, democratic administration? Recognizing that the overwhelming majority of the southerners, given a genuine choice, would prefer to secede from the North, to what extent will the rebellions in the North and a nationwide "African renaissance" influence the attitude of the southerners to vote for unity? Looking at the situation from the perspective of the North, to what extent has the message of the SPLM/A been sufficiently understood and accepted by the northern establishment, so that the concept of the New Sudan is now seen as plausible, credible, and laudable?

The agreement between the government and the SPLM/A gives the people of Abyei the right to decide through a referendum whether to join the South or remain in the North, while also maintaining its position as a North-South bridge through a dual North-South citizenship during the six-year interim period. The Missiriya, Abyei's Arab neighbors to the North, are, however, hostile to the prospects of the Ngok Dinka joining the South and are openly threatening violence in retaliation. There is genuine fear among the Ngok Dinka that as people return after the peace agreement, Abyei could once again be a theater for a genocidal Arab onslaught.

Ironically, the Missiriya Arabs are the prototype of the identity crisis the country is experiencing. Although they are the closest to the black African race and culture, they are paradoxically among the proudest of their Arab identity. Their case confirms the general observation that the more ambiguous the identity in the context of racial mixture, the more a fictional or mythical purist identity is asserted to compensate for the discrepancy. It is popularly acknowledged that those "Arabs" with a known Dinka ancestral connection are among the most ferocious fighters in Arab-Dinka wars, as they must prove their Arab identity and loyalty beyond any doubt, a case of being "more royal" than the king or "holier" than the pope.

Social scientists generally emphasize self-identification as the pivotal factor in determining identity.[9] In the Sudanese context, two sets of discrepancies need to be addressed: the extent to which self-identification with Arabism conforms with the objective factors, in which the African element is conspicuously dominant, and the degree to which the Arab-Islamic model can be said to be representative of a country that is otherwise pluralistic in race, ethnicity, religion, and culture. Where identity is a subjective factor that does not affect the rights of others, there is reason to consider it a purely personal matter, with no public policy significance. But when self-identification by a particular group is projected as the national identity framework, with normative principles that determine participation in the shaping and sharing of power, national wealth, social services, development opportunities, and the rights of citizenship, it ceases to be a personal matter and becomes a public policy concern. To facilitate the development of a framework of justice and equality, distorted and divisive self-perceptions become legitimate targets for scrutiny. In addition to the principle of mutual accommodation within a framework of unity in diversity, commonalities of identities should be explored to foster a common ground for national unity and equitable integration.

What is new and requires closer observation and investigation is that significant developments now appear to be playing out in a way that is challenging dualistic characterization of the conflict. This would seem to favor unity in diversity in the short run, with longer-term prospects for an equitable integration of the country. However, the likelihood, indeed the probability, of the North remaining committed to some version of the Arab-Islamic vision and the South opting for secession cannot be ruled out. On the other hand, even if the South were to secede, the myth of northern identity as Arab has already begun to be challenged, not only by the non-Arab groups in the North, but also by many among the "Arabs," who are increasingly acknowledging the African component of their identity or who believe in a more equitable national identity framework. The persistent efforts to preserve the hegemony of the Arab-Islamic identity, however, cannot be underestimated. Indeed, although the ultimate outcome of the current development on the ground is by no means certain, the demand for a new, secular Sudan, in which there would be no discrimination on the ground of race, ethnicity, religion, culture, and gender, while increasing in popularity, is being countered with the assertion of an extremist version of the Arab-Islamic model for the country.

Wider Relevancy of the Study

Although the Sudan is an extreme case in Africa, the cleavages of identity reflected not only in diversity, but also in gross inequities that contribute to racial, ethnic, or religious conflicts, constitute a widely shared problem of statehood and nation building not only in Africa but indeed around the world. During my twelve years as representative of the secretary-general on internal displacement, a crisis affecting 25 to 30 million people in more than fifty countries, I have undertaken more than thirty missions to countries experiencing conflict-induced displacement and witnessed firsthand the parameters of the national identity crises in those countries.[10] These are acutely divided nations, where some groups enjoy the rights and dignity of citizenship, while others are marginalized and relegated to a status of virtual statelessness. Although the tragic consequences of these conflicts have been treated largely as humanitarian concerns, all these countries are challenged to explore a national common ground and to develop an inclusive sense of belonging, with the rights and obligations of full citizenship.

Notes

1. For a historical background on how identities were shaped by racial, cultural, and religious interaction with the Arabs, see Yusuf Fadl Hasan, *The Arabs in the Sudan* (Edinburgh: Edinburgh University Press, 1967). For the role slavery played in the process, see Amir H. Idris, *Sudan's Civil Wars: Slavery, Race and Formational Identities* (Lewiston, NY: Edwin Mellen, 2001).

2. As Professor Ali Mazrui, the renowned African scholar, observed, "Disputes as to whether such and such a family is really Arab by descent or not, and evaluations of family prestige partly in terms of lighter shades of color, have remained an important part of the texture of Sudanese life in the North." Ali Mazrui, "The Black Arabs in Comparative Perspective," in Dunstan Wai, ed., *The Southern Sudan: The Problem of National Integration* (London: Frank Cass, 1973), p. 69. Michael Wolfers argues: "So much of the debate on race relations is conducted on the interaction of black and white groups and peoples that we do not have a ready terminology for what is occurring in a country like the Sudan," in *Races and Class*, vol.23 no.1 (Summer 1981), pp. 65-79.

3. For background, see: Mohamed Omer Bashir, *The Southern Sudan: Background to Conflict* (London: C. Hurst and Company, 1968, republished by Khartoum University Press, 1979). See also Dunstan Wai, *The Problem of National Integration, op cit.*, Wai, *The African-Arab Conflict in the Sudan* (New York and London: Africana Publishing, 1981); Cecil Eprile, *War and Peace in the Sudan: 1955-1972* (London: David and Charles: World Realities, 1974); Abel Alier, *Southern Sudan: Too Many Agreements Dishonored* (Exeter:

Ithaca, 1990); Francis M. Deng, *War of Visions: Conflict of Identities in the Sudan* (Washington DC: Brookings Institution, 1995); and Ann Mosley Lesch, *Contested National Identities*, (Indianapolis: Indiana University Press, 1998).

4. For a deeper analysis of the country's crisis of national identity in historical perspective, see Francis M. Deng, *Dynamics of Identification: A Basis for National Integration in the Sudan* (Khartoum: Khartoum University Press, 1973); Deng, *War of Visions*; and Lesch, *Contested National Identities*.

5. For an update on these developments see Ahfad University for Women: *Building Peace through Diversity Series, Inter-Communal Conflicts in the Sudan: Causes, Resolution, Mechanisms and Transformation*, including Vol. 1, *Introduction and Summary*, Vol. 2 *Darfur*, Vol. 3 *Dinka-Nuer*, Vol. 4 *Eastern*, Vol. 5 *Nuba Mountains*, and Vol. 6 *Shendi*, (Khartoum: Ahfad University for Women, 2005). See also Francis M. Deng, "Sudan's Turbulent Road to Nationhood," in Ricardo Rene Laremont, ed., *Borders, Nationalism, and Nation in Africa: The African State* (Boulder, CO: Lynne Riener, 2005).

6. See Gerard Prunier, *Darfur: The Ambiguous Genocide* (Ithaca, NY: Cornell University Press, 2005).

7. See Francis M. Deng, *The Man Called Deng Majok: A Biography of Power, Polygyny and Change* (New Haven: Yale University Press, 1986); *The Recollections of Babo Nimir* (London: Ithaca, 1982); *War of Visions*, Part Four, "North-South Microcosm"; "Abyei: Bridge or Gulf? The Ngok Dinka on Sudan's North-South Border," in Jay Spaulding and Stephanie Beswick, eds., *White Nile Black Blood* (Lawrenceville: Red Sea, 1999).

8. The power-sharing arrangements give the South a large measure of autonomy, with its own legislative and judicial branches, while also participating on equitable bases in the Government of National Unity, with the President of the South becoming First Vice President of the Republic in a collegiate presidency. Security arrangements give the South the right to keep its own army (SPLA) at par with the Sudan Armed Forces of the Central Government, and provides for Joint Integrated Units that would constitute a nucleus for the future national army, should the South vote for unity. Wealth-sharing arrangements give the North 50 percent of revenues from oil produced in the South and 50 percent of national non-oil revenues generated in the South. A third source of revenue will be taxation by the Government of Southern Sudan. There will be a National Central Bank, but the South will have its own branch, which will follow a conventional financial system, while the Northern branch of the Bank will follow the Islamic banking system. The comprehensive peace agreement also makes special arrangements for Abyei, Nuba Mountains, and Southern Blue Nile areas, which were allied with the South in the SPLM/A.

9. See e.g., Frederick Barth, *Ethnic Groups and Boundaries: The Social Organization of Culture Difference* (Boston: Little, Brown, 1969), pp. 10-11. See e.g. Crawford Young, *The Politics of Cultural Pluralism* (Madison: University of Wisconsin Press, 1976), pp. 23-24; Nelson Kasfir, "Peace Making and Social Cleavages in the Sudan" in Joseph V. Montville, ed., *Conflict in Multiethnic Societies* (Lexington, MA: D.C. Heath, 1990), pp. 365-66.

10. My annual reports to the Commission on Human Rights and bilineal reports to the General Assembly, including reports on my country missions, are available as documents of the Commission and the Assembly.

The development of democracy in the Arab world does not always pay sufficient attention to the cultural foundations of Arab political and social life. Concepts of the person, time, memory, and relationship need to be considered as vital elements of the political cultures of these countries. Against that background, it may be possible to suggest elements of constitutional and legal organization that are more in keeping with Arab cultural orientations, rather than supposing that the imposition of Western constitutional forms will necessarily suit local needs in the Middle East.

Keywords: democracy; Arabs; Middle East; constitutionalism

Expecting the Unexpected: Cultural Components of Arab Governance

By
LAWRENCE ROSEN

Discussions about governance in the Arab world tend to revolve around the prospects for democracy. One of several models tends to dominate these discussions. Either it is assumed that an electoral model based on competing political parties must cast up leaders whose legitimacy stems from the process itself, or a middle class must develop whose eagerness to affect the distribution of power coincides with those enlightened self-interests and unseen market forces that conduce toward representative government. It is not that these models lack merit but that they tend to exist in a partial cultural vacuum. To understand the relation of democratic forms and contemporary Arab political life it may, therefore, be useful to explore some aspects of Arab culture more broadly con-

Lawrence Rosen is William Nelson Cromwell Professor of Anthropology at Princeton University and an adjunct professor of law at Columbia Law School. As an anthropologist, he has worked mainly in North Africa; as a lawyer, he has concentrated on the rights of indigenous peoples and American family law. Named to the first group of MacArthur Award winners, he has held visiting appointments at Oxford and Cambridge Universities and been named a Carnegie Corporation Scholar and fellow of the Woodrow Wilson International Center for Scholars. His books include Bargaining For Reality *(1984),* The Anthropology of Justice *(1989),* The Justice of Islam *(2000),* The Culture of Islam *(2002), and* Law as Culture *(in press).*

DOI: 10.1177/0002716205282329

ceived and to consider how they interact with the forms of governance that have been developing.

I come at these issues as both an anthropologist and a lawyer. While some scholars seek to derive, by historic or contemporary comparison, the "foundations" of a given political form like democracy, the approach of an anthropologist like myself, while not overtly "antifoundational," is more concerned with the ways in which seemingly unconnected social and cultural factors may contribute to the development and perpetuation of a particular political pattern. Thus, among the features I want to consider are the ways in which concepts of person and time affect the idea of power, the nature of reciprocity and ingratiation in the development of bonds of obligation and institutionalized ways for leveling difference, and the relation between Arab concepts of chaos and their views of the moral/religious underpinnings of human nature. As a legal scholar I am, in addition, interested in the ways in which cultural assumptions inform the institutions through which power is distributed and differences addressed. I will, therefore, with full recognition that these themes vary considerably in different parts of the Arab world, try to show how such cultural concepts and institutional forms are vital to any understanding of Arab governance and how they may be drawn upon in fashioning culturally responsive constitutions.

Cultural Components of Arab Social Life

In the Arab world, it may be argued, a person is primarily identified in terms of his or her network of obligations. Envisioning the world as a terrain for interpersonal negotiation—and supported by the Islamic view that central to human nature and divine injunction is the need to govern one's passions with reason—the individual is largely defined by the ability to marshal dependencies and overcome opponents on behalf of himself and those with whom interdependent ties have been formed. Because the community of believers constitutes the broader unit within which one operates and one's local community is its everyday manifestation, to fabricate a network of associations is to connect one's own actions with a world whose universal vision of humankind and its proper organization appear both true and natural. Successful construction of a network of dependents thus implies both self-mastery and worldly effect. As elements of the cultural paradigm emerge in distinctive contexts, the synergistic quality of each upon the whole reinforces the sense of a universe that is both orderly and consonant with the structure established by God. Consider some of the specific cultural correlates through which this pattern is expressed.

By contrast to the West, where property is primarily seen as the relation of a person to things, in the Arab world the emphasis is more clearly on ownership as a focus of the relations between persons as they concern things. Moreover, it is vital that a man be able to move freely, forming attachments wherever they prove most advantageous. To be tied up is, both metaphorically and literally, to be unmanned, indeed to be rendered less than fully human. Rituals may heighten this emphasis:

in particular marriage rites, for example, a man is bound with a cord and then released, in a demonstration of his moving from a female-like position to that of a man. Similarly, an apprentice's situation is often analogized to that of a woman, and being freed from the master to become a master in one's own right is to be unbound (Hammoudi 1997). Jews, too, were characteristically analogized to women, unable to move with genuine freedom in the world of men. (The equation of the feminine with the lack of free movement is captured in the common North African saying: "Never trust a man who does not move about or a woman who does.") These two aspects—of property as relationship and the freedom to move in the world—are vital to the Arab understanding of one's ability to navigate the world of reality.

[T]he idea of the self as a unity rather than potentially fractionable is central to Arab concepts of personhood, moral worth, and social place.

The normal state of matters in Arab culture, it may be argued, is that because free movement and property as relationship are linked and as long as one can establish oneself in a place and replicate relationships there, the specific site at which one may once have established such ties carries little in the way of mystical or romantic meaning. One may, therefore, hypothesize that where networks of relatedness could be moved, as Rémy Leveau (1985) has noted for Morocco, attachment to a home territory was not particularly intense. A person's name may be associated with a given place from which one's predecessors are said to have originated. But the combination of genealogical amnesia and genealogical manipulation frequently yield identifying family place names that are either of recent creation or simple fabrication.[1] Attachment to a particular territory may, however, be intensified if people are not in fact free to reproduce the network of associations enjoyed in one domain in another territory. Thus, among the Algerians and Palestinians, for example, who have been hampered in their ability to re-create social ties in another place, the attachment to particular places may become quite intense. The idea, therefore, that the state must preserve property, as personal possession, to possess legitimacy may, in such instances, be less central than ensuring freedom of movement, the ability to enact one's capacity to forge interpersonal ties wherever they prove most beneficial. Put differently, any attempt to restrict movement—whether through educational or economic opportunity—cuts deeply into the Arab sense of justice, maturity, and legitimate authority.

Another factor has to do with the conception of the self. It may be argued that in the West a kind of fractionation of the self occurred—apparently more than once—that contributed to the separation of one's personal viewpoint from the role one might be playing at a given moment. In ancient Greece, this segmentation of the self may have been represented (indeed, perhaps, partly created) in tragedy and comedy, where an individual may be seen, often wearing a mask, enacting some aspect of his or her personality and perspective that varies as situation and role themselves vary. During the twelfth-century renaissance, this may have taken an added turn, as religious thinkers like Bernard of Clairvaux and Peter Abelard argued that God would punish one for having the wrong intention even though one performed the right act, an idea that contributed to the development of a language of interiority and separation of self into various components previously regarded as indissoluble.

By contrast, the idea of the self as a unity rather than potentially fractionable is central to Arab concepts of personhood, moral worth, and social place. To say that the fractionation of the self is not a point of emphasis in Arab culture is in no sense meant as a criticism or comparison by negation.[2] To the contrary, it is a feature of conceptual unity that has profound consequences. The idea that a person may play a role in one context wholly separable from other roles is, in the Arab conceptual system, largely inconceivable. Thus, informants raise doubts, say, that a Western judge can play a role separate from what he or she personally believes: the idea that persons and institutions are separable, that officials might rule contrary to their personal disposition, conflicts with the idea of the person as a unity of traits and ties. Power, then, is unlikely to be limited by such an imagined fragmentation of the self. Indeed, while such fractionation is certainly not a prerequisite to democracy, its counter—the focus on the unity of the person—renders the idea of institutions less a separable entity upon which to build a political system and more an aspect of the individual who combines multiple attachments—including positions within political structures—as part of a unified social persona.

Time, too, plays into this pattern. Events are commonly categorized not by strict chronology but by whether they have a continuing effect on relationships. Events that occurred in the more distant past but are perceived as having a continuing effect may be far more important than recent events that are seen as having no continuing relational impact. For example, aspects of the colonial period may seem very current to people in some Arab cultures, but not, as some of the Orientalists would claim, because they are constantly mired in a past from which they cannot shake free or because they look to this past as a way of blaming others for their present circumstances (Lewis 2002). Rather, if one looks at the highly selective references to the past that are being made, one can see that the principle of selection is not one of self-justifying misrepresentation of the past but whether persons or events are seen as having a continuing impact on current relationships. Thus, if one sees the French, say, as still having an impact on the politics and culture of Morocco by having relented in their postcolonial attempt to have French used as the primary language of instruction through the high school level only to succeed in having it used as the key language for texts and lectures at the university level, people may understandably feel that colonial pressures are still being brought to bear since anyone who hopes to go on to higher education will effectively have to learn French in the earlier grades. The old saw that colonialism has never worked so well as since the end of colonialism is, then, not a diversion from reality: it is of the essence of how time and context are perceived against the fundamental criterion of the continuing or absent effect on people's relationships to one another.

The ways in which memory is manipulated by the state, or the ways in which time is used to legitimate or delegitimate ongoing structures, may, then, bear on the course of political development. If, for example, one looks at monuments or pictures of present or past leaders in the Arab world, some common elements appear to be present. Historic monuments are particularly noteworthy for their absence: one sees rather few memorials to the past. In some instances, of course, this is connected to the Islamic prohibition on idols, to which statues may be easily equated. But it is also, perhaps, connected to the points made above, namely, that if what is vital for one to know is how a person fashions his relationships and how those relationships continue to have effect in the world such a culturally acceptable mode of monumental portrayal may never have been a cultural priority. Instead, it is in various utterances that such memorials may be found—the stories told, the words identified with a given leader, the allusions to a powerful man's effect in a continuous world. Graveyards, after all, commonly have either no markers or extremely modest ones: people are usually buried in rows ordered only by when they died rather than family groupings, and although people visit cemeteries on particular occasions and even eat a meal at the site of a relative's grave, after forty years a cemetery may be bulldozed and turned to another purpose altogether. The common saying in North Africa is that three days after one's death, one's property dispersed and the mourning rituals complete, one no longer exists. Thus, the emphasis found in other domains of Arab culture—the emphasis on continuing social impact in the world—is shown to be not just disrupted by death but to focus attention on social ties in this world through rituals relating to the next.

To monitor the way politicians, among others, negotiate these categories is thus to gain insight into what is imagined to have effects in the world of relationships. If statues are (Saddam Hussein and a few others aside) too close to idols to be broadly acceptable representations of leaders, one might imagine that a similar contradiction exists if portraits are employed since it is often thought that any sort of pictorial representation is, if not actually forbidden, at least frowned upon in Islam. But in truth, there is no formal prohibition on pictures. To the contrary, it may be suggested that portraits are not common simply because they cannot tell the viewer what he or she needs most to know about another person—how that person goes about arranging his or her associations with others.[3] By contrast, film and television are readily accepted modes of representation precisely because one can see the individual moving in a world of relationships, creating ties wherever desired. The use of photographs of leaders in the Arab world might seem to contradict this proposition. But if these images are not portraits as that medium is commonly regarded in the West—not merely an identifying image but an entry point to an understanding of the personality of the figure represented—then such portraits must be seen in the Arab context as signs of the persons rather than insights into them. The latter could only be implied from a moving form working in the world. Thus, it is not a religious prohibition that is at work but a cultural emphasis on what it is that one needs and can know from a given form of representation.

> *If, in sum, this is a system in which persons make institutions, and not the other way around, one will have to address the process by which legitimacy is ascribed and whether it can be transformed into institutions far less dependent on personal bonds than on institutionalized powers.*

Several aspects of social organization also correlate with this pattern of relationships. Although most Arabs do not belong to actual tribes, these political forms have features that continue to affect many perceptions and relations. We might even speak of a "tribal ethic" separable from its initial source. There are several components to this tribal ethic. First, tribes themselves are a distinct type of political form, but their shape is not the defining or constant feature about them. Indeed, they are political forms capable of shifting shape. Elsewhere I have analogized them to amoeba inasmuch as one does not capture the distinctive quality of that life form by asking what shape it possesses but rather about some of its capabilities such that it can indeed alter its appearance (Rosen 2002, 39-55). Tribes, too, manifest their characteristic qualities not by their momentary organizational form: their foundational quality lies not in the design they take on at a given moment but in their ability to take on such variations while retaining certain central features. Indeed, tribes commonly coexist with other political forms: it has been shown, for example, that tribes often only come into existence in response to the formation of states, not as some evolutionary precursor to that more elaborated form (Fried 1966). Bands, defined as extended families that operate as producing and consuming units, may be the form out of which a broader identity may precipitate under various circumstances—ranging from predatory expansion and common defense to spiritual unification in the face of religious competition or threat. But if the form is not the central feature of tribes, other features may lie closer to the heart of these distinctive political forms. Two features in particular may be vital, namely, the existence of mechanisms for internal leveling and the moral equivalence of constituent units.

Leveling keeps too much power from flowing into too few hands for too long a period of time. It may take many institutionalized forms, from joking relations that knock people down to size, or avoidance patterns (as when Arab men keep a distinct distance from their fathers but expect emotional support from their maternal uncles, who are not part of their lineage). These leveling devices may limit certain forms of collective action, but they work, more importantly, to dispel the felt disadvantages of hierarchy. If we now connect this first point about leveling to the second, that of moral equivalence, we can see the synergy that results. For if one regards every social unit as standing on the same moral footing—that no one family or person or lineage is inherently and permanently of greater moral worth than any other (Dresch 1990)—then leveling devices can be seen as supporting this image of the moral equivalence of each social unit. The result is a political and social form of enormous resilience, one that may even appear and reappear at different moments, as the stimulus of other political entities operates to bring them into action. And if we see the features of leveling and moral equivalence as no longer necessarily connected to the existence of actual tribes—any more than one must be a Protestant concerned about one's soul to possess all the characteristics of the Protestant ethic—then the forces of this tribal ethic may still pervade much of Arab political culture.

For example, the legitimacy of any leader may be primarily a function of his effectiveness in putting together a network of dependents, a constellation of others who owe him support just as he must support them through his much larger network of connections. The flip side of this "big man" pattern, in the context of a tribal ethos, however, is that anyone who can put together a competing, indeed superior, network will ipso facto be legitimate: the process of demonstrating such effective movement in the world is the indispensable index of legitimacy, not some inherited or elective position. Since, as we saw earlier, roles are not segregated but coalesced, legitimacy lies in the fabrication of culturally recognizable capabilities and social consequences. And if every unit is morally equivalent, anyone can try his hand at the game.

We may even think of this notion of the tribal ethic (to continue poaching from Max Weber) as related to what might be called the *spirit of reciprocity*—that all obligations are interchangeable and subject to bargaining. Power, as we have seen, tends to be both personal and susceptible to limitation. It is accumulated by getting others indebted and then, given the ability to convert debts formed in one way into obligations that may be called up in quite a different domain, to be able to play the expectation of reciprocity to advantage. Thus, a favor done to help another raise a bridewealth payment may be drawn upon when one seeks help in a political election, or help offered in an economic venture may be called up in asking another to serve as one's intermediary in a dispute. This interchangeability of reciprocal obligations and the constant quest for information about others' networks of obligation form a central component of the political cultures of the Arab world and the changes that may be taking place in them.

Limiting Power: Culture and Democracy

If, then, one is looking for democratic forces at work on Arab political structures, the perpetuation of leveling devices, the reinforcement of morally equal social units, and the backdrop of interchangeable obligations may be crucial to the sense of authenticity of any practice or innovation. For example, discussions of democracy in the Arab world often call forth mention of several classic modes of collective decision making, or at least decision ratification. *Shura*, or consultation, generally refers to some group either sitting with the ruler as an advisory panel or being contacted by the ruler for their input and/or approval. The group, however, does not have a clear, universal, institutional definition: it may be as unspecific as the notables (*ᶜayan*) of the area—usually men of substance, education, and familial connection—or it may refer to those regarded as particularly learned in the sacred texts (*ᶜulamāʾ*). As is the case with political leaders and important persons in all other domains, it is by taking on the qualities ideally associated with a given position that one comes to be treated as someone in that position. Proof of position is by worldly consequent acts rather than formal induction into an institutionalized position. Thus, when consultation does occur it is predominantly with those who have acquired the status of being acknowledged rather than ex officio occupants of particular roles. The type of consultation can also vary quite widely, from pro forma ratification and mere rubber stamping by those picked by the ruler to a far more profound, indeed sometimes courageous, willingness to tell truth to power, or at least oppose that power on some personal or principled grounds. Stories are told, for instance, of a local big man who would try to steal land by having the local religious officials ratify his duress only to find that such figures were willing to risk prison or death to oppose the theft on religious grounds. Proponents of modern democratization who point to the practice of *shura*, however, may have to contend with the issue of its cultural form of legitimacy rather than expect that by mere election or appointment, by the mere formalization of constitutional powers, one can indeed expect this body to act in the way that checks and balances may in some other democratic systems.

Similarly, the institution of the *bayᶜa*, or ratification of the ruler in his position, is seen by some as a practice on which one could build democratic institutions. Here, too, however, the acknowledgment is traditionally not by a group whose membership is prescribed, much less institutionalized, but is made up of those regarded as knowledgeable and worldly. If one were to claim either that the election of the leader constituted the *bayᶜa* of "the people" or if such endorsement were to take place through an established body, such as a senate of elected or appointed persons, the legitimacy issue would still remain: can one acquire legitimacy in this cultural system merely by garnering the necessary votes or group ratification or must one demonstrate, through favor and obligation, that one can indeed construct a network of obligations that stands above and beyond institutional position alone? If, in sum, this is a system in which persons make institutions, and not the other way around, one will have to address the process by which legitimacy is ascribed and whether it can be transformed into institutions far less dependent on personal bonds than on institutionalized powers.

Similarly, corruption forms an important indicator of the concept of power itself. Surveys by Transparency International and others show just how extensive corruption is in many Arab countries. But these studies seldom explore the meaning of corruption in people's everyday lives. Arabs tend to characterize corruption not as abuse of some formal set of criteria associated with a given position but as the failure to share whatever largesse comes one's way with those to whom one has forged ties of obligation. To be told, as some informants only half jokingly put it, that "corruption is our form of democracy" because it means one can undercut an autocrat by bribing a person below him to disregard the superior's orders, is but to suggest how such an idea, however ironic, implies a limitation on power.

[W]hatever else may be said of [Arab] autocratic regimes, one cannot simply assert that they are utterly devoid of legitimacy.

Identifying certain moments as ones of chaos may also fit this patterned emphasis on the relational and the negotiable. After the invasion of Iraq in March 2003, Americans were told that there was a period of anarchy, chaos, and looting. The implication of these terms was that there was no order to people's acts beyond the personally expedient. But such moments always have a distinctive set of characteristic features—whether it be the anarchy of Russia at the time of the Bolshevik Revolution or the mayhem wrought in seventeenth-century Britain by such "libertine" groups as the Ranters. The Arabic word for chaos in this context, *fitna* (far more than its milder corollary, *fauda*), calls forth notions of the social universe not holding together.[4] But it also implies a reshuffling of the deck, of leveling the playing field so that others may have a chance at the game. We have not been told how this played out in the recent Iraqi context, but from many such historic examples we know to look at such practices as new marital arrangements, the revitalization of such voluntary associations as religious brotherhoods, and the redistribution of wealth to see how people are securing themselves in an uncertain social environment. To understand acceptable order one may, therefore, need to understand the meaning and structure of acceptable disorder.

Language is central to the ability of any Arab to maneuver in such a world. A person of importance is said to "have word": a person who can capture the definition of a situation can turn it to advantage. The structure of Arabic is itself important in this context. Arabic may be thought of as organized like a kind of periodical chart: there are elements (composed of three, and more rarely four, consonants) that can be varied by the use of prefixes, infixes, and suffixes—especially through vowel variations—to produce words whose theoretical places in the chart are known but whose specific overtones may be open to variation. Thus, a root applied in a given verb form may mean "to cause X," but the specific implications of what this causation means will vary with the contexts and uses to which it may be put.

The result is that control of language as an instrument for capturing the terms of discussion is an enormous asset to be used in forming relationships: if I can define a situation as one of commonality rather than hierarchy, or as one in which collective duty takes precedence over monetary advantage, I can control the repercussions of the relationship. It is for this reason that political rhetoric, which to outsiders may at times seem extravagant and out of touch with reality, may more accurately be seen as trying out a concept that, if it takes, will capture the situation in a particular way. Like a price mentioned in the marketplace, it is not inherently true; instead it only becomes "true" when relationships get formed in and through it. Similarly, the poet is vital to Arab political culture, for it is the poet who, above all others, explores language and may create terms that forge a new reality. Transferred to the realm of politics this means, among other things, that the man who wishes to build a following must not only *have word* (in the sense that his words have an impact on relationships) but must demonstrate, directly or through surrogates, his ability to capture relationships through words. One of the questions an anthropologist of the Middle East would, therefore, want to know about the period immediately following the end of major military action in the Iraqi war is what was happening in the coffeehouses: were poets using words in new ways, were they speaking about relationships in a language of democracy, were they expanding the use of standard references to reconceptualize the meaning of the property that had been (stolen, liberated, reallocated?) during the period of chaos? Indeed, did they refer to this period as *fitna* or in some other way? One would like to know if items that were stolen were ever returned (perhaps with the expectation that the hospital or school from which they were taken would be expected to favor the allies of the person returning the items should the latter have need of medical or educational assistance) and how this recirculation of items—like the recirculation of words—was used as an instrument for rearranging relationships of interdependence.

Even Islamic law, when seen against this cultural backdrop, appears somewhat different than it is often portrayed. Islamic law as it is actually practiced (as opposed to its theological and scholarly renderings) tends to focus on the local: judges use experts and witnesses from the area to inform them of both the facts and the customs relating to various actions, and even where national codes apply they are commonly informed by these localized fact-finding mechanisms. Just as political and religious leaders must build followings, so too a judge's credibility depends not on his office alone but on the ways in which he (or sometimes now, she) has built a reputation for knowledge and acceptable discretion. While this may appear true of almost any legal system, this emphasis is particularly important in Islamic law. Moreover, every Islamic legal variant has a proposition that basically asserts that, short of violating one of the very few clear prohibitions in the Quran, custom takes precedence over the law. Even though the traditional absence of appeals has been modified by most modern legal systems, judges have extremely wide discretion. The personalistic element in fashioning believability, the use of the local in the calculation of consequences, and the enormous creativity of the courts in fashioning approaches to the cases before them are all consonant with a system that displays similar features in many other cultural domains.

Seen in this overall cultural context, the Arab variants of political culture are also enormously flexible: people are not simply held to category, nor are events reducible to prefigured occurrence. Rather, like an elaborate game of chess—that most theologically correct of games Arabs may play—the moves can be infinitely alluring without additional pieces or altered rules being essential to variation. The old saying that a man can be poor in the morning, a vizier of the king in the afternoon, and hanged in the public marketplace the next day is only one way in which Arabs underscore the need to maintain this flexibility and its promise at all times. Yet it may also be true—and here as a proposition of rather universal import—that at moments when the world seems disorderly people have a strong tendency to revert to role expectations. What parent has not insisted at a frustrating moment on a child doing what he or she is told simply because "I am your father (mother)." What individual has not felt more prone to revert to expected behavior when challenged by uncertain circumstance? The key, of course, is to understand what constitutes such challenges in different cultures as well as for different personalities. But if there is some merit to this argument, then we must also ask, for example, whether Arabs who feel they are living in a continual state of disorder and injustice are, like any others, prone to revert to traditional roles—to claims of honor or paternalistic authority or exaggerated solidarity, all elements that under less stress are occulted by the advantages of ambiguity and ambivalence. We need to understand what constitutes disorder in these cultures, then, if we are to ask what actions may prove most effective when Arabs change their structure of political/religious leadership or fashion such foundational documents as a new constitution.

Indeed, the failure to see how such key ideas as time and person, property and "chaos" play out in the context of political culture may lead to a view of future Arab politics that is far too dependent on ideas of democracy and legitimacy derived from the Western experience. To commentators like Thomas Friedman, this leads to the untenable assertion that all of the Arab regimes are regarded as illegitimate by their people, and if these regimes were to be removed truly legitimate ones could take their place. But whatever else may be said of such autocratic regimes, one cannot simply assert that they are utterly devoid of legitimacy. Any Arab leader must put together his following in a highly personalized way, and anyone who fails to accomplish this through culturally recognizable ways will not be legitimate. Put differently, legitimacy comes not from the ballot box or other institutionalized mechanisms alone but from the fabrication of networks of indebtedness that demonstrate a person's ability to marshal allies in the real world. And whoever does that will, by definition, be legitimate.

As a thought experiment, we can now take a series of these cultural issues and try to relate them to the building of democracy in a hypothetical, average Arab country. Let us also assume that the keystone to democracy in this exercise is not the presence of elections or political parties alone but, much more centrally, that a democracy is a government of limited powers. Then, given the emphasis we have described on Arab personalism, it can be argued that it is indeed possible to construct a government of structurally balanced powers even in the absence of a clear set of institutionalized roles, that is, even though people do not fragment themselves into roles through which they might act contrary to their own private beliefs. Moreover, the balance of powers need not be a static one, in the sense that a formal list of the powers accompanying a given position articulates the limits of their range. To the contrary, the limitations may be at the margins, rather than at the core of each position. A phrase that constantly recurs in the Quran is, "These are the limits of God, do not trespass them." Islam makes a clear distinction between the "rights (sing. *haqq*) of God" and "the rights of man," and it is part of both religious doctrine and the concept of humankind that God intended humanity to control all those aspects of life through their God-given reason that are not fully and clearly proscribed by divine ordinance. Since these latter are very few in number—the Quran not being an intensely lawlike document, as is the Hebrew Bible—a very great deal is left to humans to determine. Thus limitations may be forged at the boundaries in terms that are consonant with those prescribed by Islam. We could even specify some of these restraints on personalistic power more precisely. For example, courts might take cases for purposes of issuing advisory opinions, truth and reconciliation mechanisms could expose abuses of power without threat of conviction, supermajorities might be required for the passage of certain types of legislation (thus requiring some cooperation across ethnic or regional boundaries), and military leaders may have a specified term of office (as do members of the Joint Chiefs of Staff in the United States). Each of these modes of limiting power may, therefore, have greater hope of success for partaking of the cultural and religious assumptions that give meaning to relationships in social life at large.

Creating Culturally Responsive Constitutions

Since the late nineteenth century, many Islamic countries have adopted constitutions, usually based on specific Western models. Frequently, these constitutions have been changed at the whim of autocratic rulers or simply been ignored when their tenets were regarded by a ruler as inconvenient. In response to the Iraq war, a new round of constitution writing has begun. The question arises as to how one can develop a constitution that is in accord with the sentiments of a people. If constitutional provisions are to be responsive to cultural concerns, several foundational notions may be worth keeping in mind. If one asks people in the West what is the opposite of freedom, most would probably respond that it is tyranny. In the Arab world, the common response is that the opposite of freedom is chaos (*fitna*). Given this concern, one might consider that, to avoid this predominant threat of social chaos, some of the following freedoms might be of particular importance to Arabs:

1. Freedom of movement. We have seen how vital mobility is to Arabs—in the sense of being able to freely negotiate their networks wherever advantageous. This mobility incorporates both spatial and relational elements. Spatially, it would be important that people be able to own land wherever they are able to purchase it and that the government underscore its desire to supply adequate housing for each family.[5]

Simply drawing constitutional models from the West, as if even those documents were without cultural and historical foundation but were the manifestation of some natural phenomenon, is to court failure or meaningless legislation.

Similarly, it is very important in some Arab countries that collective ownership of land and resources be placed on as sound a footing as private property titles. Tribal lands, in particular, could be specifically protected as the private property of a group—the internal divisions and uses of the land being entirely a matter of their own organization—thus merging whatever laws apply to collective land with that of private holdings as a way of securing the former through homology with the latter. The seizure of any property by right of eminent domain should require (along the lines of the U.S. Constitution's Fifth Amendment guarantee) that it must be devoted to a clear public purpose with owners receiving full compensation for the taking. Relationally, it is important that there be clear definitions of what constitutes corruption and that the entitlement to education should include clear statements about the process by which rules for obtaining degrees can be altered.[6]

2. Freedom of law. From its earliest days, the central government in Islamic countries had control over criminal law, but each confessional community or school of Islamic law followed its own laws of personal status. This pattern was continued in the Ottoman lands and was common even beyond that empire's borders. To Arabs, this is more than a matter of jurisdiction: it is a matter of being free from the potential chaos that they fear may be engendered by having to follow a legal regime that is not locally responsive. Addressing this legal/cultural concern, Arab states might constitutionally authorize local confessional groups to apply their own laws of marriage, divorce, filiation, and inheritance, but with two provisos—that any individual may opt out of the local system and be granted jurisdiction in a national court operating by national codes and that such laws shall not be inconsistent with what might be called "the cultural repugnancy clause" of the constitution. To put this latter proposition in context: much of the debate about Islam and democracy concerns the role of Islamic law in the state system, and often the discussion is set either in terms of whether Islamic law shall govern or whether laws shall only be consistent with the general principles of Islam. To get away from this divisive perspective, one might say that no law shall be inconsistent with such prophetic values as balance, moderation, and proper intent. Alternatively, it could be said that laws must be demonstrated to further the Quranic principles of avoiding evil and doing good (Cook 2000). The inclusion of a repugnancy clause places the burden on those proposing a law to show that it is not inconsistent with these religious, cultural values. Like "the limits of God," it focuses attention on a constitution as a vehicle for drawing outer boundaries more than prescribing details of life that may vary with locality and custom.

3. *Freedom of the local.* Islamic law is only one manifestation of the importance of the local in Arab cultures. As has been noted, the "tribal ethos" incorporates a strong component of building local networks that may coalesce at moments into larger groupings and that one's personal identity (origins, *asl*) is deeply informed by the relational practices of the peopled place in which one is situated. To build on this element, regional, devolved legislative bodies may be particularly appropriate. Models to be studied may include those of Spain or the United Kingdom. There should be no fear that semiautonomous zones would be coincident with ethnic or confessional boundaries. To the contrary, concern about local groupings should be replaced by support for them. A brief comparison may be informative here. The writers of *The Federalist Papers* were greatly concerned about "faction" as a threat to an independent America: they thought that such groups would threaten the new republic by their inherent divisiveness. In fact, the fear was largely misplaced. Political groupings, if roughly balanced or required by the structure of legislative decision making to need one another as allies for various endeavors, may actually fortify democracy rather than undermine it. We have seen how for the Arabs it was often the approval of one's enemies that was vital to one's own legitimacy. In a similar spirit, it may prove true that the structured interdependence of local groups may be a strength of emergent Arab democracies, one that should be encouraged rather than feared.

4. *Freedom of personality.* A sense of distinctive personal identity is culturally emphasized among the Arabs: force of personality is key to navigating the world. While, as with all the features being considered, the content of this proposition varies from one area to another, some common features may require articulation in a foundational document. Everyone, for example, should be assured of an identity. This means that immigrants, women, and illegitimate children, like all others,

should be entitled to civil identity documents and passports drawn in their own name, not that of a husband or (as is sometimes the case for the illegitimate) denied documentation altogether. Similarly, the right to privacy—to a home immune to invasion without warrant, to the retention of information about oneself that is not available to the government—has particular relevance insofar as the quest and control of knowledge about others is vital to building alliances. Indeed, the sense of fair play in this process includes the need for protecting confidential knowledge. At the same time, public places—which are often those terrains for which no one feels any individual responsibility since they are not involved in the development of their bonds of affiliation—should be reconceptualized as joint space for which some investment of personality becomes at least possible. As in each of the other freedoms mentioned above, the key to this kind of approach is to determine what the cultural values are that relate to personal identity and to attempt protections that are drawn in their terms.

Of the twenty-two Middle East Muslim countries, none is commonly regarded as a democracy. Yet if the keystone to democracy is not elections or parties as such but a government of limited powers, then we may hypothesize that institution building where personalism informs relationship, time, memory, and property may very well follow a different course than in the West. Nothing inherent in Arab cultures (it should go without saying), much less Islamic thought, is antithetical to the development of democracy. Simply drawing constitutional models from the West, as if even those documents were without cultural and historical foundation but were the manifestation of some natural phenomenon, is to court failure or meaningless legislation. For the Arabs, perhaps, constitutions that not only reflect underlying cultural assumptions but are built analogically from "the limits of God" and the "rights of man," that serve less as the scaffolding for the construction of a state than as an exoskeleton that protects vital organs, and that recognize the continuing force of personalism over institutionalized roles, will have far more meaning than some artificial construct imposed from on high. What we in the West need to understand, as we watch these developments at a distance, is that quite fundamental aspects of person, time, and relationship will deeply inform whatever changes take place and that treating democracy or legitimacy or institutions in a cultural vacuum is, at the very least, to diminish our own chances of being able to expect the unexpected.

Notes

1. Some groups—the descendants of the Prophet or particular saints—are the exceptions that prove the rule, inasmuch as their predecessors' shrine may be vital to both their claimed legitimacy and the income produced by their attachment.

2. This point requires careful emphasis. It is quite common, in discussions of the Middle East, for scholars and commentators to speak in terms of something that is missing in the Muslims' cultures. Phrases like "what went wrong" (to cite the title of Bernard Lewis's [2002] best-selling book) convey the impression that Arabs or Persians have missed out on something the West has come to possess—whether it be modern science or democratic institutions or concern for the rights of women and minorities. But to couch such issues of comparison as a lack of something in the one that is found in the other is to do an injustice to the peoples of the region and

scholarship alike. The comparisons drawn here are, therefore, intended simply as that—attempts to highlight the features of one entity through an understanding of another—rather than as an evaluation or criticism. Any other reading of the comparisons drawn here would be wholly incorrect.

3. The meaning of portraiture in Arab cultures is one of the topics discussed in my forthcoming book *Re-Presenting Islam*.

4. The importance of the fear of *fitna* is strikingly revealed in an anecdote about one of the 9/11 suicide bombers, Mohamed Atta, who was taken by a friend to a crowded theatre where they saw the Disney cartoon *The Jungle Book*. Atta reportedly kept "muttering over and over again in disgust, 'Chaos, chaos'" (McDermott 2005).

5. Many people in the Arab world are unable to marry unless they have a place to move to outside of the parental home. Egypt, for example, actually requires one to show that some dwelling place is available to a couple before the marriage itself may be authorized. The older pattern of residing with the husband's family is regarded by most men as highly limiting of their freedom to entertain and ingratiate in their own name, and moving out of the father's house is often the occasion of considerable stress.

6. Corruption is commonly seen as the failure to share with those to whom one has bonds of interdependence whatever largesse comes one's way, rather than doing favors for friends, relatives, and political patrons or clients. The pervasive nature of petty corruption and its affect on people's sense of civility is one of the primary obstacles to both the freedom of movement and the ability to negotiate in the world in accordance with rules that give "the game" a sense of fairness. Whether anticorruption measures should involve alterations in the form of civil service organization or the like will have to be matters of local choice, but a clear commitment to its eradication—as it is conceptualized culturally by those concerned—is increasingly vital to the stability of many Arab nations. For a story of corruption and its local effects, see Rosen (2002, 3-20).

Similarly, parents often make enormous sacrifices for their children's education only to find that the government changes the rules for how many are permitted, for example, to receive the baccalaureate degree in a given year. This has occasionally resulted in violent protests. Some guarantees about educational opportunities may be vital to the sense of justice that is itself at the heart of many Arabs' concerns. For more on my own assessment of Islamic ideas of justice, see Rosen (2000).

References

Cook, M. A. 2000. *Commanding right and forbidding wrong in Islamic thought*. Cambridge: Cambridge University Press.

Dresch, Paul. 1990. Imams and tribes: The writing and acting of history in Upper Yemen. In *Tribes and state formation in the Middle East*, ed. Philip S. Khoury and Joseph Kostiner, 252-87. Berkeley: University of California Press.

Fried, Morton H. 1966. On the concepts of "tribe" and "tribal societies." *Transactions of the New York Academy of Sciences* 28 (4): 527-40.

Hammoudi, Abdellah. 1997. *Master and disciple: The cultural foundations of Moroccan authoritarianism*. Chicago: University of Chicago Press.

Leveau, Rémy. 1985. Public property and control of property rights: Their effects on social structure in Morocco. In *Property, social structure, and the modern Middle East*, ed. Ann Elizabeth Mayer, 61-84. Albany: State University of New York Press.

Lewis, Bernard. 2002. *What went wrong?* Oxford: Oxford University Press.

McDermott, Terry. 2005. *Perfect soldiers: The hijackers: Who they were, why they did it*. New York: HarperCollins.

Rosen, Lawrence. 2000. *The justice of Islam*. Oxford: Oxford University Press.

———. 2002. *The culture of Islam*. Chicago: University of Chicago Press.

Rule of Law and Lawyers in Latin America

By
ROGELIO
PÉREZ-PERDOMO

From the nineteenth century onward, lawyers have been the leading members of Latin American political elites. Nevertheless, Latin American countries have been plagued with caudillos and dictators, and lawyers have been these strongmen's collaborators. The article explains the dissonance between the constitutionalism and legalism taught at the universities and the sordid political practices that resulted from the lack of independence of the legal profession: there was not a market for lawyers' services, so lawyers depended on those who controlled the political apparatus. The situation started changing in the late twentieth century. During this recent period, lawyers and judges have shown more independence and have become active political players, using the law as an instrument for opposing arbitrary political practices. The new trend is explained not only by the increased awareness of the rule of law values but also by the existence of a market for legal services.

Keywords: lawyers' political roles; Latin American politics

N owadays we tend to associate rule of law with notions of liberty and democracy. The linkage with liberty comes from the limits that are imposed on public officials. The state is perceived as the most influential apparatus of power, which is why the restrictions imposed on the role of public officials and the protection of citizens' rights are perceived as a guarantee of liberty. It is also believed that the rule of law protects the electoral system and ensures the rights of minorities. In this sense, the rule of law is perceived as a political value.

Rogelio Pérez-Perdomo is dean of the Facultad de Estudios Jurídicos y Políticos, Universidad Metropolitana, Caracas, Venezuela. He has served as the academic director of the Stanford Program for International Legal Studies (California) and of the International Institute for the Sociology of Law (Onati, Spain). He has published in the fields of history and sociology of law. His most recent book is Latin American Lawyers: A Historical Introduction *(Stanford University Press, 2006).*

NOTE: I thank Richard Schwartz for the invitation to write this article and Manuel Gómez for his assistance in the research and editing.

DOI: 10.1177/0002716205283132

Rule of law can be considered an important achievement of civilization but shall not be treated as a factual situation. The citizens' aspiration is that public officials perform their duties within the boundaries set forth by the constitution and other legal instruments, and they expect their rights to be preserved. In this sense, the rule of law is a normative model. By so understanding the rule of law, we also imply that it can be used as an instrument to evaluate the performance of the real political and legal systems. For example, the statement that Spain during the early twenty-first century is a model of rule of law does not mean that all public officials operate within their boundaries and that everybody's rights are dully safeguarded. If we say that Spain under Franco's ruling was not a model of rule of law, we do not imply that law was not important at all during that time or that no public official operated within the legal boundaries. What we are really trying to convey is that today's Spain is closer to the rule of law's normative model than during Franco's era. In general, it is believed that those who exercise public duties today are more constrained (legally and constitutionally) than in the past and that any abuses or violations are more likely to be prosecuted than under Franco's ruling. In other words, today there is more freedom and democracy. We are doing a value assessment on Spain's legal and political system.

Naturally, the rule of law is closely related to the idea of law. In the notion and name of *rule of law*, law is deemed to impose limits on the state's power and, specially, on each one of its different branches. *Law* implies the constitution and other legal instruments but also encompasses the entire apparatus in charge of interpreting and enforcing it, to wit: the courts, lawyers, police, military, and in general, all citizens. This article is about legal professionals, their relationship with the state, and their role in making it work.

The operation of a political-legal system is closely related to economic, social, and cultural aspects. Our awareness about its complexity does not prevent us from being able to analyze the role of certain social or professional groups in making the system work. It is possible that lawyers, military forces, landowners, businesspeople, and also foreign superpowers have had an influence in the direction that different Latin American countries have taken in different historical moments. That is why we will make an effort to analyze the particular group formed by legal professionals. The way in which a political-legal system works is undoubtedly linked to economic, social, and cultural factors.

Democratization is a common feature in Latin America during the beginning of the twenty-first century. Today, the presidents of all countries, with the exception of Cuba, have been democratically elected. This differs from the 1970s and 1980s, a time during which the majority of Latin American countries were in hands of dictators, some of whom became known for the massive violation of human rights. The rule of law has been linked to democratization because our notion of democracy is liberal,[1] but has the rule of law in Latin America achieved similar progress to that accomplished by democratization?

According to the general perception, the adoption of the rule of law faces more difficulties than the functioning of democracy (Schor 2003; Pereira 2000). Even in countries that hold elections periodically, and where the opposition has a chance of winning, the judiciary can perform poorly, and public officials—from police officers to the president—can commit abuses against citizens. This is why strengthening the judiciary has become a critical task in each of these Latin American countries as a way to improve the rule of law.

[I]ndependent judges, who administer justice
in a transparent and accountable manner
through the most modern means, are the
best guarantors of the rule of law.

The basic idea is that independent judges, who administer justice in a transparent and accountable manner through the most modern means, are the best guarantors of the rule of law. Following this reasoning, since the 1990s, each country has invested important resources to improve judicial and administrative procedures, to strengthen the training of judges, and to invest in new technologies geared to modernize and improve courts' management (Pásara 2004). An important portion of the resources devoted to these reform processes have come through loans from the World Bank and the Inter-American Development Bank, or through donations from the United Status and some European countries for specific projects. This has helped to create a homogeneous agenda (Domingo and Sieder 2001; Hammergren 2003; Rodríguez 2001).

We might want to ask if by focusing on the judiciary and, in general, on the legal rules, democracy and rule of law would become stronger in Latin America. This article offers an analysis of some general aspects of the experiences that we, as Latin Americans, currently have. I will make frequent references to history, in particular to recent history, and give special attention to the role of lawyers. In the first part, I explore the Latin American tradition and its connection with the rule of law and, in particular, with respect to the role of lawyers and their relationship with the political system. In the second part, I will analyze the most recent initiatives and will assess their chance of succeeding.

Rule of Law and the Social Position of Lawyers

The countries that we now call Latin American became independent from Spain and Portugal during the first decades of the nineteenth century.[2] Independence required them to adopt constitutions modeled after those common in that time. Among the essential features were the distribution of the state apparatus in different branches and the bill of rights. The obvious question for us in light of this article is why during the nineteenth and twentieth centuries, the idea of a constitutional government, as stated in documents, was so difficult to put in practice? From our standpoint, the answer might be partially in the role of lawyers in the tension between stated ideals and real policies put into practice.

The truth is that lawyers were very important long before independence. Law graduates were used widely by the Iberian monarchies that founded the great colonial empires as administrators of their interests. These monarchies, however, followed opposing policies in relationship with the legal education. Spain favored the establishment of universities in its American provinces; law schools were among the main priorities. Since the mid-sixteenth century, universities were established, and by the early nineteenth century, each important city in Spanish America had at least one university. Legal studies, along with theology, were at the heart of university courses. The number of law graduates (as in general, the number of university graduates) was low. The number of lawyers was even lower since clerics had restrictions to practice law. Toward 1800, the number of lawyers in all Spanish America was probably around one thousand (around ten for every ten thousand inhabitants). The total of law graduates was at least twice that number since many of them were direct officials of the monarchy or the Catholic Church without having obtained the habilitation as lawyers (Pérez-Perdomo 2004).

Portugal followed a different educational policy by avoiding the establishment of universities in Brazil. Wealthy Brazilians had to go to Coimbra to pursue their careers. As a consequence of this restrictive policy, the number of law graduates in 1800 was around 250, in a country with less than 3 million inhabitants.[3] That is 8 for every 100,000 inhabitants.

In spite of these low figures,[4] the general perception at the time, at least in Spain and its colonies, was that there were too many lawyers. The reason probably lies in the fact that lawyers and law graduates saw themselves as potential officials for the crown. The number of positions was limited due to the prohibition against the "sons of the country" (hijos del pais) to serve as high officials in their own countries and also because most of the tasks performed by today's lawyers (like representing private citizens in courts) were left to solicitors (procuradores). The solicitors did not have a formal legal training but were very knowledgeable of the practice of law. Lawyers deemed these tasks unworthy of their prestige and social position.

A lawyer was seen as a socially important person, related to an audiencia or high court. The normative image of the lawyer was closer to an official of the state than to a defender of the citizens. Lawyers were men of "honor," but that honor derived from their service to the monarch and, later on, to the state (Uribe-Urán 2000; Gaitán Bohórquez 2002).

As owners of the political knowledge of the time and members of the colonial high class, lawyers had the most independence, and in fact, they became its civil leaders. In the period of independence, the lawyers drafted the constitutions, the laws, manifests, and proclamas; in other words, they were the architects of the state. Between 1811 and 1830, the Latin American countries were the great producers of constitutional texts. Each country adopted at least one constitution, and frequently several, enacted one after another. All these constitutions contained provisions about the division of the state in separate branches (generally, the executive, the legislature, and the judiciary) and also about certain rights.

Legal education experienced an important transformation after independence. In Brazil, universities and legal studies were established. In every country, the programs of study and the teaching methods also changed. New courses were added to the traditional teaching of Roman and canonical law. One of these new courses covered constitutional law. The most successful book for this course was Florentino González's *Lecciones de derecho constitucional*, which in general terms describes the constitutional government.[5]

In sum, since the inception of independent states, Latin American legal scholars became familiar with the central ideas of the constitutional government that we now call rule of law. It can be said that rule of law is within the Latin American legal tradition, at least in relationship to the knowledge and culture of legal scholars. Under the traditional idea of constitutional government, the emphasis is on the limit imposed upon the different organs of the state more than on the citizen's rights.

During the nineteenth century and at the beginning of the twentieth century, the number of lawyers remained low and their main role was to fill high government positions (Serrano 1994; Pérez-Perdomo 2004, 1981). Well into the twentieth century, working for the government was still the main job for lawyers in Brazil (Falcão 1979), but by midcentury, lawyers became business advisers and started representing individual clients. Also in Chile, a tension between the state and the market as potential competitors for legal services has been reported (de la Maza 2001). One could state that this is the general trend (Pérez-Perdomo 2004).

During this long period, lawyers were always part of cabinets, parliaments, and also served as leaders of political parties. In some countries like Chile, lawyers were also chiefs of state. This is how lawyers became important members of the political elite. Countries were well equipped with parliaments, judicial systems, and an initially small—but steadily increasing—number of lawyers. At the beginning, legal knowledge was not restricted to lawyers: cultivated people were familiar with the fundamental works in law, and among those who wrote about law there were a certain number of nonlawyers (Pérez-Perdomo 2004). During the twentieth century, however, legal knowledge became more specialized.

On the other hand, there is a general perception that political life occurred in a different fashion than the way for which the constitution and other legal instruments provided. The variation among different countries and between different times within each country might be relevant. In each country, there were relatively stable periods when institutions functioned well and also other times of enormous turmoil including civil wars. In general terms, Latin American political systems during the nineteenth and twentieth centuries can be labeled as personalist *(personalistas)*. By this, we mean that the system's axis was an individual who set the pace of the political apparatus and was its most predominant player. There is no

doubt that Santa Ana or Porfirio Díaz in Mexico, Juan Vicente Gómez in Venezuela, Vargas in Brazil, Perón in Argentina, Pinochet in Chile, and Fujimori in Peru
were dissimilar characters who ruled their countries under very diverse political
systems in different times. However, they all had in common the important presence that each of them played in their political arenas and also the absence of constitutional constraints to their power and the safeguard of individual rights.

How is it possible that prominent lawyers helped these governments? How is
possible that many distinguished legal professionals served in high positions during
these regimes and, to some extent, acquiesced the massive violation of constitutional rights? Why did the lawyers who were judges or Supreme Court justices not
put their efforts in stopping the abusive conduct of those in power?

A complete study would require that we analyze the particular features of each
regime, the attitude of lawyers toward the system, and the motivations that prominent legal professionals had to actively participate in it. Such study is beyond the
scope of this article, but at least we may be able to highlight some hypotheses.

The cooperation of lawyers with dictators and strong men is not a Latin American peculiarity. Judges and lawyers did not offer any resistance to Hitler in Germany, and the resistance to Mussolini in Italy was weak at best (Müller 1991).
Leading law professors, as Schmidt and Rocco, became important actors of those
totalitarian regimes. Most French judges and prosecutors applied the repressive
and anti-Semite Nazi law as part of their ordinary activity during the Vichy regime
(Bancaud 2002). The lack of resistance or the collaboration may have several explanations. In first place, collaborating with authoritarian regimes can be seen as an
opportunity to amass a personal fortune and to enjoy the privileges of power. It can
also be that once somebody is tied to a particular regime, it is very difficult to separate from it, as often occurs with criminal networks or mafias. Wealth, power, and
fear could encourage a particular conduct, but they are not absolute values. It is
probably an exaggeration to think that well-educated jurists would renounce the
values that were inculcated to them to embrace a regime that overtly contradicts
the fundamentals of the law. We could understand such weakness in some jurists,
but we should not believe this moral abjection to be the rule.

A more plausible explanation has to do with the belief that leaning toward an
authoritarian ruler might be seen by lawyers as a lesser harm or even as a relatively
good thing under difficult circumstances. The majority of Latin American countries are socially and ethnically heterogeneous, with a high echelon that has control
over most of the wealth. This stratum is predominantly formed by European
ascendants; most lawyers came from this group. The majority of the population is
from mixed (mestizo) ascendance, with indigenous features. Conflicts within the
upper class have allowed others to become part of the political scenario, thus
inducing fear of a general turmoil. The collaboration with rulers like Porfirio Díaz,
Juan Vicente Gómez, Pinochet, or Fujimori, who were known for rising into power
during grave domestic commotions, might be explained with this motivation.

Another hypothesis may have to do with their intellectual linkage with the state
and with market conditions. During the nineteenth century and part of the twentieth century, lawyers were seen as state officials. In fact, the state was the great

employer; there was not really a need for legal services that would allow an important number of lawyers to practice on their own and be able to make a living out of it. Lawyers may feel rewarded by being allowed to participate in governmental or parliamentary decisions or by acting as judges, and this could make them overlook the negative features of the regime. This is even more enticing when the lawyer does not have other gratifying options.

In general terms, Latin American political systems during the nineteenth and twentieth centuries can be labeled as personalist (personalistas).

In sum, there are conceivable reasons why people educated within the idea of a constitutional government and well versed about the need to protect human rights feel compelled to collaborate—without any moral guilt—with dictatorial regimes that often violate human rights. Toward the end of the nineteenth century and during the first half of the twentieth century, the idea that law was completely unrelated to ethics and its notion as a neutral discipline became popular. Positivism claimed the total separation of law and ethics. The law was seen as a neutral technology that could be at the service of any cause or regime.

Recent Tensions

During the past fifteen years, many efforts and significant changes have occurred. Democratization or the replacement of military governments with democratically elected governments was the feature of the 1980s and 1990s. Argentina, Brazil, Chile, Ecuador, Paraguay, Peru, Uruguay, and several Central American countries followed this path. In Mexico, a regime based on a hegemonic party became a truly pluralistic democracy. However, this is far from being a clear path. Several democratically elected presidents became authoritarian rulers with a tendency to corrupt the political system. Menem in Argentina and Fujimori in Peru are clear examples of democratically elected authoritarian presidents with no respect for human rights or limitations on their power. Colombia and Venezuela, with party-controlled democracies during the second half of the twentieth century, have elected clearly authoritarian presidents (Uribe, Chávez) who made important constitutional changes to strengthen their power.[6] Gutiérrez, in Ecuador, also tried to amass power with much less success and was forced out.

At the same time of this tremulous democratization, there has been an important effort to reform the judiciary. These projects are not totally alike. Almost every Latin American country had reformed procedures (mostly in the context of the criminal trial). As a result, the power of judges has been limited in a transition from the written, inquisitorial style to the oral and adversarial system. Courts have adopted new technologies and managerial practices. Judges have undergone training; small-claims justice and alternative dispute resolution mechanisms have gained attention (Pásara 2004). The World Bank, the Inter-American Development Bank, and various countries and donor organizations have contributed to these projects, even though the beneficiary countries by themselves have been the ones to set their priorities (Domingo and Sieder 2001; Hammergren 2003; Jensen 2003). This explains why, in each country, the emphasis put into the different aspects of the judicial reform vary and also why the results are different.

The balance of these efforts is not easy to assess. It is true that in almost all countries, the courts are now equipped with more computers, and function in new and better buildings where modern technologies are applied; but it does not seem that justice is more accessible to everyone, that it protects better the rights of citizens, or that judges are more independent and impartial.

In general, judges have not had the power to circumvent the uncontrolled authoritarianism of rulers like Fujimori, Menem, or Chávez. Judges have not even been able to protect the rights of those citizens or groups of citizens who oppose these governments. In other countries like Costa Rica, Chile, Mexico, Brazil, and Colombia, judges have been more independent and have become political arbitrators. It is also true that these judges have encountered more plural political systems and more moderated presidents.

The novelty is in the use of the judiciary as a tool for political participation. This means, in the first place, that citizens and lawyers have used the courts to protect their own political interests. Latin America has a long tradition of human rights violations, electoral fraud, and apparently legal decisions geared to exclude certain groups from the political arena. Irregularities have not ceased with democratizations, and they are not likely to cease in the immediate future. Now the citizens have turned to the courts. When we look back to fifty years ago, political wrongdoings were retaliated with political means, not with judicial actions.

Fifty years ago, the separation between politics and law was greater. In the perspective of the analysis of the professions, this means that lawyers avoided filing politically controversial claims before the judges, who also stood away from ruling on those cases. Certainly, governments were not less abusive than those in present times, but citizens and especially lawyers were not willing to use legal remedies and the justice system to defend their rights. An example from Venezuela may help us illustrate this point. Colonel Pérez Jiménez won the presidential election of 1952 through fraudulent means. In 1957 (after becoming a general), he tried to get reelected through a plebiscite, which was a questionable procedure from the constitutional point of view. This triggered a general opposition within the population, and in January 1958, he was forced to resign. In 2004, similar behavior on the part of Lieutenant Colonel Chávez generated a fierce judicial activity.

Another example is the fourth chamber (or constitutional chamber) of the Costa Rican Supreme Court, which every year has decided thousands of cases challenging judicial rulings that in other times were complied with, with virtually no resistance. Among those thousands of claims is the case of former president Oscar Arias, who challenged the constitutional provision that forbade the reelection of former presidents, under the argument that such rule violated his constitutional rights. The chamber decided in his favor, thus introducing a new element in the Costa Rican political system. The constitution was enacted in 1949, and nobody had challenged it before.

Fifty years ago, people opposed corrupt governments, but none of them used the legal system as a tool for challenging the government.

It is interesting to see how citizens and lawyers have decided to step forward and take enormous risks to protect their rights against authoritarian regimes in light of the likelihood of an adverse ruling and the risk to the claimant's personal safety. As an example, during Pinochet's dictatorship in Chile, many people "disappeared." This occurred when the government's security forces, sometimes in uniform, detained citizens without allowing them to contact their relatives. When others began inquiring, the government simply denied that the detentions took place. Some of the disappeared people were released after being tortured; others were simply never found. In spite of the enormous risk that it posed to the victims, their relatives, and lawyers, many claims were filed. Some Chilean judges made brave decisions, even though the Supreme Court justices leaned toward the government and ruled that judges should not take action after the authorities declared that an individual was not detained (Frühling 1984; Correa Sutil 1997).

Judges at times rule against the interests of the political establishment, despite the political leaders' lack of respect for the judges. One such case is Venezuela. The judges of the First Court for Administrative Contentious matters issued several important rulings against some policies enacted by President Chávez's government. After several incidents, the government's special police took over the court building and the judges were fired. A similar event took place at the Electoral Chamber of the Venezuelan Supreme Court. A decision favoring the opposition created a conflict in which the Constitutional Chamber (the majority of its members progovernment) got involved. As a result, several justices of the court were forced to resign, and the government drafted and enacted a new law that allows appointing and firing justices very easily (Pérez-Perdomo 2005). More than two hundred judges have been fired in 2004 and 2005 (of a total of approximately fifteen hundred in the country), and in many cases it was due to political motivations.

Interestingly, the Constitutional Chamber of the Costa Rican Supreme Court, the Colombian Constitutional Court, and the Venezuelan Supreme Court during the 1990s were first-class political arbitrators. This has been achieved because lawyers have been eager to bring claims against the government, and courageous judges have been willing to decide them. Also, the features of the political system have allowed a more pluralistic judicature and more independent judges. Clearly, judges have stopped being the Cinderella of the state's branches and have assumed the role given to them by the constitution even if they never exercised it in the past.

In sum, the novelty is not in the abusive power exerted by authoritarian governments in having control over the judges and firing those who oppose the regime. The innovation is that now, some lawyers and judges have taken a step forward to challenge the establishment through legal means. It is remarkable how in some cases this has lead to a stronger and truly independent judiciary.

Most impressive are when judges take a stand knowing that they will be fired or sanctioned and when lawyers take actions in spite of their practical futility and the risk that it poses for them.

The reason for this could be political. We have seen that an important number of judges and lawyers who lined up with Pinochet, Fujimori, or Chávez shared or currently share their political projects (or maybe simply for opportunistic reasons). At the same time, some judges and lawyers oppose those regimes. The distinctiveness is in the use of the law as an instrument for political struggle. Fifty years ago, people opposed corrupt governments, but none of them used the legal system as a tool for challenging the government.

The second motivation is the identity with the values of rule of law. A legal professional might feel ideologically close to a political leader or program, but such loyalty shall be limited by the rule of law. We should assume that judges and lawyers, at least from time to time, deem justice and legality as their cardinal values.

Going further in the analysis of the motivations might be like walking on quicksand, but the most important are the social manifestations. Lawyers who use the court system to voice their rights in spite of a very difficult political situation—for example, the risk of becoming political prisoners—do it simply because they believe that there are still some judges guided by high professional values who can decide according to the law. Such lawyers might also be guided by a merely selfish interest: a politically controversial legal action may bring them fame and publicity. Perhaps there is a market for the lawyer who after becoming famous may get referrals.

On the other hand, whoever chooses to hide real motivations and uses the principles of the legal system as a façade ends up legitimating it. The saying, "hypocrisy is the homage that the vice gives to the virtue," is appropriate. Lip service is not innocuous.

The independence that we can now see in a growing number of lawyers has a material substratum: a market for legal services that did not exist fifty years ago. This gives force to the idea of law detached from politics. We feel farther away from the rule of law, but as a social conscience we are closer (López-Ayllón and Fix-Fierro 2003; Vianna et al. 1999). The studies on legal or constitutional culture show the same ambiguity. A study on Mexico (Concha-Cantú et al. 2004) concluded that the public values the equality in law enforcement and the good work of justice but criticizes impunity. In simple terms, people are for the rule of law. At the same time, people have a weak knowledge of the constitution and do not esteem the performance of judges and other law enforcement officials. Probably the situation for the rest of Latin America is not very different.

Could we affirm that the investments and efforts put into judicial reform in Latin America are making the rule of law ingrained? The answer is a nuanced negative. It seems uncontested that there is a bigger conscience about the greater importance of the law (Smulovitz 2002), which explains the enormous investments and efforts. However, it is more difficult to accept that the adoption of new technologies geared to improve the courts' management or that the adoption of new procedural laws could have a direct impact.

We are convinced that a more expedite, transparent, and accessible justice strengthens the rule of law, but we have yet to see the effects of the judicial reform efforts.

An aspect that has been left aside is the training of jurists in the values of the rule of law. The legalistic positivist teaching typical of Latin America might reinforce the notion of law as a neutral value, as a mere social technology. Some reform agendas have paid special attention to the training of judges. Perhaps the most salient case is that of Chile, where the program emerged after the concern that the majority of the judges—starting with the Supreme Court justices—were insensitive to the massive violation of human rights during the seventeen years of dictatorship. Nonetheless, in general, the efforts geared to educate the judges seem to have done and achieved little (Binder 2001). Perhaps the obstacle is before that stage, in the legal education. In this respect, the law and development movement of the 1970s had a better aim, except for the fact that it tended to make law subordinate to the economy without giving credit to its own values.

Notes

1. Democracy, rule of law, and respect of human rights are closely linked in the Inter-American Democratic Charter (2001), an international treaty signed by all hemispheric countries for the strengthening of democracy. Rule of law is considered today as equivalent to the concept of *estado de derecho*, in Spanish (*état de droit* and *Rechtstaat* in French and German, respectively). They were quite distinct concepts in the past. Both rule of law and *estado de derecho* were not originally associated with democracy or liberal democracy, as it is today (Pereira Menaut 2003; Joujan 2003; Heuschling 2002; Böckenförde 2000; Halliday and Karpik 1997).

2. Latin America includes also Haiti, a former French colony, whose history and legal systems are poorly known in other Latin American countries. The conflicts leading to the independence started in 1808, in rela-

tion with the Napoleonic invasion of Spain. Most countries became effectively independent in the decade of the 1820s.

3. Between 1776 and 1800, 236 Brazilian men graduated in law at Coimbra (Barman and Barman 1976). The number of lawyers was probably smaller.

4. The number of lawyers is low if we compare it with the priests' numbers. There were fewer lawyers in Latin America than priests and monks in Mexico City. For a discussion on numbers and the perception of excess, see Pérez-Perdomo (2004, 61).

5. González (1869) was probably the best-known constitutional law handbook in the second half of the nineteen century in Argentina, Colombia, and Venezuela. The book has thirty-seven lectures, and only four deal with rights. For earlier times, the book used was Constant (1825). García Pelayo (1949) is probably the most influential constitutional handbook in the second half of the twentieth century. None of these books give much importance to constitutional rights. The *Manual político del venezolano* by Francisco Javier Yanes (1959) is an important exception. The book is an analysis of fundamental rights. This brief book was originally published in 1839 but did not have an impact till later.

6. There is a vast bibliography on transition to democracy in Latin America. For example, see O'Donnell, Schmitter, and Whitehead (1986); and Agüero and Stark (1998).

References

Agüero, Felipe, and J. Stark, eds. 1998. *Fault lines of democracy in post-transition Latin America*. Miami, FL: North/South Center Press.

Bancaud, Alain. 2002. *Une exception ordinaire. La magistrature en France 1930-1950*. Paris: Gallimard.

Barman, Roderick, and J. Barman. 1976. The role of the law graduate in the political elite of imperial Brazil. *Journal of Interamerican Studies and World Affairs* 18.

Binder, Alberto. 2001. Los oficios del jurista: la fragmentación de la profesión jurídica y la uniformidad de la carrera judicial. *Sistemas judiciales* 1 (1).

Böckenförde, Ernest W. 2000. *Estudios sobre el estado de derecho y la democracia*. Madrid, Spain: Trotta.

Concha-Cantú, Hugo A., Héctor Fix-Fierro, Julia Flores, and Diego Valadés. 2004. *Cultura de la constitución en México*. Mexico City: Universidad Nacional Autónoma de México.

Constant, Benjamín. 1825. *Curso de política constitucional*. Paris: Librarie Parmentier.

Correa Sutil, Jorge. 1997. "No victorious army has ever been prosecuted" . . . The unsettled story of transitional justice in Chile. In *Transitional justice and the rule of law in new democracies*, ed. A. J. McAdams. South Bend, IN: University of Notre Dame Press.

de la Maza, Íñigo. 2001. Lawyers: From the state to the market. Master's thesis, Stanford Law School, Stanford, CA.

Domingo, Pilar, and R. Sieder, eds. 2001. *Rule of law in Latin America. The international promotion of rule of law*. London: Institute of Latin American Studies.

Falcão, Joaquim. 1979. Lawyers in Brazil: Ideals and praxis. *International Journal of the Sociology of Law* 7.

Frühling, Hugo. 1984. Poder judicial y política en Chile. In *La administración de justicia en América Latina*, ed. J. de Belaúnde. Lima, Peru: Consejo Latinoamericano de Derecho y Desarrollo.

Gaitán Bohórquez, Julio. 2002. *Huestes de Estado. La formación universitaria de los juristas en los comienzos del estado colombiano*. Bogotá, Columbia: Centro Editorial de la Universidad del Rosario.

García Pelayo, Manuel. 1949. *Manual de derecho constitucional comparado*. Madrid, Spain: Editorial Revista de Occidente.

González, Florentino. 1869. *Lecciones de derecho constitucional*. Buenos Aires, Argentina.

Halliday, Terence C., and L. Karpik. 1997. *Lawyers and the rise of Western political liberalism*. Oxford: Clarendon.

Hammergren, Linn. 2003. International assistance to Latin American justice programs: Toward an agenda for reforming the reformers. In *Beyond common knowledge. Empirical approaches to the rule of law*, ed. E. Jensen and T. Heller. Stanford, CA: Stanford University Press.

Heuschling, L. 2002. *État de droit, Rechstaat, rule of law*. Paris: Dalloz.

Jensen, Eric. 2003. The rule of law and judicial reform: The political economy of diverse institutional patterns and reformers' responses. In *Beyond common knowledge. Empirical approaches to the rule of law*, ed. E. Jensen and T. Heller. Stanford, CA: Stanford University Press.

Joujan, Olivier. 2003. État de droit. In *Dictionnaire de la culture juridique*. Paris: Presses Universitaires de France.

López-Ayllón, S., and H. Fix-Fierro. 2003. "Faraway, so close!" The rule of law and legal change in Mexico 1970-2000. In *Legal culture in the age of globalization. Latin America and Latin Europe*, ed. L. Friedman and R. Pérez-Perdomo. Stanford, CA: Stanford University Press.

Müller, Ingo. 1991. *Hitler's justice. The courts of the Third Reich*. Cambridge, MA: Harvard University Press.

O'Donnell, Guillermo, Philippe Schmitter, and Laurece Whitehead, eds. 1986. *Transitions from authoritarian rule. Latin America*. Baltimore: Johns Hopkins University Press.

Pásara, Luis, comp. 2004. *En búsqueda de una justicia distinta. Experiencias de reforma en América Latina*. Lima, Peru: Consorcio Justicia Viva.

Pereira, Anthony. 2000. An ugly democracy? State violence and rule of law in post-authoritarian Brazil. In *Democratic Brazil: Actors, institutions and processes*, ed. P. Kingstone and T. Powers. Pittsburgh, PA: University of Pittsburgh Press.

Pereira Menaut, Antonio-Carlos. 2003. *Rule of law o estado de derecho*. Madrid, Spain: Marcial Pons.

Pérez-Perdomo, Rogelio. 1981. *Los abogados en Venezuela. Historia de una elite intelectual y política 1780-1980*. Caracas, Venezuela: Monte Ávila.

———. 2004. *Los abogados de América Latina. Una introducción histórica*. Bogotá: Universidad del Externado de Colombia.

———. 2005. Judicialization and regime transformation: The Venezuelan Supreme Court. In *The judicialization of politics in Latin America*, ed. R. Sieder, L. Schjolden, and A. Angell. London: Palgrave Macmillan.

Rodríguez, César. 2001. Globalization, judicial reform and the rule of law in Latin America: The return of law and development. *Beyond Law*, 23.

Schor, Miguel. 2003. The rule of law and democratic consolidation in Latin America. Paper presented at the meeting of the Latin American Studies Association, Dallas, TX.

Serrano, Sol. 1994. *Universidad y nación. Chile en el siglo XIX*. Santiago, Chile: Editorial Universitaria.

Smulovitz, Catalina. 2002. The discovery of law: Political consequences in the Argentina case. In *Global prescriptions—The production, exportation, and importation of a new legal orthodoxy*, ed. Yves Dezalay and B.Garth, 249-75. Ann Arbor: University of Michigan Press.

Uribe-Urán, Victor M. 2000. *Honorable lives. Lawyers, family, and politics in Colombia, 1780-1850*. Pittsburgh, PA: University of Pittsburgh Press.

Vianna, Luis Werneck, Maria Alice Rezende de Carvalho, Manuel Palacios Cunha Melo, and Marcelo Bauman Burgos Vianna. 1999. *A judicialização da política e das relações sociais no Brasil*. Rio de Janeiro, Brazil: Editora Revan.

Yanes, Francisco Javier. 1839/1959. *Manual político del venezolano*. Caracas, Venezuela: Academia Nacional de la Historia.

Law and Development of Constitutional Democracy: Is China a Problem Case?

By
RANDALL PEERENBOOM

China is frequently portrayed as a problem case for the law and development movement because it has achieved economic growth with a weak legal system, has resisted the third wave of democratization, and has a poor record on civil and political rights. Is China a problem case? The author thinks not, or at least that it is too early to tell. China is now following the path of other East Asian countries that have achieved sustained economic growth, established rule of law, and developed constitutional or rights-based democracies, albeit not necessarily liberal rights-based democracies. At this stage of development, for all of its problems, China is meeting or exceeding expectations on most measures. China outperforms the average country in its income class in terms of economic growth, rule of law and most human rights measures, and other indicators of human well-being with the notable exception of civil and political rights.

Keywords: law and development; comparative law; China; human rights; democracy; constitutionalism; economic growth

China is frequently portrayed as a problem case for the law and development movement. For some, the problem is that China has enjoyed remarkable economic growth in the past several decades, apparently without the benefit of "the rule of law," thus challenging the prevailing view that a legal system that enforces property rights is necessary if not sufficient for sustained economic growth.

For others, the problem is political in nature. China has resisted the third wave of democratization and remains officially a socialist state,

Randall Peerenboom is a professor of law at UCLA Law School. He often serves as an expert witness on PRC legal issues and has been a consultant to the Ford Foundation and the Asian Development Bank on legal reforms and rule of law in China. He has written more than sixty articles and authored and edited several books on Chinese law and philosophy. Recent works include China's Long March toward Rule of Law (Cambridge University Press, 2002); Asian Discourses of Rule of Law: Theories and Implementation of Rule of Law in Twelve Asian Countries, France and the US (ed., RoutledgeCurzon, 2004); and Human Rights in Asia (Peerenboom, Petersen, and Chen, eds., RoutledgeCurzon, 2006).

DOI: 10.1177/0002716205281505

albeit a unique twenty-first-century version of a socialist state that has endorsed a market economy and rule of law.

Setting aside the issue of democracy, for others the problem is China's poor record on civil and political rights.

Is China a problem case? I think not, or at least it is too early to tell. China is now following the path of other East Asian countries that have achieved sustained economic growth, established the rule of law, and developed constitutional or rights-based democracies, albeit not necessarily liberal rights-based democracies. This appears to be the most successful "model" for relatively large countries in the contemporary era to achieve high levels of economic growth, implement rule of law, and eventually democratize and protect the full range of human rights through some form of constitutionalism.

China is now following the path of other East Asian countries that have achieved sustained economic growth, established the rule of law, and developed constitutional or rights-based democracies, albeit not necessarily liberal rights-based democracies.

Five East Asian countries or jurisdictions rank in the top quartile on the World Bank's rule of law index: Singapore, Japan, Hong Kong, Taiwan, and South Korea. This is a remarkable achievement given the well-documented failures of the earlier law and development movement in the mid-1960s and 1970s and of its more recent reincarnation under the banner of rule of law and good governance in the past twenty years. Despite large sums of money and the best efforts of international and domestic actors, the results have on the whole been rather poor (Carothers 2003; Dezalay and Garth 2002). Apart from North American and Western European countries, Australia, and Israel, the only other countries in the top quartile are Chile and French Guiana from Latin America, Slovenia as the lone (non)represen-

NOTE: This short excerpt summarizes my comments at the conference in honor of Richard Schwartz, the original title of which was "Legal Evolution: Toward a World Rule of Law." After some discussion, the title was changed to "On Law and Democratic Development," with the focus on the development of constitutional democracy. China was included in the panel on problematic cases, along with Africa and the Mid East. The longer article from which this excerpt was drawn will appear as Peerenboom (forthcoming).

tative from Eastern Europe, and a handful of small island states and oil-rich Arab countries.[1]

The seemingly random countries in this odd grouping have one thing in common: wealth. All of the countries in the top quartile of the World Bank rule of law index, including the East Asian countries, are high- or upper-middle-income countries. This is consistent with the general empirical evidence that rule of law and economic development are closely related ($r = .82, p < .01$) (Peerenboom 2005) and tend to be mutually reinforcing (Chang and Calderon 2000; Rigobon and Rodrik 2005).[2] Indeed, notwithstanding theoretical arguments for and against the claim that rule of law contributes to economic development, the empirical evidence is surprisingly consistent and supportive of the claim that implementation of rule of law is necessary though by no means sufficient for sustained economic development.[3]

The (East) Asian Path to Constitutional Democracy

The "East Asian path"—a notion that admittedly serves a useful purpose only at a high level of generalization, if at all, and conceals considerable diversity when subject to closer scrutiny—involves the sequencing of economic growth, legal reforms, democratization, and constitutionalism, with different rights being taken seriously at different times in the process. In particular, the "model" involves the following:

1. An emphasis on economic growth rather than civil and political rights during the initial stages of development, with a period of rapid economic growth occurring under authoritarian regimes.
2. As the economy grows and wealth is generated, the government invests in human capital and in institutions, including reforms to establish a legal system that meets the basic Fullerian requirements of a procedural or thin rule of law;[4] over time, as the legal system becomes more efficient, professionalized, and autonomous, it comes to play a greater role in the economy and society more generally.
3   Democratization in the sense of freely contested multiple party elections is postponed until a relatively high level of wealth is attained.
4. Nascent but limited constitutionalism begins during the authoritarian period, including the development of constitutional norms and the strengthening of institutions; the emergence of social organizations and the development of "civil society," albeit often with a different nature and political orientation than in Western liberal democracies, and with organizations with a political agenda subject to limitations (Peerenboom 2004b); citizens enjoy economic liberties, rising living standards for most, some civil and political rights although with limitations especially on rights that involve political issues and impinge on the control of the regime; moreover, judicial independence remains limited, with the protection of the full range of human rights and in particular politically sensitive rights suffering accordingly.
5. After democratization, citizens have greater protection of civil and political rights although with ongoing abuses of rights in some cases and with rights frequently given a communitarian or collectivist rather than liberal interpretation.

This very roughly describes the arc of several Asian states, albeit with countries at various levels of economic wealth and legal system development, and with political regimes ranging from democracies to semidemocracies to socialist single-party states (Peerenboom 2004c). South Korea and Taiwan have high levels of wealth, rule of law compliant legal systems, democratic government, and constitutionalism. Japan does as well, although it is a special case given its early rise economically and the postwar influence of the United States on legal and political institutions. Hong Kong, Singapore, and Malaysia are also wealthy, with legal systems that fare well in terms of rule of law, but are either not democratic (Hong Kong) or are nonliberal democracies (Singapore and Malaysia). Thailand, less wealthy than the others, has democratized but has a weaker legal system and has, under Prime Minister Thaksin, adopted policies that emphasize growth and social order rather than civil and political liberties. China and Vietnam are at an earlier stage. They are lower-middle-income countries and have legal systems that outperform the average in their income class but are weaker than the rest. They remain single-party socialist states, with varying degrees and areas of political openness.

There are also examples of less successful paths in Asia (and elsewhere) measured in terms of wealth, rule of law, human rights, and other indicators of well-being. Some involve countries that democratized at lower levels of wealth. Others involve authoritarian systems that failed to invest in human capital and institutions. They tend to have the weakest legal systems and to be mired in poverty, with all of the human suffering that entails.

China

Given the high correlation between wealth and rule of law and virtually all human rights measures and indicators of human well-being, countries are arguably best evaluated relative to other countries in their income class. At this stage of development, for all of its problems, China is meeting or exceeding expectations on most measures. The legal system has played a greater role in economic growth than often suggested and is likely to play an even greater role in the future, which is consistent with the experiences of other countries in Asia and elsewhere (Peerenboom 2002, 450-512).

China has made remarkable progress in a short time in improving the legal system, having essentially begun from scratch in 1978. As of 2002, China's legal system ranked in the 51st percentile on the World Bank's rule of law index, having risen from the 32nd percentile in 1996.[5] While far from perfect, China's legal system outperforms the average in the lower-middle income class.

Moreover, notwithstanding the repeated attempts by the United States and its allies to censure China for human rights violations and the steady stream of reports from human rights groups claiming deterioration in rights performance, Chinese citizens enjoy more freedoms, including civil and political freedoms, than ever before. In fact, despite many problems, China outperforms the average country in its income class on most major indicators of human rights and well-being, with the exception of civil and political rights (Peerenboom 2004a).

Of course, this process of development will take decades at least to reach a relative state of equilibrium. Even then, the process of change will continue, if perhaps in less dramatic fashion, just as it does in Euro-America. Moreover, capitalism, rule of law, democracy, and human rights are sufficiently contested in theory and varied in practice that the final outcome in China cannot be specified at this point—much to the chagrin of those who would choose to impose a highly idiosyncratic version of liberal democracy on China. As China negotiates modernity, and indeed postmodernity, it may very well give rise to one or more novel varieties of capitalism, rule of law, democracy, and human rights (Peerenboom 2002). On the other hand, there is enough minimal determinate—dare I say universal—content to each of these four aspects of modernity to provide a teleological orientation to the process that is likely to survive into the next decades, barring extraordinary catastrophes that change radically the nature of contemporary society.

Conclusion: China—Problem or Paradigm?

It is still too early to sit in final judgment of China's efforts to establish rule of law and constitutional democracy. We do not know whether China will succeed in its efforts to achieve the same level of wealth as Japan, South Korea, Taiwan, Singapore, or Hong Kong. Nor do we know whether it will be as successful in implementing rule of law as they are, or in achieving the same level of success on human rights measures and other indicators of human well-being. Nor do we know when it will democratize in the sense of general elections for even the highest level of office or when, if ever, it will obtain a rank of 8-10 on the Polity IV index. However, China's performance to date has exceeded expectations, and it appears to be progressing well along the same general path of its East Asian neighbors.

To be sure, China today will be judged a failure by those for whom the metrics are civil and political rights and democracy now, not later. But then the other East Asian countries would also have been deemed failures at similar points in the developmental arc. Indeed, these East Asian states might still be judged a failure by those who insist on a liberal interpretation of rights, as these countries continue to score lower on civil and political rights measures than others in their income class and to limit rights in ways consistent with a communitarian or collectivist interpretation. But then, many in Asia would judge Western countries a failure by their preferred normative standards (Peerenboom 2003).

If China is not a problem case, is it a possible model or paradigm for other developing countries, as some have suggested (Zakaria 2003)? It is doubtful that China or the "East Asian path" more generally can serve as a model for other states. First, the developmental state has been undermined by economic globalization and democratization in most countries. Moreover, legal reforms are path dependent and in that sense inherently local. Thus, no single model is likely to work everywhere given the diversity of initial starting conditions and the complexity of the reform process. Indeed, the East Asian model presented here is stated at too high a level of abstraction to be of much use to policy makers. Any attempt to be much more specific, however, runs into the uncomfortable fact that these Asian countries varied in significant ways in their economies, legal systems, political systems, and societies. In any event, many international actors and important domestic constituencies would object to the "East Asian model" given the delayed transition to democracy and the limits on civil and political rights.

[D]espite many problems, China outperforms the average country in its income class on most major indicators of human rights and well-being, with the exception of civil and political rights.

In short, China may be neither problem nor paradigm. Indeed, if we have learned anything about law and development, it is the need to be pragmatic about legal reforms. The reform process inevitably involves many discrete decisions, which produce winners and losers. As such, the process is not only inherently local but inherently political. China, like other developing countries, is struggling to overcome a host of problems with limited resources. It has for the most part been able to resist international pressure to conform to a particular legal paradigm, in part because of its size and geopolitical importance and in part because the leadership remains fundamentally pragmatic. While the scientific background of state leaders is often cited as a negative, such a background fosters a pragmatic, problem-solving outlook determined more by consequences than ideology, the latest theory of development, or the latest version of the Bretton Wood/Washington consensus. Much as China's leaders resisted the advice of international experts to go for big bang economic reforms in favor of a more gradual approach, so have they resisted efforts to blindly ape a liberal democratic rule of law. And just as the slower approach to economic reforms resulted in impressive economic growth without many of the severe negative consequences of shock therapy, so has the contextualized approach to legal reforms resulted in steady progress.

To be sure, critics would argue that the slow pace of reforms has delayed the day of reckoning and increased the ultimate costs of more fundamental reforms. Which side will have the better of the argument remains to be seen and hinges on the ability of Chinese reformers to continue to improve the legal system and ultimately to address the political obstacles that are currently barriers to the full realization of rule of law and likely to become even more serious barriers in the future. There is a real danger that government leaders will move too slowly on political reforms and fail to implement in a timely way deep institutional reforms of the legal system, including greater independence and authority for the judiciary.

Pragmatism has always been about the application of creativity and intelligence to contemporary problems to devise novel and ameliorative solutions—which themselves will lead to further problems and the need to continue to experiment with an open mind. Open-minded reformers cannot afford to look only West or only East; only up to the state or down to civil society; or only to culture, politics, or economics. They need a more context-sensitive approach. Fortunately, no one seriously engaged in legal reforms in China seems to think there is any other alternative.

Notes

1. These include Antigua and Barbuda, Barbados, the Bahamas, Bermuda, the Cayman Islands, Malta, Martinique, Mauritius, Puerto Rico, and Samoa, in addition to Oman, Qatar, Bahrain, Kuwait, and the United Arab Emirates. Several of the island states rely heavily on tourism and the provision of financial services to companies looking for tax havens for economic development. Most have populations between fifty and five hundred thousand.

2. Using time series data, Chang and Calderon (2000) found that the causal relationship between institutions and economic growth runs in both directions, although the impact of greater growth on institutional development is stronger than the impact of institutions on growth.

3. I summarize the main theoretical arguments for the relationship between rule of law and economic development as well as the critiques elsewhere (Peerenboom 2002, 451-58).

4. On the differences between thin (procedural) and thick (substantive) theories of rule of law, see Peerenboom (2002, 65-71), and the citations therein.

5. For a more extensive treatment of legal reforms in China, see Peerenboom (2002). The index is part of the World Bank's Good Governance Indicators (Kaufmann, Kraay, and Mastruzzi 2003, 32). According to the authors, the rule of law index measures the extent to which people have confidence in and abide by the rules of society, how fair and predictable the rules are, and how well property rights are protected. The indicators include perceptions of incidence of crime, the effectiveness and predictability of the judiciary, and the enforceability of contracts. Interestingly, the authors "cautiously conclude" that there is no evidence of "any significant improvement in governance worldwide, and if anything the evidence is suggestive of a deterioration, at the very least in key dimensions such as rule of law, control of corruption, political stability and government effectiveness."

References

Carothers, Thomas. 2003. Promoting the rule of law abroad—The problem of knowledge. Rule of Law Series, Carnegie Paper no. 34. New York: Carnegie Endowment for International Peace.

Chang, Alberto, and Cesar Calderon. 2000. Causality and feedback between institutional measures and economic growth. *Economics and Politics* 12 (1): 69-81.

Dezalay, Yves, and Bryant G. Garth. 2002. *The internationalization of palace wars: Lawyers, economists, and the contest to transform Latin American states.* Chicago: University of Chicago Press.

Kaufmann, Daniel, A. Kraay, and M. Mastruzzi. 2003. *Governance matters III: Governance indicators for 1996-2002.* http://www.worldbank.org/wbi/governance/pdf/govmatters3.pdf.

Peerenboom, Randall. 2002. *China's long march toward rule of law*. Cambridge: Cambridge University Press.

———. 2003. Beyond universalism and relativism: The evolving debates about "values" in Asia. *Indiana International and Comparative Law Review* 14 (1): 1-85.

———. 2004a. Assessing human rights in China: Why the double standard? *Cornell International Law Journal* 38 (1): 71-172.

———. 2004b. Social networks, civil society, democracy and rule of law: A new conceptual framework. In *The politics of affective relations: East Asia and beyond*, ed. Chaihark Hahm and Daniel Bell, 249-76. Lexington, MA: Lexington Books.

———. 2004c. Varieties of rule of law. In *Asian discourses of rule of law: Theories and implementation of rule of law in twelve Asian countries, France and the U.S.A.*, ed. Randall Peerenboom. London: RoutledgeCurzon.

———. 2005. Show me the money: The dominance of wealth in determining rights performance in Asia. *Duke International Law Journal* 15 (1): 75-152.

———. Forthcoming. Law and development of constitutional democracy in China: Problem or paradigm? *Journal of Asian Law*.

Rigobon, Roberto, and Dani Rodrik. 2005. Rule of law, democracy, openness, and income: Estimating the interrelationships. *Economics of Transition* 13 (3): 533-64.

Zakaria, Fareed. 2003. *The future of freedom: Illiberal democracy at home and abroad*. New York: Norton.

International Processes

Toward a World Rule of Law: Freedom of Expression

KURT WIMMER

Freedom of expression is guaranteed by international treaties, but countries differ significantly in their view of the meaning of "free expression" and how it should be protected. Before the emergence of the Internet, each country could workably set its own ceiling for the protection of expression without having an adverse impact on other countries that might make a different choice. The borderless nature of the Internet makes it more difficult for despots and dictators to limit the access of their citizens to information from outside their countries' borders. But the conflict represented by this medium expresses itself in legitimate disputes over the application of national law. Each nation must apply its own rules of law without diminishing the freedoms available to citizens of other states. This article suggests that nations focus on applying the law of the country in which speech originates, following the view of the European Union.

Keywords: free expression; First Amendment; Internet; international law; hate speech; choice of law; jurisdiction

Introduction

Freedom of expression and of the media is inextricably tied to freedom of conscience, freedom of thought, and the ability to exercise political will. It has long been seen as a necessary condition for effective civil society (Emerson 1970, 6-8; Bickel 1976, 62-63). More recently, others involved in fostering civil society in developing countries have noted that free expression is

Kurt Wimmer is a partner in the Washington, D.C., office of international law firm Covington & Burling and is the cochair of its technology, media, and communications group. He is chair of the First Amendment Advisory Council of the Media Institute, president of the Defense Counsel Section of the Media Law Resource Center, and chair of the board of directors of the International Research Exchanges Board. In addition to representing media companies in the United States, he has advised journalists and legislators on free expression issues in some twenty countries. From 2000 to 2003, he was managing partner of Covington & Burling's office in London. He earned his J.D. from Syracuse University College of Law.

DOI: 10.1177/0002716205282120

essential for building working economies and stable societies (Wolfenson 1999). Anecdotal evidence at least bears out this view. Societies that support speech freedoms—including the Member States of the European Union, the United States, Australia, and Canada—have become stable, long-term democracies. States that limit speech freedoms—Belarus, Cuba, North Korea, Sudan, and Zimbabwe, for example—are characterized by a stability that can only be maintained by brute force.

Yet various countries differ significantly in their view of the meaning of "free expression" and how it should be fostered. At the most basic level, a core of agreement on a floor-level protection for free expression is reflected in organic documents such as the United Nations' International Covenant on Civil and Political Rights (ICCPR),[1] the European Convention for Human Rights (ECHR),[2] the American Convention on Human Rights (ACHR),[3] and the African Charter on Human and Peoples' Rights (ACHPR).[4] The basic structure is that individuals are guaranteed the right to receive information and to freedom of expression through media of their choice. This right, however, is tempered by permissible restrictions to protect national security, individual privacy and reputation, the impartiality of courts, and the like.[5] But there is widespread disagreement on the extent to which each country permissibly may build on the minimal levels of free expression ensured by international norms. Laws dealing with protection of reputation vary dramatically from country to country, as do laws and regulations addressing the electronic media, political speech, and commercial speech.

Before the emergence of the one true global medium of communication—the Internet—each country could workably set its own ceiling for the protection of expression without having an adverse impact on other countries that might make a different choice. The publication of *Mein Kampf* could be prohibited in Germany and France but protected as free speech in the United States and Australia. Criticism of a ruler could be criminalized in Zimbabwe but unrestrained in South Africa. Injunctions against speech could be strictly limited in the United States but commonplace in Britain and Australia. The Internet has placed new and unprecedented strains on national protections for free speech. Content published on a Web server in California can be accessed in France, and an auction for Nazi paraphernalia that would be illegal on French soil can take place between French citizens on that server. Chinese dissidents can use electronic means to distribute content within China from outside the country. Broadcasters shut down in Serbia can transmit content via the Internet to outside the country's borders, where that signal can be transmitted back into the country by satellite. Injunctions against speech ordered in England can be vitiated by publication of the enjoined content in Poland. The borderless nature of the Internet makes it more difficult (but by no means impossible) for despots and dictators to limit the access of their citizens to information from outside their countries' borders. But needless to say, the conflict represented by this medium expresses itself in legitimate disputes over the application of national law.

The challenge will be to ascertain how a nation can apply its own rules of law without diminishing the freedoms available to citizens of other states. If the United

States wishes to protect Nazi speech, the domestic law of France should not be able to undermine the United States's ability to do so. But should those who would be willing to avoid the laws of their country be able to establish virtual web presences within the United States to frustrate the application of their own states' laws against them? And on the other hand, should a court in Australia or Canada be able to try a U.S. publisher for defamation under their own countries' standards when the only connection between that publisher and the forum state is the publication of content that can be downloaded from the Internet in that state?

The Internet has placed new and unprecedented strains on national protections for free speech.

Countries currently have no realistic process for even beginning to discuss how to achieve an accommodation between one country's ability to support the free speech of its citizens and another country's desire to restrict the availability of certain content. Strongly held views on all sides of these debates make it questionable whether international treaties on issues such as jurisdiction, choice of law, and enforcement of judgments will ever succeed. Despite heroic efforts, recent attempts to amend the Hague Convention on the Recognition and Enforcement of Foreign Judgments to address these issues have not succeeded. There is no successor on the horizon. And case-by-case adjudication of disputes has led to the virtually universal result of the forum state applying its own law, regardless of whether the forum state is truly central to the act of Internet publication. These cases are characterized less by thoughtful analysis of international norms than simple nationalistic determinations that "publication" occurs wherever the citizens of any state in the world can be injured by speech published on the Internet.

The dialogue typically focuses on three issues: when a state may apply its laws against citizens of another state, when it may exercise jurisdiction over citizens of another state, and whether and to what extent states must enforce judgments of foreign courts. It is possible, given the strength of the ideological objections on all sides, that no set of principles can be crafted for this purpose. If that is the case, the resolution of this issue will be left to nonlegal means—that is, the basic code of the Internet will need to make up for the failure of nations to agree on accommodations of differing speech freedoms.

Publishers could adopt strict "in country only" approaches to their works, limiting their availability to individuals outside their borders if the risk of the application of foreign law against them becomes too great. Another option for publishers is to adopt the "least common denominator" approach to publishing, under which the speech standards of the most restrictive country with a nexus to a particular piece of expression would define the standards by which that expression will be published (Werley 2004, 226; Geist 2003, 385). Governments also can impose barriers, as Singapore and China have, that would limit their own citizens' access to information published outside of their borders (and information published inside their borders with which their governments disagree). But ultimately, the widespread adoption of any of these strategies means that the essential character of the Internet will be altered and its capacity to act as a universal source of information will be lost.

If [no set of principles can be crafted], . . . the basic code of the Internet will need to make up for the failure of nations to agree on accommodations of differing speech freedoms.

Legal institutions are making efforts to accommodate these conflicting principles. One set of examples that bears inspection is various courts' attempts to exercise jurisdiction over Internet content (notably Australian, English, and Canadian court decisions concerning defamation and French and American court decisions concerning prohibited content). Another example, which may provide a structure that could be useful in provoking an accommodation between countries, is the European Union's efforts to legislate in the area of jurisdiction and choice of law—that is, the questions of which countries can exercise legal authority over the resolution of a dispute and which countries' laws will apply to that dispute.

The Problem of Libel, Privacy, and Content Litigation

In the past five years, a number of high-profile cases have demonstrated the difficulty of moving toward a single rule of law for global free expression because of the Internet. The most important cases have involved Dow Jones in Australia and Yahoo! in France.

In *Dow Jones & Co. v. Gutnick*,[6] the High Court of Australia held that Dow Jones was subject to suit in Victoria for allegedly defamatory material that appeared in the online version of *Barron's*, despite the fact that the Web site is published and hosted in New Jersey. The court's decision rested, in part, on the subscription nature of the site by which *Barron's* is accessed in Australia. Because the publication at issue was available through a subscription service with a handful of subscribers who paid using Australian credit cards, the court found that Dow Jones had accepted the risk of being sued in Australia and would be required to defend the suit there.

Dow Jones argued against a finding of jurisdiction in Australia, pointing out that the material on which the complaint was based was published in New Jersey and that 99 percent of the circulation of *Barron's* three hundred thousand subscribers are in the United States. The online version of the magazine had only five hundred thousand subscribers, and only seventeen hundred of these were in Victoria. The High Court focused on where "publication" occurs in an Internet publication, and rejected Dow Jones's argument that publication occurs where the material is last edited before being placed online. "Harm to reputation is done when a defamatory publication is comprehended by the reader, the listener, or the observer," the Court said. "This being so, it would be wrong to treat publication as if it were a unilateral act on the part of the publisher alone. It is not. It is a bilateral act—in which the publisher makes it available and a third party has it available for his or her comprehension."[7] This "comprehension" rule in print or broadcast defamation cases commonly leads to the result that jurisdiction will be found at the place where the damage to reputation occurred, which is most often the country of residence of the claimant. The High Court had no difficulty extending this concept to Internet publication, finding that "the material is not available in comprehensible form until downloaded" and thus that "it is where that person downloads the material that the damage to reputation may be done."[8]

The High Court disposed quickly of Dow Jones's arguments that this rule led to the result that Internet publishers would be required to assume that they could be subject to suit anywhere in the world under this rule:

> The spectre which Dow Jones sought to conjure up in the present appeal, of a publisher forced to consider every article it publishes on the World Wide Web against the defamation laws of every country from Afghanistan to Zimbabwe, is seen to be unreal when it is recalled that in all except the most unusual of cases, identifying the person about whom material is to be published will readily identify the defamation law to which that person may resort.[9]

The High Court also pointed out that other limiting factors would be at play, including the fact that a claimant ordinarily will be able to win damages only in a jurisdiction where the claimant has a reputation and that any judgment rendered in such a jurisdiction would only be of practical concern if it could be enforced in a jurisdiction where the defendant has assets. Faced with the prospect of defending a case under Australian law, under which Dow Jones was essentially guilty until it proved itself innocent, Dow Jones settled the case. William Alpert, the author of the article that is the subject of the lawsuit, has filed a petition with the Office of the High Commissioner for Human Rights in Geneva arguing that the assertion of jurisdiction over the case violates the ICCPR, but there has been no action on this petition.[10]

The danger of the *Gutnick* case to Internet publishers was made clear last year, when a court in Canada found jurisdiction against an American publisher proper in Canada over distribution of just one Internet download and seven paper copies. In *Bangoura v. The Washington Post*,[11] the Ontario Superior Court of Justice exercised jurisdiction over *The Washington Post* for an article that reached only seven subscribers in Ontario when it was published and was accessed only once over the Internet—by the plaintiff's lawyer. In sweeping language, the Canadian court found that *The Washington Post* should anticipate being sued in any court in the world.

The plaintiff, Cheickh Bangoura, was the head of a United Nations program in Kenya when *The Washington Post* published three articles in 1997 alleging mismanagement of the program. Bangoura moved to Canada in 2001 and sued *The Washington Post* in Toronto, some four years after the article was published, alleging that the article damaged his reputation in his new country. *The Washington Post* moved to dismiss the case, but the court maintained that jurisdiction was proper. Although the court conceded that the *Post* had "no connection to Ontario," it noted that "the *Washington Post* is a major newspaper in the capital of the most powerful country in the world now made figuratively smaller by, inter alia, the Internet. . . . Frankly, the defendants should have reasonably foreseen that the story would follow the plaintiff wherever he resided."

The court further reasoned that it would be fair for the case to be tried in Canada because "the *Post* is a newspaper with an international profile." The court noted that it "would be surprised if [the *Post*] were not insured for damages for libel or defamation anywhere in the world, and if it is not, then it should be." The court cited the decision of the Australian High Court in *Gutnick* with approval and specifically noted that "those who publish via the Internet are aware of the global reach of their publications." *The Washington Post* has appealed to the Ontario Court of Appeal. On July 30, 2004, more than fifty newspaper, magazine, and Internet publishers; trade associations; and nongovernmental organizations promoting free expression filed an amicus brief in support of the appeal. On September 16, 2005, the Ontario Supreme Court reversed the trial court's decision, holding that it was not reasonably foreseeable that *The Washington Post* would have been sued in Ontario based on Internet publication of the article in question.

The application of foreign laws against Internet speech is not limited to defamation and privacy cases. In perhaps the most famous case of the line, *Association Union des Etudiants Juifs de France v. Yahoo! Inc.*, a French court ordered Yahoo!—a U.S. company—to use all means necessary to prevent French users from accessing its auction site, which featured Nazi paraphernalia in violation of French laws.[12] French law generally prohibits the possession, sale, and public display in France of uniforms, insignias, or emblems worn by Nazi organizations prior to or during World War II and the publication of "revisionist" statements and literature disputing Nazi war crimes or inciting racism or anti-Semitism. The Union des Etudiants Juifs de France (UEJF) and Ligue Contre Le Racisme et L'Antisémitisme (LICRA) claimed that Yahoo! Inc. and Yahoo! France had made available to French residents, operating from French territory, auction sites displaying and proposing the sale of approximately one thousand items of Nazi memorabilia. The UEJF claimed in addition that Yahoo! Inc. and Yahoo! France had made available to French residents, either directly or through hyperlinks, two works of anti-Semitic literature (*Mein Kampf* and *Protocole des Sages de Scion*) as well as photographic depictions purportedly proving that the gas chambers operated by the Nazis never existed.

On May 22, 2000, the Tribunal de Grande Instance de Paris rejected requests that had been made by Yahoo! Inc. and Yahoo! France for summary dismissal of the case on jurisdictional and standing grounds. According to the court, permitting the visualization in France and/or the sale to French residents of Nazi-related messages and memorabilia constitutes "a wrong on the territory of France . . . regardless of the fact that the activity complained of is marginal in relation to the entire business of the auction sales service offered on the Yahoo.com auction site." The court ordered Yahoo! Inc. "to take any and all measures of such kind as to dissuade and make impossible any consultations by surfers calling from France to its sites and services . . . which infringe upon the internal public order in France, especially the selling of Nazi objects." The court gave Yahoo! Inc. two months to formulate compliance proposals.

Yahoo! France—the local French subsidiary of Yahoo! Inc. that operates the French-language Web site www.yahoo.fr—responded to the court's May 22 order by adding a section to the conditions of use section of the Yahoo! France Web site.[13] If a user of Yahoo! France initiated a category search having a clear relationship to Nazism, the following warning appeared: "Warning: By continuing your search on Yahoo! US you may be led to consult revisionist sites whose content is illegal under French law and whose consultation, if you continue, is punishable." Yahoo! Inc., the main www.yahoo.com site, also discontinued its link to the *Protocole des Sages de Sion*. But Yahoo! Inc. resisted the court's May 22 order in other respects by renewing its jurisdictional and standing arguments and arguing that full compliance with the court's order was technically impossible. Yahoo! Inc. also emphasized that the Yahoo.com server was located in the United States, the Yahoo.com auction site was addressed primarily to users based in the United States, and the messages and memorabilia at issue in the case were protected by the First Amendment to the United States Constitution.

After having rejected again the jurisdictional and standing arguments lodged by Yahoo! Inc., the Court de Grande Instance de Paris held on November 20, 2002, that Yahoo! Inc. had failed to comply with the core provisions of its earlier order. The court gave Yahoo! Inc. three months to comply with the November 20 order, after which time Yahoo! Inc. was made subject to a penalty of FRF $100,000 (approximately US$13,300) "for each day of delay until perfect accomplishment." The court received evidence that technical mechanisms could be used to block at least some—but certainly not all—access to the content by French nationals. Vinton Cerf, who is widely acknowledged as one of the major developers of the Internet, was part of a panel of experts that testified to the methods that could be employed.[14]

Yahoo! Inc. did not appeal the French court's decision further but instead sued LICRA and UEJF in federal court in its home district in California, arguing that it would offend the First Amendment for the French judgment to be enforced against it in the United States. In *Yahoo! Inc. v. La Ligue Contre Le Racisme et L'Antisemitisme*,[15] Yahoo! prevailed in its arguments that the French court's orders are not recognizable or enforceable because they violate the U.S. and California public policy of protecting free speech and because they constitute an unconstitutional prior restraint on speech that is protected by the First Amendment to the U.S. Constitution and by Article I of the Constitution of California. The district court granted summary judgment to Yahoo! Inc., preventing enforcement of the French judgment against it.

On August 23, 2004, however, the U.S. Court of Appeals for the Ninth Circuit reversed the district court's decision. In a two to one decision, the panel held that the district court did not have jurisdiction over LICRA and UEJF because LICRA and UEJF had not "wrongfully" sought to avail itself of the benefits of California's laws:

> France is within its rights as a sovereign nation to enact hate speech laws against the distribution of Nazi propaganda in response to its terrible experience with Nazi forces during World War II. Similarly, LICRA and UEJF are within their rights to bring suit in France against Yahoo! for violation of French speech law. The only adverse consequence experienced by Yahoo! as a result of the acts with which we are concerned is that Yahoo! must wait for LICRA and UEJF to come to the United States to enforce the French judgment before it is able to raise its First Amendment claim. However, it was not wrongful for the French organizations to place Yahoo! in this position.[16]

Judge Brunetti issued a strong dissent, arguing that the actions of LICRA and UEJF—demanding that Yahoo! Inc. reengineer its U.S. servers to observe French law, suing Yahoo! Inc. in French court, and availing themselves of U.S. marshals to serve their papers on Yahoo! Inc.—were in fact sufficient to exercise jurisdiction over them. Although it did not reach the First Amendment issue, as did the district court, the Ninth Circuit's decision forestalls the merits of the dispute until LICRA and UEJF actually seek to enforce the judgment against Yahoo! in the United States, despite the fact that damages against Yahoo! Inc. continue to mount under the French court's judgment. The Ninth Circuit has granted Yahoo!'s petition for rehearing en banc, although no decision has yet been issued.

Cases raising the difficulty of one country applying its own, often more restrictive, laws against Internet content have been raised in many contexts. In Germany, a court has found that an Australian citizen operating a Web site in Australia can be prosecuted for violating German laws against denial of the Holocaust and "denigration of the memory of the dead."[17] In Italy, an Italian court has applied criminal libel laws against an Israeli Web site operator.[18] In England, the House of Lords permitted a Russian businessman to sue the American magazine *Forbes* in London, even though only 2,000 of the magazine's 787,000 copies were distributed in England.[19] London accordingly has become a world capitol of "libel tourism." In Zimbabwe, the Mugabe government prosecuted an American journalist writing for the *Guardian*, a London newspaper, for violating the so-called Access to Information and Protection of Privacy Bill on the basis of an article that was not distributed at all in Zimbabwe but could be accessed by a prosecutor searching the Internet (Robertson 2002). These cases demonstrate the ability of a country with relatively lower standards for free expression to thwart the efforts of other countries with differing legal constructs.

The European Union's Legislative Efforts

In almost all cases, the issue of whether a publisher will be subject to the jurisdiction of national courts is a matter of the internal laws of that nation. One of the few exceptions to this principle is the European Union, which is one of the few multinational entities that has established principles of jurisdiction and choice of law that apply to multiple countries (in this case, of course, the twenty-five Member States of the European Union).

The EU was one of the earliest entities to focus on issues presented by cross-border Internet publication. On June 8, 2000, the EU adopted Directive 2000/31/EC on electronic commerce (the "E-Commerce Directive"), which establishes basic harmonized rules in such areas as electronic contracts, electronic commercial communications, and online provision of professional services. Under the E-Commerce Directive, which applies only to electronic commerce activities within the EU, companies are subjected only to the jurisdiction and the law of the Member State in which they are established. This approach has become known as the "country of origin" principle. The concept of a single "country of origin" for information hosted on the Internet is not, of course, an entirely self-evident concept in an age when reporters, photojournalists, and editors can upload electronic information to a publication from literally anywhere on the globe and the location of servers hosting content can be manipulated easily to locate foreign content in a jurisdiction where it may be safely published (in the United States, for example). In an attempt to provide definition to the country of origin approach, the E-Commerce Directive speaks in terms of the Member State where the publisher is "established":

> Information society services should be supervised at the source of the activity, in order to ensure an effective protection of public interest objectives; to that end, it is necessary to ensure that the competent authority provides such protection not only for the citizens of its own country but for all Community citizens; in order to improve mutual trust between Member States, it is essential to state clearly where the services originate; moreover, in order to effectively guarantee freedom to provide services and legal certainty for suppliers and recipients of services, such information society services should in principle be subject to the law of the Member State in which the service provider is established (E-Commerce Directive, recital 22).

This principle is sensible because only the country in which a publisher is "established" can fully regulate its activities; it also is a concept that is sensitive to general principles of international law, which recognize that one state should not prescribe its laws in a manner that interferes with a sister state's ability to prescribe its own legal concepts.

In an attempt to make the "country of origin" approach more precise, media advocates have suggested the additional application of a "single point of publication" rule to determine which country's law should apply to a particular content claim. Under this framework, claims would be governed by the law of the nation in which the publisher last had an opportunity to exercise editorial control over the publication. This proposal, which members of the U.S. media industry have advanced before the European Commission and the High Court of Australia in an amicus curiae brief in the *Gutnick* litigation discussed below, is designed for an Internet publishing context in which content can be viewed instantaneously in many locations but there is only one place from which the publisher controls content as a final matter—that is, the point at which final editorial decisions are made and final technical work is done to upload the material (Media Law Resource Center 2002). The advocates of the "single point of publication" rule point out that it complements the country of origin rule by ensuring that there is a principal place of publication, and therefore the country of origin, for every article. The proposal also accounts for the widespread phenomenon of inadvertent digital publishing—even publishers who attempt to prevent their publications from being distributed in certain countries may fail to control circulation completely, especially if a publisher releases content online. The content may be forwarded without the publisher's consent to other individuals, or it may be recirculated at a later point in time by others. The single point of publication rule accounts for this fact because "publication" would be deemed to take place at the point at which there is a final opportunity for the publisher to exercise control over content.

The E-Commerce Directive applies to information society services provided on the Internet, but it does not apply to cross-border content disputes that do not relate to Internet content (and its application to Internet defamation, privacy, and other actions has not been adjudicated). Two seminal accords, the Brussels convention,[20] dealing with interstate enforcement of judgments, and the Rome convention,[21] dealing with enforcement of contracts, deal with broader jurisdictional principles. Both, however, provide that under particular limited circumstances, consumers should be allowed to rely on local consumer protection laws instead of the country of origin's laws.[22] Although this "local loophole" does not apply to disputes over Internet content, it does demonstrate a potential precedent in favor of permitting individuals to take actions against Internet companies in their own countries.

The European Union currently is debating whether this approach will be applied to disputes related to Internet content. In 2002, the Justice and Home Affairs Council of the European Commission commenced a consultation proposing to apply the law of the country in which the plaintiff resides to any tort action based on Internet content.[23] This effort, the so-called Rome II initiative, resulted in a draft general rule that would provide that "The law applicable to a non-contractual obligation shall be the law of the country in which the damage arises or is likely to arise, irrespective of the country in which the event giving rise to the damage occurred and irrespective of the country or countries in which the indirect consequences of that event arise" (Article 3.1). This approach would in virtually all cases, lead to the result in which the law of the plaintiff would apply because damages are most likely to be felt by a claimant in his or her own country. Accordingly, an Internet publication from England (with relatively free standards for expression) may be governed by the laws of Poland (with lesser protections for free expression) if a Polish citizen claims damage. The European Commission also added a provision under which another country's law could apply if it "would be contrary to the fundamental principles of the forum as regards freedom of expression and information" for the law of the claimant's country to apply (Article 6.1).

[M]edia advocates have suggested the additional application of a "single point of publication" rule to determine which country's law should apply to a particular content claim.

This approach did not find approval among European publishers, who prefer the country of origin approach. As stated by the United Kingdom House of Lords, the publishing industry strongly favors an approach by which the law of the country of publication would determine a publisher's obligations in defamation and privacy actions:

> A country of origin rule would have certain advantages, notably simplicity and certainty. It would point to one law. . . . To adopt a country of origin rule would also accord with, though not necessarily in all cases replicate, the host country/place of establishment regimes found in the E-Commerce and other Single Market measures. A country of origin rule would encourage enterprise, education and the widest dissemination of knowledge, information and opinion.[24]

The European Commission's draft rule now is being considered by the European Parliament. Amendments released by the legal affairs committee of the Parliament on June 21, 2005, would create an important exception and move the document closer to the country of origin principle. If there is a "manifestly closer connection" to a country other than the country of the claimant, the country of the publisher could be applied. Whether such a connection exists would be judged by whether the "country to which a publication or broadcast is principally directed" is different from the claimant's country, or whether "the language of the publication or broadcast or sales or audience size in a given country as a proportion of total sales or audience size, or a combination of these factors" indicates that there is a closer connection to a country other than the claimant's country. This proposal, which explicitly applies to Internet publication, would move the Rome II doctrine closer in line to the E-Commerce Directive principle. (The next step is for the Council of Ministers to draft a common position that will attempt to resolve the language finally, after which Parliament will give the document a second reading.)

This approach promises a potential resolution of some, but clearly not all, of the issues confronting a uniform rule of law for free expression. In many cases, Internet publishers are legitimately concerned that they will be unable to control the legal obligations that Internet content may trigger. Because the Internet is available almost universally, the law of any country could apply to content published online. A publisher in France could be sued under the laws of Zimbabwe and risk liability for content that would not violate French law. The country of origin approach from the European Union would solve some of the most vexing issues this scenario represents—the law of the publisher's country would follow that content on the Internet. The publisher thus would be able to predict, when considering its obligations before publication, the type of obligation that would be triggered by the publication. It would know the scope of legal liabilities beforehand, a crucial element of foreseeability. It still would not be able to require that all suits against it be taken in the courts of its own country, of course, so it still may be subjected to unpredictable liability. But if the EU approach were to be followed universally, accommodating the diverse interests surrounding free expression in a world rule of law would be more straightforward.

Conclusion

It may be impossible to forge a world rule of law on free expression that goes beyond the floor established by the major human rights treaties binding on virtually all countries. The enlightened approach being followed by the European Union, however, may constitute a structural solution that could eliminate many problems. If the law of the country of origin is applied to judge Internet publications, many of the most difficult issues dealt with in international content litigation could be minimized. For example, the French litigation involving Yahoo! would have resulted in the French-language Yahoo! site, www.yahoo.fr, being subjected to French law because it publishes from France but the international site being subjected to American law because it publishes from the United States. In the *Gutnick* litigation, the obligations of Dow Jones would have been governed by U.S. law because Dow Jones published in the United States. Countries' unrestrained application of their own, often more restrictive, laws against Internet content could provide incentives for publishers to avoid extending beyond their borders, thus denying large portions of the world's population the ability to receive diverse sources of information. The EU approach, if it became widespread, could provide a mechanism by which these incentives would be removed and many of the most difficult disputes could be avoided. It is perhaps the only current proposal by which a world law of freedom of expression can be forged in the Internet age, and there may be reason to hope that its logic could be influential beyond the twenty-five countries of the European Union.

Notes

1. Article 19 of the ICCPR provides,
   1. Everyone shall have the right to hold opinions without interference.
   2. Everyone shall have the right to freedom of expression; this right shall include freedom to seek, receive and impart information and ideas of all kinds, regardless of frontiers, either orally, in writing or in print, in the form of art, or through any other media of his choice.
   3. The exercise of the rights provided for in paragraph 2 of this article carries with it special duties and responsibilities. It may therefore be subject to certain restrictions, but these shall only be such as are provided by law and are necessary:
      (a) For respect of the rights or reputations of others;
      (b) For the protection of national security or of public order (ordre public), or of public health or morals.
2. Article 10 of ECHR provides,
   1. Everyone has the right to freedom of expression. This right shall include freedom to hold opinions and to receive and impart information and ideas without interference by public authority and regardless of frontiers. This article shall not prevent States from requiring the licensing of broadcasting, television or cinema enterprises.
   2. The exercise of these freedoms, since it carries with it duties and responsibilities, may be subject to such formalities, conditions, restrictions or penalties as are prescribed by law and are necessary in a democratic society, in the interests of national security, territorial integrity or public safety, for the prevention of disorder or crime, for the protection of health or morals, for the protection of the reputation or rights of others, for preventing the disclosure of information received in confidence, or for maintaining the authority and impartiality of the judiciary.
3. Article 13 of the ACHR provides as follows:
   1. Everyone has the right to freedom of thought and expression. This right includes freedom to seek, receive, and impart information and ideas of all kinds, regardless of frontiers, either orally, in writing, in print, in the form of art, or through any other medium of one's choice.
   2. The exercise of the right provided for in the foregoing paragraph shall not be subject to prior censorship but shall be subject to subsequent imposition of liability, which shall be expressly established by law to the extent necessary to ensure:
      a. respect for the rights or reputations of others; or
      b. the protection of national security, public order, or public health or morals.
   3. The right of expression may not be restricted by indirect methods or means, such as the abuse of government or private controls over newsprint, radio broadcasting frequencies, or equipment used in the dissemination of information, or by any other means tending to impede the communication and circulation of ideas and opinions.
   4. Notwithstanding the provisions of paragraph 2 above, public entertainments may be subject by law to prior censorship for the sole purpose of regulating access to them for the moral protection of childhood and adolescence.
   5. Any propaganda for war and any advocacy of national, racial, or religious hatred that constitute incitements to lawless violence or to any other similar action against any person or group of persons on any grounds including those of race, color, religion, language, or national origin shall be considered as offenses punishable by law.

4. Article 9 of the ACHPR provides,

1. Every individual shall have the right to receive information.

2. Every individual shall have the right to express and disseminate his opinions within the law

5. Some countries, of course, do not agree on the floor-level protections for human rights set out in the treaties of the United Nations, the Council of Europe, the Americas, or Africa. But those countries who refuse to recognize even the floor may legitimately be seen as outliers that are simply out of compliance with international norms and, indeed, their own global obligations. Political and diplomatic mechanisms for bringing these nations back into the fold exist, even though their efficacy can be debated.

6. [2002] HCA 56 (Dec. 10, 2002) (available at http://www.austlii.edu.au/au/cases/cth/high_ct/2002/56.html/).

7. *Id*. at para. 26.

8. *Id*. at para. 44.

9. *Id*. at para. 54.

10. See *Alpert v. Australia, Communication Submitted for Consideration Under the First Optional Protocol to the International Covenant on Civil and Political Rights* (April 15, 2003).

11. 235 D.L.R. (4th) 564 (Jan. 27, 2004).

12. T.G.I. Paris, Nov. 20, 2000, 6 ILR (P&F) 434. An English translation of the case also is available at www.cdt.org/speech/international/001120yahoofrance.pdf/.

13. The message, translated from French, stated as follows:

Lastly, if in the context of a search made on www.yahoo.fr based on a tree structure, key words, the results of this search were to lead to sites, pages or chats the title and/or the content of which constitute a breach of French law, in particular due to the fact that Yahoo! France cannot control the content of these sites and external sources (including the content referenced on other Yahoo! sites and services around the world), you should cease your consultation of the site concerned on penalty of incurring the sanctions applicable under French law or of having to respond to lawsuits brought against you.

14. In particular, the panel focused on "Internet protocol addresses," the unique identifiers used by each computer that accesses the Internet. IP addresses often—but do not always—reflect the geographic origin of the computer that is attempting to access a Web site. By blocking access to IP addresses assumed to be of French origin and taking a few other measures, the panel found that some 90 percent of French nationals could, in fact, be blocked from accessing content that violates French law. (IP addresses are not a perfect mechanism for blocking access because a sophisticated user can configure a computer to utilize an IP address from a different geographic area.)

15. 169 F. Supp. 2d 1181 (N.D. Cal. 2001), *rev'd*, No. 01-17424 (9th Cir. Aug. 23, 2004).

16. *Id*., slip op. at 11933 (footnote omitted). The issue of whether LICRA and UEJF "wrongfully" sought to invoke jurisdiction arose not because of the Ninth Circuit's application of traditional U.S. Supreme Court cases on jurisdiction, including *Calder v. Jones*, 465 U.S. 783 (1984), but by a gloss applied to the *Calder* test by an earlier Ninth Circuit case, *Bancroft & Masters, Inc. v. Augusta Nat'l Inc.*, 223 F.3d 1082 (9th Cir. 2000). In that case, the Ninth Circuit noted that it would be overinclusive to hold that *Calder* would apply to any targeting, however minor, of the forum state by the defendant. Rather, it held, *Calder* would be satisfied when "the defendant is alleged to have engaged in *wrongful* conduct targeted at a plaintiff whom the defendant knows to be a resident of the forum state." *Id*. at 1087 (emphasis added).

17. See Kettmann, *German Hate Law: No Denying It* (http://www.wired.com/news/politics/0,1283,40669,00.html) and Weisman, *Germany Bans Foreign Web site for Nazi Content* (www.newsfactor.com/perl/story/6063.html). German law contains several provisions that address speech offenses. A section on "incitement of the people" criminalizes incitement to violence by appeals to racial or ethnic hatred. A section on "incitement to racial hatred" criminalizes the display of "documents which incite racial hatred" or depict violence against humanity in a positive light. A section on "slander on confessions, religious groups and association of world views" criminalizes slandering the views of religious groups in an attempt to breach the peace. Another provision includes a prohibition against the Auschwitlfüge, the denial of the Holocaust, and denigrating the memory of the dead.

18. See Corte di Cassazione, closed sez., 27 deC. 2000, n.4741, V (English translation available at http://www.cdt.org/speech/international/001227italiandecision.pdf/). The names of the complainant or the Web sites attempted to be prosecuted are not published in the court's decision.

19. *Berezovsky v. Michaels*, [2000] E.M.L.R. 643 (H.L. 2000).

20. http://www.curia.eu.int/common/recdoc/convention/en/c-textes/brux-idx.htm/.Jurisdiction .Enforcement.Judgments.Civil.Commercial.Matters.Convention.Brussels.1968.html.

21. http://www.rome-convention.org/instruments/i_conv_orig_en.htm/.

22. On November 3, 1998, the Consumer Affairs Council of Ministers adopted a resolution on consumer protection in the Information society. See http://europa.eu.int/comm/dg24/library/legislation/ap/ap01_en.html/.

23. See http://www.europa.eu.int/comm./justice_home/unit/civil/consultation/index_en.htm/, consultation for a Preliminary Draft Proposal for a Council Regulation.

24. United Kingdom House of Lords, European Union Committee, *The Rome II Regulation, Report with Evidence* [2004] 8th Report of Session 2003-04 at paras. 117-30.

References

Bickel, Alexander. 1976. *The morality of consent*. New Haven, CT: Yale University Press.

Emerson, Thomas I. 1970. *The system of freedom of expression*. New York: Vintage Books.

Geist, Michael. 2003. Cyberlaw 2.0. *Boston College Law Review* 44:359-98.

Media Law Resource Center. 2002. Comments to the European Commission. http://www.europa.eu.int/comm/justice_home/unit/civil/consultation/contributions/mlrc_en.pdf (accessed July 11, 2005).

Robertson, Geoffrey. 2002. Mugabe versus the Internet. *The Guardian*, June 17. http://www.guardian.co.uk/Archive/Article/0,4273,4435071,00.html (accessed July 11, 2005).

Werley, B. P. 2004. Aussie rules: Universal jurisdiction over Internet defamation. *Temple International and Comparative Law Journal* 18:199-232.

Wolfenson, James D. 1999. Voices of the poor. *Washington Post*, November 10, p. A 39.

Divided Nations: The Paradox of National Protection

By

FRANCIS M. DENG

Internal displacement, which in many cases leads to refuge across international borders, has emerged as one of the major crises confronting the world today. The assumption, clearly erroneous, is that unlike refugees, who have lost the protection of their own governments by crossing international borders, the internally displaced remain under the protection of their national governments. In most cases, these same governments are actually the cause of their displacement, and worse—they neglect and even persecute them. This article aims to develop a new international response to the global crisis of internal displacement in acutely divided nations. It suggests the problem is more than a humanitarian and human rights issue; the underlying causes have much to do with gross inequities in the shaping and sharing of values and the gross discrimination and marginalization of certain groups. Citizenship becomes largely of paper value. The crisis is ultimately a challenge of nation building.

Keywords: United Nations; displaced people; state responsibility; humanitarian crises

Overview of the Problem

The United Nations Millennium Declaration of September 8, 2000, states that in addition to their separate responsibilities to their individual societies, the heads of state and government recognize that they have a collective responsibility to uphold the principles of human dignity, equality, and equity at the global level. This is explicitly stated as entailing a duty to all the world's people, especially the most vulnerable, and in particular, children. The declaration elaborates on this theme by stating, "We will spare

Francis M. Deng is director of the Center for Displacement Studies at the School of Advanced International Studies (SAIS) and research professor of international law, politics, and society at Johns Hopkins University. He serves as representative of the UN secretary-general on internally displaced persons and is a nonresident senior fellow at the Brookings Institution. He served as the ambassador of Sudan to Canada, the Scandinavian countries, and the United States as well as Sudan's minister of state for Foreign Affairs.

DOI: 10.1177/0002716205283019

no effort to ensure that children and all civilian populations that suffer dispropor-tionately the consequences of national disasters, genocide, armed conflicts and other humanitarian emergencies are given every assistance and protection so that they can resume normal life as soon as possible." The tension between interna-tional protection of the vulnerable and respect for the sovereignty of the states comes across strikingly in the declaration, as the heads of state and government rededicate themselves "to support all efforts to uphold the sovereign equality of all states, respect for their territorial integrity and political independence . . . non interference in the internal affairs of states."[1] This tension is perhaps unavoidable. If progress is to be made in promoting the universal principles of human dignity and providing a comprehensive system of protection for all, however, this paradox must be confronted and openly addressed.

The paradox is that most of the member states of the United Nations are in vary-ing degrees divided nations, suffering from acute national identity crisis as both cause and effect, and a factor in the official response to humanitarian crises. The attention of the international community tends to be focused on the humanitarian dimension, specifically the need for providing assistance and, to a lesser extent, respect for human rights. If humanitarian and human rights principles were holis-tically interpreted and implemented, they could provide a comprehensive system of protection. Oftentimes, however, the application of these principles falls short of the objectives and certainly do not address the underlying causes of the conflicts and the humanitarian crises.

This article will build largely on the experience of the author with the plight of those forcefully displaced within their national borders by armed conflicts, com-munal violence, egregious violations of human rights, and other human-made or natural disasters.[2] Most of the victims are women, children, and the elderly.[3] The internally displaced should not, however, be viewed as an isolated category but should, instead, be seen as a microcosm of the wider civilian population that is affected by internal wars.[4]

The Internally Displaced: A Sample of the Vulnerable

Some 25 million people in more than fifty countries are internally displaced per-sons (IDPs), denied safety and dignity and deprived of the essentials of life, includ-ing shelter, food, medicine, education, community, and a resource base for self-reliant livelihood.[5] The internally displaced are paradoxically assumed to be under the care of their own governments, despite the fact that their displacement is often caused by the same state authorities.

NOTE: The author was the representative of the UN secretary-general on Internally Displaced Persons from 1992 to 2004. This article builds largely on the experience of his mandate.

The principle of state responsibility to guarantee the protection and general welfare of its citizens and all those under state jurisdiction poses practical problems in countries experiencing sharp cleavages with differentiated identities based on race, ethnicity, religion, language, or culture. The worst affected are minority or marginalized groups in conflict with the dominant group. Instead of being protected and assisted as citizens, members of these groups tend to be identified as part of the enemy, neglected and even persecuted. For them, citizenship becomes of little more than paper value. Disconnected from the enjoyment of the rights normally associated with the dignity of being a citizen, their marginalization becomes tantamount to statelessness.

Identity Cleavages and Vacuums of Responsibility

In some cases the differences involved are visible and clearly marked, but in many situations the differences are more subjective than a reflection of objective factors. Even then, the less visible the differences, the more they tend to be asserted to remove any ambiguities that might challenge the integrity of self-perception.

Whether the differences are apparent or perceived, what generates conflict is not merely the differences but their implications in terms of participation in the shaping and sharing of political power, national wealth, social services, development opportunities, and the overall sense of belonging with pride and dignity.[6] In most cases, identity differences imply stratification and discrimination. Internal conflicts are, in essence, a desperate reaction to injustice, real or perceived, which in turn provokes ruthless counterinsurgency that only aggravates the crisis. The innocent civilian populations become the victims of these internal wars. As they cannot depend on their national authorities, they must look to the international community to fill the vacuum of responsibility.

The Challenge of International Response

Identity conflicts involve not only competition over power and material resources but also a contest for the soul of the nation. So divided are the parties that their perceptions of the conflict become a zero-sum game that, in some cases, tend to make the conflict genocidal. Third-party involvement becomes essential to both addressing the immediate humanitarian crises and mediating the conflict. Whatever the rights and wrongs, saving face is an important aspect of mediation. And yet, the mediator cannot be neutral on the rights and wrongs involved. Any constructive resolution must envisage a normative framework that promotes justice and respects diversity, while also exploring a common ground for national unity. However, governments intent on preserving the status quo are likely to resist outside involvement by invoking sovereignty as a barricade against international involvement.

Postulating Sovereignty as Responsibility

The principle of national sovereignty is still the cornerstone of international relations, despite significant modifications in its application. While international humanitarian and human rights instruments offer legally binding bases for international protection and assistance to needy populations within state borders, those people are, for the most part, still left to national authorities for their security and general welfare.

A pragmatic basis for dialogue is to postulate sovereignty positively as a concept of state responsibility to protect and assist its citizens in need. Where lack or inadequacy of resources and operational capacities necessitates, they are expected to invite or at least welcome international assistance to complement their efforts.[7] An implicit assumption of accountability lies behind the concept of responsibility. This means that where the needs of sizeable populations are unmet under the exercise of sovereignty, and large numbers suffer extreme deprivation and are threatened with death, humanitarian intervention becomes imperative. The best guarantee for sovereignty is therefore for states to discharge minimum standards of responsibility, if need be with international cooperation.

The normative principle of sovereignty as responsibility has recently been strengthened and mainstreamed by the Canadian-sponsored Commission on Intervention and State Sovereignty, whose report, "The Responsibility to Protect," has received considerable international attention.[8] But the concept needs to be expounded, sharpened, and given teeth for effective application. How that can be done is an open but challenging question. Among the core questions that will continue to engage the international community are what precisely the concept of protection entails and who is best equipped to provide it. Much work is already done and still being done to respond to these questions. Both substantively and operationally, international efforts have focused on "soft" protection entailing monitoring and reporting of human rights violations. The challenge is how to continue to improve the provision of "hard" protection, to ensure the safety and dignity of the civilian population. In situations where the United Nations has undertaken peacekeeping operations, "hard" protection would entail mandating, training, and equipping the peacekeepers and civilian police to safeguard the security of the civilians in conflict situations. Experience so far indicates that there is still a wide gap between what ought to be done and what is being done. Much of whatever protection is provided remains "soft," and sovereignty continues to be an obstacle to "hard" protection.

Protection of the Internally Displaced

The post–cold war era has witnessed the proliferation of internal conflicts, pitting governments against insurgency groups. At the same time, human rights and humanitarian concerns began to challenge strategic national interest as a driving force in international politics. Concomitantly, the rigid observances of sovereignty as a barricade against international monitoring and scrutiny began to fall under pressure. The narrow view of sovereignty became increasingly challenged as the media and nongovernmental organizations exposed the plight of millions who fell victim to the new types of wars that were fought internally, with devastating loss of lives, egregious violations of human rights, and dehumanization of the civilian populations. It was under these emerging circumstances that the crisis of internal displacement began to surface on the international scene.[9]

The internally displaced are paradoxically assumed to be under the care of their own governments, despite the fact that their displacement is often caused by the same state authorities.

Since the Commission on Human Rights created a mechanism for protecting and assisting the internally displaced and the secretary-general appointed a Representative on Internally Displaced Persons, work on the mandate has been carried out in a number of interconnected areas: raising the level of awareness of the crisis; developing an appropriate normative framework for protection and assistance; fostering effective international and regional institutional arrangements; focusing attention on specific situations through country missions involving advocacy and constructive dialogue with all concerned; reinforcing and building regional, national, and local capacities for effective response; and undertaking policy and action-oriented research to broaden and deepen understanding of the problem in its various dimensions. While all these areas of activity are important to the cause, the development of normative and institutional frameworks and engagement in dialogue with governments are critical to an effective international response to the challenge.

A set of Guiding Principles on Internal Displacement has been developed based on restating existing human rights and humanitarian law and covering all phases of internal displacement[10] from prevention of arbitrary displacement; to protection and assistance during displacement; to finding durable solutions that lead to return in safety and dignity, alternative resettlement, and reintegration and self-sustaining development. The Principles apply equally to both states and nonstate actors with control over displaced persons. In the short time since their presentation to the commission in 1998, the Principles have gained remarkable recognition internationally, regionally, and most important, at the national level. Indeed, a number of governments have adopted policies and/or laws based at least in part upon the Guiding Principles, and several other states are considering plans for legislation and policies based on the Principles. Some rebel movements have also begun to make active use of the Principles in developing policies and strategies of response to the displacement crisis in the areas under their control. The Principles have also been a source of empowerment to the internally displaced, who are entitled to demand protection and assistance from their governments and others exercising control over them, as a matter of right, rather than humanitarian favor.[11]

While the growing acceptance of the Guiding Principles is encouraging, the development of effective institutional mechanisms for protecting and assisting the internally displaced is also crucially important. At the inception of the commission's mandate on the issue, three options were presented for response: creation of a new agency for the internally displaced; the designation of an existing agency, such as the United Nations High Commissioner for Refugees (UNHCR), to assume full responsibility; and collaboration among all the existing agencies. To date, the preferred response has been the "collaborative approach," according to which existing human rights, humanitarian, and development agencies and organizations work collectively to address the needs of the internally displaced within their respective mandates and with regard to their comparative advantages. Important steps have been taken to solidify this approach, including the designation of resident and humanitarian coordinators as officials charged with ensuring coordination of assistance to, and protection of, the internally displaced at the country level, the designation of the emergency relief coordinator (ERC) who chairs the Inter-Agency Standing Committee (IASC) as the focal point for issues of internal displacement at the headquarters level, and the creation of the Office for the Coordination of Humanitarian Affairs (OCHA) IDP Unit recently upgraded to a division to assist the ERC in his task.[12] The prevailing view now is that virtually every organization and every field-worker has a protection role to play.

Nevertheless, coordination remains problematic and challenging; many IDPs continue to fall through institutional cracks, leaving their pressing protection and assistance needs unmet. Important practical questions still need to be answered: How are responsibilities assigned? What are the most effective ways to address protection? How does the system ensure that appropriate accountability mechanisms are in place? In what way should the secretary-general exercise his leadership to reinforce the collaborative approach? How can the Security Council be more effective in enforcing the principle of sovereignty as responsibility without bias or favor based on particular national interests or concerns of its members, especially the permanent five? On a positive note, the Security Council has in recent years recognized the need to address the lack of effective protection for civilians in armed conflict, including IDPs. It has recognized that situations of internal displacement can constitute a threat to international peace and security and has specifically requested that situations where IDPs are under threat of harassment and harm be brought to its attention.

Conclusion: The Persistent
Challenge and a Call for Action

Since the Millennium Declaration was adopted by heads of state and government in September 2000, significant developments have taken place in the world. The cause of peace has progressed in a number of countries. Humanitarian response to crises continues to receive focused attention, and millions of people around the world are receiving assistance and a degree of international protection. But conflicts persist in many parts of the world. The statistics of those forcefully displaced within the borders of their countries and therefore within the war zone, have remained at 25 million. Overwhelmingly, these vulnerable people are women, children, and the elderly. Allegations of genocide continue to challenge the slogan of "never again."

There are, of course, normative and operational constraints on what the United Nations can do to provide effective and comprehensive protection and assistance, where sovereignty continues to be used as a barricade against effective action. The international community is urgently called upon to resolve the tension between the global responsibility to assist and protect "all the world's people, especially the most vulnerable," and the restrictive interpretation of sovereignty, compounded by the vacuums of responsibility resulting from acute crises of national identity in divided nations. Based on the author's experience with the internally displaced, several lines of action can be proposed:

First, the principle of sovereignty as responsibility, now advanced by the report of the Commission on Intervention and State Sovereignty, "The Responsibility to Protect" should be condensed into a forceful statement of a fundamental norm to be endorsed by the General Assembly and the Security Council.

Second, the reports of the human rights mechanisms should receive executive support beyond being presented to the commission and "softly" acted upon. The backing of the high commissioner for human rights, the ERC, the undersecretary for political affairs, and the secretary-general, in their dialogue with governments, would reinforce and enhance the standing and influence of these reports and their recommendations.

Third, while binding instruments have legal authority, the invocation of values and moral principles in the dialogue with governments, based on the fundamental norm of sovereignty as responsibility, is likely to provoke less defensiveness and generate a morally compelling common ground on what is noble and humane.

Fourth, since the issues of protecting and assisting vulnerable people in conflict situations, marked by crises of national identity, involve not only humanitarian and human rights issues, but also security and political concerns that are relevant to the challenges of nation building, the Inter-Agency Standing Committee, the core body for the collaborative approach, should include in its membership all the relevant bodies of the UN system, such as the Department of Peacekeeping Operations and the Department for Political Affairs.

Fifth, those whose mandates are relevant to the protection of the vulnerable, such as the representative of the secretary-general on the human rights of IDPs, should be given access to address the Security Council, at least in situations where the risks to the populations concerned are high.

Finally, it is crucial to break through the barriers of sovereignty and stipulate the concept positively as entailing responsibility with accountability. While this article does not provide an answer on how that can be effectively achieved, it has tried to draw the attention to the urgent need to address the crises of divided nations. The normative principles for action are in place; they only need to be effectively acted upon.

Notes

1. United Nations, *The Millennium Declaration* (New York: United Nations Secretariat, 2000).

2. In 1994, Roberta Cohen and I cofounded and codirected The Brookings Project on Internal Displacement to assist my mandate with research and outreach activities, including collaboration with regional organizations and nongovernmental organizations. When I left Brookings in 2002 to join the City University of New York Graduate Center and then to the Johns Hopkins University School of Advanced International Studies (SAIS) the Project changed names to reflect the Brookings collaboration with these institutions. In 2004, when Professor Walter Kalin of Bern University in Switzerland, the Project became Brookings-Bern Project on Internal Displacement.

3. See Roberta Cohen, "Protecting Internally Displaced Women and Children," in Norwegian Refugee Council, *Rights Have No Borders*, Worldwide Internal Displacement, 63-74 (1998).

4. For a detailed overview of the crisis of internal displacement, see Roberta Cohen and Francis M. Deng, *Masses in Flight: The Global Crisis of Internal Displacement*, and *The Forsaken People: Case Studies of the Internally Displaced* (Washington DC: Brookings Institution, 1998). See also Francis M. Deng, *Protecting the Dispossessed: A Challenge for the International Community*, (Washington DC: Brookings Institution, 1993) and David Korn, *Exodus Within Borders: An Introduction to the Crisis of Internal Displacement*, 1999. Other publications on the global crisis of internal displacement include: Norwegian Refugee Council Global IDP Project, *Rights Have No Borders: Worldwide Internal Displacement*, (1998). See also Norwegian Refugee Council, Global IDP Project, *Internally Displaced Persons: A Global Survey*, Second Edition (London, Earthscan, 2002).

5. Initially, the working definition of the United Nations described internally displaced persons as "persons who have been forced to flee their homes suddenly or unexpectedly in large numbers, as a result of armed conflict, internal strife, systematic violations of human rights or natural or manmade disasters, and who are within the territory of their country." Analytical Report of the Secretary General on Internally Displaced Persons, U.N. Doc. E/CN.4/1992.23 (1992). For a preliminary discussion of definitional issues on the basis of this definition see Report of the Representative of the Secretary General on Internally Displaced Persons, U.N. ESCOR, 51 Sess., Agenda item 11(d) 116-27, U.N. Doc. E/CN.4/1995/50 (1995). Further points for consideration and the rational for refining the definition appear in Cohen and Deng, *Masses in Flight*, p. 10. The present definition in The Guiding Principles on Internal Displacement, Principle 2, is: a persons or group of persons who have been forced or obliged to flee or to leave their homes or places of habitual residence in particular as a result of, or to avoid the effects of, armed conflict, situations of generalized violence, violations of human rights, or natural or human-made disasters and who have not crossed internationally-recognized State border."

6. See Crawford Young, *The Politics of Cultural Pluralism* (Madison: University of Wisconsin Press, 1970); Frederick Barth, ed., *Ethnic Groups and Boundaries: The Social Organization of Culture Differences* (Boston: Little, Brown, 1969); and Francis M. Deng and I. William Zartman, eds., *Conflict Resolution in Africa* (Washington DC: Brookings Institution, 1991). See, in particular, the chapters by Ted Gurr, Donald Rothchild, Otieno Odhiambo, I. William Zartman, Crawford Young, and Stephen John Stedman. See also Joseph V. Montville (ed.), *Conflict and Peacemaking in Mulitethnic Societies* (Washington DC: Heath, 1991).

7. For the initial development of the concept in the Brookings Africa Program which I founded and directed from 1998 until 2001, see Francis M. Deng et al., *Sovereignty as Responsibility: Conflict Management in Africa* (Washington DC: The Brookings Institution, 1991) and Francis M. Deng and Terrence Lyons (eds.), *African Reckoning: A Quest for Good Governance* (Washington DC: Brookings Institution, 1998).

8. The International Commission on Intervention and State Responsibility, *The Responsibility to Protect, Report of the International Commission on Intervention and State Sovereignty 2001*. See also Brookings Institution-University of Bern Project on Internal Displacement, *Addressing Internal Displacement: A Framework for National Responsibility*, 2005; and Edward J. Keller and Donald Rothchild, eds., *Africa in the New State Sovereignty and Regional Security* (Boulder, CO: Lynne Reiner, 1996).

9. When internally displaced persons were first counted in 1982, it was estimated that there were 1.2 million IDPs. By 1992, when the issue was considered by the Commission on Human Rights, the numbers had increased to between 20 and 24 million. With the end of the Cold War, super power rivalry ended and Western governments geopolitical advantage in accepting refugees began to wane, which led to the desire to find solutions that would keep potential refugees within their own borders. Today, the number of IDPs in estimated at 24 million in about 50 countries. Norwegian Refugee Council, Global IDP Project, 2004.

10. Work on the Guiding Principles began with the compilation of all existing standards in human rights law, humanitarian law, and analogous refugee law that were pertinent to the protection of IDPs. This resulted in *Compilation and Analysis: Report of the Representative of the Secretary-General*, U.N. Doc. E/CN.4/1996 add 2 (1996), submitted pursuant to the Commission on Human Rights resolution 1995/57. See also Report of the Representative of the Secretary-General on Legal Aspects Relating to the Protection Against Arbitrary Displacement, UN.ESCOR, 54th Sess., Agenda item 9(d), U.N. Doc. E/CN.4/1998/53/add.1 and Report of the Representative of the Secretary-General on the Guiding Principles on Internal Displacement, U.N. Commission on Human Rights, 54th Sess., Agenda item 9(d) U.N. Doc. E/CN.4/1998/53/Add.2 (1998). *The Guiding Principles* were finalized in January, 1998. For a comprehensive review of how the Guiding Principles were developed, see Simon Bagshaw, *Developing the Guiding Principles on Internal Displacement: The Role of a Global Public Policy Network*, available at www.globalpublicpolicy.net.

11. For responses to *The Guiding Principles* within the U.N. see *Strengthening of Coordination of Emergency Humanitarian Assistance of the United Nations*, U.N. Doc. A/53/139-E/67 (1998); Report of the Secretary-General to the Security Council, 409 1st mtg. U.N., U.N. Doc. SC/RES, 1286 (2000); and G.A. Res.167, U.N., GAOR, 54th Sess. U.N. Doc. A/RES/54/167 (2000); For a study of the sources of the law that guided the development of *The Guiding Principles on Internal Displacement: Annotations* (Washington DC: American Society of International Law and the Brookings Project on Internal Displacement, 2000). For other publications on *The Guiding Principles* see Susan Forbes Martin, *The Handbook for Applying the Guiding Principles*, Brookings Project on Internal Displacement and the Office for the Coordination of Humanitarian Affairs (OCHA) 2000, available at http://www.reliefweb.int/rw/lib.nsf/db900SID/LGEL-5CTJBU?OpenDocument, and *Manual on Field Practice in Internal Displacement*, Inter-Agency Standing Committee Policy Paper Series No.1, Office for the Coordination of Humanitarian Affairs (OCHA. For reports on how NGOs around the world have made use of the *Guiding Principles*, see Brookings Institution, Brookings Project on Internal Displacement, *Report of the International Colloquy on the Guiding Principles on Internal Displacement* (2000).

12. See the report of the Secretary-General Kofi Annan, *Renewing the United Nations: A Program for Reform*, U.N. Doc. A/51/950 (1997); The Inter-Agency Standing Committee policy paper, *Protection of Internally Displaced Persons*, 1999, at http:/www.idpproject.org; and at the same website, the Inter-Agency Standing Committee, *Supplementary Guide to Humanitarian Resident Coordinators on Their Responsibilities in Relation to Internally Displaced Persons.*

Views on the Ground: The Local Perception of International Criminal Tribunals in the Former Yugoslavia and Sierra Leone

By
DONNA E. ARZT

If international criminal courts are to achieve their aims—one of which is to contribute to the consolidation of democracy and the triumph of the rule of law over the instinct for revenge after prolonged periods of communal violence—perception of their legitimacy by the local population is a crucial factor. After laying out and comparing the basic features of the International Criminal Tribunal for the former Yugoslavia and the Special Court for Sierra Leone as to their respective origins, objectives, and programs of outreach, the article examines local reception from three standpoints: perceptions of overall legitimacy, perceptions of tribunal impartiality, and the effect of public perceptions of the tribunals on the respective countries' reconciliation process.

Keywords: international criminal tribunals; war crimes; Yugoslavia; Sierra Leone

Since 1993, a revolution in public international law has taken place through the creation of seven international criminal tribunals to prosecute war criminals.[1] It had taken forty-eight years since the Nuremberg and Tokyo tribunals were in operation for the international community to begin creating new institutions to hold individuals criminally responsible for wartime atrocities committed by them or under their command. The area of law that the tribunals apply, known as international criminal law, has grown from the domain of a handful of scholars[2] during the cold war era to a vast literature, along with an exponentially expanding jurisprudence, today.

Donna E. Arzt is Dean's Distinguished Research Scholar at Syracuse University College of Law. In her capacity as director of the school's Center for Global Law and Practice, she codirects the Sierra Leone Project, a team of students and faculty that prepares research memos at the request of the Office of the Prosecutor (OTP) of the Special Court for Sierra Leone. She worked for the OTP in Freetown, Sierra Leone, during the summer of 2003, and among other courses in the field of public international law, she teaches a seminar in international criminal law. Research assistance for this article was provided in part by Syracuse law students Jennifer Nash Liu and Alan Pereira.

DOI: 10.1177/0002716205281443

How have the new tribunals been received by the local populations that they have been created for? How have the resident constituencies perceived the legitimacy, impartiality, and objectives of the tribunals? These questions have rarely been formally studied in any of the seven settings.[3] Yet if international criminal courts are to achieve their aims—one of which is to contribute to the consolidation of democracy and the triumph of the rule of law over the instinct for revenge after prolonged periods of communal violence—perception of their legitimacy by the local population is a crucial factor. Indeed, the "building of state institutions and capacity, especially in the rule of law sector," has been identified as a vital aspect of postconflict peace building by the UN Secretary General's High-Level Panel on Threats, Challenges and Change (*A More Secure World* 2004, 5). These tribunals must also have popular credibility to serve as effective deterrents to future war crimes. Indeed, in a joint statement, the prosecutors of four of the international criminal tribunals have stated, "Only when a culture of accountability has replaced the culture of impunity can the diverse people of the world live and prosper together in peace" (Prosecutors 2004).

This article will examine popular reactions to the first post-Nuremberg tribunal, the International Criminal Tribunal for the Former Yugoslavia (ICTY), along with local responses to one of the newer "hybrid" or "internationalized" tribunals, the Special Court for Sierra Leone (SCSL).[4] Assuming that public perceptions affect cultural change, these data can be used to tentatively assess the tribunals' impact or legacies regarding the rule of law and democratization in the respective countries. To the extent that the local reception of international criminal tribunals in regions as diverse as the Balkans and West Africa is a rough gauge of the prospects for reception of the permanent International Criminal Court (ICC), which will have complementary jurisdiction to that of national courts[5] in the ninety-nine countries that have now become ICC members,[6] this study may have wider value. It may also help illumine why some transitional governments, such as in Iraq, decide to forego international assistance and instead to prosecute their former regime's leadership largely on their own.

After laying out and comparing the basic features of the ICTY and SCSL as to their respective origins, objectives, and programs of outreach, this article will examine local reception from three standpoints: perceptions of overall legitimacy, perceptions of tribunal impartiality, and the effect of public perceptions of the tribunals on the respective countries' reconciliation process.

Origins, Objectives, Outreach

Institutional overviews

It is useful to first appreciate some of the special characteristics of each tribunal: the ICTY was created in 1993 by a mandatory resolution of the UN Security Council, in the face of opposition by all the warring countries of the former Yugoslavia, whereas the SCSL was established by a 2002 treaty between the United Nations and the government of Sierra Leone, at the latter's invitation.[7] The ICTY is located in The Hague, nine hundred miles outside of the Balkans, making it physically and psychologically remote to the population of the former Yugoslavia. By contrast, the

---

The underlying nature of the conflicts was sufficiently dissimilar. . . . Nevertheless, the [International Criminal Tribunal for the Former Yugoslavia and the Special Court for Sierra Leone] share similar objectives for their respective operations.

SCSL is situated within Sierra Leone's capital, which allows it to contribute to the country's reconciliation process but also poses security risks, especially for witnesses. Although the subject matter jurisdiction of the two tribunals overlap to a great extent, regarding war crimes, crimes against humanity, and violations of the Geneva Conventions—with some specific deviations[8]—and both have primacy but concurrent jurisdiction with the respective national courts, the SCSL is explicitly limited to prosecuting "persons who bear *the greatest responsibility* [italics added] for serious violations of international humanitarian law" (Special Court Statute, art. 1). Thus, only thirteen indictments have been issued in the Special Court's three and a half years of operation, with nine persons currently on trial, compared to 107 who have appeared in proceedings before the ICTY since 1993, in addition to 18 still at large.[9]

The underlying nature of the conflicts was sufficiently dissimilar: in the former Yugoslavia, the war was ethnically motivated and territorial; in Sierra Leone, it was primarily economic and political. While Yugoslavia broke into three separate sovereignties, secessionism was not a condition in Sierra Leone's civil war. Nevertheless, the two institutions share similar objectives for their respective operations. The ICTY mission is said to be fourfold: (1) to bring to justice persons allegedly responsible for serious violations of international humanitarian law, (2) to render justice to the victims, (3) to deter further crimes, and (4) to contribute to the restoration of peace by promoting reconciliation in the former Yugoslavia (ICTY n.d.-b). Similarly, as aspirations for the SCSL have expressed,

It is hoped that the Special Court will contribute to revitalizing Sierra Leoneans' belief in the rule of law—that, in the face of future crimes, they will turn to the judicial system for recourse instead of either seeking revenge or fatalistically accepting what happened as "the way it is." This is necessary to meaningfully combat the culture of impunity that has prevailed in Sierra Leone, to build respect for the rule of law, and to bring a sense of justice for the horrific crimes committed. (Human Rights Watch [HRW] 2004, 32)

Equally important, the UN Security Council wanted the Special Court to address the "negative impact of the security situation on the administration of justice in Sierra Leone" and to assist "in strengthening the judicial system," which had ceased to function due to the war (UN Security Council 2000).

Each tribunal has produced landmark rulings that have contributed to the developing jurisprudence of international criminal law. As the first international tribunal since the Nuremburg and Tokyo tribunals of the 1940s to hold individuals responsible for violations of international law, the ICTY has had numerous achievements, including the following:

- It has expanded upon the legal elements of the crime of grave breaches of the Geneva Conventions of 1949 by further defining the test of overall control, identifying the existence of an international armed conflict, and also the extended and exact definition of protected persons under the Conventions.
- It has narrowed the differences that are perceived between the laws or customs of war applicable in internal and in international conflicts, thus approaching both standards for the protection of individuals.
- It has made significant advances in international humanitarian law pertaining to the legal treatment and punishment of sexual violence in wartime.
- It has identified and applied the modern doctrine of criminal responsibility of superiors, so-called command responsibility, clarifying that a formal superior-subordinate relationship is *not* necessarily required for criminal responsibility. (ICTY n.d.-a)

In its short history, the SCSL has also had its share of noteworthy decisions. After the indictment of Charles Taylor while he was president of Liberia and his subsequent exile in Nigeria, the Special Court held that heads of state are not immune from prosecution before an international criminal tribunal or court (SCSL Appeals Chamber 2004a). The SCSL has also ruled that it has jurisdiction to try the recruitment or use of children under the age of fifteen as soldiers because it was a crime under international law even before the court's creation and during the entire period covered by its authority (SCSL Appeals Chamber 2004b).[10] It is also the first international criminal tribunal to have established a permanent Defense Office to give legal representation to arrestees before they could acquire their own counsel.

The ICTY has been ordered by the Security Council to conclude all its open trials by 2007 and all appeals by 2010 (UN Security Council 2003). The SCSL is slated to cease operations even sooner, just four years after its commencement in 2002.[11] In anticipation of these deadlines, the ICTY has begun to accept plea bargains in exchange for defendant cooperation, refer cases to national war crimes courts, and make other procedural adjustments (ICTY President 2005). The SCSL has also begun planning for what will happen after its three present trials finish their appeals (Kendall and Staggs 2005, 35).

Outreach efforts

The ICTY proceedings have generally been broadcast by radio in the former Yugoslavia, while selected trials—notably that of Slobodan Milosevic—have also been televised there. In its early years, ICTY personnel were focused on the tasks of institution building and did not pay much attention to the continual fanning of

---

It is one thing for the tribunals to articulate their own objectives and achievements but quite another to ask whether these have been popularly understood.

---

the flames of ethnic hatred by regional leaders and media, who were simultaneously spewing paranoid rhetoric against the tribunal itself. In 1999, more than five years into its operation, the ICTY finally established an Outreach Programme to counter the widespread propaganda against it in the region, particularly in Belgrade, by promoting the tribunal's impartiality and independence. Using live audio and video Web broadcasts in the Bosnian, Croatian, and Serbian languages; press releases to regional media, television interviews; and an array of roundtables, training sessions, and conferences with national officials, nongovernmental organization (NGO) representatives, and in particular, victims groups (McDonald 2004, 15-22). As explained by Judge Gabrielle Kirk McDonald, former presiding judge of the ICTY, "The people for whom the Tribunal was established must have access to the judgments and must be educated about its procedures and processes. They must 'buy into' the Tribunal if it is to help achieve a lasting peace and lay the groundwork for reconciliation" (McDonald 2004, 22).

Obviously learning the lesson of the ICTY's initial neglect of its constituency, the SCSL prioritized an outreach program from its first days to educate the population about the court's mission and procedures and to invite local civil society groups to offer their views on developments. Seventeen staff members operate fourteen district offices throughout the country (International Center for Transitional Justice [ICTJ] 2004, 18). Outreach activities have included town hall meetings at the district and chiefdom level; sessions with targeted groups such as the police, the army, the bar association, journalists, victims groups, and students at every level; the creation of brochures and posters (some using pictorial materials, for a largely illiterate population, as well as others in braille); and radio and video programs in the country's four main languages (President of the SCSL 2004, 26-27; HRW 2004, 34).

The Special Court's Public Affairs Unit, in addition to issuing frequent press releases, provides weekly audio and video trial summaries in English and Krio; however, local media find the unit to be mainly concerned with the foreign press (Gberie 2003, 647). Perhaps most significant, the chief prosecutor has taken the unusual step of making occasional public statements on contentious prosecution strategies, such as not to indict child soldiers and not to subpoena testimony from the Truth and Reconciliation Commission (TRC) (ICTJ 2004, 5; Kendall and Staggs 2005, 32-34).

The value of outreach is demonstrated by the study of ex-combatant knowledge and views concerning the SCSL and the Sierra Leone TRC before and after "sensitization sessions" conducted by a Freetown-based NGO. Support for and understanding of the Special Court greatly increased through sensitization: before the sessions, 59 percent of ex-combatants said they support the court, whereas this number grew to 79 percent postsensitization. Similarly, after sensitization, 63 percent of female ex-combatants, up from 14 percent, expressed willingness to testify before the court, probably due to increased confidence in the court's witness protection effectiveness. As the study's authors note,

> Ex-combatants need the Truth and Reconciliation Commission (TRC) and the Special Court (SC) to help them make sense of the war and reintegrate and reconcile with their communities. . . . Anyone wanting to shape the relationship between ex-combatants and the accountability institutions in a way that promotes reconciliation, justice and peace in Sierra Leone must understand what ex-combatants know of, fear about and expect from the TRC and the SC. (Post-conflict Reintegration Initiative for Development and Empowerment [PRIDE] 2002, 16, 2)

Popular Reception

It is one thing for the tribunals to articulate their own objectives and achievements but quite another to ask whether these have been popularly understood. Evidence as to this must be gleaned from a variety of indirect and incomplete sources, as very little reliable data on popular opinion have been gathered systematically in either setting. Moreover, in both contexts, it will be necessary to distinguish between various constituency groups, including victims, former combatants (who can belong to different factions), witnesses to atrocities, indigenous NGO activists, local journalists and other professionals, as well as government and opposition leaders—not to mention the different nationalities in the former Yugoslavia. Nevertheless, both there and in Sierra Leone, the extent of the devastations was so vast that virtually everyone is a "survivor" of some sort.

Perceptions of tribunal legitimacy

"Just because an institution is international," noted a panelist at a conference to assess whether international war crimes trials are making a difference, "does not mean that local populations necessarily think it's better or that it has enhanced moral authority to punish wrongdoing in the place in question" (Drumbl 2004, 32). The objectives of the international community in establishing the tribunals do not automatically translate into popular acceptance, not only when, as with the ICTY, the process was imposed "top-down." Naturally, the perception of the tribunal among Bosnian Muslims has always been much more positive than among Serbs or Croats in the region.

Local victim groups often express bitterness when they learn of [International Criminal Tribunal for the Former Yugoslavia] plea bargains—which are unheard of in their national legal systems—for atrocities committed by their former tormentors.

Public opinion surveys were conducted in Serbia between December 2000 (a few months after Milosevic resigned) and July 2003.[12] More than 72 percent of those polled in December 2000 thought the "Hague Tribunal" threatened the safety of Serbs, more than any other international institution besides NATO; this percentage gradually lowered to 40 percent in May 2003 (while the perceived threat of NATO was reduced to 39 percent). In July 2003, 59 percent of the 1,545 polled still thought that Serbia should not cooperate with the tribunal, although 64 percent admitted that they had little or very little knowledge about it (Bandovic 2004, 95-96). As summarized by the project coordinator of the Belgrade human rights organization that conducted the surveys,

> Serbia's citizens do not see the ICTY as an international court whose task is to try persons who violated international law for war crimes, or an institution working to reconcile the peoples of the former Yugoslavia. Most people view the ICTY as an unavoidable and enforced precondition for Serbia's full return to the world community and simply the price that Serbia has to pay. These views completely sideline the issue of the guilt of those indicted by the ICTY. (Bandovic 2004, 93)

He attributes these continued beliefs, despite the country's democratic changes, to the lingering effects of the distrust and negative attitudes propagated during the Milosevic regime and the publicly known opposition to the tribunal of leading Serbian experts on international law (Bandovic 2004, 92, 98).[13]

2455 Teller Road • Thousand Oaks, CA 91320 • U.S.A.
PHONE: (800) 818-7243 or (805) 499-9774 • FAX: (805) 499-0871
E-MAIL: journals@sagepub.com
WEBSITE: www.sagepublications.com

1 Oliver's Yard • 55 City Road • London EC1Y 1SP • U.K.
PHONE: +44 (0) 20-7324-8500 • FAX: +44 (0) 20-7324-8600
E-MAIL: subscription@sagepub.co.uk
WEBSITE: www.sagepublications.co.uk

H03409

FOR MORE INFORMATION ABOUT THIS JOURNAL, TO SIGN UP FOR E-MAIL OR PRODUCT ALERTS, TO VIEW A SAMPLE ISSUE ONLINE, OR TO SUBSCRIBE, PLEASE VISIT: http://theannals.sagepub.com OR FILL OUT THIS POSTCARD AND RETURN IT TO Ⓢ SAGE PUBLICATIONS.

THE ANNALS OF THE AMERICAN ACADEMY OF POLITICAL AND SOCIAL SCIENCE-PAPERBOUND

Frequency: 6 Times/Year

Please start my subscription to The Annals of the American Academy of Political and Social Science-Paperbound (J295) ISSN: 0002-7162

In North America, South America, Central America, the Caribbean, and Asia

☐ Individuals (Print only): $84 *
☐ Single Copy Price: Individuals (Print only): $34

☐ Institutions (Combined print & online): $577
☐ Single Copy Price: Institutions (Print only): $102

In the United Kingdom, Europe, Australasia, the Middle East, and Africa

☐ Individuals (Print only): £55 *
☐ Single Copy Price: Individuals (Print only): £22

☐ Institutions (Combined print & online): £373
☐ Single Copy Price: Institutions (Print only): £66

* (All individual subscriptions are handled through the Annals of the American Academy of Political and Social Science at www.aapss.org)

Name

Title/Department

Address

Address

City/State or Province / Zip or Postal Code / Country

Phone

E-mail

Subscriptions will begin with the current issue, unless otherwise specified. Customers outside of the United States will receive their publications via air-speeded delivery.

BUSINESS REPLY MAIL

FIRST-CLASS MAIL   PERMIT NO. 90   THOUSAND OAKS, CA

POSTAGE WILL BE PAID BY ADDRESSEE

SAGE PUBLICATIONS
PO BOX 5084
THOUSAND OAKS CA 91359-9989

NO POSTAGE
NECESSARY
IF MAILED
IN THE
UNITED STATES

In neighboring Croatia, also within the ICTY's jurisdiction, a similar though more moderate pattern prevails: in the 1990s, the nationalistic government under Tudjman took a scornful view of ICTY investigations of Croats (which were much fewer than those of Serbs), while the liberal Mesic government, which in February 2000 was swept into power, takes a more pragmatic stance of cooperation with the tribunal, as a means of distancing the Croat nation from collective guilt for Croat wartime behavior. However, this approach is not necessarily popular with the public, more than 52 percent of which in August 2000 believed that "The Hague wants to criminalize the Homeland War." More than 78 percent opposed extradition of citizens to the ICTY, although some Croats supported trials in national courts (Akhavan 2001, 22-23).

In Sierra Leone, by contrast, receptiveness toward the Special Court is rather broad, with concerns expressed more in regard to details and implementation than overall legitimacy. For instance, a controversial feature of the limited-budget SCSL is the small number of persons (thirteen to date) indicted, only those who bore "the greatest responsibility" for wartime atrocities. Local reaction to this seems to depend on one's status: average villagers repeatedly express approval ("It was the big, big ones who sent the children to do bad things") (Shaw 2005, 11) while local NGO activists tend to be frustrated that many midlevel commanders will escape prosecution (HRW 2004, 5-6; Bangura 2005, 56). Sierra Leone's judicial personnel were reportedly asking, Is the world only interested in the prosecution of a handful of notorious criminals while the country must make do with a collapsed judicial system and the same venal petty officials who compounded the problems that plagued society before, during, and after the war? (Gberie 2003, 643).

Nevertheless, one such NGO worker has written, "Despite endless debate about its cost and legitimacy . . . Sierra Leoneans welcomed the court. We saw it not only as a mechanism for transnational justice but also as an instrument to transform our judicial system. . . . Nobody therefore challenged the court's existence" (Bangura 2005, 56). Moreover, now that the trials are under way, he writes, "Sierra Leoneans are amazed at the revelations coming out of the court" (Bangura 2005, 56). Similarly, a handbook produced by a Freetown-based NGO states, "We can move forward only if we address the conditions that caused the war. . . . [This] requires punishing those with the greatest responsibility, to show that people cannot mastermind terrible acts in our country and get away with it" (Gberie 2003, 637). Accordingly, the SCSL may have grown in stature in many local eyes when its indictment of Charles Taylor became public, even if the initial attempt to serve him with an arrest warrant appeared to be bungled (see Standard Times 2003).

Perceptions of tribunal impartiality

According to the same July 2003 survey described above, the Serbian population overwhelmingly distrusts the ICTY, believing it is politically motivated and biased against those defeated in the war. Particularly, "that an international conspiracy exists against the Serbs and that all other peoples enjoy better cooperation with and more support from the big powers; and that only Serbs are on trial and that they receive harsh punishment, while all the other trials are just a farce and an excuse for prosecuting the Serbs" (Bandovic 2004, 93). Almost 70 percent of Serbs surveyed in July 2003 distrusted the ICTY to act impartially concerning the Serbian defendants, while 57 percent gave it an impartiality grade in general (Bandovic 2004, 96). Among Croats, more than 60 percent in August 2000 believed it to be unfair compared to 15 percent who graded it as fair (Akhavan 2001, 22).

The SCSL from its beginning has contended with the local (if not global) perception that it is an American demonstration project, either serving a U.S. agenda to undercut the ICC, or as a covert instrument to gather intelligence on al-Qaeda's alleged presence in West Africa (International Crisis Group 2003, 14-17; Gberie 2003, 643). "These local suspicions of extra-judicial U.S. objectives may well have little plausibility but they are undoubtedly affecting the Sierra Leone people's sense of ownership in the process," one NGO noted (International Crisis Group 2003, 17).[14] Surely, however, more than one person in the country noticed the coincidence of U.S. backing for the Special Court during the very period when it was vigorously pressing developing countries (including Sierra Leone) to sign agreements not to hand over American soldiers to the ICC (see Kamanda 2003).

Ironically but understandably, an effort by the SCSL prosecutor to be fair and evenhanded in serving indictments initially so shocked the population that temporarily, at least, its credibility was called into question. Many contend that arresting Sam Hinga Norman, a tribal chief then serving as a government minister, at the same time as indicted rebel leaders, was inappropriate because he had led the Civil Defense Forces to put down the rebel coup. It was also probably difficult for Sierra Leoneans to understand why the SCSL would prevent Norman—then in pretrial custody—from giving televised testimony to the TRC to protect his right to a fair trial (see Kamanda 2003).

Effects on reconciliation of tribunal perceptions

Since the creation of each tribunal, portions of the respective local populations have been concerned that the tribunal's operation would endanger the fragile peace and reconciliation processes (International Crisis Group 2003, 4-5). This was especially true for the ICTY; although the tribunal is located outside the region, the war between Serbs and Bosnians was still ongoing when legal proceedings commenced. The SCSL was established just as the war ended, but because it is located inside the country, where most ex-combatants (including associates of the detained defendants) remain at large and often still live under the "protection" of their commanders, the potential for unrest and destabilization is ever present.

Many people in Sierra Leone, including ex-combatants, were confused about the difference between the Special Court and the preexisting TRC (International Crisis Group 2003, 7). The court's indictments were announced just as the TRC was holding hearings and taking testimony, which may have been an unfortunate coincidence of timing. Because many ex-combatants feared that the TRC would convey their testimony to the SCSL—despite the prosecutor's public denials—

their participation was low, sometimes going into hiding during TRC hearings, sometimes driving TRC staff away (Shaw 2005, 4).

A joint TRC for the entire region of the former Yugoslavia might be desired but is highly unlikely; even a proposed one to serve Croatia alone was cancelled before it got started. So any attempt to measure the ICTY's effect on reconciliation must take account of actions by the tribunal itself. Local victim groups often express bitterness when they learn of ICTY plea bargains—which are unheard of in their national legal systems—for atrocities committed by their former tormentors. No explanation had been given to the public as to what was being pled to and what was the institutional advantage of taking pleas. Some local observers saw the practice as "a way of covering up something or somebody. And that is always done at the expense of the victims" (McDonald 2004, 26). Relatives of wartime prison camp victims were furious when a guard who pleaded guilty to killing five inmates was sentenced to eight years, whereas lower-level guards who went to trial got twenty (Simons 2003). Moreover, the population as a whole is robbed of the historical record that trials create. Concerning one Serbian defendant who pleaded guilty and is serving her sentence in Sweden,[15] it has been noted, "The polls say that most of the population (93 percent) do not know that Plavsic was responsible for ethnic cleansing in 32 communities in Bosnia, for which she pleaded guilty. But they know that there is a sauna in her prison" (Mladjenovic 2004, 63). As observed by one scholarly commentator, "Institutions like the ICTY can impair the very reconciliation they seek to advance if the rewards that they hand out in appreciation for reconciliation become themselves an additional source of bitterness" (Coombs 2002, 14).

On the other hand, a counselor from a Belgrade women victims organization reports that many Bosnian survivors of the Srebrenica massacre gain strength and emotional relief from watching TV broadcasts of ICTY trials. She quotes one survivor who has since said, "We Bosnian Muslims no longer have to prove we were victims. Our friends and cousins, fathers and brothers were killed—and we no longer have to prove they were innocent." Validation, alleviating shame, and confirmation of the facts are thus some of the tribunal's major functions (Mladjenovic 2004, 61-63). Even the plea bargains have had a positive effect in one respect: the confessions have made the tribunal more acceptable to Serbs and Croats who previously believed it was biased (Simons 2003).

Conclusion

How can one compare or assess the perceptions of these two tribunals and predict their impact on the long-term development of democratization and the rule of law in these locales when the evidence is so incomplete and uneven? This suggests that much more data should be collected—or at least, more time must pass for the "views on the ground" to develop into "facts on the ground." This article has simply tried to demonstrate the axiom that "justice must not only be done but be seen to be done." Ultimately, however, whether justice is done will depend on more than just public observations of a particular justice system's fairness in operation. In the words of a forty-five-year-old internally displaced Sierra Leonean, "If the boy who cut off my arm goes to prison now, well, then maybe that's called justice. But even if that boy goes to jail, I will never get my arm back" (Rehrl 2004, 17).

Notes

1. The seven, with their years of creation, are the International Criminal Tribunal for the Former Yugoslavia (ICTY; 1993), the International Criminal Tribunal for Rwanda (1994), "Regulation 64" Panels in the Courts of Kosovo (1999), Special Panels for Serious Crimes of the District Court of Dili (East Timor 2000), the Special Court for Sierra Leone (SCSL; 2002), the International Criminal Court (ICC; 2002), and the Extraordinary Chambers in the Courts of Cambodia (2004).

2. Predominantly the work of one scholar in particular, M. Cherif Bassiouni (1974, 1980, 1986a, 1986b).

3. It may be too early to assess long-term perceptions because five of the tribunals are still holding trials and the two most recently established, the ICC and the Cambodian Extraordinary Chambers, have not yet held any trials.

4. Along with the courts created for Kosovo, East Timor, and Cambodia, the SCSL is called a "hybrid" or "internationalized" tribunal because it combines international and national elements (primarily in the personnel making up the bench and the prosecutor's office) (see Romano, Nollkaemper, and Kleffner 2004). In this article, the terms *tribunal* and *court* will be used interchangeably to refer to both the ICTY and SCSL, as well as to international criminal courts generally. The Federal Republic of Yugoslavia ceased to exist in February 2003, when the Yugoslav Parliament adopted a charter that proclaimed the new name to be Serbia and Montenegro. However, this article, like the ICTY itself, generally uses the phrase "the former Yugoslavia" to incorporate reference to Croatia and Bosnia-Hercegovina as well as Serbia.

5. The ICC will exercise jurisdiction only when national courts are unwilling or unable to investigate or prosecute someone accused of violating international criminal law. By contrast, both the ICTY and the SCSL have concurrent but primary jurisdiction in relation to the national courts in the former Yugoslavian countries and Sierra Leone.

6. Ninety-nine as of June 15, 2005 (Coalition for the ICC 2005).

7. In June 2000, after numerous peace accords had failed to end the war and after the Revolutionary United Front abducted five hundred UN peacekeepers, the Sierra Leone president, Ahmad Tejan Kabbah, wrote Kofi Annan, requesting UN assistance in setting up a court "to try and bring to credible justice those members of the Revolutionary United Front (RUF) and their accomplices responsible for committing crimes against the people of Sierra Leone and for the taking of United Nations peacekeepers as hostages" (International Crisis Group 2003, 2, n.8).

8. Notably, the ICTY but not the SCSL can prosecute genocide while the SCSL also has jurisdiction over certain crimes under Sierra Leone law. However, no indictments have included any national crimes.

9. Dividing the number of indictments by the years of operation yields figures of 4.33 for the SCSL and 11.36 for the ICTY. A significant problem for the ICTY has been in obtaining custody over its accused, both those known to be residing in the former Yugoslav territory and those who had fled elsewhere (Kerr 2004, 156-69). For instance, although the Republika Srpska National Assembly, under intense international pressure, adopted a law in 2001 on cooperation with the ICTY, it has never been implemented and not a single indicted war criminal has been arrested (Alic 2004).

10. The SCSL Statute is the first treaty in force that criminalizes the conscripting of child soldiers. While the Rome Statute of the ICC, which does the same, came into force six months after the SCSL Statute, the ICC has not yet indicted anyone for that crime.

11. No international instrument limits the temporal mandate of the SCSL, but it is only funded (through voluntary contributions) for at most four years. See International Crisis Group (2003, 3).

12. Milosevic resigned on October 6, 2000, following mounting pressure to quit over allegations of vote rigging. The Yugoslav Constitutional Court, which annulled the September 24 presidential elections, acknowledged Kostunica as the true winner. The Yugoslav army also publicly withdrew its support for Milosevic (see *On This Day* 2000). Another opinion survey in Serbia, conducted in April 2001, showed that

the 2,171 respondents got most of their news during the Balkan wars from Serbia's state-controlled media, the main propaganda arm of then-president Milosevic. More than half could not name a single war crime committed by Serbs. Only 15 percent could name three. Asked to name the greatest defenders of the Serbian nation during the 1990s, the 75 percent who responded named Ratko Mladic and Radovan Karadzic most frequently ("Perceptions in Serbia" 2001). Those are the two most notorious ICTY indictees who are still evading custody. The new democratically elected Serbian government continues to avoid opening public debate on Serbian war crimes (Devic 2003).

13. See, for instance, The Hague Tribunal—Conclusions from the Seminar held on 19 June 2004 at the Faculty of Laws, Belgrade, by the International Committee to Defend Slobodan Milosevic (2004), which argues against the ICTY's legitimacy, stating, "The analysis of indictments shows that the prosecution of the ICTY leans on the well known CIA report from the beginning of the 1990s according to which the guilt of the Serbs for the Yugoslav crisis and civil wars in Croatia and BiH is apportioned at 70 percent, that of Croats at 20 percent and Bosnian Muslims at—10 percent. This assessment engineering was used in the preparation of the indictments [sic] against the highest representatives of Serbian people. More than two thirds of those indicted at the ICTY are the Serbs. It is the fact that only the Serbian leadership has been indicted and deprived of liberty, while the leaders of other former Yugoslav states have been pardoned. It seems as if non-Serbian indictees are in the Hague only to unsuccessfuly mask the anti-Serbian character of the Tribunal."

14. The first chief prosecutor was a U.S. national, and at the beginning, a significant number of Americans worked in his office, but by 2003, British and Canadian nationals had outnumbered them. In fact, of the 255 total personnel in all divisions of the SCSL in 2003, 154 (or 60 percent) were Sierra Leoneans (President of the SCSL, 2004, 20). All three countries have made proportionately large voluntary contributions to the court's budget.

15. Because there are no international prison facilities at The Hague, the ICTY has "contracted out" the enforcement of sentences through agreements with ten other countries (see http://www.un.org/icty/legaldoc/coopgarde.htm). The SCSL signed its first agreement on the enforcement of sentences outside of Sierra Leone in October 2004 (see Kendall and Staggs 2005, 35).

References

Agreement between the United Nations and the Government of Sierra Leone on the Establishment of the Special Court for Sierra Leone. 2002. January 16.

Akhavan, Payam. 2001. Beyond impunity: Can international criminal justice prevent future atrocities? *American Journal of International Law* 95:7-31.

Alic, Anes. 2004. Demand for arrests. June 7. Transitions Online. Retrieved January 9, 2005, from WL (Westlaw) 62509513.

Bandovic, Igor. 2004. Remarks of Igor Bandovic. In *International war crimes trials: Making a difference?* ed. Steven R. Ratner and James L. Bischoff. Austin: University of Texas Press.

Bangura, Zainab. 2005. Sierra Leone: Ordinary Courts and the Special Court. February. http://www.justiceinitiative.org/db/resource2/fs/?file_id=15283 (accessed December 10, 2004).

Bassiouni, M. Cherif. 1974. *International extradition and world public order.* Dobbs Ferry, NY: Oceana.

———. 1980. *A draft international criminal code and draft statute for an international criminal tribunal.* Boston: M. Nijhoff.

———. 1986a. *International criminal law.* Dobbs Ferry, NY: Transnational.

———. 1986b. *International crimes: Digest/index of international instruments, 1815-1985.* New York: Oceana.

Coalition for the ICC. 2005. World signature and ratifications. http://www.iccnow.org/countryinfo/worldsigsandratifications.html (accessed June 19, 2005).

Coombs, Nancy Amoury. 2002. Copping a plea to genocide: The plea bargaining of international crimes. *University of Pennsylvania Law Review* 151:1-157.

Devic, Ana. 2003. War guilt and responsibility: The case of Serbia. March. Social Science Research Council. Available on Columbia International Affairs Online.

Drumbl, Mark. 2004. Remarks of Mark Drumbl. In *International war crimes trials: Making a difference?* ed. Steven R. Ratner and James L. Bischoff. Austin: University of Texas Press.

Gberie, Lansana. 2003. Briefing: The Special Court of Sierra Leone. *African Affairs* 102:637-48.

Human Rights Watch (HRW). 2004. Bringing justice: The Special Court for Sierra Leone: Accomplishments, shortcomings, and needed support. September. http://hrw.org/reports/2004/sierraleone0904/ (accessed May 6, 2005).

ICTY President to UN Security Council. 2005. June 13. http://www.cij.org/index.cfm?fuseaction=viewReport&reportID=690&tribunalID=1 (accessed June 22, 2005).

International Center for Transitional Justice (ICTJ). 2004. The Special Court for Sierra Leone: The first eighteen months. http://www.ictj.org/downloads/SC_SL_Case_Study_designed.pdf (accessed June 21, 2005).

International Committee to Defend Slobodan Milosevic. 2004. The Hague Tribunal—Conclusions from the Seminar held on 19 June 2004 at the Faculty of Laws, Belgrade. http://www.icdsm.org/more/BF1906 .htm (accessed June 23, 2005).

International Criminal Tribunal for Yugoslavia (ICTY). n.d.-a. Bringing justice to the former Yugoslavia: The tribunal's five core achievements. http://www.un.org/icty/cases/factsheets/achieve-e.htm (accessed December 10, 2004).

———. n.d.-b. General information. http://www.un.org/icty/cases/factsheets/generalinfo-e.htm (accessed December 10, 2004).

———. n.d.-c. Key figures of ICTY cases. http://www.un.org/icty/cases/factsheets/procfact-e.htm (accessed January 17, 2005).

International Crisis Group. 2003. The Special Court for Sierra Leone: Promises and pitfalls of a "new model." http://www.crisisgroup.org/home/index.cfm?action=login&ref_id=1803 (accessed January 9, 2005).

Kamanda, Joseph. 2003. Is the Special Court truly independent and neutral? *Concord Times* (Sierra Leone), December 11. Retrieved January 12, 2005, from Global News Wire—Asia, Africa.

Kendall, Sara, and Michelle Staggs. 2005. From mandate to legacy: The Special Court for Sierra Leone as a model for "hybrid justice." April. U.C. Berkeley War Crimes Study Center. http://ist-socrates.berkeley.edu/~warcrime/SLSC_Report.pdf (accessed May 11, 2005).

Kerr, Rachel. 2004. *The International Criminal Tribunal for the Former Yugoslavia: An exercise in law, politics and diplomacy.* Oxford: Oxford University Press.

McDonald, Gabrielle Kirk. 2004. Assessing the impact of the International Criminal Tribunal for the Former Yugoslavia. In *International war crimes trials: Making a difference?* ed. Steven R. Ratner and James L. Bischoff. Austin: University of Texas Press.

Mladjenovic, Lepa. 2004. The ICTY: The validation of the experiences of survivors. In *International war crimes trials: Making a difference?* ed. Steven R. Ratner and James L. Bischoff. Austin: University of Texas Press.

A more secure world: Our shared responsibility, Report of the High-Level Panel on Threats, Challenges and Change. 2004. New York: United Nations.

On this day 2000: Milosevic quits, street celebrations continue. 2000. October 6. Retrieved http://news.bbc .co.uk/onthisday/hi/dates/stories/october/6/newsid_2516000/2516673.stm (accessed June 23, 2005).

Perceptions in Serbia. 2001. *USIP Peace Watch* 7 (June): 6.

Post-conflict Reintegration Initiative for Development and Empowerment (PRIDE). 2002. Ex-combatant views of the Truth and Reconciliation Commission and the Special Court in Sierra Leone. September 12. http://www.ictj.org/downloads/PRIDE%20report.pdf (accessed June 22, 2005).

President of the Special Court for Sierra Leone (SCSL). 2004. First annual report for the period 2 December 2002-1 December 2003. http://www.sc-sl.org/specialcourtannualreport2002-2003.pdf (accessed June 20, 2005).

Prosecutors of the International Criminal Court, the International Criminal Tribunal for the Former Yugoslavia, the International Criminal Tribunal for Rwanda, and the Special Court for Sierra Leone. 2004. Joint Statement. November 27. http://www.sc-sl.org/prosecutor-092004.pdf (accessed June 22, 2005).

Rehrl, Annette. 2004. Sierra Leone: We want reconciliation. We will never forget. But we try to forgive. *Refugees Magazine* 136 (September): 15-18.

Romano, Cesare P. R., Andre Nollkaemper, and Jann K. Kleffner, eds. 2004. *Internationalized criminal courts*. Oxford: Oxford University Press.

Shaw, Rosalind. 2005. Rethinking Truth and Reconciliation Commissions: Lessons from Sierra Leone. Special Report no. 130. February. Washington, DC: United States Institute for Peace.

Simons, Marlise. 2003. Plea deals being used to clear Balkan war tribunal's docket. *New York Times*, November 18.

Special Court for Sierra Leone (SCSL). 2002. Statute of the Special Court. January 16.

———. n.d. About the Special Court. http://www.sc-sl.org/about.html (accessed January 10, 2005).

Special Court for Sierra Leone, Appeals Chamber. 2004a. Prosecutor v. Charles Ghankay Taylor. Decision on immunity from prosecution. May 31. http://www.sc-sl.org/Documents/SCSL-03-01-I-059.pdf (accessed December 10, 2004).

———. 2004b. Prosecutor v. Sam Hinga Norman. Decision on preliminary motion based on lack of jurisdiction (child recruitment). May 31. http://www.sc-sl.org/Documents/SCSL-04-14-AR72(E)-131-7383.pdf; and http://www.sc-sl.org/Documents/SCSL-04-14-AR72(E)-131-7398.pdf (accessed June 20, 2005).

Standard Times. 2003. Sierra Leone: President Charles Taylor's escape. *Africa News*, June 16.

United Nations Security Council. 1993. Resolution 808 [establishment of ICTY]. U.N. Doc. S/RES/808. February 22. New York: United Nations Security Council.

———. 2000. Resolution 1315 [establishment of SCSL]. U.N. Doc. S/RES/1315. August 14. New York: United Nations Security Council.

———. 2003. Resolution 1503 [ICTY completion strategy]. U.N. Doc. S/RES/1503. August 28. New York: United Nations Security Council.

Global Rule of Law or Global Rule of Law Enforcement? International Police Cooperation and Counterterrorism

By
MATHIEU DEFLEM

With increasing vigor since the events of September 11, 2001, police institutions across the globe have proliferated their counterterrorism strategies, including participation in international police organizations such as the International Criminal Police Organization (Interpol). This article discusses some of these developments in light of the prospects of the development toward a global rule of law. Based on the theory of police bureaucratization, it is shown that police institutions have independently developed international structures and practices irrespective of international accords. This article reveals the dynamics of such international police efforts by examining the counterterrorist policies of Interpol. It is argued that the outcome of the relative separation between international police practices, on one hand, and global legal developments, on the other, will be critical in assessing any efforts to counteract the societal processes and conditions that may facilitate the development of terrorism on a global scale.

Keywords: international police cooperation; Interpol; international terrorism; counterterrorism; rule of law

In the modern state, real authority . . . rests necessarily and unavoidably in the hands of the bureaucracy.

—Max Weber

In the context of democratic societies, the rule of law is guaranteed by the legitimacy legal norms enjoy from those to whom such norms apply, on one hand, and by the threat of enforcement from specialized agents of control, on the

Mathieu Deflem is an associate professor in the Department of Sociology at the University of South Carolina. His research interests include the police dimensions of counterterrorism, international police cooperation, abortion policy, the sociological profession, and sociological theory, especially in the area of the sociology of law. His writings have appeared in dozens of journals and books. Deflem is the author of Policing World Society *(Oxford, 2002) and editor of* Terrorism and Counter-Terrorism: Criminological Perspectives *(Elsevier, 2004) and* Habermas, Modernity, and Law *(Sage, 1996). He maintains an extensive professional Web site: www.mathieudeflem.net.*

DOI: 10.1177/0002716205282256

other. With respect to the threat of force, modern states have monopolized the function of internal coercion in specialized police institutions. But the function of policing is also articulated at the international level, as law enforcement institutions engage in a variety of international activities and have forged international cooperative structures and organizations that aim to foster collaboration in the fight against crimes that are of an international nature. Increased concerns over the threat of international terrorism since September 11, 2001, have sharply accelerated these developments. Thus, police institutions across the globe have proliferated their counterterrorism strategies, both domestically and abroad, while international police organizations have likewise stepped up their campaigns against terrorism.

Based on existing research of the dynamics of international police cooperation (Deflem 2002, 2004b), substantial evidence suggests that the security and intelligence agencies of national states engage in collaboration across national borders, in matters of terrorism and other crimes, despite the fact that critical differences may exist in their respective countries' attained level of and formal commitment to constitutional democracy. To the extent that police institutions across nations have already forged a global order against terrorism, it can be said that terrorism has effectively been criminalized under a world rule of law enforcement. Yet it is not clear whether the legitimacy requirements of a global democratic order are realized by these developments, as research has also revealed that international police operations can take place outside the confines of legal safeguards and human rights restrictions. A central question, then, is if and how a global order of law enforcement can lead the way to a global order of law. In this article, I will address this question on the basis of an analysis of selected developments in the policing of international terrorism in the post-9/11 context. I will specifically focus on the counterterrorism strategies devised by the International Criminal Police Organization, the police organization better known as Interpol. My analysis relies on the bureaucratization theory of international police cooperation that has been developed in a comparative-historical context (Deflem 2000, 2002).

International Police Cooperation and the Bureaucratization of the State

The bureaucratization theory of international police cooperation was developed to analyze the behavior of modern police institutions under conditions of increasing globalization from the middle of the nineteenth century onward (Deflem 2000, 2002). Yet the theory can also be applied to account for important dimensions of the contemporary conditions of counterterrorism, especially at the level of international policing activities (Deflem 2004a, 2004b). In these variable contexts, the

NOTE: A previous version of this article was prepared for a conference on "Legal Evolution: Toward a World Rule of Law," Syracuse University's College of Law, April 16-17, 2005. I am grateful to Richard Schwartz for inviting me to participate in the conference.

theory predicts a high degree of autonomy of police institutions to determine the means and objectives of activities related to crime control and order maintenance. As state bureaucracies always remain related to the political power of governments, the degree of a police institution's institutional autonomy will vary and have variable implications, depending on social conditions, especially attempts by governments to politicize police activity during periods of intense societal upheaval.

[P]oliticization efforts occur progressively at times when police institutions continue to expand and solidify a position of autonomy that enables them to better resist such attempts at political control.

The bureaucratization theory of policing is founded on the work of the sociologist Max Weber (1922/1980), who forwarded the conception of police institutions as state bureaucracies when he specified among the functions of the modern state "the protection of personal security and public order (police)" (p. 516). Weber attributed special significance to the police function by arguing that the expansion of the bureaucratization process was particularly accelerated by "the increasing need, in a society accustomed to pacification, for order and protection ("police") in all areas" (p. 561).

The bureaucratization theory maintains that public police institutions, since at least the formation of national states in the nineteenth century, reveal a tendency toward independence from the governments of their respective national states. Police bureaucracies achieve institutional autonomy on the basis of a purposive-rational logic to employ the most efficient means (professional expertise) given certain objectives that are rationalized on the basis of professional systems of knowledge (official information). The theory does not deny that policing is related to state control but holds that the behavior of police agencies is not wholly determined by reference to their relation to the political center of states. Instead, bureaucracies are shaped by organizational transformations related to a more general rationalization process affecting bureaucratic activity. In the case of social control, it is most crucial that police bureaucracies gradually adopt criminal enforcement tasks, irrespective of political directives, and develop professional techniques to fulfill these goals.

The theory of bureaucratization accounts for change and continuity in the development of state institutions. Most interesting in this respect are the conditions that impact bureaucratization during periods of momentous societal change. Intense social disturbances typically lead to attempts to redirect bureaucratic activity to again play a role intimately related to the political goals of national states (politicization). In the case of policing, periods of societal upheaval are seen to affect the institutional autonomy of police institutions in functional and organizational ways. Drawing from work on the evolution of international policing in the context of Europe and the United States, several historical examples can be mentioned (Deflem 2002).

In 1851, the first modern international police organization was established in the form of the Police Union of German States. Active until 1866, the Police Union brought together police of seven sovereign German-language states, including Prussia and Austria, with the express purpose of policing the political opposition of established autocratic regimes. Ironically, from such political efforts would gradually grow police organizations and practices with distinctly criminal objectives. Throughout the latter half of the nineteenth century, police institutions indeed developed and expanded professionally justified systems of policing and forged cooperation on the basis thereof. In 1898, a striking repoliticization attempt occurred when the Italian government organized the Anti-Anarchist Conference of Rome. Attended by government representatives of twenty-one European nations, the conference sought to organize an international police structure against the anarchist movement. Although a follow-up meeting was held in St. Petersburg in 1904, three years after the assassination of U.S. President McKinley, independent developments in the bureaucratization of the police function prevented these politically directed efforts from interrupting the antianarchist and other international policing strategies that police institutions had already begun to develop beyond any political policies and intergovernmental conventions.

Next to the disruptive impact of World War I, another striking example of the momentary shifts brought about in bureaucratization during sudden crises occurred after the Bolshevik Revolution, when police institutions in Europe and elsewhere turned attention to the presumed spread of a global communist movement. But once again, such politically motivated police activities would be only temporarily relevant, or they were redirected in terms that did not necessarily harmonize with government power, with implications that lasted until long after World War II. This is most clearly revealed in the case of the FBI during the Hoover era, when anticommunist police activities formed part of a generalized policing of "each and all," including the politically powerful (Deflem 2002).

Efforts to politicize police institutions and other bureaucracies during moments of intense societal change are not especially surprising, as national crises typically bring about a centralization of power in the executive branch. What is ironic is that these politicization efforts occur progressively at times when police institutions continue to expand and solidify a position of autonomy that enables them to better resist such attempts at political control. Thus, on theoretical grounds alone, the degree to which the autonomy of state bureaucracies has been accomplished in periods of relative stability cannot be assumed to be without consequences during moments of upheaval.

September 11 as World Event

Offering an interesting parallel to historical incidents of attempts to politicize policing during periods of war and revolution are the dynamics of international policing that have taken place since September 11, 2001 (Deflem 2004b). Indeed, the function and organization of policing in many nations across the global as well as at the international level have changed very significantly in response to the terrorist events of 9/11. Among the most important external determinants of counterterrorism policing are political pressures by means of new legislations and other forms of official policy. In the decades before September 11, government policies and legislation against terrorism at the national and international level developed only slowly. Internationally, the regulation of terrorism dates back to 1937 when the League of Nations adopted a convention on the Prevention and Punishment of Terrorism. The convention found little support among the nations of the world, and from then on, international policies on terrorism developed piecemeal, focusing on specific elements associated with terrorism (plane hijackings, bombings, hostage taking). In the United States, formal policies against terrorism also developed slowly and piecemeal until the Clinton administration secured passage of the Antiterrorism and Effective Death Penalty Act of 1996.

Legislative and other policy responses to the terrorist attacks of 9/11, especially in the United States, have gone far beyond what could have been predicted on the basis of developments during the 1990s. While the military intervention in Afghanistan mirrored the strikes launched against al-Qaeda by order of President Clinton in 1998, the U.S. military effort was now more resolute, backed by new policies to justify the militarization of the judicial processing of foreign terrorists and new legislation aimed to broaden counterterrorist police strategies. About a month after 9/11, the PATRIOT Act (the "Provide Appropriate Tools Required to Intercept and Obstruct Terrorism Act") received congressional approval. Next to the PATRIOT Act, the creation of the Department of Homeland Security in November 2002 has been among the most concrete political efforts to unite and oversee the various U.S. security agencies involved in the "war on terror."

Despite the various political and legal efforts to control counterterrorist policing, however, it also makes sense to expect that police institutions will resist politicization attempts to remain focused on an efficiency-driven treatment and depoliticized conception of terrorism. The reason for this autonomy of policing is that the bureaucratization of modern police institutions is now at an unparalleled high level. Unlike in the late nineteenth and early twentieth centuries, modern police institutions have presently attained a level of bureaucratic autonomy that is unprecedented in scale. Police can therefore more effectively resist political influences in a manner congruent with achieved professional standards of expertise and knowledge with respect to the means and objectives of bureaucratic activity. In what follows, I will make this case by focusing on the counterterrorism strategies of the international police organization Interpol.[1]

Interpol and Counterterrorism

Interpol is an international police organization that aims to provide and promote mutual assistance between criminal police authorities within the limits of national laws and the Universal Declaration of Human Rights. Originally formed in Vienna in 1923, the organization has steadily grown in membership but never substantially changed in form or objectives (Deflem 2000, 2002). Interpol is not a supranational police agency with investigative powers or an organization sanctioned by an international governing body such as the United Nations. Rather, it is a cooperative network formed independently among police agencies to foster collaboration and provide assistance in police work across nations. To this end, Interpol links a central headquarters, located in Lyon, France, with specialized bureaus, the so-called National Central Bureaus (NCB), in the countries of participating police agencies. At present, Interpol counts 181 member agencies.

The diversity among Interpol's member agencies, however, has also hindered the organization's effectiveness in its missions, as members do not always trust one another.

For several decades now, Interpol has passed various resolutions to combat terrorism and terrorist-related activities (Anderson 1997; Bossard 1987; Interpol Web site, http://www.interpol.int/). During the 1970s, Interpol passed resolutions that pertained to certain crimes that are typically involved with terrorist activities, such as criminal acts conducted against international civil aviation and the holding of hostages. Such terrorism-related resolutions were considered valid only within the context of a 1951 Interpol resolution that the organization would not concern itself with matters of a political, racial, or religious nature, a restriction that has since been adopted explicitly as Article 3 of the Interpol constitution.

Following resolutions on organized groups that engage in acts of violence and on explosive substances, an Interpol resolution passed in 1984 concerning Violent Crime Commonly Referred to as Terrorism. The resolution encouraged the member agencies to cooperate and combat terrorism within the context of their national laws. An additional Interpol resolution that year acknowledged that it was not possible to give a more precise definition of political, military, religious, or racial matters and that each case had to be examined separately. In 1985, however, a resolution passed that called for the creation of a specialized group, the Public Safety and Terrorism (PST) subdirectorate to coordinate and enhance cooperation in matters of international terrorism.

Following certain highly publicized terrorist incidents during the 1990s (such as the World Trade Center bombing on February 26, 1993), the Interpol General Assembly stepped up its counterterrorist initiatives. In 1998, at the General Assembly meeting in Cairo, Interpol's commitment to combat international terrorism was explicitly confirmed in a Declaration against Terrorism, condemning terrorism because of the threat it poses with regard to security, democracy, and human rights. In 1999, at the Interpol General Assembly meeting in Seoul, it was again affirmed that the fight against international terrorism was one of Interpol's primary aims.

Interpol since September 11

A few weeks after the terrorist attacks in the United States, the Interpol General Assembly held its 70th meeting in Budapest, Hungary. At the meeting, the Interpol General Assembly passed Resolution AG-2001-RES-05 on the 9/11 terrorist attack to condemn the "murderous attacks perpetrated against the world's citizens in the United States of America on 11 September 2001" as "an abhorrent violation of law and of the standards of human decency" that constitute "cold-blooded mass murder [and] a crime against humanity" (Interpol Web site). It was also decided to tackle terrorism and organized crime more effectively and that the highest priority be given to the issuance of so-called Red Notices (i.e., international Interpol warrants to seek arrest and extradition of a suspect) for terrorists sought in connection with the 9/11 attacks. In October 2001, Interpol held its 16th Annual Symposium on Terrorism to discuss new antiterrorism initiatives, such as the feasibility of setting up a special aviation database, the financing of terrorism, and anti-money-laundering measures. In October 2002, 450 representatives from 139 of Interpol's 181 member agencies attended the 71st General Assembly meeting in Yaoundé, Cameroon. Acknowledging September 11 as a catalyst in the development of global approaches to crime, the meeting paid even more distinct attention to the matter of terrorism. The assembly attendants agreed to draft a list of security precautions for the handling of potentially dangerous materials (such as letters and parcels that might contain anthrax), while bioterrorism was specified as deserving special attention.

Since 1998, a formal set of Interpol Guidelines for Co-operation in Combating International Terrorism more explicitly addresses the relationship of terrorism to Article 3 of Interpol's Constitution, forbidding Interpol to undertake matters of a political, military, religious, or racial character. Basically, terrorist incidents are broken down into their constituent parts, only the criminal elements of which can then be identified and subjected to police investigations.

Interpol pays special attention to the financing of terrorist activities since it is assumed that the frequency and seriousness of terrorist attacks are often proportionate to the amount of financing terrorists receive. Interpol's emphasis on financing is aided by the fact that Interpol Secretary General Ronald K. Noble, the organization's chief executive (and a New York University Law School professor), has a long-standing interest in monetary crimes as president of the Financial Action Task Force, a twenty-six-nation agency established to fight money laundering. In 1999, a first specific Interpol resolution on the financing of terrorism was passed in Seoul.

In matters of the fight against terrorism, Interpol also maintains liaisons with other international organizations. In November 2001, for example, Interpol signed an agreement with Europol to foster cooperation in the policing of terrorism and other international crimes. In December 2001, Interpol and the U.S. Department of the Treasury similarly pledged to cooperate more closely and create an international database of organizations and persons identified as providing financial assistance to terrorist groups. In March 2002, Interpol reached an agreement to cooperate closely with the Arab Interior Ministers' Council to facilitate the exchange of information with the Arab police community.

Especially in matters of international terrorism, U.S. police agencies typically conduct international activities unilaterally rather than participate in an international organization such as Interpol.

The terrorist attacks of September 11 were considered an Interpol matter because of the international dimensions of the case. Shortly after 9/11, Interpol Secretary General Ronald Noble argued that while the terrorist attacks took place on U.S. soil, "they constituted attacks against the entire world and its citizens" (Interpol Web site). Immediately following September 11, Interpol issued fifty-five Red Notices for terrorists who had committed or were connected to these terrorist attacks. Interpol also increased its circulation of Blue Notices, that is, requests for information about or the location of a suspect, of which nineteen concerned the hijackers who carried out the September 11 attacks.

From a practical viewpoint, Interpol reorganized in several key respects after September 11, although some of these organizational changes had already begun before the terrorist attacks. Most concretely, during a press conference in Madrid on September 14, 2001, Secretary General Noble announced the creation of 11 September Task Force at Interpol's headquarters in Lyon, France, to coordinate international criminal police intelligence received at Interpol's headquarters and relating to the recent terrorist attacks in the United States. Also instituted following the September 11 attacks was a General Secretariat Command and Co-ordination Center that is operational twenty-four hours a day, seven days a week. A new Financial and High Tech Crimes Sub-directorate was created that specialized in money laundering. In April 2002, Interpol announced the creation of an Interpol Terrorism Watch List, which provides direct access by police agencies to information on fugitive and suspected terrorists who are subject to Interpol warrants. Also, at the Interpol meeting in Cameroon in 2002, a new global communications project was announced as Interpol's highest priority. This project involves the launching of a new Internet-based Global Communications System (called I-24/7) to provide for a more rapid and more secure exchange of data between the member agencies.

Global Rule of Law and International Police Cooperation

The theory of bureaucratization suggests that structures and processes of international police cooperation rely on a high degree of institutional independence among police institutions. Unlike a legally binding and/or politically attained global rule of law, the global rule of law enforcement relies on professional expertise and efficiency considerations. Interpol indeed places most emphasis on a smooth coordination of and direct contacts between the various participating police agencies. Only a few days after September 11, Interpol Secretary General Noble flew to New York and Washington to meet with U.S. police chiefs and plead for international cooperation. Interpol pays much attention to establishing direct international police communications that can be used efficiently, further aided by technologically advanced means of police technique.

As an important consequence of Interpol's orientation to efficiency in counterterrorist and other police objectives, the organization has managed to attract cooperation from police agencies representing nations that are ideologically very diverse and not always on friendly terms in political respects. For example, shortly after the war in Iraq, authorities from France and the United States agreed to cooperate toward the development of biometric techniques to prevent the forgery of passports as part of their efforts against terrorism, despite these countries' profound disagreements over the Iraqi conflict. On the occasion of the signing of the agreement, U.S. Attorney General John Ashcroft also visited the Interpol headquarters in Lyon to attend an international conference aimed at stepping up the recovery of Iraqi works of art stolen in the aftermath of the fall of the Saddam Hussein regime. The diversity among Interpol's member agencies, however, has also hindered the organization's effectiveness in its missions, as members do not always trust one another. Therefore, unilaterally executed transnational police operations may be preferred instead of participation in the multilateral structures of Interpol. In that sense, Interpol is not always a particularly effective organization because "major powers, like the United States, do not fully trust it" (Bassiouni 2002, 93). Especially in matters of international terrorism, U.S. police agencies typically conduct international activities unilaterally rather than participate in an international organization such as Interpol.

The emphasis on efficiency in international counterterrorist police work reveals the relevance of formal rationalization processes that have been observed in many modern bureaucratic institutions. In terms of the objectives of social control, the bureaucratization of policing involves most noticeably a depoliticization of the target of counterterrorism. This criminalization of terrorism is accomplished by defining terrorism very vaguely ("a crime against humanity") and/or by identifying and isolating the distinctly criminal elements (bombings, killings) from terrorist incidents. Bureaucratization processes have historically been influential across Western societies (Jacoby 1969/1973), so that an important implication is that cooperation among state bureaucracies policing terrorism can take place irrespective of the similarities and/or differences among nations in political, legal, cultural, and other respects. The relative independence of police thereby exposes the limitations of state-centered theories in terms of the specific roles played by police and other state institutions. The autonomy of state bureaucracies creates the potential for bureaucratic activity, such as policing efforts against terrorism, to be planned and implemented without regard for considerations of legality, justice, and politics.

Conclusion

Ideological and political sentiments on terrorism are very divided in the world of international politics and diplomacy. Yet efforts at the level of police agencies and international police organizations, such as Interpol and its member agencies, can be based on a common ground surrounding terrorism through its treatment as a depoliticized crime. Terrorism is thereby fought in ways that are considered to be efficient, irrespective of normative concerns. As such, the bureaucratization of modern police institutions harmonizes with Weber's (1922/1980) perspective of societal rationalization as having gone in the direction of an increasing reliance on principles of efficiency in terms of a calculation of means. It is under those conditions, Weber argued, that the modern state bureaucracy becomes an "almost unbreakable formation," with little political control and democratic oversight (p. 570).

It is important to recognize that the processes and structures of policing and other state activities are composed of a multitude of dimensions and institutions that are not necessarily in tune with one another. For our theorizing of the rule of law, an important implication of the developments of bureaucratization at the level of policing is that we need to recognize a fundamental irony of the modern political state from its origins through its further evolution. The centrality of the state in any discussion on law and police needs no introduction, but it is also important to contemplate the evolution of the state and its functionally divided components, specifically the legal system and the forces of internal coercion. Developing a bureaucratic apparatus to fulfill the state's concentrated and growing arsenal of functions, the state's powers are dispersed across a multitude of institutions, the organization and activities of which the state can no longer carefully control. As the case of international police cooperation shows, the institutions that develop and multiply during the state's continued development cannot be assumed to always be carefully disciplined by the center of the state.

Not only does the evolution of the modern state bring about that the spontaneous collective attention of society is inevitably relaxed (Durkheim 1893/1984), the functionally divided state institutions that are created in response to the weakening influence of tradition also lead to a diversification of the objectives of state power. The expansion of state bureaucracies such as the police has ironic consequences. For as the state grows, the relative power of its center weakens. There is no common end to the state, of course, but it also does not suffice to merely enumerate the state's multiple functions. What is particularly important is that the many functions of the state are not always neatly harmonized, for they each have their own instruments and institutions that develop in relative autonomy to one another and with respect to the center of the state. A state with many means will also have many ends. Therefore, whatever model that is suggested toward the adoption of constitutional-democratic principles at the global level of law and politics to decrease the chances of terrorism must also take into account the manner in which effective control of terrorism is currently accomplished by international cooperation among public police agencies.

Note

1. The following analysis selectively draws from Deflem and Maybin (2005).

References

Anderson, Malcolm. 1997. Interpol and the developing system of international police cooperation. In *Crime and law enforcement in the global village*, ed. William F. McDonald, 89-102. Cincinnati, OH: Anderson.
Bassiouni, M. Cherif. 2002. Legal control of international terrorism: A policy-oriented assessment. *Harvard International Law Journal* 43:83-103.
Bossard, André. 1987. The war against terrorism: The Interpol response. In *International terrorism: The domestic response*, ed. Richard H. Ward and Harold E. Smith, 1-10. Chicago: Office of International Criminal Justice.
Deflem, Mathieu. 2000. Bureaucratization and social control: Historical foundations of international policing. *Law & Society Review* 34 (3): 601-40.
———. 2002. *Policing world society: Historical foundations of international police cooperation*. Oxford: Oxford University Press.

————. 2004a. The boundaries of international cooperation: Problems and prospects of U.S.-Mexican police relations. In *Police corruption: Challenges for developed countries*, ed. Menachem Amir and Stanley Einstein, 93-122. Huntsville, TX: Office of International Criminal Justice.

————. 2004b. Social control and the policing of terrorism: Foundations for a sociology of counter-terrorism. *American Sociologist* 35 (2): 75-92.

Deflem, Mathieu, and Lindsay C. Maybin. 2005. Interpol and the policing of international terrorism: Developments and dynamics since September 11. In *Terrorism: Research, readings, & realities*, ed. Lynne L. Snowden and Brad Whitsel, 175-91. Englewood Cliffs, NJ: Prentice Hall.

Durkheim, Emile. 1893/1984. *The division of labor in society.* New York: Free Press.

Jacoby, Henry. 1969/1973. *The bureaucratization of the world.* Berkeley: University of California Press.

Weber, Max. 1922/1980. *Wirtschaft und Gesellschaft: Grundriss der verstehenden Soziologie.* Tübingen, Germany: J.C.B. Mohr/Paul Siebeck. (English translation: *Economy and society*, ed. Guenther Roth and Claus Wittich, University of California Press, Berkeley, 1986).

This article explores the links between international environmental law and the law of free trade. Democratic countries have tended to favor both environmental law and free trade more so than other countries. The more interesting question is whether the converse is true, that is, do environmental law and free trade aid democracy and the development of the rule of law? This article addresses that question.

Keywords: environmental law; international law; free trade; democracy; rule of law

Environmental Protection, Free Trade, and Democracy

By
DAVID M. DRIESEN

We know that environmentalism played a key role in the revolutionary changes in Central Europe. (Bowman and Hunter 1992, 923). In what was then Czechoslovakia, an environmental group wrote an exposé demanding a solution to the industrial pollution in and around Bratislava (ibid., 926). The circulation of this publication, and the subsequent attempt to jail its authors, was "a central rallying point" for the prodemocracy revolution in 1989 (ibid.). In the same year, "when five thousand people gathered in Sofia, Bulgaria, to protest environmental pollution, it was the country's first public protest in forty years" (ibid.). One week later, the Bulgarian leader resigned (ibid.).

David M. Driesen is the Angela R. Cooney Professor of Law at Syracuse University College of Law, an affiliate of the Maxwell School of Citizenship Center for Environmental Policy and Administration, and an adjunct professor at the State University of New York College of Environmental Science and Forestry. Professor Driesen is the author of The Economic Dynamics of Environmental Law *(MIT Press, 2003), the winner of the Lynton Keith Caldwell Award for the best book of the year on science, environment, and technology. He has written numerous law review articles on national and international environmental law and on constitutional law. Professor Driesen holds a J.D. from the Yale Law School (1989) and served as an attorney for the Natural Resources Defense Council, a leading citizen group, prior to joining the Syracuse University faculty.*

NOTE: I would like to thank Noelle Valentine for research assistance. Any errors belong to me.

DOI: 10.1177/0002716205281493

Environmental damage was a very visible flaw of communist rule in countries such as Hungary, Bulgaria, and Slovakia. Citizens could actually see, taste, and smell the pollution, but they were not allowed to talk about it (ibid.). This dichotomy between the visible effects of industrial pollution and the inability to speak about them was one of the intolerable aspects of daily existence. The communist regime did permit "nature protection" activities and groups formed to transplant native plants, build tunnels for native frogs, and the like (ibid., 927). These groups allowed citizens to discuss environmental problems and slowly evolved into hotbeds of dissident activity, which spawned many postrevolution leaders.

Professor Schwartz has asked me to describe how the law of environmental protection and free trade might contribute to the development of democracy around the world, a key aspect of the development of the world rule of law. In this dramatic case, the demand for a clean environment played a significant role in stimulating democracy. But usually the relationship between environmental law (and free trade) and democracy is more subtle. I will argue that both bodies of law have some capacity to aid development of democracy but that the relationship between environmental protection, free trade, and democracy is somewhat complex.

I will begin this analysis by providing some basic background on international environmental law and international trade law, emphasizing how both bodies of international law interact with domestic legal regimes. I will then discuss the relationship between these bodies of law and more general democratic and rule of law ideals.

International Environmental Law

Notwithstanding some early-twentieth-century conservation treaties, modern international environmental basically came into being in the 1970s. It includes both global environmental agreements with large numbers of parties; regional pacts, such as agreements managing various transboundary water bodies and airsheds; and some customary law.

A lot of classic international law involves states agreeing to some restraints on their own conduct. Examples include conventions limiting the use of force.

International environmental law, however, often addresses problems that have their roots in some of the unfortunate by-products of private productive activities. Thus, the Convention to Regulate International Trade in Endangered Species of Flora and Fauna (CITES) addresses the sale of animal parts in international trade, an economically valuable activity. Unfortunately, the sale of these animal parts encouraged those hoping to profit from the trade to kill so many animals that some species became endangered (Reeve 2002, 7-15). The Montreal Protocol on Ozone Depleting Substances addresses substances serving valuable economic functions, refrigerating food, cooling down cars, acting as solvents in a variety of industrial processes, and protecting crops from pests. The manufacturers of these substances, however, unwittingly unleashed forces destroying the stratospheric ozone layer, which shields us from ultraviolet radiation capable of causing widespread skin cancer (Ozone Secretariat 1993). The Kyoto Protocol to the United Nations Framework Convention on Climate Change addresses the burning of fossil fuels, an economic activity at the heart of transportation, manufacturing, and the production of electricity for homes and offices. Unfortunately, we have abundant evidence that burning fossil fuels has warmed the earth's average mean surface temperature and will do so to a greater degree in the future absent basic changes in how we carry on these basic economic activities (Houghton et al. 1996, 3-7). Scientists expect this rise in mean surface temperature to cause sea levels to rise, inundating coastal areas and some islands, and causing infectious diseases to spread (ibid., 449). They also predict a host of ecological changes, many of them troubling (Watson, Zinyowera, and Moss 1998, 2-6; Fischman 1991, 565).

Because international environmental treaties often address problems coming from private conduct, treaties start rather than end the establishment of an environmental rule of law. A nation that agrees to limit trade in endangered species, to phase out production of ozone-depleting chemicals, to reduce greenhouse gas emissions, or to otherwise limit environmental destruction must then pass and enforce domestic laws encouraging or requiring individuals and firms to change their conduct to allow the country to meet its treaty obligations.

Thus, international environmental law encourages the development of domestic environmental law (Driesen 2000). And one may ask whether this law creation function helps establish democracy and the rule of law more generally, a question I will take up in due course.

Free Trade

At the same time, a body of law has grown up seeking to encourage free trade. This body of law grew out of the postwar General Agreement on Tariffs and Trade (GATT), an agreement designed to keep the peace by encouraging friendly commercial relations among the developed countries. Over time, the regime has gained strength, and participation in free trade agreements has become much more widespread (Strauss 1998, 815). Economic theory predicts that free trade will contribute to prosperity, so economists, many development specialists, and, increasingly, the political leadership of developing countries see free trade as an essential element in efforts to spread the blessings of economic development to countries afflicted with serious poverty (Spriggs and Stanford 1993; Holbein 1992).

This body of law has a more classic structure. It seeks to limit the conduct of states, in this case by discouraging them from banning imports and enacting discriminatory tariffs to protect their domestic industries. Hence, it seeks to prevent the enactment of laws that might discourage international commerce, rather than to encourage laws limiting private activities, as international environmental law does.

Until recently, international trade law and international environmental law proceeded along completely separate tracks, even though trade restraints have always been used as a means of encouraging the development of international environmental law and of enforcing treaty obligations. When some of those involved in creating the Montreal Protocol on Ozone Depleting Substances asked about the legality under GATT of prohibiting trade in ozone-depleting substances from countries that refused to sign on to the emerging international environmental treaty, the GATT expert they consulted saw no problem (Driesen 2001, 305).

The separation between trade and environmental law, however, began to erode in the 1980s. Two GATT panel decisions held that U.S. laws forbidding importation of tuna caught in ways that endanger dolphins violates GATT (GATT 1993, 155, 195, 200-201, 205; GATT 1994, 889-90, 894, 898-99). These decisions, and a later one declaring a ban on importation into Europe of beef made from cattle fed with growth hormones contrary to a later trade agreement, the Agreement on Sanitary and Phyto-Sanitary Measures, spurred widespread dissatisfaction with the trade regime among many people in developed countries, even leading to street demonstrations in Seattle, the site of a meeting to further develop the trade regime in the 1990s. A subsequent decision struck down a ban on importing shrimp caught without using devices to protect endangered sea turtles (World Trade Organization [WTO] 1999). Even though this decision had an antienvironmental result, it reflected some narrowing of the antienvironmental doctrine that had led to the tuna-dolphin decisions, which might reflect some response to the political pressures on the free trade regime. Subsequently, the WTO issued its first decision ever upholding a challenged environmental regulation, a ban on asbestos (Driesen 2001, 294-95; WTO 2000).

Just as the WTO began to modify its antienvironmental stance, international panels arbitrating disputes under the North American Free Trade Agreement (NAFTA) began to articulate new legal principles providing a greater potential threat to environmental law than the WTO decisions. In one case, a NAFTA panel held that a Mexican municipality's denial of a permit to dispose of hazardous waste constituted an expropriation in violation of NAFTA, thereby incorporating an expansive concept of regulatory takings into NAFTA (*United States v. Metalclad Corp.* 2001). The U.S. law creating the doctrine of regulatory takings makes the United States a bit of an outlier in this realm. Neither Canadian nor Mexican law uses takings doctrine to limit regulation. But the NAFTA decision went far beyond even the most property protective conceptions of a legitimate regulatory takings doctrine (Been and Beauvais 2003).

Some of the anxiety these free trade decisions created has led to charges that trade institutions, like the WTO, are antidemocratic. Yet many of the trade regimes supporters would see the trade regime as an engine for democracy. We now turn to the question of what, if anything, international law on the environment and on international trade have to contribute to democracy.

Trade, Environment, and Democracy

Generally, a case can be made that environmental protection and free trade coincide with democratic government. Most Western democracies have relatively strong environmental protection regimes (Neumayer, Gates, and Gleditsch 2003), but the Soviet Union was an environmental disaster. Similarly, many Western democracies became members of the WTO, but China only became eligible as it began to take steps toward some degree of democratization. It is not so clear, however, that either of these bodies of law creates democracy. It might be that democracies tend to favor free trade and environmental protection.

The issue of creating a world rule of law involves both international and domestic legal components. To some extent, the idea of a world rule of law envisions a set of restraints on nation-states. GATT formed a minor part of the post–World War II restraints. The United States' unilateralism arguably constitutes the greatest contemporary threat to that rule of law, as the United States substitutes a doctrine of "regime change" and a concept of "enemy combatants" for international laws providing for humane treatment of prisoners and limiting the use of military force.

The point is that the rule of law and democracy sometimes reinforce each other but sometimes exist in tension with each other.

Yet the international rule of law as conventionally conceived exists in some tension with democratic ideals. The conventional conception saw international law as the product of the consent of states. International law's legitimacy depended on the consent of the states themselves, even antidemocratic states, not upon the consent of the people within those states.

Democratic legitimacy, however, only comes from consent by democratically elected states through processes offering some possibility for democratic participation. GATT's enactment through executive agreement constituted a democracy deficit in the eyes of many (Jackson 1967). Yet Congressional ratification of the Uruguay Round Agreements, which reaffirmed the GATT, did not silence democracy-based criticism of the WTO. This may reflect the large role the Uruguay Round gives to binding dispute resolution. Ironically, a measure that probably greatly strengthened the rule of law in international trade, by providing a judicial process to settle disputes requiring interpretation of the general principles in trade agreements, gave rise to a perception that the agreements were antidemocratic.

The Kyoto Protocol might offer a mirror image of this. One might view the U.S. rejection of the Kyoto Protocols as democracy in action. The Senate passed a resolution disapproving of the Kyoto Protocol by a wide margin, and President Clinton considered passage so unlikely that he never submitted the agreement to Congress (Driesen 1998, 21). President Bush's repudiation of the agreement, however, greatly hurt the rule of law, undermining international cooperation needed to solve international problems and contributing to the perception of the United States as a "rogue nation" (Karon 2001). But if his action reflects the views of the majority of people in the United States, then this blow to the rule of law represents a victory for democracy.

The point is that the rule of law and democracy sometimes reinforce each other but sometimes exist in tension with each other. Indeed, the rule of law ideal presupposes official adherence to laws, even if the particular application is unpopular, and thus appears, in a sense, antidemocratic.

Some critics of the WTO seek to cure the democracy deficit that inheres in any high-level international decision by creating a greater role for direct participation by civil society. They suggest that we need an international assemblage of citizens to directly create international law (Falk and Strauss 2001; Strauss 1999). While such a notion may seem far-fetched, the idea of a European Parliament, which performs precisely this sort of role in Europe today, probably seemed insane decades ago.

Also, a number of recent international agreements address the democracy deficit directly. They only allow democratically elected governments to participate (Fox and Roth 2000). The traditional conception of international law accepted state consent by whoever was in power, even a dictator.

On the national level, the relationship between international trade law, international environmental law, and democracy is also complex. I will argue that both bodies of law have some capacity to contribute to democracy, but they do not necessarily perform this function.

But does international environmental law have anything to do with encouraging this domestic rule of law development? I am not sure that I can fully answer that question, but an affirmative answer becomes easier if we expand the definition of international law to include what one might call transnational law. Nation-states influence each other's law through means other than formal treaty agreements. International conferences and other mechanisms for sharing ideas often lead one country to emulate features of another country's laws. For example, the United Nation's Development Program has been working with the Iranian government to deal with the problem of water scarcity (World Resources Institute 2003). Since the late 1990s, the Sustainable Management of Land and Water Resources program has developed a model of participatory decision making, where facilitators work with villagers in communities along the Hable River to identify the environmental problems and solutions. The results have encouraged the Iranian government to replicate the project's community-led methods to counter other natural resources problems such as soil erosion, land degradation, and drought in other rural regions.

Countries around the world have adopted variants on the theme the United States created when it enacted the National Environmental Policy Act (NEPA). This law requires assessment of the environmental consequences of government actions before they are undertaken. Most important, it requires public participation in the assessment process. To the extent that other countries have adopted the public participation model of NEPA, transnational law has promoted democracy by giving people a greater say in decisions impacting the environment in which they live. Similarly, many countries have run with the idea of "right-to-know" laws, which require industrial facilities to report information about their pollution to the public. These laws empower citizens to demand changes based on some knowledge of what is being done to the environment. Again, the spread of these laws might be seen as international environmental law spreading democratization.

International environmental treaties generate a demand for laws in the signatory nations. It does not necessarily follow that the laws stimulate democracy. For example, CITES has limited international trade in elephant tusks (Glennon 1990). Kenya, a corrupt dictatorship, became very serious about meeting its conservation obligations. It hired a leading anthropologist, Richard Leakey, to run its largest game reserve and employed helicopter gunships to keep poachers away from the elephants. Kenya's president, Daniel arap Moi, acted very environmentally, but not democratically.

> *My own view is that democracy encourages
> environmental law because most people usually
> favor environmental protection.*

On the other hand, South Africa and Botswana created participatory community-based management of elephant herds (Heimert 1995). They allowed local communities to get some of the proceeds from the sale of elephant tusks and to participate in deciding how to manage the elephants. Yet this limited sale of tusks creates some potential to aid poachers of less-well-managed elephant herds to launder tusks, thus potentially undermining the international rule of law. On the other hand, these programs created some resources for local communities and some public participation.

Even where country officials are eagerly embracing the concept of public participation, the result is not necessarily an increase in democracy. The Aarhus Convention, for example, is an international agreement created to implement the three pillars of Rio Principle 10: (1) public access to information, (2) public participation in decision making, and (3) equal access to justice in environmental matters

(Hunter, Salzman, and Zaelke 2002, 436). Signed by sixteen former Soviet bloc countries, some heralded the treaty as a unique instrument for democratization that would create a massive movement toward opening the doors to participatory democracy. While the treaty may be a unique instrument, this massive movement toward a participatory democracy has not occurred. In exploring the reasons why, researchers interviewing officials in these countries found that while committed to the convention, they were unable to overcome fundamental characteristics of their former regimes (Zaharchenko and Goldenman 2004). Programs to provide information to the public were described as "propaganda and education" (ibid.). A general attitude of paternalism was pervasive, with one top official likening public requests for information to a child asking questions with officials being the proverbial parents who know which answers the child may have (ibid.). Economics also played a role, where state salaries have been cut, inflation has increased, and the information that government officials possess may be the only asset and a source of pride as well as professional recognition (ibid.).

One of the difficulties in creating a world rule of law involves the problem of creating legitimacy for both international and domestic legal institutions at the same time.

My own view is that democracy encourages environmental law because most people usually favor environmental protection. I suspect that the converse is true as well. Environmental law may strengthen democracy. But if it does so, it must do so through creating public participation possibilities that strengthen the engagement of civil society with the creation of law.

Furthermore, there are limits to environmental law's capacity to encourage democracy. CITES may have inspired Moi to protect elephants, but his government may have been too corrupt to succeed at it. Low-paid rangers are susceptible to bribery. Environmental law may further democratize governments already having some of the basic requisites of democracy in place.

Moreover, the Czech case shows that demand for environmental protection can sometimes motivate a demand for democracy where none exists. Generally, movements for democracy reflect not only an abstract embrace of democratic ideals but also reactions to concrete failings of existing institutions. A failure of a nondemocratic regime to protect the environment can help catalyze democratic movements, but often other kinds of issues, such as human rights and economic issues, have proven even more central.

The picture regarding international trade is equally complex. Free traders argue that free trade aids democracy because it aids in the project of creating sufficient wealth to make democracy possible. But perhaps it is the other way around. Maybe democracy creates the conditions to make free trade a viable policy.

On the other hand, if people want protectionist policies, and sometime they do, then the rule of law undermines democracy, at least in the short term. It obligates national governments to avoid protecting domestic industries, even if their people want to in particular cases.

Some might argue that the tension I have described simply reflects too simplistic a conception of democracy. Democracy is not only rule by the people. It includes countermajoritarian institutions like courts. Maybe so. But the case that judicial decisions are part of democracy, rather than in opposition to it, rests on public acceptance of the judicial role. One of the difficulties in creating a world rule of law involves the problem of creating legitimacy for both international and domestic legal institutions at the same time. From that perspective, the WTO may suffer from a democracy deficit, not because of a lack of participation in writing free trade rules—free trade rules are written much like other international legal rules—but by virtue of a trade-specialist-dominated judicial process straying into areas where a trade orientation is not sufficient as a source of legitimacy (Driesen 2001, 312-16). Still, perhaps we need a political process to gain acceptance for a richer conception of democracy, one that accepts, at least presumptively, that countries should choose, at least most of the time, to adhere to international legal norms and that civil society should participate in their creation.

Conclusion

Public participation in environmental law can aid democracy. Free trade law can spread democracy to the extent that it helps create the material basis for it in civil society. But in neither case is the relationship between international law, the rule of law, and democracy simple and straightforward.

References

Been, V., and Joel Beauvais. 2003. The global fifth amendment? NAFTA's investment protections and the misguided quest for an international regulatory takings doctrine. *New York University Law Review* 78:30-143.

Bowman, M., and David Hunter. 1992. Environmental reforms in post-communist Central Europe: From high hopes to hard reality. *Michigan Journal of International Law* 13:921-80.

Driesen, D. M. 1998. Free lunch or cheap fix? The emissions trading idea and the climate change convention. *Boston College Environmental Affairs Law Review* 26:1-87.

———. 2000. Choosing environmental instruments in transnational legal context. *Ecology Law Quarterly* 27:1-52.

———. 2001. What is free trade? The real issue lurking behind the trade and environment debate. *Virginia Journal of International Law* 41:279-366.

Falk, R., and Andrew L. Strauss. 2001. Toward global parliament. *Foreign Affairs* 80:212-20.

Fischman, Robert L. 1991. Global warming and property interests: Preserving coastal wetlands as sea levels rise. *Hofstra Law Review* 19:565-602.

Fox, G., and Brad Roth, eds. 2000. *Democratic governance and international law.* New York: Cambridge University Press.

GATT Dispute Settlement Panel Report on U.S.-Restrictions on Imports of Tuna, Sept. 3, 1991, GATT B.I.S.D. (39th Supp.) (1993).

GATT Dispute Settlement Panel Report on U.S.-Restrictions on Imports of Tuna, July 1994, 33 I.L.M. 839 (1994).

Glennon, M. 1990. Has international law failed the elephant? *American Journal of International Law* 84:1-34.

Heimert, A. 1995. Note, how the elephant lost its tusks. *Yale Law Journal* 104:1473-1506.

Holbein, J. R. 1992. The case for free trade. *Loyola of Los Angeles International and Comparative Law Journal* 15:19-32.

Houghton, J. T., L. G. Meira Filho, B. A. Callander, N. Harris, A. Kattenberg, and K. Maskell, eds. 1996. *Climate change 1995: The science of climate change.* New York: Cambridge University Press.

Hunter, D., James Salzman, and Durwood Zaelke. 2002. *International environmental law and policy.* New York: Foundation Press.

Jackson, J. H. 1967. The General Agreement on Tariffs and Trade in United States domestic law. *Michigan Law Review* 66:249-332.

Karon, K. 2001. When it comes to Kyoto, the U.S. is the "rogue nation." *Time,* July 24.

Neumayer, E., Scott Gates, and Nils Petter Gleditsch. 2003. *Environmental commitment, democracy and inequality. A background paper to World Development Report 2003.* Washington, DC: World Bank.

Ozone Secretariat. 1993. *Handbook for the Montreal Protocol on Substances that Deplete the Ozone Layer.* 3rd ed. Nairobi, Kenya: United National Environment Programme.

Reeve, Rosalind. 2002. *Policing international trade in endangered species: The cites treaty and compliance.* London: Earthscan Publications.

Spriggs, W. E., and James Stanford. 1993. Economists' assessments of the likely employment and wage effects of the North American Free Trade Agreement. *Hofstra Labor Law Journal* 10:495-536.

Strauss, A. L. 1998. From Gattzilla to the Green Giant: Winning the environmental battle for the soul of the World Trade Organization. *University of Pennsylvania Journal of International Economic Law* 19:769-821.

———. 1999. Overcoming the dysfunction of the bifurcated global system: The promise of a people's assembly. *Transnational Law and Contemporary Problems* 9:489-511.

United States v. Metalclad Corp., 2001. British Columbia Supreme Court 664 (May 5, 2001).

Watson, R. T., Marufu C. Zinyowera, and Richard H. Moss, eds. 1998. *The regional impacts of climate change: An assessment of vulnerabilities.* New York: Cambridge University Press.

World Resources Institute. 2003. *World resources 2002-2004: Decisions for the Earth: Balance voice and power.* Washington, DC: World Resources Institute.

WTO Appellate Body Report on U.S.-Import Prohibition of Certain Shrimp and Shrimp Products, Oct. 12, 1998, 38 I.L.M. 118 (1999).

WTO Dispute Settlement Panel Report on E.C.-Measures Affecting Asbestos and Asbestos-Containing Products, 2000 WL 1449942 (Sept. 18, 2000).

Zaharchenko, T., and Gretta Goldenman. 2004. Accountability and governance: the challenge of implementing the Aarhus Convention in Eastern Europe and Central Asia. *International Environmental Agreements: Politics, Law and Economics* 4:229-51.

Global Business: Oversight without Inhibiting Enterprise

This article is focused on the role of international business in wealth creation. It discusses the issue of what regulations should be imposed, country by country, to encourage legal and ethical conduct by international firms. In a libertarian view, many excesses are self-correcting because businesses wish to operate in individual countries on a long-term basis. Serious abuses are rare but take place nonetheless, sometimes with disastrous consequences. The only effective way to control abuses is through tighter scrutiny of foreign direct investment (FDI) at a local level. Abuses affect individual countries and must therefore be policed in those countries, despite sometimes endemic corruption. Local politicians and bureaucrats—who issue FDI licenses—must be motivated by concern for public welfare and nothing else.

Keywords: global business; capitalism; foreign investment; foreign subsidiaries; corporate social responsibility

By
JOHN PHILIP JONES

In this article, global business means two things: first, the export of goods and services, mostly from large countries to small ones; and second, the establishment of separate enterprises in foreign countries, with capital from (and therefore much control exercised by) private companies in the home market. I am mainly concerned with the latter. This article does not discuss the transfer of capital sums as loans and grants through public aid programs run by governments and United Nations agencies. These

John Philip Jones entered academe in 1981 after a twenty-five-year career in advertising with J. Walter Thompson in Europe and is a tenured professor in the Newhouse School at Syracuse University. He has published twelve books on advertising and numerous journal articles. Among his many awards are Distinguished Advertising Educator by the American Advertising Federation (1991), a leadership award from Cowles Business Media and the American Association of Advertising Agencies (1996), the Telmar Award for extending the concept of Short-Term Advertising Strength (STAS) from television to print media (1997), and the Syracuse University Chancellor's Citation for Exceptional Academic Achievement (2001).

DOI: 10.1177/0002716205282264

have a very patchy history and have been subject to great abuse.[1] Private investment is evaluated by the criteria of the marketplace. In other words, foreign investments are made on the basis of their perceived economic soundness.

Politicians, journalists, academics, and members of the public at large form themselves into two separate and opposing groups when they think about global business. The libertarians see global business as an extension into the international sphere of the principle of the division of labor: something that provides unquestioned benefits in terms of economic efficiency.[2] Opposing them are people who see global business as an expression of economic and social (and perhaps even political) imperialism.[3] It is sometimes known as the "McDonaldization" of the world: an epithet hardly characterized by subtle understatement.

I believe that the weight of evidence supports the libertarian position, and some of the facts will be briefly reviewed. The background arguments in favor of global business are (1) that it provides work in overseas markets at wage rates usually above those ruling in those markets (although not in the United States). This means (2) that wealth is created, and (3) goods are produced relatively cheaply, which is something of great value to everybody, including American consumers. At the same time, (4) the United States demonstrates its usual adaptability through the willingness of American workers to move from declining industries to expanding ones and to move home from the "rust belt" to the "sun belt." This is a process not without pain. But American workers, with their accustomed resilience, accept it in large numbers. They are after all mostly the descendents of immigrants who made longer journeys before they caught their first glimpse of the Statue of Liberty.

As a result of these processes, China does things that it does best because of the structure of the Chinese economy; and the United States does what it does best because of the different structure of its own economy. This is Adam Smith's Invisible Hand at work.

The libertarian argument does not claim that the path of global business is strewn with orchids, and it certainly does not mean that it will inevitably lead to a situation (familiar to readers of *Candide*) that can be described as the best possible of all conceivable worlds. On the contrary, global business needs to be scrutinized in such a way that its potential excesses (which can have dangerous consequences) are detected and corrected, without at the same time inhibiting the enterprise of the system: the enterprise that is its basic raison d'être.

The Positive Side

Substantial batteries of data exist to demonstrate the overall benefits of global business. I shall merely quote one series of robust estimates published by *The Economist*.[4] The data compare two years, 1980 and 1997; and they cover twenty-four "more globalized" countries (carefully defined) and forty-nine "less globalized" ones. The 1997 populations of the first group were 2.9 billion and of the second group 1.1 billion.

- In the more globalized countries, gross domestic product (GDP) advanced by 3.1 percent per annum; in the less globalized, it grew by 0.5 percent per annum.
- The average number of years of primary schooling in the more globalized countries advanced from 2.4 to 3.8 and in the less globalized from 2.5 to 3.1.
- In the majority of countries, the productivity per worker and the wage per worker are closely correlated. The economic benefit is therefore shared by the labor force as well as by the owners of capital.

Different tranches of data demonstrate that the idea that globalization is to the exclusive benefit of rich countries is a total fallacy.

Global business has a long history. Exporting has taken place for centuries. Separately established organizations funded by foreign direct investment (FDI) have existed for a hundred years. I have direct personal knowledge of such "daughter companies" that were established well before World War II. In all cases, they have developed a strong local culture that has been impregnated into the American (or British or Japanese or other) culture of the firms that established them.

In the majority of cases, problems correct themselves. The reason for this is that firms are in business for the long term, and they are fully aware that they must show themselves to be good citizens. But good citizenship can be interpreted in a number of different ways.

[G]lobal business needs to be scrutinized in such a way that its potential excesses (which can have dangerous consequences) are detected and corrected, without at the same time inhibiting the enterprise of the system.

The most fashionable concept at the moment is corporate social responsibility (CSR).[5] This has a wonderfully ethical ring to it, and as a result it is discussed and widely applauded by academics and social commentators who have an optimistic disposition. Have we arrived finally at "capitalism with a conscience"?

I am not enthusiastic about CSR. I see it as a dangerous fallacy, for two separate reasons. First, it has little real influence on the operating policy of major companies. From a large sample of such companies, it was found for instance that their donations to charity account for *less than 1 percent* of their pretax profits. To such companies, CSR may have benefits from the public relations standpoint, but that is about all. A perhaps more serious point is that the real purpose of capitalistic enterprise is for firms to make things that people will buy and thereby earn a profit. If they concentrate on this process while maintaining their respect for the letter and spirit of the law, they can compete most efficiently in a vigorously competitive marketplace. And from this the real benefits of capitalism flow. This is really what global business is all about.

We nevertheless need to remind ourselves of the problems.

The Negative Side

We now come to an examination of specific widely known examples, supplemented by my personal experience of the field of international business. There are two broad groups of problems: those derived from different (and less stringent) controls over foreign than over home operations and those stemming from investment and financial policies.

Consider these three notorious examples in which the controls over foreign subsidiaries have been less rigorous than over domestic ones:

- The shockingly lax way in which Union Carbide operated its plant in Bhopal, India, which led to the leakage of lethal gas in 1984, causing the death of twenty thousand people.
- The long-established policy of Altria (the company that markets Philip Morris cigarettes) in marketing cigarettes in vast quantities to third world countries, especially to China and (most recently) to Indonesia, which have few legal controls over such operations. At the same time, the company has advertised widely in the United States to try to persuade people not to start smoking: a preemptive strategy pursued for fear of stricter legal sanctions. By operating so differently in the Pacific countries and in the United States, the company is saying explicitly that Asian lives are less valuable than American ones.
- During the 1970s and 1980s, Nestlé, the largest food company in the world, generated enormous business through selling its Infant Formula milk products in third world countries. This was, prima facie, perfectly ethical, except that many such countries lack plentiful supplies of pure drinking water. The result of mixing the Nestlé product with contaminated water was a series of major health crises. Should Nestlé have been held responsible? Many observers think so, and I share their view.

Next consider these two examples of problems relating to investment and financial controls:

- A number of major companies, especially those in the oil sector, pump large quantities of capital into third world countries that are run by savagely autocratic and corrupt political regimes. The profit made locally from this investment is in effect used to curtail the liberty and prosperity of the population of those countries.
- Cases in which individual companies transfer profits from countries that levy high corporate taxes to those that levy lower ones. This practice may be legal (or on the fringe of legality). But it strikes many people as unethical, and it is certainly not an admirable example of good citizenship.

Overcoming Abuses

Citizens are fairly aware of the problems; these are not just the concern of the antiglobalist factions. The worries are shared by the better global firms themselves. The traditional response to the problems, however, has taken the form of either (1) (generally weak) legal regulations within the individual countries where global businesses are established; or (2) sanctions imposed by the companies themselves: in the home countries, in the outlying countries, or (most commonly) in both. I shall call these sanctions "self-regulation," and they will be discussed first.

My own experience of the local affiliates of major global companies has been very favorable. These include Unilever, Pepsi-Cola, Ford, Gillette, Nestlé (despite the problem just mentioned), and a number of slightly less important companies. Over time, these firms have developed a strong local culture in the individual countries where they operate. They invest in education and training of their local staff. Much of their success has been due to the importation of knowledge and expertise that has been exploited by the local companies.

Unilever, a joint British/Dutch enterprise, is run by a board of directors from these two countries. It is significant that the first director who was neither British nor Dutch was an Indian executive, who had been chairman of Unilever's highly successful subsidiary, Hindustan Lever (which has been established for almost eighty years). He was one of the most respected business leaders in India, and Unilever was perfectly aware of what he could contribute to its business as a whole.

[International corporate scandals] dramatically highlight the need for the government of a receiving country to act rigorously and proactively.

But with the investment and financial policies of less scrupulous organizations, the potential abuses need to be more strictly investigated than they are at present. Where they are open (e.g., investment in countries with undesirable political regimes), the system is *not* self-correcting. Questions raised by individual stockholders at company annual general meetings usually have no effect whatsoever. And the problems of accounting practice remain *sub rosa* and are never put on the table.

The logical forum where such problems should be addressed is the United Nations. This raises serious questions, however, discussed below. Assuming that the problem can be handed to an organization set up by one of the established United Nations agencies, how will it do its work, remembering that its deliberations need to be carried out with full transparency and publicity?

A model for this type of organization is the way in which the Better Business Bureaus in the United States have set up a voluntary mechanism to handle complaints (from all sources) about advertising claims. The bodies in question are called the National Advertising Division and National Advertising Review Board (NAD/NARB). These systems are run by a small but highly qualified staff supplemented by experienced volunteers from the advertising industry, and the findings of specific investigations are published monthly. In this way, self-policing can be made to work because it is generally recognized that high ethical standards are to the benefit of all.[6]

I must, however, return to my doubts about the ability of the United Nations to address abuses such as those described in this article. This body seems to me to be sinking into the ocean beneath the weight of its own bureaucracy plus the added weight of the large number of separate parties with conflicting self-interests. I believe that it is absolutely necessary to devise a system that is likely to be implemented more rigorously and with stronger sanctions than the United Nations is at present capable of providing. This is certainly true of the types of problems that carry safety and health hazards.

Foreign Direct Investment

FDI is in the interest of both the investing organizations and the receiving countries. Investors are keen to make it because they will only put up the money if the proposal meets commercial criteria. Receiving countries—specifically politicians in those countries—are in favor of it because they know that it is good for employment, income, and tax revenues. The only opposition that makes itself heard comes from local politicians who are either xenophobic or proponents of economic self-sufficiency or both. For this reason, in some countries, for example, India and Norway, foreign owners are only allowed to hold a minority stake in the equity of their subsidiary companies.

FDI plans should be subject to tough negotiation between the two parties. Conditions should be required. Leverage can be applied. All details should be scrutinized.

FDI is always regulated by the receiving countries, and licenses are granted by politicians and bureaucrats. These provide obvious opportunities for corruption, although direct evidence is difficult to find. But it has certainly been prevalent and may indeed be endemic. A highly informed analyst once described investment decision making in third world countries as the transfer of money from poor people in rich countries to rich people in poor countries.[7]

FDI is enormously important and can make an almost immediate difference to the economic health of developing countries. As an illustration of this, the different rules in India and China regarding FDI have had strikingly contrasting effects in the retail field. In China, retail FDI has been liberalized, and as a result the retail sector has developed rapidly, with a significant reduction in margins that has been of great benefit to the Chinese buying public. In contrast, retail FDI is still rigidly restricted in India. As a result, retailing remains atomized, with high margins and vast wastage (estimated at $11 billion per annum) because food stores are small and lack air-conditioning. This is strikingly evident to visitors to the subcontinent.

Even more important, the Union Carbide, Altria, and Nestlé scandals should have been addressed by legal regulations, yet they were not. They dramatically highlight the need for the government of a receiving country to act rigorously and proactively. It must only agree to accept FDI on condition that there will be a tough and formal evaluation of how the global company intends to conduct its business in the new country. At this stage, it should be made quite clear that matters as important as safety standards and marketing policy should be applied uniformly across all parts of the company: the home country and the foreign subsidiaries. There should be no holes in the net.

If receiving countries are to avoid disasters like the ones described in this article, politicians must think exclusively of the economic and social welfare of their people. I wish I knew how to achieve this wonderfully utopian objective. I am nevertheless convinced that this is the only way in which excesses can be avoided.

Analysts can advise. It is up to politicians to take action. Can the first group influence the second? We might remember the wise words of a Harvard economist who is now in his nineties but who thinks as clearly and trenchantly as ever: "Conservatives worry about universities being centers of disquieting innovation. Their worries may be exaggerated, but it has occurred."[8]

Notes

1. Peter T. Bauer, *Dissent on Development* (London: Weidenfeld & Nicolson, 1976), 34-36. Also see Peter T. Bauer, *Reality and Logic* (Cambridge, MA: Harvard University Press, 1984), 38-62.

2. See for instance Martin Wolf, *Why Globalization Works* (New Haven, CT: Yale University Press, 2004).

3. See for instance Naomi Klein, *No Logo* (New York: Picador USA, 1999). This book's strongest feature is tendentious argument rather than empirical demonstration.

4. Wolf, *Why Globalization Works*, 138-72.

5. See for instance "The Good Company. A Survey of Corporate Social Responsibility," *The Economist*, January 22, 2005.

6. Rana Said, "The National Advertising Division, National Advertising Review Board, and the Self-Regulation of Advertising," in *Advertising Organizations and Publications. A Resource Guide*, ed. John Philip Jones (Thousand Oaks, CA: Sage, 2000), 203-16.

7. Bauer, personal communication.

8. John Kenneth Galbraith, "How Keynes Came to America," *Economics, Peace and Laughter* (Harmondsworth, UK: Penguin, 1979), 40.

The "Good Governance" Concept Revisited

By
VED P. NANDA

The term "good governance" is unsettled in its meaning. Through the 1980s and 1990s, donor countries and institutions trended to make aid conditional upon reforms in the recipient country, which was found largely ineffective in encouraging real policy changes. More recently, donors, such as the International Monetary Fund, the World Bank, and the United States, are increasingly insisting upon performance and good governance as a prerequisite for aid, a practice called "selectivity." This is a means of requiring a recipient state to demonstrate the seriousness of its commitment to economic and social reforms. There are no objective standards for determining good governance: some aspects include political stability, the rule of law, control of corruption, and accountability. High levels of poverty and weak governance are linked, making selectivity difficult to implement. For reforms to succeed, domestic support, ownership, and commitment are crucial, as are the recipient's cultural context and history.

Keywords: good governance; aid; conditionality; rule of law; accountability; cultural context; International Monetary Fund; World Bank

"Good governance," a term that came into vogue in the 1990s with the World Bank leading the charge, has assumed the status of a mantra for donor agencies as well as donor countries for conditioning aid upon the performance of the recipient government. This is

Ved P. Nanda is the Thompson G. Marsh Professor of Law and director of the International Legal Studies Program at the University of Denver Sturm College of Law. He has served as the U.S. delegate to the World Federation of the United Nations Associations, Geneva, and as vice chair of its Executive Council. He is a member of the advisory council of the United States Institute of Human Rights and serves on the Board of Directors of the United Nations Association of the United States of America. He also serves as an elected member of the American Law Institute and as a council member-at-large for the American Bar Association Section of International Law and Practice. Widely published in law journals and national magazines, he has authored or coauthored more than twenty books and more than 150 chapters and major law review articles.

DOI: 10.1177/0002716205282847

intended to ensure that the development assistance is used effectively.

The G-8 leaders, who met in Gleneagle, Scotland, on July 7-8, 2005, with a major focus of the summit on combating poverty in Africa, reiterated the requirement in their final *Communiqué* (Gleneagles Communiqué 2005, para. 27). They noted that the aid is to be focused "on low income countries which are committed to growth and poverty reduction, to democratic, accountable and transparent government, and to sound public financial management" (ibid., para. 30; see White and Mahtani 2005).

On making this commitment, the leaders endorsed the earlier report by the G-8 Africa Personal Representatives on implementation of the Africa Action Plan (Progress Report 2005).[1] The report stated,

> Improving the effectiveness of aid is a vital complement to increasing the volume of resources. . . . The evidence shows that aid is particularly effective when provided to governments with sound policies, strong leadership and capacity to absorb resources. The Millennium Challenge Account, a major new US initiative in development effectiveness, allocates aid resources according to these principles. (Ibid., para. 80)

In the debate surrounding the issues of debt forgiveness and increases in aid, experts, policy makers, and long-time observers stressed the need for governance reform and policy prescriptions to ensure transparency and rule of law, accountability in public finances, improvement in governance standards, and creation of a productive private sector (Bhagwati and Gambari 2005; Blitz 2005; Oppenheimer 2005; Wolf 2005).

To spend the new aid productively, suggestions were made to increase aid beyond its current levels to countries with "good governance" (Bhagwati and Gambari 2005) and to give debt relief only to countries "with good performance and tolerable political accountability" (Wolf 2005). Accordingly, Nigerian Finance Minister Ngozi Okonjo-Iweala announced two initiatives to be taken by the Nigerian government: (1) Nigeria will establish a monitoring system to ensure that savings to the country of $1 billion a year in a debt deal it has reached to settle $30 billion it owes to its creditors, members of the Paris Club countries, will be earmarked for health, education, agriculture, and power and water supply; and (2) the government of Nigeria will send to the National Assembly a draft Fiscal Responsibility Bill requiring greater accountability in the management of government finances (White and Mahtani 2005).

Economist Jagdish Bhagwati and UN Under Secretary General and Special Advisor for Africa Ibrahim Gambari responded to those calling for debt relief only to those countries with good governance:

> Debt relief for the very poor nations makes sense. It should be extended regardless of bad governance. Would you collect a pound of flesh from a dictator if the flesh is actually going to come from his emaciated and oppressed subjects? (Bhagwati and Gambari 2005)

As there is no consensus on the criteria for measuring good governance, however, the term remains ambiguous and hence imprecision results. Should economic performance be the sole or a primary measuring rod, or should the term be extended to encompass the governance of political entities, be they central or state governments or even municipalities? What is the political content of good governance? Are liberal, democratic values included as an element of that content, and, if so, how important are they? What kind of participation in decision making is envisaged and by whom? What kind of accountability is required? How universal are or should be the standards used to evaluate good governance?

This article will provide a historical context in the next section, which will be followed by examining the World Bank's and the International Monetary Fund's approaches to governance in developing states that are recipients of aid from these international financial institutions (IFIs). The sections following will comprise a review of a donor country's—the United States's—approach to the issue of governance and a few concluding remarks, respectively.

Historical Context

Prior conditions on countries seeking debt relief and financial help in the form of loans and development aid are not new. Several decades ago, the International Monetary Fund and the World Bank instituted structural adjustment programs imposing specific conditions upon a country suffering from economic malaise caused by balance of payments deficits, high inflation, and sluggish GDP, and seeking financial help to meet those challenges. Initial short-term measures prescribed by the IFIs were usually aimed at ensuring fiscal and monetary discipline. These include curtailing of spending and austerity measures, devaluation, trade liberalization, market-oriented policies and privatization, and incentives for private savings and investments. Long-term measures have included restructuring the role of the state aimed at market allocation of resources. This typically resulted in erosion of the state's role for public action and the substitution of the private sector for state involvement in the economy. Voluminous literature exists on the socioeconomic and political impacts of the austerity measures and other Structural Adjustment Programs (SAPs) prescribed by the IFIs for, and their implementation in, many developing countries since the 1980s, especially in Sub-Saharan Africa (Crisp and Kelly 1999; Hilson 2004; Devarajan, Dollar, and Holgren 2001; Dollar and Svensson 1998; Donkor 1997; Gwin and Nelson 1997; International Monetary Fund [IMF] 2001a, 2001b; IMF and World Bank 2001; Reed 1996; Stokke 1995; World Bank 1998). Hence, I will not discuss these issues further, except to note briefly one such program that researchers have studied extensively: mining sector reform in Ghana.

Policy formulations in Ghana, prescribed by the IMF and implemented with the active involvement of the government since 1983, have resulted in the country's achieving continuous economic growth and macroeconomic gains. However, Ghana continues to face enormous socioeconomic problems as well. The suffering of the poor and the impoverished is exacerbated as these people have been experiencing further marginalization, large displacements of the population have occurred, a substantial portion of the mineral economy of the country is owned by foreign multinationals, and there has occurred unabated mine pollution and contamination of the fresh water resources (Hilson 2004). Thus, the SAP in Ghana has been a mixed blessing.

The World Bank and Good Governance

As a condition for lending development assistance, the Bank requires the recipient government to show effective performance and to promote further reforms. The rationale is that with good governance—that is, combating corruption, nepotism, bureaucracy, and mismanagement—and transparency, accountability, and proper procedures, aid would be effectively used to achieve the objective of reducing poverty (Doornbos 1995). Traditionally, the Bank has not considered political issues in determining whether to undertake aid programs in the recipient state, for under their traditional mandates, the World Bank and the International Monetary Fund are to remain apolitical, not involved in considering governance issues. The World Bank's core mandate under its Articles of Agreement does not encompass governance reform unrelated to its economic growth agenda. As the Bank's general counsel Ibrahim Shihata (1991, 88-91) stated, the Bank can promote legal and civil service reform and transparency and accountability in budgetary discipline and fiscal management in pursuance of that agenda.

Public sector reform aimed at efficiency and economic growth remained the Bank policy and practice until a shift took place in the 1990s following a 1989 Bank report that blamed a "crisis of governance" in Sub-Saharan African for a lack of effective use of development aid in the region (World Bank 1989). A World Bank Staff Paper in 1991 identified external agencies as "potentially key political players capable of exerting considerable influence in promoting good or bad governance. In raising the shortcomings of a country's governance, external agencies are calling into question its government's performance" (Landell-Mills and Serageldin 1991, 13).

Thus, good governance appeared on the World Bank's agenda; one of the themes of the Bank's 1991 Annual Development Economic Conference was "Good Governance" (World Bank 1992b). On the relationship between development and governance, the Bank conceptualized governance to indicate the manner in which power and authority are exercised for development "in the management of a country's economic and social resources" (World Bank 1992a, 1). Also, as former chief economist of the Bank Joseph Stiglitz acknowledged in 1999, a shift toward "broader objectives, entitling more instruments, than was the case earlier," occurred with a change of views about development in the World Bank as well as in the development community (p. F587).

A United Nations Conference on Trade and Development (UNCTAD) discussion paper suggested that the new mandate regarding governance "arrived at a moment when growing doubts regarding the purpose and effectiveness of the IFIs seemed to threaten their funding, and even their continued existence" (Kapur and

Webb 2000, 18). Since the early 1990s, the Bank has actively engaged in governance-related programs and projects. To illustrate, between 1996 and 2000, the Bank initiated significant governance reform in the public sector in at least fifty countries, while its governance-related initiatives numbered more than six hundred in ninety-five countries (Development Committee 2000).

The World Bank's emphasis has been on the economic dimensions of good governance and the state's capacity to effectively use the development assistance.

Although the Bank presents the broader objectives mentioned by Stiglitz (1999) in economic terms, they cannot be separated from political aspects. As an illustration, the Bank, acting as the secretariat for a consortium of several donor countries that set political conditions for providing aid, conveyed those conditions to the aid recipient countries and monitored their implementation as well (Gibbon 1993, 55-56). And the Bank's governance discourse reflects the tension between economic and political aspects of governance without at the same time providing precise criteria by which to define good governance and thus to evaluate a recipient country for the appropriate conditions for allocation of aid. As a starting point for the discussion here, a comment from the authors of the Bank's Staff Paper is appropriate:

> Governance may be taken as denoting how people are ruled and how the affairs of a state are administered and regulated. It refers to a nation's system of politics and how this functions in relation to public administration and law. Thus, the concept of governance goes beyond that of "government" to include a political dimension. (Landell-Mills and Serageldin 1992, 304)

With the focus on the structures of the state and its institutions as they relate to public administration and law, the Bank as the external agency prescribes these conditions purportedly to ensure transparency, accountability, and good management practices. Doornbos (2004, 377) postulated that given the World Bank's orientation, one of the key aims of the Bank's designing a good governance approach "appears to have been the creation, in developing country contexts, of state-market relationships that have been characteristic for Western neo-liberal systems." He found the end of the cold war to have been a propitious time for the Bank to open the door for imposing internally directed political conditionalities. These are to be contrasted with externally directed conditionalities that do not address internal state structures. Internally directed conditionalities, on the other hand, address the structuring and operation of the aid recipient country's institutions, and are aimed at rolling back the state systems—unwieldy structures and operations of state institutions—of many developing countries (ibid.).

The World Bank's emphasis has been on the economic dimensions of good governance and the state's capacity to effectively use the development assistance. It also continued to reiterate its apolitical approach to governance reform in the allocation of development aid by focusing on efficiency in public administration, rule of law, and transparency and accountability notions of governance as the major elements to ensure economic growth and development. Consequently, it did not explicitly question how legitimate the government and its power structures are, what the decision-making process is, how public policy is formulated and implemented, or how equitable the economic system is. In its 1997 *Development Report*, however, the Bank did refer to citizen participation and the role of the state as pertinent governance factors having a bearing on development (Martinussen 1998).

After a few years' experience with implementing the good governance agenda, it became apparent to the Bank that sociocultural and political contexts in the recipient countries and not the Western donors' preferences primarily shape the agenda. Although the recipient governments paid lip service to conditionalities for promoting transparency and political reform, little change in fact occurred because of resistance from entrenched socioeconomic and political interests (Bayart 1993; Harrison 1999; Doornbos 2004, 380-382). Democracy, multipartyism, and prescribed changes in aid-receiving countries' policy structures and processes are cases in point (Doornbos 2004).

Acknowledging that conditionalities have failed to induce reforms and good governance in the recipient countries, the World Bank and the donors have increasingly shifted their focus from conditionality to selectivity in allocating aid. A 1998 World Bank report assessing aid stated that the governments better able to use aid are those with good economic performance (World Bank 1998). The report thus recommended that aid be linked with performance and targeted to countries with effective institutions and sound policies. Subsequently, David Dollar, the main author of the Bank report, collaborating with other Bank researchers, conducted a case study of ten Sub-Saharan African countries and reaffirmed his earlier finding that conditionalities had not succeeded in inducing policy changes (Devarajan, Dollar, and Holgren 2001). Another World Bank study likewise posited that since "corruption can significantly impair aid effectiveness," the Bank has learned to allocate aid taking into account corruption in the recipient country (Collier and Dollar 2001, 21).

Consequently, the World Bank and several donor countries have shifted their focus from attempting to induce good governance in a recipient country by providing aid and attaching political conditionalities to requiring performance and good governance as a prerequisite from a recipient government. To illustrate, Anne Krueger, a former Bank vice president who subsequently became IMF's deputy managing director, said that the Bank "will need to differentiate carefully between countries where reforms are serious and stand a reasonable prospect of success and those in which window dressing is used as a means of seeking additional funding" (Krueger 1998, 2009). Aid policies of the Dutch government (Netherlands Ministry of Foreign Affairs 2000) and the U.S. government (National Security Council 2002) reflect this policy shift.

Another recent apt example is the Norwegian ambassador's announcement in July 2005 that Norway had suspended $4 million in aid to the Ugandan government for its "mishandling the transition to multiparty democracy, stifling opposition parties, failing to combat corruption and abusing human rights." The President of Uganda's spokesman called the move "unfair" ("Norway Freezes Aid to Press Government" 2005). A critic of this policy, Jan Pronk (2001, 626), has observed, "Policy improvement and better governance should not be seen as preconditions for development aid, but also as development objectives themselves." Also, as there is no consensus about the contents of good governance, and hence no universally accepted objective standards to decide what government, political, and administrative practices qualify as good governance, there is validity to the criticism that the allocation of aid might be made on political grounds and simply justified under the rubric of good governance (Doornbos 2004, 385).

Graham Harrison (2005, 240) asserted that although the World Bank shows primary concern with economic efficiency, economic growth, and administrative reforms, its governance agenda is "subject to political and ideological influence and how governance reform can have a variety of effects on power relations." This assertion is based on prior analysis by several observers (Harriss 2002; Marquette 2001; Nelson 1995). After extensively studying the Bank's interventions in Sub-Saharan Africa (Harrison 2004), Harrison (2005, 241-42) concluded that the Bank has a liberal worldview, which it has imposed on African states in promoting governance reforms through its interventions—lending and technical assistance. It is worth noting that African states have been the subject of the bulk of Bank-funded governance reform. Harrison attributed this new liberal worldview, steeped in a combination of Western culture and history and American political thought, to shape the Bank's strategy of reducing the capacity and scope of the recipient state for public action (ibid.).

Harrison suggested that the World Bank theory of political change stems from the Bank's belief that those responsible for change in the recipient state act with *rational choice*, that the state should intervene as little as possible in the economy, that incentives for state agents will work, and that the state should act as a market-complementing institution (ibid., 245-46). He found this liberal-capitalist worldview at odds with the worldview and the theory of political change in Tanzania and Uganda, the countries he studies. Contrasting these divergent theories, he concluded that both the earlier class-based theory of the African state and the subsequent theory relying upon a network of clientelism based in ethnic-social relations are steeped in cultural traditions and history and are not comprehended by the Bank, which doggedly pursues governance reforms it considers appropriate. These prescribed reforms, he suggested, cannot succeed, for, although the African states make cosmetic changes in response to the Bank's demands, not much in fact changes (ibid., 251-56).

In a study released in May 2005, the World Bank presented the latest update of its aggregate governance indicators for 2004 for 209 countries and territories, designed to measure the following six dimensions of governance—voice and accountability, political stability and violence, government effectiveness, regulatory quality, rule of law, and control of corruption (Kaufmann, Kraay, and Mastruzzi 2005). The study documents that "there is little evidence of any trends—for better or worse—in global averages of governance" (ibid., 2). It argues that based upon existing evidence "most of the correlation between governance and per capita income reflects causation from the former to the latter," and that misgovernance in a country or region leads to low incomes (ibid., 3-4).

Based upon the past experience and current trends, for governance reforms to succeed, the history and culture of the recipient country matter the most and must be given top priority. The World Bank, in applying its own conceptualization of good governance and seemingly not showing enough sensitivity to these issues in the developing states, may not be able to succeed in achieving the results it seeks.

IMF and Good Governance

The IMF was established to act as a forum to facilitate international monetary cooperation and to regulate monetary relationships. However, the traditional IMF role as international coordinator and regulator on monetary issues among states came under heavy pressure because of a combination of the rise of capital flows and a breakdown of international exchange rate obligations. In the 1980s the number of developing countries seeking assistance grew, the World Bank/IMF intrusions into states' policies grew, and hence the number of SAPs became the norm and the scope of conditionality expanded. IFIs imposed severe austerity measures.

The IMF had initially gotten involved in capital account issues because of its role in addressing the debt crisis but subsequently began justifying conditionality under the rationale that in inducing capital flows and thus enhancing market confidence, it was acting as a catalyst (Thirkell-White 2003, 104; Dhonte 1997, 7; for a critical account, see Bird and Rowlands 1997). During the late 1980s, a backlash began against the SAPs in developing countries, and by the mid-1990s according to one estimate, more than half of IMF programs were failing implementation (Killick 1995).

Despite the research findings that conditionality does not work, its expansion during the course of the 1990s is striking, as the share of programs with structural conditions and the average number of conditions per program increased significantly during that period—programs with structural conditions increased from 60 to 100 percent from 1989 to 1999, and the average number of structural conditions per program increased from three to twelve (Santiso 2001, 10; Kapur and Webb 2000, 5-7).

Two factors are primarily responsible for the Fund's governance agenda: "the rise of capital account openness and . . . the difficult political consequences of its adoption of structural adjustment in the 1980s" (Thirkell-White 2003, 105). Those driving the agenda were financial technocrats—financial ministers and central bankers in developed as well as developing states and nongovernmental organizations (NGOs) in developed states (ibid.). It was not, however, until 1997 that the IMF fully articulated its governance policy. Although the policy guidelines announced then were couched in economic terms, there were strong political undertones. After explicitly stating that the IMF should focus on the improvement and support of "the development and maintenance of a transparent and stable economic and regulatory environment" (IMF 1997, para. 5), the document provides the rationale for the Fund's concern with governance issues: "Poor governance would have a significant current or potential impact on macroeconomic performance in the short and medium term and on the ability of the government credibly to pursue policies aimed at external viability" (ibid., para. 9).

[F]or governance reforms to succeed, the history and culture of the recipient country matter the most and must be given top priority.

Thirkell-White (2003), who studied the IMF's response to the financial crises in the 1990s in Korea and Indonesia, criticized the Fund's governance policy as applied to middle-income countries on two grounds: first, the policy was being steered by the IMF's Executive Board with unbridled discretion to make decisions no longer controlled by a rules-based framework, and second, the decisions did not necessarily reflect the primacy of the needs or interests of those the IMF purported to help but rather of Western countries and Western NGOs that were far less affected by those decisions (pp. 120-21).

He argued that both economic and political forces are driving the Fund's governance. Financial technocrats in the Fund and the financial elites in government ministries and banks in the countries that the Fund assists lead the economic forces; and the liberal and democratic agenda is driven by political concerns and potentially addresses the criticism in the West that traditionally the Fund has been too narrowly focused on macroeconomic considerations in the formulation and implementation of its aid policies (ibid., 99-100).

As in the World Bank, there is tension between the Fund's economic and political governance agendas, especially when the Fund's goals on governance are not clearly defined and articulated. It should be noted that the Fund's economic governance agenda is concerned with traditional economic management and the political governance agenda is aimed at enhancing market confidence.

Thirkell-White raised a question of principle by suggesting that the Fund's major proposed reforms in Korea—enhancing corporate transparency, accountability, and competition; and disciplining and structuring the huge industrial conglomerates, the *chaebols*, to favor small business—cannot be justified as interventions in pursuance of the Fund's traditional technocratic and politically neutral mandate, even though at the heart of the crisis was the lack of market confidence. These were interventions dovetailing President Kim Dae Jung's political agenda, and the Korean people adopted them not as measures devised to enhance economic efficiency but to further nationalism and democracy (ibid., 108-12).

Similar was the case in Indonesia, which was suffering reversal of market confidence caused primarily by corruption and nepotism and poor governance by the Suharto regime. This had led to the financial crisis. The IMF's structural reform measures aimed at the prevalent corruption and bank mismanagement did not work. Subsequently, the Suharto government agreed to IMF prescriptions for governance reform, including new bankruptcy, consumer, and corporate governance laws, capital and current account liberalization, modification of several subsidies, ending cartels and monopolies, and independent audits of government departments and state-owned enterprises (Government of Indonesia 1998).

However, the program was not effectively implemented and hence did not succeed in establishing market confidence. According to some critics (Radelet and Sachs 1998), the Fund should have directly addressed Indonesia's debt burden, which it failed to do initially. It did, however, belatedly take measures to provide the needed debt relief. Others saw the problem as mainly political (Haggard 2000). IMF intervention, seeking to end corruption and nepotism, the main reasons for Suharto's downfall, could perhaps be seen as the Fund's positive role in Indonesia (Thirkell-White 2003, 116). What is noteworthy is that on the economic front IMF's intervention in Indonesia was a failure. If the governance agenda brought about a political change in the government, however, questions then arise about the Fund's political authority to do so, and especially its decision-making mechanisms in striking a balance between democracy on one hand and markets and liberal economics on the other. It may be argued that without meaningful participation of the recipient country's political leadership, the Fund's decisions on macroeconomic management may not garner the political receptivity essential for the success of the Fund's governance agenda.

Thirkell-White's observation is apt:

Transparent administration sounds positive from a political point of view but, in the hands of economists, can slip from a means of accountability (transparency about decision-making procedures) to a requirement for "predictable" policy-making that takes away government discretion. The most benign form of that is central bank independence but the agenda rapidly broadens to include, for example, ideas like a fiscal constitution to limit government spending. Is transparency over country economic policy transparency for developing country citizens or a free source of data for the markets? Concern with the "rule of law" can similarly be subverted to outlaw land reform and ethnic redistribution of wealth or, with an economic focus, can divert judicial resources from grass roots justice to training judges for the commercial courts. (Ibid. 118)[2]

In a nutshell, unlike the Fund's current practice, decision making at the Fund about the direction of its governance agenda in each country must be responsive to the country's cultural and political traditions, preferences, and sensitivities.

The United States and Good Governance

The National Security Strategy of the United States, announced by President George W. Bush in September 2002, provides the rationale and the framework for new U.S. development assistance under a new Millennium Challenge Account (MCA) (National Security Strategy of the United States of America 2002, sec. VII). Noting that massive development assistance has not resulted in economic growth in many countries and "has often served to prop up failed policies," the president said that the MCA is

> for projects in countries whose governments rule justly, invest in the people, and encourage economic freedom. Governments must fight corruption, respect basic human rights, embrace the rule of law, invest in health care and education, follow responsible economic policies, and enable entrepreneurship. The Millennium Challenge Account will reward countries that have demonstrated real policy change and challenge those that have not to implement reforms. (Ibid.)

This policy statement has set the tone for U.S. aid agencies to opt for selectivity. In November 1998, the U.S. Agency for International Development's (U.S. AID) Center for Democracy and Governance provided a conceptual framework that recognized the importance of linkages between democratization and economic growth (Center for Democracy and Governance November 1998, 3). It identified four categories that describe the agency's democracy and governance activities— rule of law, elections and political processes, civil society, and governance (ibid., 5). Noting that ultimately the process of governing is most legitimate "when it is infused with democratic principles such as transparency, pluralism, citizen involvement in decisionmaking, representation, and accountability," the center organized its governance work in five areas—democratic decentralization, legislative strengthening, government integrity, policy implementation, and civil-military relations (ibid., 19).

U.S. AID builds on the National Security Strategy statement to formulate and implement its development goals. In a January 2004 white paper on U.S. foreign aid, the agency noted that donors have learned lessons about aid effectiveness, including the following: "Allocate aid across and within countries more selectively," since "progress is primarily a function of commitment and political will to rule justly, promote economic freedom, and invest in people" (U.S. Foreign Aid 2004, 6). It stated that it will work in a complementary fashion with another independent agency, the Millennium Challenge Corporation (MCC), "employing principles of selectivity based on commitment and performance in countries that can aspire to MCC eligibility or are good candidates for transformational development" (ibid; see also ibid., 20).

U.S. AID has identified nine principles of development and reconstruction assistance to achieve development objectives including economic growth, democracy and governance, and social transition: ownership, capacity building, sustainability, selectivity, assessment, results, partnership, flexibility, and accountability (U.S. AID 2005b). The United States coordinates its international aid policies with major donor governments, regional organizations, and multilateral lending bodies including the World Bank (U.S. AID 2005a).

The MCC uses five of the six World Bank indicators—rule of law, government effectiveness, voice and accountability, control of corruption, and regulatory quality—as part of the set of sixteen indicators it uses to select countries to qualify to submit proposals for MCA funding (Radelet, Siddiqi, and Dizolele 2005). A country must score better than the median score in its group in half of the indicators in each of three broad areas—ruling justly, investing in people, establishing economic freedom—to pass the indicators test, and must surpass the median on corruption as part of the "ruling justly" indicators (ibid., 2).

In a discussion on the future of the MCA in May 2005, the focus was on economic growth, donor ownership, and free markets (Center for Global Development 2005). There was consensus on linking assistance to performance, measuring results, monitoring and evaluation, and "ownership" as the direction taken by the MCA in the selection of the recipient countries. Experts also agreed that the country's commitment to change and its allocation of resources are important factors to assure effective use of aid in reducing poverty (ibid.).

Concluding Remarks

Conditionalities have not necessarily brought about policy reforms that are sustainable over the long term (Killick 1998; Gwin and Nelson 1997). Based on the failure of conditionality in Africa, one critic argues that if it is pursued as a means of general economic policy making, conditionality is often "dysfunctional" because it implies a "transfer of sovereignty" that undermines the domestic political process (Collier 1999). For reforms to succeed, domestic support, ownership, and commitment are crucial; otherwise, as a World Bank researcher has reported, development aid dependence had a negative impact during 1982 and 1995 on corruption, rule of law, and quality of governance (Knack 2000).

It is difficult to implement selectivity for high levels of poverty and weak governance go together. As one critic has aptly stated, selectivity as a "form of ex-post conditionality should not penalize least developed countries by concentrating aid exclusively on good performers, most of which are middle-income countries. The poor in poorly performing countries already have to bear the burden of inept governments and authoritarian regimes" (ibid., 11).

Past performance cannot be an effective indicator and guide to future performance (Hansen and Tarp 2000). For the success of governance reforms, the state and governing institutions must be reformed and strengthened; effective democratic institutions established; and effective participation, strengthened accountability, and enhanced rule of law instituted to ensure sustainable good governance.

The good governance agenda of multilateral aid agencies and donor countries is being refined. Although it is impossible to have a clear-cut demarcation between economic and political aspects of governance, the current confusion and ambiguities need to be further clarified. Notwithstanding the lack of clarity about the concept, however, a reiteration of good governance and efforts at governance reforms, despite many pitfalls, have served a useful function in identifying the problem areas hampering the success of development aid. It bears reiterating that the concept can be used effectively only when the cultural context and history are understood and sensitively taken into account. Finally, without effective participation and meaningful ownership by the recipient government and the people in the recipient country, development aid cannot accomplish its objectives.

Notes

1. The G-8 leaders, along with other donor countries, committed to double aid to Africa by 2010 as compared to 2004 and to increase official development assistance (ODA) to around $50 billion a year by 2010, compared to 2004 (Gleneagles Communiqué 2005, para. 28). Also, they agreed on a proposal to cancel 100 percent of eligible Heavily Indebted Poor Countries' (HIPC) debt to the International Monetary Fund, International Development Association (IDA), and African Development Fund (ibid., para. 29).

2. As Robison (2001, as quoted in Thirkell-White 2003) explained in the context of the Fund's intervention in Indonesia, "The neo-liberal agenda is embedded in coalitions of interest and power," which has not succeeded in "assembling a broad and powerful political coalition."

References

Bayart, J.-F. 1993. *The state in Africa: The politics of the belly*. London: Longman.

Bhagwati, J., and I. Gambari. 2005. Political will, not just aid, can lift Africa out of despair. *Financial Times*, July 5, p. 13, col. 2.

Bird, G., and D. Rowlands. 1997. The catalytic effect of lending by the international financial institutions. *World Economy* 20 (7): 967-91.

Blitz, J. 2005. Brown attacks trade policies of the rich. *Financial Times*, June 20, p. 4, col. 8.

Center for Democracy and Governance. 1998. *Democracy and governance: A conceptual framework*. November. Washington, DC: U.S. AID.

Collier, P. 1999. Learning from failure: The international financial institutions as agencies of restraint in Africa. In *The self-restraining state: Power and accountability in new democracies*, ed. A. Schedler, L. Diamond, and M. Plattner. Boulder, CO: Lynne Rienner.

Collier, P., and D. Dollar. 2001. *Development effectiveness: What have we learnt?* Washington, DC: World Bank.

Crisp, B., and M. Kelly. 1999. The socioeconomic impacts of structural adjustment. *International Studies Quarterly* 43:533-52.

Devarajan, S., D. Dollar, and T. Holgren. 2001. *Aid and reform in Africa: Lessons from ten case studies*. Washington, DC: World Bank.

Development Committee. 2000. Update on the IBRD's financial capacity. World Bank Document DC/2000-07/Rev.1, April 10. Washington, DC: World Bank.

Dhonte, P. 1997. Conditionality as an instrument of borrower credibility. IMF Papers on Policy Analysis and Assessment, PPAA/97/2. Washington, DC: IMF.

Dollar, D., and J. Svensson. 1998. What explains the successor failure of structural adjustment programs? Policy Research Working Paper 1938. Washington, DC: World Bank.

Donkor, K. 1997. *Structural adjustment and mass poverty in Ghana*. London: Ashgate.

Doornbos, M. 1995. State formation processes under external supervision: Reflections on "good governance." In *Aid and political conditionality*, ed. Olav Stokke. London: Frank Cass.

———. 2004. "Good governance": The pliability of a policy concept. *Trames: A Journal of the Humanities & Social Sciences* 8 (4): 372-87.

Gibbon, P. 1993. The World Bank and the new politics of aid. In *Political conditionality*, ed. Georg Sorensen. London: Frank Cass.

Gleneagles Communiqué on Africa, Climate Change, Energy and Sustainable Development. 2005. July. G-8, www.g-8.org.

Government of Indonesia. 1998. Memorandum of economic and financial policies. January 15. Jakarta: Government of Indonesia.

Gwin, C., and J. Nelson, eds. 1997. *Perspectives on aid and development*. Washington, DC: Institute for International Economics.

Haggard, S. 2000. *The political economy of the Asian financial crisis*. Washington, DC: Institute for International Economics.

Hansen, H., and F. Tarp. 2000. Aid effectiveness disputed. *Journal of International Development* 12: 375-98.

Harrison, G. 1999, Clean-ups, conditionality and adjustment: Why institutions matter in Mozambique. *Review of African Political Economy* 26:323-34.

Harrison, G. 2004. *The World Bank and Africa: The construction of governance states*. London: Routledge.

———. 2005. The World Bank, governance and theories of political action in Africa. *British Journal of Politics & International Relations* 7 (2): 240-60.

Harriss, J. 2002. *Depoliticizing development. The World Bank and social capital*. London: Anthem.

Hilson, G. 2004. Structural adjustment in Ghana: Assessing the impacts of mining-sector reform. *Africa Today* 51 (2): 52-77.

IMF and World Bank Sponsored Structural Adjustment Programs in Africa: Ghana's Experience, 1983-99. 2001. K. Konadu-Agyemang, ed. London: Ashgate.

International Monetary Fund. 1997. *Good governance: The IMF's role*. Washington, DC: IMF.

———. 2001a. *Structural conditionality in fund-supported programs*. February 16. Washington, DC: IMF Policy Development and Review Department.

———. 2001b. *Structural conditionality in fund-supported programs—Policy issues*. Washington, DC: IMF Policy Development and Review Department.

Kapur, D., and R. Webb 2000. Governance-related conditionalities of the international financial institutions. G-24 Discussion Paper Series 6. New York: United Nations Conference on Trade and Development.

Kaufmann, D., A. Kraay, and M. Mastruzzi. 2005. *Governance Matters IV: Governance indicators for 1996-2004*. Washington, DC: World Bank.

Killick, T. 1995. *IMF programmes in developing countries*. London: Routledge and Overseas Development Institute.

———. 1998. *Aid and the political economy of policy change*. London: Overseas Development Institute.

Knack, S. 2000. Aid dependence and the quality of governance: A cross-country empirical analysis. Policy Research Working Paper 2396. Washington, DC: World Bank.

Krueger, A. 1998. Whither the World Bank and the IMF? *Journal of Economic Literature* 36:1983-2020.

Landell-Mills, P., and I. Serageldin. 1991. Governance and the external factor. Staff Paper, World Bank Annual Conference on Development Economics 1991. Washington, DC: World Bank.

———. 1992. Proceedings of the World Bank annual conference on Development Economics 1991. Washington, DC: World Bank.

Marquette, H. 2001. Corruption, democracy, and the World Bank. *Crime Law and Social Change* 36 (4): 395-409.

Martinussen, J. 1998. Challenges and opportunities in Danish development co-operation. In *Danish foreign policy yearbook 1998*, ed. Bertel Heurlin and Hans Mouritzen. Copenhagen: Danish Institute of International Affairs.

National Security Council. 2002. *National security strategy of the United States of America*. Washington, DC: NSC.

Nelson, P. 1995. *The World Bank and non-governmental organisations. The limits of apolitical development*. Houndmills, UK: Macmillan.

Netherlands Ministry of Foreign Affairs. 2000. *Afrika Nottite*. The Hague: Netherlands Ministry of Foreign Affairs.

Norway freezes aid to press government. 2005. *International Herald Tribune*, July 20, p. 4, col. 1 (Associated Press).

Oppenheimer, N. 2005. Aid fatigue—Enough handouts for Africa. *International Herald Tribune*, July 12, p. 6, col. 3 (Associated Press).

Progress Report by the G-8 Africa Personal Representatives on implementation of the Africa Action Plan. 2005. July 1. London: Stairway Communications.

Pronk, J. 2001. Aid as a catalyst. *Development and Change* 32 (4): 611-29.

Radelet, S., and J. Sachs. 1998. *The East Asian financial crisis: Diagnosis, remedies, prospects*. Cambridge, MA: Harvard Institute for Economic Development.

Radelet, S., B. Siddiqi, and M. Dizolele. 2005. *New global governance indicators and the possible impact on MCA qualification*. Washington DC: Center for Global Development, Millennium Challenge Corporation.

Reed, D., ed. 1996. *Structural adjustment, the environment, and sustainable development*. London: Earthscan.

Robison, R. 2001. The politics of financial reform: Recapitalising Indonesia's banks. Mimeograph, Murdoch University, Perth, Australia.

Santiso, C. 2001. Good governance and aid effectiveness: The World Bank and conditionality. *Georgetown Public Policy Review* 7 (1): 1-22.

Shihata, I. 1991. *The World Bank in a changing world: Selected essays*. Dordrecht, the Netherlands: Martinus Nijhoff.

Stiglitz, J. 1999. The World Bank at the millennium. *Economic Journal* 109:F577-97.

Stokke, O., ed. 1995. *Aid and political conditionality*. London: Frank Cass.

Thirkell-White, B. 2003. The IMF, good governance and middle-income countries. *European Journal of Development Research* 15 (1): 99-125.

U.S. AID. 2005a. *International donor coordination*. Washington, DC: U.S. AID.

———. 2005b. *Policy—Nine principles of development and reconstruction assistance*. www.usaid.gov/policy.

U.S. Foreign Aid—Meeting the challenges of the twenty-first century. 2004. January. www.usaid.gov/policy.

White, D., and D. Mahtani. 2005. Nigeria vows to track use of debt relief funds. *Financial Times*, July 9-10, p. 4, col. 1.

Wolf, M. 2005. Aid will not make poverty history—But it is worth trying. *Financial Times*, July 6, p. 13, col. 2.

World Bank. 1989. *Sub-Saharan Africa: From crisis to sustainable growth: A long term perspective study*. Washington, DC: World Bank.

———. 1992a. *Governance and development*. Washington, DC: World Bank.

———. 1992b. *Proceedings of the World Bank annual conference on Development Economics 1991*. Washington, DC: World Bank.

———. 1998. *Assessing aid. What works, what doesn't, and why*. New York: Oxford University Press.

Sociolegal Evolution: An Afterword

By
RICHARD E. D. SCHWARTZ

The Syracuse Conference brought together a substantial number of Law and Society scholars. Their papers, published here and in the *Syracuse Journal of International Law and Commerce*, add to our store of information about societies that have moved in the direction of democratic government and a rule of law. These case studies are only a sample, and an unsystematic one at that, of the societies that have moved in that direction. In this Afterword, I want to mention some cases, whether or not covered in this volume, and add a brief word about their significance.

In an article on "Roads to Democracy," conference participant Lawrence Friedman discusses three routes by which societies can move toward democracy. These he gives as top down (as in Britain), bottom up (as in the United States), and imposed from outside (as in Japan). That set of possibilities provides a valuable framework for analyzing changes in the direction of democratic governance and rule of law. Several cases fit quite well within Friedman's categories.

Japan

Japan after World War II moved to a more fully democratic government than before the American occupation. During the first years, paramount power was exercised by General Douglas MacArthur, who handled it in a way that accorded formal deference to the emperor. The arrangement fit with Japanese tradition in the sense that MacArthur acted as the supreme authority while the emperor assumed a ceremonial role. This relationship resembled the pattern of authority during previous periods in which a powerful noble family exercised control, as in the period of the Tokugawa shogunate that preceded the Meiji restoration.

DOI: 10.1177/0002716205282662

ANNALS, *AAPSS*, 603, January 2006

During the American occupation, Japan shifted toward democratic institutions of governance. The legal process, however, remained relatively inactive during and following the occupation. Some have attributed the disuse of the courts to the Japanese cultural base that specified proper behavior so completely that the courts were seldom invoked. Recently, however, the use of law in Japan seems to have increased, as evidenced by the establishment in the fall of 2004 of sixty-eight new law schools.[1]

India

India seems to fit Friedman's outside category, but with reservations. During the period when India was dominated by the British, governance was largely in the hands of local rajas, supervised by the British East India Company, and then by the British government. Indigenous legal institutions are said to have proved quite unsatisfactory for regulating commerce and ensuring order. The British did institute courts in a number of coastal cities where their control was stronger. In time, these courts were increasingly used by Indians to settle disputes. An Indian nationalist I knew put it thus, "We did not like the British, sir, but one good thing they left with us was with was English jurisprudence." That sentiment was widely held.

Russia

The Russian move toward democracy and the rule of law cannot be attributed to external imposition. Dictators had used law in the Soviet Union as a mechanism for implementing their imperatives. The rise of constitutional governance under Gorbachev, Yeltsin, and Putin is largely attributable to internal dynamics. The West may have precipitated the shift from one-party to multiparty governance by its victory in the cold war, but the adoption of parliamentary democracy seems to reflect the top-down decisions of leaders who had had significant positions in the Communist Party. Their decisions might have reflected popular discontent with the Communist Party rule, but the direction of change seems to have been decided more from the top down than from the bottom up.

If there was a groundswell from the public in favor of democratic rule of law, it should be traceable by scholars. While such a dynamic has been noted by Inga Markovits in East Germany and by other students of Eastern European countries emerging from Soviet domination, we do not yet have a definitive account of the role played in the Russian transformation by the population. Except for a brief period after 1905, Russian governance remained essentially in the hands of the czar and his court. If anything, history and culture in Russia seem to support absolute monarchical rule.

Why, then, would the Russians have changed their governance in the direction of democracy? There is a suggestion here that the idea of democratic governance convinced people in positions of leadership that this is the direction in which to go—even for a nation that has had very little experience with democracy in the past. Cultural traditions and popular sentiment played a part, to be sure, as James Richardson points out in his article in this volume.

One is tempted, however, by the Russian case to suggest a trend, attributable perhaps to a wave of public opinion and leadership that makes democracy a favored choice. A hunch of that kind cannot be accepted, however, until there is a much more comprehensive analysis not only for the occurrence of movement toward democracy but also of the underlying dynamic. Are we dealing here with a tide that will reach high water and recede? Or will a strong tendency toward legal democracy survive to become the prevailing mode of governance? What are the determinants that would lead in one direction or the other?

South Africa

Some other cases come to mind. Among the most compelling is the transformation of South Africa from apartheid to an inclusive democracy. Here, the dynamic includes elements of all three of the routes outlined by Friedman. We know that South Africa was subject to pressure from outside of South Africa. The boycott that arguably contributed to the end of apartheid was supported by virtually all other nations.[2]

The principle of formal, racial discrimination embedded in law and practice was judged by the international community to be unacceptable. Also operative was the decision of F. W. de Klerk to cooperate with Nelson Mandela in the transformation of South Africa into a democratic state with equal protection of laws for all racial groups. This change can be viewed as top down, but the status of Nelson Mandela as leader of the nonwhites brought in the element of change from below.

The South African case is also of interest because of the innovation that helped to some extent (as James Gibson's [2004] work shows) in making the change more widely acceptable than had been anticipated. Truth and reconciliation, a remarkable process, represented an innovation in healing wounds resulting from apartheid. As that follow-up to conflict has come to be more widely known, it might be duplicated with comparable success in other nations struggling with the problems of ethnic, religious, and racial conflict.[3]

South Korea

Another instance of democratic transformation is that of South Korea. The story there involved a major effort to build the economy, and a good start was achieved with the help of American economic experts. The industrial and scientific success of South Korea seems to have been a major factor in social change there, a change that took hold during a period of dictatorship. But the trend in governance in South Korea has been toward constitutional democracy, in which the change is at least as much a matter of the inclination of the public, expressed in elections, as it has been the product of foreign influence.

West Germany

The case of Germany also tells us something of the paths to democracy. Germany had had during the Weimar period an experience with democracy that lasted only fourteen years. The capacity of the Weimar Republic to survive in the face of divisive forces of right and left, and in view of the punitive policies of the World War I victors, was in retrospect very limited. Germany in that period can be counted as an example of how international influence can diminish the chances of democracy. Yet the example of Germany achieving stable democracy during the period following World War II is a dramatic one. The working of the West German Constitutional Court, as described by Donald Kommers in his article and earlier work (1997) represents an innovation that seems to have functioned to preserve German democracy against the threat of authoritarianism. Some psychologists (Fromm 1941; Waelder 1939; Adorno et al. 1993) have attributed Nazism to personality traits in the German population, but that explanation is called into question by the developments in West Germany, and now in a reunited Germany since World War II.

To some extent, West German democracy could be attributed to foreign influence. The Western democracies stationed large military forces in West Germany, to be sure, and some are still there. But the dynamics of democratic development hardly seem attributable to the occupation alone. West Germany adopted its own governance institutions in many ways independently of the occupation. And as these institutions developed and gained respect in the population, they became an impressive case of how democracy can work even where first efforts along those lines, as in Weimar, ended in failure.

Quasi-Experimental Governance

In the two cases last mentioned, Korea and Germany, we have seen quasi-experimentation, or an experiment in nature, in which two systems of governance have been tried by initially similar populations. To some extent, external force led in both cases to the differences. East Germany was forced into the communist mold by the Soviets, while West Germany was forced into the democratic form by the Western Allies. Something similar set up the governmental difference between North and South Korea. Once established, these modes of government persisted for decades in Germany, and they continue in Korea.

The democratic capitalist method seems, by multiple measures, to have met with success in both cases. There are many indications that the population of North Korea would, if given the choice, favor the democratic path. In the case of East Germany, the choice was available, and the evidence strongly suggests that East

Germans generally preferred the West German mode of government and law. There are no signs that West Germans or South Koreans would favor a return to the one-party rule that was adopted in the communist world.

The positive reaction toward democracy and the rule of law has not gone unnoticed elsewhere in the world. Taken together with many other factors, it seems to have contributed to a favorable evaluation around the world of democratic, rule-of-law governance. That evaluation, if sustained, can greatly affect the inclinations of populations to press for comparable governments in their own nations.

If so, that leaves us with two major questions: (1) How can democratic development be encouraged if at all from outside? (2) What internal developments facilitate and sustain democracy in various countries? Neither of these questions can be generally and definitively answered at this time, if ever. Yet we cannot avoid these issues. Isolation is no longer an option, and intervention can lead to enormous problems, as in Afghanistan and Iraq, for which solutions are not yet available.

In this Afterword, I have spoken of democracy as if its meaning were palpable. The overt indicia can be enumerated by way of definition, but the underlying mechanism on which this form of governance depends is less certain. We do not know whether the trend in the democratic direction will continue and how well the processes that develop will fulfill the potential of an idea "whose time [perhaps] has come."

Notes

1. The *Japan Times Online*, March 31, 2004, www.japantimes.co.jp.

2. See speech by F. W. de Klerk, June 14, 2004, for an appraisal of the mixed effects of the boycott: http://www.fwdklerk.org.za/speeches.php.

3. Truth and reconciliation commissions have been set up by the following countries:

Argentina
   National Commission for Forced Disappearances (Comisión Nacional de Desaparición Forzosa de Personas)

Chile
   National Truth and Reconciliation Commission (Comisión Nacional de Verdad y Reconciliación; Rettig report)
   National Commission on Political Imprisonment and Torture (Valech report)

El Salvador
   Truth Commission (Comisión de la Verdad)

Guatamala
   Historical Clarification Commission (Comisión para el Esclarecimiento Histórico)

Panama
   Truth Commission (Comisión de la Verdad)

Peru
   Truth and Reconciliation Commission (Comisión de la Verdad y Reconciliación)

South Africa
   Truth and Reconciliation Commission

Sierra Leone
Truth and Reconciliation Commission

Timor-Leste (East Timor)
Commission for Reception, Truth and Reconciliation in East Timor (Comissão de Acolhimento, Verdade e Reconciliação em Timor Leste)

References

Adorno, Theodor W., Else Frenkel-Brunswik, Daniel J. Levinson, and Nevitt Sanford. 1993. *The authoritarian personality*. New York: Norton.

Fromm, Erich. 1941. *Escape from freedom*. New York: Henry Holt and Company, Inc.

Gibson, James L. 2004. *Overcoming apartheid: Can truth reconcile a divided nation?* New York: Russell Sage Foundation.

Kommers, Donald. 1997. *The constitutional jurisprudence of the Federal Republic of Germany*. 2nd ed. Durham, NC: Duke University Press.

Waelder, Robert. 1939. Psychological aspects of war and peace. vol. 10, Geneva Studies 2 (monograph volume): 85-150.

SECTION FOUR

Quick Read Synopsis

QUICK READ SYNOPSIS

Law, Society, and Democracy: Comparative Perspectives

Special Editor: RICHARD E. D. SCHWARTZ
Yale Law School

Volume 603, January 2006

Prepared by Herb Fayer, Jerry Lee Foundation

DOI: 10.1177/0002716205284197

I. THE RULE OF LAW: WHAT IS IT?

Democracy and Equality

Robert Post, Yale Law School

Background   This article closely examines the meaning of democracy and discusses the logical and practical connections between it and various forms of equality.
- Democratic forms of government are those in which the laws are made by the same people to whom they apply.
- In autocratic forms of government the lawmakers are different from those to whom the laws are addressed.
- The question is, What is the relationship between autonomous forms of government and equality?

Autonomy   What does it mean for a form of government to be autonomous?
- Democracy is not the same thing as popular sovereignty because a people can decide to enact antidemocratic rules.
- Nor is democracy equivalent to majoritarianism, in which the majority of the people exercise control over their government.
NOTE: These examples suggest that popular sovereignty and majoritarianism may be intimately associated with the practice of democracy, but they themselves do not define democracy. We can coherently speak of enactments of popular sovereignty or of majorities that are antidemocratic.

Democracy   Democracy refers to the values associated with collective self-determination.
- Governments do not become democratic merely because they hold elections in which majorities govern.

- It is a mistake to confuse democracy with particular decision-making procedures and to fail to identify the core values that democracy as a form of government seeks to represent.
- The values of autonomy are essential to democracy—values associated with the practice of self-determination.

Self-Determination

Self-determination is more than making decisions or electing those who make decisions.

- The practice of self-government requires that a people have the warranted conviction that they are engaged in the process of governing themselves.
- Self-determination turns on the difference between making particular decisions and recognizing particular decisions as one's own. It is about the authorship of decisions.
- Collective decision making is democratic when there is a connection between the particular wills of individual citizens and the collective will of the state.
  - When citizens feel alienated from the general will, voting on issues is merely a mechanism for decision making, a mechanism that can easily turn oppressive and undemocratic.
  - The value of democracy can be fulfilled only if there is a continual mediation between collective self-determination and the self-determination of individual citizens.
  - Democracy requires that citizens experience their government as their own and responsive to their own values and ideas.

First Amendment

The First Amendment protects democracy by safeguarding the communicative processes by which citizens seek to construct an uncoerced agreement that is responsive to their views.

- Citizens are free to engage in public discourse so as to make the state responsive to their ideas and values.
- Modern democracies must regard their citizens, insofar as they engage in public discourse, as equal and autonomous persons.
- It is the essence of democracy to replace the unilateral respect of authority by the mutual respect of autonomous wills.

Democracy

Democracy requires that persons be treated equally insofar as they are autonomous participants in the process of self-government.

- Democracy must regard each citizen as an autonomous, self-determining person, at least insofar as is relevant to maintaining a living identification with the self-government of the state.
- The purpose of communication within public discourse is to empower citizens to participate in ways that will permit them to believe that public opinion will potentially respond to their views.
  - If the state too closely regulates when and how a person may speak, speech may lose its ability to mediate between individual and collective self-determination.

Democratic Legitimacy

The equality required by democracy can easily be experienced as thin and formal, in contrast with the robust forms of substantive equality associated with theories of distributive justice.

- Much depends on our understanding of the logic of democratic legitimacy.
- This logic requires that citizens be treated equally with respect to the requirements of autonomous participation in the practice of self-government.
- Democracy presupposes an equality measured in terms of the autonomous agency required by democratic legitimacy.

Moral Equality

As democracy is a form of government committed to self-determination, democracy must also encompass self-determination about the meaning of the moral equality of citizens.
- A democracy will decide the meaning of moral equality in the context of public discussion and debate.
- Advocates of strong egalitarian principles regard debate as offering inadequate protection for distributive justice because they believe the judgment of citizens may be distorted by prejudice and bias.
- Democracy and strong egalitarian principles do not have to be in opposition to each other.
  - Strong egalitarian principles may have significant democracy-reinforcing effects.
  - Systematic violation of these principles may sometimes lead to the failure of democratic legitimacy—democracy requires only that inequities that undermine democratic legitimacy be ameliorated.

NOTE: Inequities need not be resolved for reasons of fairness or distributive justice but simply because such inequities undermine democratic legitimacy.

The Implication

The unsettling implication of the above reasoning is that democracy is quite compatible with important forms of status subordination, as long as these forms of subordination are not experienced by citizens as alienating.
- At the time that disempowering of women was accepted, democracy did not require that this subordination be ended.
- Democracy requires self-determination by the people, but it does not itself define who the people are.
- Insofar as egalitarian norms developed that made the disempowerment of women alienating, precluding the identification of citizens with the general will of the state, democratic arguments emerged for ending this status subordination. This suggests that strong egalitarian principles are in a dynamic and dialectical relationship to democracy.
- As egalitarian principles become politically salient, as they make inequities visible and oppressive, as they create alienation, they prepare the way for democracy-based arguments for amelioration of inequities.
  - Thus democracy and strong egalitarian principles are intimately related.
  - Democracy does not entail these principles but is itself affected by them because it must reckon with the threats to democratic legitimacy generated by these principles.
  - Democracy is in this sense tightly connected to egalitarian commitments.
  - Democracy and equality are bound in an indissoluble knot, mutually reinforcing and mutually antagonistic.

Reflecting on the Rule of Law:
Its Reciprocal Relation with Rights,
Legitimacy, and Other Concepts
and Institutions

Samuel J. M. Donnelly, Syracuse University College of Law

Q
R
S

Background

Central to discussion of law and social change is a discernable relationship between legitimacy, the rule of law, and respect for human rights.
- To the extent that a government is subject to the rule of law, the human and civil rights of its citizens are advanced.
- When citizens can bring disputes concerning rights to court rather than fight in the streets, the rule of law is advanced.
- Respect for rights and the rule of law are likely to make a government more acceptable and hence more legitimate.
- A basic requirement of legitimacy is that government advances everyone's share of primary social goods, their opportunity to participate in society, and hence their basic rights.
- Rights are not only statements of ideals or entitlements but goals and tools for pursuit of these goals, the means for pursuing law reform and enhancing society's legitimacy.

NOTE: From the end of WWII until the present time has been one of the greatest periods in the development of international law and the world rule of law. The EU and European Covenant on Human Rights are particularly remarkable as is the development and recognition of human rights in the EU since WWII.

Law and Social Change

To study the promotion of human rights and the establishment of a world rule of law, we must think about social change both worldwide and in individual countries and the role of law in social change.
- Legal, political, and cultural events and circumstances just prior to and following the 1954 decision in *Brown v. Board of Education* show how the interaction of law and culture results in social change.
- An example is the period between 1937 and 1954, which was a tumultuous time including the end of the Great Depression, WWII, the Holocaust, the Korean War, and the beginning of the cold war.
- *Brown* has led to a quarrel over method; legal philosophers creating or criticizing decision-making methods should struggle to understand the relationship between social forces and the work of decision makers.

NOTE: The *Brown* decision has a quality the author describes as ultimate legitimacy, yet in its aftermath to the present the decision produced legitimacy costs.

Rule of Law

Why is it that the protection of civil liberties should be associated historically with the advance of the rule of law?
- One thing is that the rule of law governs those in authority as well as the public.

- Under the rule of law, citizens should be protected by law against their government as well as against private violence.

World Rule of Law From the experience of English-speaking countries one can develop some ideas that are not particularly original for advancing the world rule of law.
- *Control of private violence:* On the world stage, the UN or some similar institution must have the authority to authorize the international use of violence by one country against another—at this time the move is in that direction.
- *Role of courts:* Courts have two connected roles: to protect civil liberties and to control private violence. Encouraging citizens to use the courts is a positive contribution to the rule of law.
- *Establishing international rule of law:* Using European developments as a model, regional courts can be established—international investment and commercial activity will be advanced as a result. See also international commercial arbitration.

Political Friendship An inquiry, using tools of social science, into the qualities that make law or changes in law more likely to be acceptable would seem to advance our understanding of how to promote the rule of law and human rights advances.
- Dworkin (1986) contended that the legitimacy of law is grounded in fraternity, community, and their attendant obligations.
- Political friendship would seem to present both problems and opportunities for furthering the world rule of law.
  - A new institution like an international court does not fit easily into the existing pattern of political friendships and interactions.
  - Commercial activity will be an important element of the interactions that lead to political friendships.
- Personalist theory offers a foundation for political friendship saying that we are more fully persons when in relation with other persons.
  - At the foundation is a commitment to afford each person deep respect and concern.
  - Political friendship, in that view, then leads to a theory of rights, obligations, and legitimacy.

Primary Social Goods Each person under personalist theory has a right to participate in the common action of society and a right to the means necessary for that participation.
- The means necessary could be described as primary social goods—those goods necessary or important for participation in the common action of a society.
- In personalist theory, primary social goods are very helpful in constructing a theory of rights. As in the U.S. Constitution, basic rights are those designed to protect primary social goods.
  - Rights protecting against the deprivation of the personal, economic, and political goods necessary to basic participation.
  - Legitimacy in personalist thought then shares a common grounding with the theories of rights and obligations.
  - A society is legitimate to the extent that it strives to advance and protect everyone's and each one's share of the primary social goods.

Rights Related to "Horizons" International human rights scholars taking positions related to their horizons question whether economic rights are more important than civil liberties or vice versa.

- Horizons, the normal human condition of having "limited knowledge and understanding," affect our understanding of rights.
  - Every rights statement is made within a horizon and from a point of view that is limited in scope.
- Both judges and law reform attorneys should be conscious of horizons.
  - A law reformer must find a way to make his or her arguments comprehensible within the narrow horizons of the judge.
  - He or she must persuade the judge to cross beyond those narrow horizons to see the problems of his or her client.
- A law reformer and one concerned with the advance of the rule of law and human rights should be conscious of the phenomenon of horizons, of the experiences that open the opportunity for expanding our understanding.
- Judges who recognize their horizons—their limited knowledge and understanding—should be able to cross horizons.
  - Commitment to crossing horizons is a means for promoting human rights and is a topic for legal philosophers and social scientists.

Q
R
S

Advance of Rights

The advance of rights is related to the advance of the rule of law and to the legitimacy of new governmental arrangements.
- The availability and regular use of the process of law reform to establish rights should contribute to the legitimacy and stability of governments and regional organizations.
- The regular use of law reform campaigns should contribute to strengthening and expanding the rule of law.

Natural Law

Government's subjectivity to the rule of law lays a strong foundation for the development of civil liberties and the advance of human rights.
- The institutionalization of higher law for this purpose is in the mainstream of the natural law tradition.
- Natural law in its many incarnations over the ages has served as a vast storehouse of resources to advance the rule of law.
- The notion of a higher law is the essential contribution of the natural law tradition to the advance of the rule of law and the promotion of human rights.
- International law could serve as the higher law that could subject otherwise unrestrained rulers to the rule of law and the respect for the human rights of their citizens—this process has begun.

NOTE: Natural law is not a set of propositions or even ideals, important as *they* are to natural law, but a process of human experience by which our regard for our fellow human beings grows, is generalized into ideals and commitments, is institutionalized, and regularly changes by crossing horizons.

Can the Welfare State Survive in a Globalized Legal Order?

Samuel Krislov, American University

Background

Neither predictions that the welfare state would endanger law and freedom nor that globalization would make the welfare state obsolete seem verified by recent history. However,

**Q
R
S**

- There has been a retrenchment, particularly in denationalization, for fundamental economic reasons.
- Most entrenchments have occurred in the United States from feelings that social benefits were overgenerous.
- Funding issues will be a challenge to social security, health care, and unemployment protections.
- Changes in "safety nets" will also challenge the rights and full-class citizenship of the unsuccessful or unlucky.
- The antiwelfare effort sees doom for welfare states in that they are luxury systems inhibiting international efficiency.
- Other problems include changing of demographics regarding wealth and the increasing percentage of the elderly in populations.

NOTE: Economic realities have curtailed the growth of U.S. governmental programs. In Europe, welfare protection has been cut back, although it is still broad in its coverage compared to the United States.

*Benefit
Reductions*

The trimming of welfare benefits came also from demonstrated costs and competitive disadvantages in international trade.

- There was a revulsion to greater and greater demands for benefits by nonproductive segments of society.
- The public supported reduced benefits but generally turned to support of welfarist parties after reductions were made—the welfarists see this as a prudent regrouping rather than the end of welfare.

Freedom

Welfare state countries show little sign of marching away from freedom.

- In spite of considerable monetary controls, economic liberty is maintained at a high level.
- Personal rights are profoundly protected—on the whole they are firmly planted in a tradition of personal freedom and liberty.
- Complex checks and balances are sources of freedom.
- Many of the conglomerates contain requirements and buttresses for freedom—most conspicuous are the EC requirements that members maintain a democratic structure and adhere to human rights.

*The Asian
Threat*

Pronouncements of the eclipse of the United States and Europe emerged with Japan's rise as a quality producer and the entry into the world markets by other Asian countries.

- The fear was of cheap foreign labor leading to relinquishment of the lead in manufacturing.
- At first, authoritarian systems seemed to succeed, but a series of predictably bad choices created a system doomed for failure—only Korea and Taiwan moved from market system to law-constrained economy and then to freedom as manifestations of Asian democracy and free expression.

NOTE: The United States has emerged as the big winner, benefiting from intellectual property in industrial know-how and its skill at training, along with the use of internationalized assembly of multinationally produced parts into finished, maximally profitable products.

Globalization

Predicted efficiency of globalization was to be a by-product largely of two factors.

- There would be an intensification of the trend toward mobility of the factors of production and coproduction of goods.
- The absence of legal barriers and minimization of physical barriers would permit products or parts of products to be made where there was the great-

est comparative efficiency, but free trade remains a fiction as one hand cuts while the other creates new barriers.

Many argue that opportunities will grow when obstacles to competitiveness are removed and the artificial barriers to the flow of goods and services are broken down.

The migration of jobs to seek cheaper labor is suggested to be efficient in reducing costs and just in reducing worldwide income disparity, but outsourcing becomes a sore point when the jobs involve highly skilled functions such as computer programmers.

Q R S

Global Legal Order

One other claimed nemesis remains: the emergence of a global legal order may inhibit many forms of welfare regulation, as it does in the European community and in NAFTA and WTO protocols.

- Larger, more established powers, however, are reluctant to yield leadership to a motley grouping of smaller nation-states.
- No one has been ingenious enough to formulate a decent structure to establish new law on a basis regarded as legitimate—the exception being violation of human rights and genocide.
- NGOs provide a vast, interlinked web of transnational structures.
  - They constitute an international civic society, although NGOs have virtually no legal power.
  - They are a foundation, a buttress, a supplement to legal order, but this structure is an unlikely matrix for world order.
- The emergence within the WTO of panels making "determinations" is the most lawlike aspect, exciting the spirits of global law enthusiasts.

Other Global Influencers

International forms of expert opinion influence legal changes.

- Policies on health and on product standards are influenced by expert opinion and by the public "voting with its purse."
- Worldwide investor confidence also is an influencer.
- NGOs inform the public or mobilize opinion.

Standards

Perhaps the purest form of claim to objectivity and expertise is expressed in the form of standards.

- Penalties for not measuring up range from refusal of delivery to confiscation.
- Standards are versatile and apply to more than quality; pricing and safety are also in the formula.
- In addition to protecting consumers, standards protect society with respect to ultimate usage and distribution—they also affect the basics of a product's manufacture, assembly, or development.
- The caveat is there is subjectivity and manipulation for gain in creating and enforcing standards.
- The move toward globalization has gone hand-in-hand with efforts to objectify standards and to eliminate tax-and-nontax barriers to trade.

NOTE: For virtually all standard developers and users, a national standard authorized by an organization like ANSI maximizes access to a national market.

Resolving Conflicts

It is increasingly likely that the underpinnings and intertwinement of competing legal orders will continue to create conflicts resolved either through political negotiations, or by the creation of agencies with limited decision power like the WTO.

QRS

Internet Communication

Internet communication generally makes the universe of information more global in all areas.
- The organization of people with similar views in NGOs and in communication networks is a dramatic change for the world.
- The difficulties governments experience in curtailing global contact among people and trying to isolate their citizenry is the strongest hope for globalization of the spirit and therefore the law.

II. CASE STUDIES
A. MOVES TOWARD DEMOCRACY

Overcoming Apartheid: Can Truth Reconcile a Divided Nation?

James L. Gibson, Washington University in St. Louis

Thesis

A major analysis of the work of South Africa's truth and reconciliation process shows the following:
- There is no evidence that the "truth" proclaimed by the Truth and Reconciliation Commission (TRC) damaged reconciliation.
- Indeed, the truth-finding process contributed to at least some forms of reconciliation among at least some groups.

Truth and Reconciliation

Two themes have dominated discussions of the truth and reconciliation process in South Africa.
- No one seems to know what "reconciliation" means.
- However, everyone was certain that "reconciliation" had failed or at least not lived up to expectations.

Reconciliation

Discussions of reconciliation in South Africa typically deal with two things:
- The micro truth about what happened to specific loved ones.
- A macro focus on the reconciliation of victims and perpetrators.
  - Reconciliation usually means acceptance of blame, apology, and forgiveness.
  - This often has deeply religious overtones (with the risk of mistakenly equating forgiveness of past enemies with reconciliation).
  - There is also the focus on who profited from apartheid and which groups and people were injured by it—coming to grips with the subjugation of the black majority by the white minority.
  - The overarching focus of reconciliation involves trying to bridge the divide between various distinct and generally separate racial communities. Reconciliation may be thought of as a continuum describing the relationship between those who were masters and slaves, not just those who were victims or perpetrators of gross human rights violations.

NOTE: The TRC is considered to be a facilitator that can improve communication and mutual tolerance of diversity.

Key to Reconciliation

The key to reconciliation is that South Africans of every race accept all other South Africans as equals, extending dignity and respect to them.
- This requires that people come to interact more and communicate more, which in turn can lead to greater understanding and perhaps acceptance.

Connecting Truth with Reconciliation

Some in South Africa believe that not only does truth not lead to reconciliation, but instead it leads to irreconciliation by exacerbating tension and conflict.
- The view is that truth finding can
  - Uncover horrific human rights abuses.
  - Reawaken long dormant memories and animosities.
  - Generally force all sides in the struggle over apartheid to confront each other.
- The alternative view is that, by documenting atrocities from the past, the process can succeed in getting people to rethink their views.

NOTE: Sharing responsibility, blame, and victimhood evens the score ever so slightly, providing a basis for dialogue.

Measuring Reconciliation

The four components of reconciliation are
- Interracial reconciliation.
- Cultural respect for human rights.
- Political tolerance.
- Institutional legitimacy.

NOTE: Based on the results of the research, one might draw the following conclusions about the levels of reconciliation among the racial groups: Africans not very reconciled, whites somewhat reconciled, coloured South Africans somewhat reconciled, and South Africans of Asian origin somewhat reconciled. Reconciliation still has a long way to go before it predominates in South Africa, even if the level of reconciliation is higher than many expected from a country so close to civil war so recently.

Acceptance of TRC's Truth

One of the objectives of the truth and reconciliation process was to create a collective memory for South Africa—an accepted version about the past.
- The TRC's multifaceted truth is not necessarily an officially sanctioned truth but is instead an amalgamation of ideas about the past with which all must now contend.
- To test whether truth contributes to reconciliation, the author developed a summary measure of the degree to which each individual accepts the TRC's historical truth about apartheid.
  - Everyone accepts that those who struggled for and against apartheid committed horrible abuses.
  - Nonetheless, a significant proportion of every racial group believes that the idea of apartheid was good.
  - Thirty-nine percent of blacks believe the struggle to preserve apartheid was just.

* A plurality is willing to attribute abuses to individuals and not to the state.
* Most important, widespread agreement exists that all sides in the struggle over apartheid did horrible things.

NOTE: The author believes the data suggest that the TRC's revelations played some role in producing a common understanding among all South Africans of the country's apartheid past.

*TRC
Successes*

At some level, the truth and reconciliation process clearly succeeded. It appears certain that something must have altered the course of the transition, avoiding the bloodbath that many predicted would accompany the transition to majority rule. More specifically, the author argues that

• The data show that truth and reconciliation do go together and are compatible with the view that the collective memory produced contributes to the levels of reconciliation.
• Certainly the data show that documenting the truth about the past does not lead to irreconciliation, as so many feared it would.

*How Truth
Leads to
Reconciliation*

Based on attitudes prior to the transition, strong impediments to reconciliation existed. Some external force was needed to provide an impetus for attitude change and to get the transition going.

• In the past, blacks and whites most likely understood and trusted each other very little, rarely interacted, held vicious stereotypes, and disliked and felt threatened by each other.
• Beliefs had to be shaken up because most people do not pay attention to a slow trickle of unwelcome information—the TRC was able to create enough noise for people to reassess their racial attitudes.
• Blacks also learned that horrible things were done by both sides.
• The frequency and quality of interaction between races has increased, allowing them to get to know each other, and this likely contributes to further reconciliation.
• Impediments were overcome by widely accessible information that had no hidden ideological messages that might cause defensiveness.

NOTE: Whites attentive to the truth and reconciliation process learned that their side was less than noble in creating and defending apartheid and that opposition was perhaps less radically evil in its efforts to create a new system.

Conclusions

In moving toward reconciliation, once one concedes that the other side has legitimate grievances, it becomes easier to accept their claims and ultimately to accept the new political dispensation.

• Truth commissions must seek to act impartially.
• There should be nonretributive forms of justice produced by the process.
• People need to be able to tell their stories and to be heard.
• A process that is open, humanized, and procedurally fair allows penetration of the consciousness of virtually all constituents.
• Most important, the process must resist resorting to "victor's justice" in which only the crimes of the defeated are criticized, and should instead cast blame for human rights abuses impartially and fairly, wherever such blame is appropriate.

The Federal Constitutional Court: Guardian of German Democracy

Donald P. Kommers, Notre Dame Law School

Background

The Federal Constitutional Court (FCC) is an important custodian of political democracy in Germany. This article is an overview of the FCC's most important decisions on election law, political parties, and parliamentary democracy.
- The FCC has promoted equality of opportunity among competing political parties while guarding the integrity of elections.
- It seeks to root Parliament's law-making powers in elections and voting.
- It has defended the principle of fair and equal representation in the system of personalized or modified proportional representation (PR).
- It has shielded minority parties against discriminatory legislation.

NOTE: By exercising its authority to pass sentence on the validity of elections and on the dissolution of Parliament, the FCC has consolidated its reputation as the ultimate guardian of both democracy and the rule of law.

The Basic Law

Germany's Basic Law—that is, its constitution—includes several provisions empowering the FCC to review the constitutionality of political parties as well as other electoral procedures and institutions.
- The Basic Law establishes political parties as major agencies of political representation for they express the political will of the people.
- Germany's electoral system provides for a modified system of proportional representation.
- The Basic Law creates a "free democratic basic order" whose defense the state is duty-bound to protect.
- Several of the Basic Law's innovations for stabilizing the political system include the diminished power of the president, the constructive vote of no confidence, the limits on the power of dissolving Parliament, and the creation of the FCC.

The FCC

Established in 1951, the FCC has evolved into one of Germany's most important policy-making institutions.
- It is the only tribunal able to declare statutes and other governmental actions unconstitutional—it is the guardian of the Basic Law.
- It handles federal/state conflicts, clashes between branches of the national government, and the constitutional complaints of ordinary citizens.

Judicial Decisions

The judicial decisions discussed in this article focus on elections, political parties, and parliamentary representation. They are important because they have helped to
- Stabilize party government.
- Make political representation responsive and responsible.
- Anchor the system more generally in the democratic values at the heart of the Basic Law.

NOTE: These studies look at
- Proportional representation.
- Voting rights and their relationship to the PR system.
- Constitutional policies related to party funding.

- Handling of election cases similar to Bush/Gore in 2000 in the United States.
- The limits of the Basic Law's power to dissolve Parliament.

Religion, Constitutional Courts, and Democracy in Former Communist Countries

James T. Richardson, University of Nevada, Reno

Background

This article makes two key arguments and attempts to combine them in a way that shows the importance of religious motivations to the development of democracies in former communist countries (FCC).

- One argument concerns the role played by religion in undermining communist governments of the former Soviet Union (FSU).
  - A corollary is that religious motivations have given impetus to democratic movements as FCC redefine themselves.
- Second is that courts, specifically constitutional courts, are playing an important role in promoting democracy in some FCC.
  - A corollary is that constitutional courts in some FCC have been very solicitous of religion and religious institutions, particularly traditional ones, and have helped define a major role for religion in a number of FCC.

Role of Religion

The Catholic Church led by Pope John Paul II contributed to the downfall of communism in a significant way.

- The pope, immediately upon becoming pope, started talking about human freedom, encouraging people to fight for their rights.
- The uprisings in Poland in the 1980s and the inability or unwillingness of the Soviets to suppress them contributed directly to oppositional developments in other Soviet republics.
- Religious motivations played a key role in the development of new constitutional democracies in the FCC.
  - The strong emphasis placed on the worth of the individual within the Christian religious tradition is a key element in the development of the democratic impulse.
  - Showing that there is a higher law above that of potentates was crucial.
  - Vatican II made a strong statement about freedom.

Constitutional Courts

The tendency to adopt constitutions has contributed to the establishment of constitutional courts to interpret and enforce those constitutions.

- In some of the FCC, constitutional courts have become quite strong with considerable popular support—Hungary being a good example.
- In other FCC, such courts have run afoul of political forces and have had their power curtailed or were not able to develop much authority.
- In Russia, the courts have regained some power by putting heavy emphasis on cases elaborating individual rights.
- The courts can force politicians to honor commitments, thus serving as an important check and balance to postcommunist governments that might

adopt different policies—in some cases they are the primary vehicles of democratic values in FCC.
- Constitutional courts have had to take on a major role of defining the place of religion in postcommunist societies.

Hungary and Russia

Below is a comparison of how constitutional courts deal with religion in Hungary and Russia.
- In Hungary, the court system in general and the constitutional courts in particular were very solicitous of the role of religion.
  - The court played a role in promoting and defending religion as deserving of a prominent place in the public square of Hungary.
- In Russia, the picture was mixed, reflective of the centuries of dominance by the Russian Orthodox Church (ROC).
  - A coalition was formed between the ROC and politicians to protect the church more so than individuals.
  - Those who want Russia's future tied to Europe succeeded in getting Russia to join the Council of Europe, which puts Russia under the sway of major European institutions such as the European Court of Human Rights.
- It seems safe to say that even within the context of a Russia dominated by the ROC and a strong presidency, the constitutional court has made some difference in terms of support for basic human rights such as religious freedom.

B. TRANSITIONS AND PROBLEM CASES

Transitions to Constitutional Democracies: The German Democratic Republic

Inga Markovits, University of Texas at Austin

Background

In totalitarian states, the waning of utopian hopes may be compensated for by an increased interest in law and rights and by the growing professionalism of a disenchanted legal class.
- The practice of legality—even the legality of a totalitarian state—can threaten and undermine the effectiveness of autocratic rule.
- In looking at GDR legal history, the author claims
  - Respect for law grew gradually over forty years.
  - The techniques of party interference with the judiciary changed from direct interference in specific cases to ideological indoctrination and control.
  - The party itself became increasingly ambivalent about its judicial policies.
- The article looks closely at the history of one East German trial court to determine what specifically it was that increased the significance of law throughout its life span and to draw conclusions about the general conditions for a global spread of the rule of law.

Late 1950s

By the late fifties, party authorities moved from directly meddling with concrete decisions to exerting their influence behind the scene and, from there, to

Q
R
S

generally impress the party line by way of the ideological and legal training of judges and their supervision by superior courts.
- The training of judges improved.
- Judges' professional self-confidence increased.
- The roles of various state authorities became more differentiated.
- The party was better at controlling and directing its own cadres.
- The Ministry of Justice and superior courts began to point to the independence of judges as an excuse for resisting local influences.

NOTE: All of this does not mean that the courts really *were* independent from the party. East Germans never believed they were.

Party Influence

How did the party exert its influence on the judiciary?
- By moving a conflict from the area of law into the area of politics. In cases in which the party was interested in a particular outcome, it would persuade the court to give it time to find what was called a political solution outside of the judicial process. The case before the court was first suspended and then withdrawn. The court cooperated in this process of displacement. But judges, as a rule, were neither willing—nor apparently expected—to break the law.
- The search for a political solution did not necessarily mean that the parties to a suit would get less than they were entitled to under the law. But it removed politically touchy issues from the authority of judges. With the dockets thus sanitized, the system could preserve a locally limited kind of judicial independence in the courtroom.
- Judges lived in two worlds.
  - As jurists, they were to apply the letter of the law.
  - As party members, they were, outside the courtroom, to do their best to realize the policy goals of the party—hence the importance of their ideological indoctrination.

Indirect Party Influence

As the party moved out of the business of directly indoctrinating judges, the Ministry of Justice and the GDR Supreme Court, staffed with party members, took over.
- By the 1980s, the political indoctrination of judges met with their increased indifference.
- Most judges seemed to like the law better than the party.
- The party no longer seemed to hope for true believers. A judge's political loyalty seemed less a matter of conviction than of political correctness.

Dwindling of Utopian Hopes

East German legal developments in the 1970s and 1980s reflect both the dwindling of utopian hopes and the entrenchment of professionalism.
- On one hand, the loss of political faith required a tight and efficient supervision. The system by which the lower courts were supervised by the superior courts became increasingly streamlined and effective.
- On the other hand, the growing professionalism of the GDR judicial bureaucracy made it push for more rule-of-law protections.
  - The GDR Supreme Court and Ministry of Justice admonished lower courts to show greater respect for defense counsel.
  - They criticized the unnecessary issuing of arrest warrants.
  - There is increasing official talk of the respect for individual rights.

Last Years of Socialism

The relationship between the party and the court became confused in the last years of socialism.
- The party wanted judges to be both obedient and more independent.

- The Supreme Court and the Ministry of Justice wanted legal change, but not the responsibility for change.
- Local judges tried to steer the right course between conflicting orders.

Conclusions   What can be learned form the study of one East German trial court for the likely development of authoritarian legal systems?
- An inverse relationship seems to exist between political and legal faith. The higher a legal system's political faith, the lower its perceived need for law. As political beliefs are fading, the search for legal solutions to social conflicts is likely to rise.
- Legal sophistication seems to encourage sympathy toward law reform.
- It would make sense to strengthen the legal systems, even of totalitarian countries, in the hope that expectations of law could help delegitimize and push back practices of injustice.

Q
R
S

Sudan: A Nation in Turbulent Search of Itself

Francis M. Deng, Johns Hopkins University

Background   Sudan is a country in painful search of itself, afflicted by a wave of regional conflicts rooted in an acute crisis of national identity.
- Three factors, Arabization, Islamization, and slavery, played a pivotal role.
- In the past, an Arab-speaking Muslim, culturally Arabized and with Arab descent, was elevated to a position of respect and dignity.
- A non-Muslim black African was deemed inferior.
NOTE: By the nineteenth century, the North was Arab-Islamic and the South was considered indigenously African in racial, cultural, and religious terms. These two are now in a zero-sum conflict of identities. Sudan faces critical choices of either equitable national assimilation or partition.

Issues   The political developments and the challenges of peace and unity pose a series of interlinked questions and issues.
- What role does religion—specifically Islam—play in shaping identities?
- How do regional conflicts challenge the Arab-Islamic establishment?
- What are prospects for a more inclusive national identity framework?
- Will the Arab-Islamic element cooperate or resist change?
- What would be the outcome if they resist?
NOTE: These questions are critical to the prospects of the Sudan remaining united or disintegrating along racial, ethnic, or religious lines. The country has the potential of being either a conciliator among its neighbors or a point of confrontation, with ripple effects extending beyond the regional context.

Conflicts   It is not mere differences that cause conflicts but the implications for the shaping and sharing of power, wealth, services, development opportunities, and the overall enjoyment of the rights of citizenship.
- By this yardstick, the South found itself, after independence, the most marginalized and oppressed region in the country.

- The first conflict went from 1955 to 1976 when the South was granted regional autonomy, but resumed in 1983 when the government unilaterally abrogated the agreement.
  - This second war's declared objective was to restructure a country that would be free from any discrimination.
  - This recasting of the issues began to gain support in the North.
- Twelve years after a Darfur rebellion was crushed in 1991, two non-Arab movements in Darfur, the Justice and Equality Movement (JEM) and the Sudan Liberation Movement and Army (SLM/A), staged a second rebellion—what is currently happening in Darfur is also happening in the South and in the bordering areas of the Nuba Mountains and the Southern Blue Nile.
  - The economic factors involved in Darfur and the mirrored situation in the South are also similar.
- Traditionally, conflicts were managed and resolved by intertribal means, but now these methods are undermined and weakened.

Peace

A path toward peace has been charted in the South, Abyei, Nuba Mountains, and the Blue Nile.
- The protocols stipulate principles for inclusivity and for addressing grievances of other marginalized areas, such as Darfur.
- The irony is, while the war in the South was coming to an end, regional conflicts were erupting in the North.
NOTE: What is unfolding in the Sudan is challenging the prevailing myths of identity and revealing the complexities of the country's racial, ethnic, cultural, and religious configuration.

Self-Identification

Self-identification is the pivotal factor in determining identity. In the Sudanese context, two sets of discrepancies need to be addressed:
- The extent to which self-identification with Arabism conforms with the objective factors, in which the African element is dominant.
- The degree to which the Arab-Islamic model can be said to be representative of a country that is otherwise pluralistic in race, ethnicity, religion, and culture.
NOTE: Where self-identification by a particular group is projected as the national identity framework, with normative principles that determine participation in the shaping and sharing of power, national wealth, social services, developmental opportunities, and the rights of citizenship, it ceases to be a personal matter and becomes a public policy concern.

New Developments

Significant developments now appear to be playing out in a way that is challenging dualistic characterization of the conflict.
- The likelihood remains that the North will stay committed to a version of the Arab-Islamic vision and the South will opt for secession.
- The myth of northern identity as Arab has begun to be challenged, not only by northern non-Arabs but also by many among the "Arabs" who increasingly acknowledge the African component of their identity or who believe in a more equitable national identity framework.
- On the other hand, the persistent efforts to preserve the hegemony of the Arab-Islamic identity cannot be underestimated.
NOTE: The demand for a new, secular, and discrimination-free Sudan is rising, but it is countered with the assertion of an extremist version of the Arab-Islamic model for the country.

Q
R
S

Wider Relevance

Problems similar to those described in Africa constitute a widely shared problem of statehood and nation building around the world.

- These others are acutely divided nations where some groups enjoy the rights and dignity of citizenship, while others are marginalized and relegated to virtual statelessness.
- Although these have been treated largely as humanitarian concerns, all these countries are challenged to explore a national common ground and to develop an inclusive sense of belonging, with the rights and obligations of full citizenship.

Expecting the Unexpected: Cultural Components of Arab Governance

Lawrence Rosen, Princeton University

Background

The development of democracy in the Arab world does not always pay sufficient attention to the cultural foundations of Arab political and social life.

- Concepts of the person, time, memory, and relationship need to be considered as vital elements of the political cultures of these countries.
- Against the above background, it may be possible to suggest elements of constitutional and legal organization that are more in keeping with Arab cultural orientations, rather than imposing Western constitutional forms assuming they will suit local needs in the Middle East.

NOTE: Simply drawing constitutional models from the West is to court failure or meaningless legislation.

Arab Culture

Before considering the imposition of Western democracy, it is useful to explore some aspects of Arab culture. Consider

- Ways in which concepts of person and time affect the idea of power.
- The nature of reciprocity and ingratiation in the development of the bonds of obligation.
- Institutionalized ways for leveling difference.
- The relation between Arab concepts of chaos and their views of the moral/ religious underpinnings of human nature.

NOTE: The cultural concepts and institutional forms are vital to any understanding of Arab governance and how they may be drawn upon in fashioning culturally responsive constitutions.

Obligations

In the Arab world, a person is primarily identified in terms of his or her network of obligations.

- The individual is defined by the ability to marshal dependencies and overcome opponents on behalf of himself and those with whom interdependent ties have been formed.
- Successful construction of a network of dependents implies both self-mastery and worldly effect.
- The emphasis is on ownership, not of things, but as a focus of the relations among persons as they concern things.

Movement

The idea that the state must preserve property as personal possession is less central than ensuring freedom of movement—the ability to enact one's capacity to forge interpersonal ties wherever they prove most beneficial.
- Any attempt to restrict movement, whether through educational or economic opportunity, cuts deeply into the Arab sense of justice, maturity, and legitimate authority.

Self-Concept

Another factor has to do with the conception of the self.
- The idea that the self is a unity rather than potentially fractionable is central to Arab concepts of personhood, moral worth, and social place.
- The idea that a person may play a role in one context wholly separate from other roles is largely inconceivable—the idea that officials or judges might rule contrary to their personal beliefs conflicts with the idea of a person as a unity of traits and ties.
- Fractionation is certainly not a prerequisite to democracy.
- The counter of fractionation—focus the on the unity of the person—renders the idea of institutions less a separable entity upon which to build a political system and more an aspect of the individual who combines multiple attachments as part of a unified social person.

Time

Events are commonly categorized not by strict chronology but by whether they have a continuing effect on relationships.
- The important thing is whether persons or events are seen as having a continuing impact on current relationships.
- The ways in which memory is manipulated by the state, or the ways in which time is used to legitimate or delegitimate ongoing structures, may bear on the course of political development.

Social Organization

Several aspects of social organization also correlate with the pattern of relationships.
- Although most Arabs do not belong to actual tribes, these political forms have features that affect many perceptions and relations.
- A tribe's political form is not the defining or constant feature about it—their foundational quality lies not in the design they take at a given moment, but in their ability to take on such variations while retaining certain central features.
- If one regards every social unit as standing on the same moral footing, that no one family or person is permanently of greater moral worth than any other, then leveling devices that knock people down to size support this image of moral equivalence.
- Power tends to be both personal and susceptible to limitation—it is accumulated by getting others indebted and being able to play the expectation of reciprocity to advantage.
  - It is this interchangeability of reciprocal obligations, and the quest for information about others' networks of obligation, that forms a central component of the political cultures of the Arab world and the changes that may be taking place in them.

Limiting Power

Power comes by taking on the qualities ideally associated with a given position and coming to be treated as someone in that position.
- Proof of position is by worldly acts rather than formal induction into an institutionalized position.
- Leaders take consultation from those who have acquired the status and power of being acknowledged.

- The ruler's position is ratified in an institution called *bay'a*, which appears to be a democratic process, but the acknowledgement is traditionally comprised of those regarded as knowledgeable and worldly.

Corruption

Corruption forms an important indicator of the concept of power itself.
- Arabs characterize corruption not as abuse but as the failure to share whatever largesse comes one's way with those to whom one has forged ties of obligation.
  - People even joke that one can undercut an autocrat by bribing a person below him to disregard the superior's orders; this presents a limitation on power.

Chaos

Identifying certain moments as ones of chaos may also fit the patterned emphasis in Arab life on the relational and the negotiable.
- To understand acceptable order, one may need to understand the meaning and structure of acceptable disorder.

Language

Language is central to the ability of any Arab to maneuver in his world.
- A person who can capture the definition of a situation can turn it to an advantage—an asset for forming relationships.
- Arab political rhetoric is the trying out of a concept, which if it takes will capture the situation in a particular way—a man builds a following with "the word" and must show others how this builds relationships.

Islamic Law

Islamic law, when seen against this cultural backdrop, appears somewhat different than it is often portrayed.
- A judge's credibility depends in part on the ways he has built a reputation for knowledge and acceptable discretion.
- Custom takes precedence over law—judges have extremely wide discretion except for strict Quran prohibitions.
- The Quran is not an intensely lawlike document, leaving a great deal left for humans to determine.

Arab versus Western Views

The failure to see how ideas such as time and person, property and chaos play out in the context of political culture may lead to a view of future Arab politics that is too dependent on ideas of Western democracy and legitimacy.
- Any legitimate Arab leader must put together his following in a highly personalized way.
- Legitimacy comes from the fabrication of networks of indebtedness that demonstrate a person's ability to marshal allies.

Creating Constitutions

Creating culturally responsive constitutions raises the question as to how one can develop a constitution that is in accord with the sentiments of the people. Some of the freedoms of importance to Arabs are
- Freedom of movement—this mobility incorporates both spatial and relational elements.
  - Spatially, it is important that people be able to own land wherever they are able to purchase it.
  - Relationally, there must be clear definitions of corruption and in education there must be clear statements about the process by which rules for obtaining degrees can be altered.

- Freedom of law—laws must be locally responsive to local culture, but an individual must be able to opt out to be judged under national law.
  - Laws must be shown to further the Quranic principles of avoiding evil and doing good.
- Freedom of the local—local groupings must be supported as part of the "tribal ethos."
- Freedom of personality—a sense of distinctive personal identity is culturally emphasized among Arabs.
  - Everyone should be assured of having civil identifying documents and passports.
  - Arabs want the right to privacy about their personal lives and want freedom from home search without warrants.

Conclusion   Of the twenty-two Middle East Muslim countries, none is commonly regarded as a democracy.
- Nothing inherent in Arab cultures is against the development of democracy.
- Simply drawing constitutional models from the West is to court failure.
- Constitutions that not only reflect underlying cultural assumptions, but also recognize the continuing force of personalism over institutionalized roles, will have far more meaning.

NOTE: What the West needs to understand is that quite fundamental aspects of person, time, and relationship will deeply inform whatever changes take place. We must recognize cultural influences. The development of democracy in the Arab world must pay sufficient attention to the cultural foundations of Arab political and social life.

Rule of Law and Lawyers in Latin America

Rogelio Pérez-Perdomo, Universidad Metropolitana, Caracas

Latin   In Latin America, presidents of all countries have been democratically
American   elected, with the exception of Cuba. Yet has the rule of law progressed?
Democracy
- Even in countries that hold periodic elections and where the opposition has a chance of winning, the judiciary may perform poorly and public officials could commit abuses against citizens.
- Strengthening the judiciary has become a critical task.

Constitutions   In the nineteenth century, Latin American countries adopted constitutions.
- Among essential features, there were distribution of the state apparatus in different branches and the bill of rights.
- The idea of a constitutional government, as stated in documents, was difficult to put into practice partly because lawyers' real practices did not necessarily follow stated ideals.
  - Lawyers were very important people even before independence and democratization.
  - Lawyers were officials of the state rather than defenders of citizens; many

erved as parts of cabinets and parliaments and as leaders of political parties.
- Under the national idea of a constitutional government, the emphasis in Latin America is on the limit imposed upon the different organs of the state more than on citizen's rights.

Political Systems and Lawyers

Latin American political systems during the nineteenth and twentieth centuries can be labeled as personalist—an individual acted as an axis and set the pace of the political apparatus.
- Many diverse political systems had in common the important presence of a dictator like Peron or Pinochet.
- Constitutional constraints to their power and the safeguard of individual rights were absent. Neither judges nor justices put their efforts in stopping the abusive conduct of those in power.
- The lack of resistance or collaboration may have several explanations:
  - Collaboration was an opportunity to amass a personal fortune and to enjoy the privileges of power.
  - Some may have thought that leaning toward an authoritarian ruler was a lesser harm or even a good thing under difficult circumstances.
  - Lawyers depended on the state for their living.
  - The idea that law was completely unrelated to ethics and its notion as a neutral discipline was popular among lawyers.

Judicial Reform

During the past fifteen years, at the time of tremulous democratization, there has been an important effort to reform the judiciary.
- The power of judges has been limited in a transition from the inquisitorial style to the oral and adversarial system.
- Courts have adopted new technologies and managerial practices.
- Judges have undergone training.
NOTE: At present, it does not seem that justice is more accessible to everyone or that it protects better the rights of citizens. Judges are not more independent or impartial.
- Judges have not been able to protect the rights of citizens or groups who oppose governments under rulers like Fujimori, Menem, or Chavez.
- In more moderate countries, judges have gained more independence and have become political arbitrators.

Risk Takers

It is interesting to see how citizens and lawyers have decided to step forward and take enormous risks to protect their rights against authoritarian regimes.
- Many judges now rule against the interests of the political establishment.
- Judges are assuming their constitutional role more and more.
- Some lawyers and judges are challenging the establishment through legal means.
- Judges are taking a stand even when they know they will be fired or sanctioned.
NOTE: As lawyers now think of themselves as associated with the people (and not mainly to the state) and can get an income outside the state, the independence or resistance of legal professionals could be considered a new trend.

Q
R
S

Law and Development of Constitutional Democracy: Is China a Problem Case?

Randall Peerenboom, UCLA Law School

Background   China is frequently portrayed as a problem case for the law and development movement.
- For some, the problem is that China has enjoyed remarkable economic growth, apparently without the benefit of "the rule of law."
- China has resisted the third wave of democratization and officially remains a socialist state.
- For others, a problem is China's poor record on civil and political rights.

NOTE: Overall, China appears to be following the path of East Asian states. This seems to be the most successful "model" for relatively large countries to achieve high levels of economic growth, implement rule of law, and eventually democratize and protect the full range of human rights through some form of constitutionalism.

Rule of Law   Five East Asian countries rank in the top quartile on the World Bank's rule of law index: Singapore, Japan, Hong Kong, Taiwan, and South Korea.
- Evidence shows that implementation of rule of law is necessary, though by no means sufficient, for sustained economic development.

East Asian Path   The "East Asian Path" involves the sequencing of economic growth, legal reforms, democratization, and constitutionalism, with different rights being taken seriously at different times in the process. It involves
- Emphasis on economic growth in the initial stages of development.
- Government investment in human capital and institutions, including reforms to establish a basic legal system.
- Democratization in the sense of free elections being postponed until a relatively high level of wealth is attained.
- Constitutionalism beginning, including the development of constitutional norms and the strengthening of institutions. Citizens enjoy economic liberties, rising living standards, and some civil and political rights.

After democratization, citizens have greater protection of rights although with some ongoing abuses.

NOTE: There are also examples of less successful paths involving countries at lower levels of wealth and authoritarian systems that did not invest in human capital and institutions. They tend to have the weakest legal systems.

China   Given the high correlation between wealth and rule of law, countries are best evaluated relative to other countries in their income class.
- China is meeting or exceeding expectations on most measures.
- The legal system played a greater role in economic growth than suggested and will play an even greater future role—China's legal system outperforms the average in the lower-middle income class.

- Chinese citizens enjoy more freedoms—including civil and political freedoms—than ever before.
- Despite many problems, China outperforms the average country in its income class on most major indicators of human rights and well-being, with the exception of civil and political rights.
- As China negotiates modernity, it may well give rise to one or more novel varieties of capitalism, rule of law, democracy, and human rights.

Conclusion Is China a problem or a paradigm? China's performance has exceeded expectations, and it appears to be progressing well along the same general path as its East Asian neighbors.
- For those who judge by civil and political rights, China today will be judged a failure, as would have other states at this development stage.
  - China's utility as a model for other states may be limited by recent economic globalization and democratization in most countries.
  - In any event, no single model is likely to work everywhere given the diversity of initial starting conditions and the complexities of the reform process.
- What we have learned is that there is a need to be pragmatic about legal reforms.
- Just as China's slower approach to economic reforms resulted in impressive economic growth, so the contextualized approach to legal reforms resulted in steady progress.
NOTE: Success hinges on the ability of Chinese reformers to continue to improve the legal system and ultimately to address the political obstacles that are currently barriers to the full realization of rule of law and are likely to become even more serious barriers in the future. There is a real danger that government leaders will move too slowly on political reforms and fail to implement deep institutional reforms of the legal system.

III. INTERNATIONAL PROCESSES

Toward a World Rule of Law: Freedom of Expression

Kurt Wimmer, Covington & Burling

Background Freedom of expression is guaranteed by international treaties, but countries differ in their view of its meaning and how it should be protected.
- The borderless Internet makes it more difficult for despots to limit their citizens' access to information from outside their borders.
- There are legitimate disputes over the application of national law—each nation must apply its own rules without diminishing the freedoms available to citizens of other states.
- This article suggests that nations should focus on applying the law of the country in which speech originates, following the view of the EU.

Treaties International treaties guarantee individuals the right to receive information and the right to freedom of expression through media of their choice.

- This right is tempered by permissible restrictions to protect national security, individual privacy and reputation, the impartiality of the courts, and the like.
- There is widespread disagreement on the extent to which countries may build on the minimal levels assured by international norms.
- Laws dealing with protection of reputation vary dramatically from country to country, as do laws addressing the electronic media, political speech, and commercial speech.

The Dilemma   Countries have no realistic process to achieve an accommodation between their own rules and another country's rules. The focus is on three issues:
- When a state may apply its laws against citizens of another state.
- When it has jurisdiction over citizens of another state.
- Whether and to what extent states must enforce judgments of foreign courts.
NOTE: Any widespread adoption of restrictive strategies means that the essential character of the Internet will be altered, and its capacity to act as a universal source of information will be lost.

Libel, Privacy,   A number of high-profile cases have demonstrated the difficulty of moving
and Content   toward a single rule of law for global free expression because of the Internet.
Litigation   Two cases involve Dow Jones in Australia and Yahoo! in France.
- *Dow Jones v. Gutnick*—Australia ruled that jurisdiction will be found at the place where the damage to reputation occurred, usually the country of residence of the claimant.
   - The High Court extended this concept to the Internet and said publishers would be required to assume that they could be subject to suit anywhere in the world.
- The Yahoo! case—A French court ordered Yahoo! to use all means necessary to prevent French users from accessing Yahoo!'s auction site, which featured Nazi items in violation of French laws.
   - Yahoo! filed suit in the United States to void the judgment in this case. The trial court found for Yahoo!, and the French groups appealed. Although fines are mounting in France, no decision has been issued in the U.S. appeals court.
NOTE: These cases demonstrate the ability of a country with relatively lower standards for free expression thwarting the efforts of other countries with differing legal constructs. In many cases, Internet publishers are legitimately concerned that they will be unable to control the legal obligations that Internet content may trigger.

The EU   One of the few exceptions to the view that a publisher is subject to the laws of
Approach other countries is the position of the European Union.
- For electronic contracts, commercial communications, and online provision of professional services, companies are subjected only to the jurisdiction and the law of the member state in which they are established.
- This principle recognizes that only the country in which a publisher is "established" can fully regulate its activities. The publisher would know the scope of legal liabilities beforehand.
- If the EU approach were to be followed universally, accommodating the diverse interests surrounding free expression in a world rule of law would be more straightforward.

Conclusion   It may be impossible to forge a world rule of law on free expression that goes beyond the floor established by the major human rights treaties binding on virtually all countries.

- If the law of "the country of origin" (following the EU) is applied to judge Internet publications, many of the most difficult issues dealt with in international litigation could be minimized.
- Laws against Internet content could give publishers incentive to avoid extending beyond their borders—denying large portions of the world's population the ability to receive diverse sources of information.

Q
R
S

Divided Nations:
The Paradox of National Protection

Francis M. Deng, Johns Hopkins University

Background   A conflict exists between the UN Millennium Declaration of September 2000 and the respect for the territorial integrity and noninterference in internal affairs of world states.

- There is a tension between international protection of the vulnerable and the sovereignty of the states.
- The paradox is that most of the member states of the UN are, in varying degrees, divided nations, suffering from acute national identity crisis as both cause and effect.
- The attention of the international community tends to be focused on the humanitarian dimension, while the states do not want interference.

The Internally Displaced   Some 25 million people in more than fifty countries are internally displaced persons (IDPs), denied safety and deprived of the essentials of life.

- The IDPs are paradoxically assumed to be under the care of their own governments, despite the fact that their displacement is often caused by the same state authorities.
- The worst affected are minority or marginalized groups in conflict with the dominant group.
  - They are seen as the enemy and are neglected and persecuted.
  - Disconnected from the enjoyment of their rights, their marginalization is tantamount to statelessness.
- In most cases, identity differences imply stratification and discrimination—internal conflicts are a desperate reaction to injustice, which in turn provokes ruthless counterinsurgency that aggravates the crisis.
- These people must look to the international community to fill the vacuum of responsibility—someone to address the humanitarian crisis and mediate the conflict.
- Any resolution must promote justice and respect diversity while exploring a common ground for national unity.

NOTE: Governments intent on preserving their status quo are likely to resist outside involvement—their people still require national authorities to provide

Q
R
S

for their security and general welfare; this despite the legally binding basis for international protection and assistance to needy populations.

*The Core
Question*

The core question is, What does the concept of protection entail, and who is best equipped to provide it?
- The challenge is to provide the safety and dignity of a civilian population.
- Experience indicates that there is still a wide gap between what ought to be done and what is being done.
- Much of the international protection is in monitoring people's rights. The states involved continue to be an obstacle to real protection and assistance.

NOTE: Ever since the UN Commission on Human Rights created a mechanism for protection and assistance, work has been carried out in a number of areas in an effort to have an effective international response to the challenge. A set of Guiding Principles has been a source of empowerment to the IDPs.

*Guiding
Principles*

While there has been a growing acceptance of the UN's Guiding Principles, the development of mechanisms for protecting and assisting the IDPs is crucially important.
- A collaborative effort of organizations now works collectively to address the needs of the IDPs, and the prevailing view is that virtually every organization and every field worker has a protection role to play.
- Important practical questions still need to be answered.
  - What are the most effective ways to address protection?
  - How should the secretary-general exercise his leadership to reinforce the collaborative approach?
  - How can the Security Council be more effective without bias based on particular national concerns?

NOTE: On a positive note, the Security Council has recognized the need to address the lack of effective protection for civilians in armed conflict. It has recognized the threat to international peace and has specifically requested that situations where IDPs are under threat of harassment and harm be brought to its attention.

Conclusion

Based on the author's experience with the internally displaced, several lines of action can be proposed.
- "The Responsibility to Protect" should be condensed into a forceful statement endorsed by the General Assembly and Security Council.
- The reports of the human rights mechanisms should receive executive support to reinforce and enhance their influence.
- The invocation of values and principles in dealing with governments is likely to provoke less defensiveness than binding legal instruments.
- The core body for the collaborative approach should include all the relevant bodies of the UN system.
- Those whose mandates are relevant to protection of the vulnerable should be given access to address the Security Council, at least in high risk situations.

NOTE: The normative principles for action are in place, they only need to be acted upon.

Views on the Ground:
The Local Perception of International Criminal Tribunals in the Former Yugoslavia and Sierra Leone

Donna E. Arzt, Syracuse University School of Law

Q
R
S

Background

Since 1993, a revolution in public international law has taken place through the creation of international criminal tribunals for war criminals.
- Perception of their legitimacy is a crucial factor.
- They must also have popular credibility to serve as effective deterrents to future war crimes.
- This article looks at the International Criminal Tribunal for the Former Yugoslavia (ICTY) and the Special Court for Sierra Leone (SCSL).

Objectives

The two institutions share similar objectives for their respective operations.
- The ICTY mission is to
  - Bring to justice persons allegedly responsible for serious violations of international humanitarian law.
  - Render justice to the victims.
  - Deter further crimes.
  - Contribute to the restoration of peace by promoting reconciliation.
- The SCSL is expected to
  - Revitalize Sierra Leoneans' belief in the rule of law.
  - Combat the culture of impunity.
  - Promote respect for the rule of law.
  - Bring a sense of justice after the horrific crimes.

Achievements

Each tribunal has produced landmark rulings contributing to the developing jurisprudence of International Criminal Law.
- The ICTY has
  - Expanded upon the legal elements involving the Geneva Conventions of 1949.
  - Narrowed the perceived differences between laws applicable in internal and international conflicts for the protection of individuals.
  - Made significant advances in international humanitarian law pertaining to sexual violence in wartime.
  - Identified and applied the modern doctrine of criminal responsibility of superiors.
- The SCSL has
  - Held that heads of state are not immune in international tribunals.
  - Ruled that it has jurisdiction to try the recruitment or use of children under fifteen years old as soldiers.
  - Established a Defense Office to give legal representation to arrestees before they acquire their own counsel.

Outreach Efforts

Both the ICTY and the SCSL have engaged in efforts to communicate with their citizenry.
- In 1999, the ICTY established a program to counter the propaganda against it by promoting the Tribunal's impartiality and independence.

- They used live audio and video web broadcasts in the Bosnian/Croation/Serbian language.
- They also used press releases, TV interviews, and roundtables and conferences with national officials, NGO representatives, and victims groups.
- The SCSL has an outreach program to educate the population about the court's mission and procedures and to invite local civil society groups to offer their views. Activities included
  - Town hall meetings.
  - Sessions with targeted groups such as the police, the army, the bar association, journalists, victims groups, and students.
  - Posters, radio, and video programs in the country's four languages.

Perceptions of Legitimacy

The objectives of the international community in establishing the tribunals do not automatically translate into popular acceptance.
- Most people in Serbia view the ICTY as an unavoidable and enforced precondition for Serbia's full return to the world community—the views sideline the issue of the guilt of those indicted by the ICTY.
- In Croatia, a similar pattern prevails regarding the ICTY:
  - More than 52 percent of people believe that The Hague wants to criminalize the Homeland War.
  - More than 78 percent opposed extradition of citizens to the ICTY.
- In Sierra Leone, by contrast, receptiveness toward the Special Court is rather broad, with concerns expressed more in regard to details and implementation than overall legitimacy.
  - People saw it not only as a mechanism for justice but also as an instrument to transform the judicial system.
  - The SCSL may have grown in stature after the indictment of Charles Taylor for war crimes and crimes against humanity.

Perceptions of Impartiality

Below is a description of perceptions of tribunal impartiality.
- The Serbian population overwhelmingly distrusts the ICTY, believing it is politically motivated and biased against those defeated in war.
  - Almost 70 percent did not believe the ICTY acted impartially concerning Serbian defendants.
- The SCSL, from its beginning, has contended with the local perception that it is an American demonstration project either to undercut the International Criminal Court or to gather intelligence on al-Qaeda in West Africa.

Effects on Reconciliation

The respective local populations have been concerned that the tribunal's operation would endanger the fragile peace and reconciliation processes.
- Because the SCSL is located inside the country where most ex-combatants remain at large and often under "protection" of their commanders—potential for unrest and destabilization is ever present.
- Many in Sierra Leone, including ex-combatants, were confused about the difference between the Special Court and the preexisting Truth and Reconciliation Commission (TRC).
  - Because many ex-combatants feared the TRC would convey their testimony to the SCSL, despite the prosecutor's denials, their participation was low.
- Regarding the ICTY, local victims groups often express bitterness when they learn of plea bargains.
  - They see it as a cover-up at the expense of victims.

- Institutions like the ICTY can impair the very reconciliation they seek to advance if the rewards they hand out in appreciation for reconciliation become a source of bitterness.

Conclusion

How can one compare or assess the perceptions of these two tribunals and predict their impact on the long-term development of democratization and the rule of law in these locales when the evidence is so incomplete and uneven?
- Much more data should be collected, or at least more time must pass so views can develop into facts.
- Justice must not only be done, but be seen to be done.

Q
R
S

Global Rule of Law or Global Rule of Law Enforcement? International Police Cooperation and Counterterrorism

Mathieu Deflem, University of South Carolina

Background

Security and intelligence agencies of national states engage in collaboration in matters of terrorism and other crimes, despite critical differences in their respective countries' attained level of and formal commitment to constitutional democracy.
- It can be said that terrorism has effectively been criminalized under a world rule of law enforcement.
- The legitimacy of a global democratic order is challenged when international police operations can take place outside the confines of legal safeguards and human rights restrictions.
- A central question is if and how a global order of law enforcement can lead the way to a global order of law.

Bureaucratization Theory

The bureaucratization theory of international police cooperation was developed to analyze the behavior of modern police institutions under conditions of increasing globalization.
- The bureaucratization theory maintains that public police institutions reveal a tendency toward independence from the governments of their respective national states.
- The degree of a police institution's autonomy will vary and have variable implications depending on social conditions, especially attempts by governments to politicize police activity during periods of intense societal upheaval.
- The theory does not deny that policing is related to state control, but holds that the behavior of police agencies is not wholly determined by reference to their relation to the political center of states.
- Periods of societal upheaval affect the institutional autonomy of police institutions in functional and organizational ways.

Politicization Efforts

Efforts to politicize police are not surprising, as national crises typically bring about a centralization of power in the executive branch.

- What is ironic is that these politicization efforts occur progressively at times when police institutions continue to expand and solidify a position of autonomy that enables them to better resist such attempts at political control.
- On theoretical grounds alone, the degree to which the autonomy of state bureaucracies has been accomplished in periods of relative stability cannot be assumed to be without consequences during moments of upheaval.

September 11   An interesting parallel to historical attempts to politicize policing during periods of war and revolution are the dynamics of international policing since September 11, 2001.
- Legislative and other policy responses, especially in the United States, have gone far beyond what could have been predicted.
- The Patriot Act and the creation of Homeland Security have been among the most concrete political efforts to unite and oversee the various security agencies involved in the "war on terror."
  - Police autonomy is unprecedented in scale.
  - Police can, thus, more effectively resist political influences.

Interpol   Following regulations on organized groups that engage in acts of violence and regulations on explosive substances, Interpol passed a resolution in 1984 concerning "Violent Crime Commonly Referred to as Terrorism."
- The resolution encouraged member agencies to cooperate and to combat terrorism within the context of their national laws.
- In 1985, a resolution called for the creation of the Public Safety and Terrorism subdirectorate to coordinate and enhance cooperation.
- In 1998, Interpol issued a condemnation of international terrorism called a Declaration against Terrorism.
- After September 11, Interpol condemned the attack as "an abhorrent violation of law and of the standards of human decency."
  - High priority was given to the issuance of Red Notices for terrorists sought in connection to the attack.

Interpol after   Interpol reorganized in several key respects after September 11.
September 11
- Interpol created an "11 September Task Force" to coordinate international criminal police intelligence.
- Interpol also instituted a command center open 24/7.
- A Financial and High Tech Crimes Sub-Directorate was created that specialized in detecting money laundering.
- In 2002, Interpol announced a Terrorism Watch List providing direct access to information on fugitive and suspected terrorists.
- A new global communications project was announced as Interpol's highest priority level.
- The organization has managed to attract cooperation from police agencies representing nations that are ideologically very diverse and not always politically friendly.
  - Members do not always trust one another.
  - Major powers like the United States typically conduct international activities unilaterally.

Depoliticization   In terms of the objectives of social control, the bureaucratization of policing involves a depoliticization of counterterrorism efforts.

- Cooperation among state bureaucracies policing terrorism can take place irrespective of the similarities and/or differences among nations in political, legal, cultural, and other respects.
- The autonomy of state bureaucracies creates the potential for policing efforts against terrorism to be planned and implemented without regard for considerations of legality, justice, and politics.

Conclusion   It is important to recognize that the processes and structures of policing and other state activities are composed of a multitude of dimensions and institutions that are not necessarily in tune with one another.
- The state's powers are dispersed across a multitude of institutions whose activities the state can no longer carefully control.
- As the case of international police cooperation shows, the institutions that develop and multiply during the state's continued development cannot be assumed to always be carefully disciplined by the center of the state.
- The expansion of state bureaucracies, such as the police, has ironic consequences.
  - As the state grows, the relative power of its center weakens.
  - The many functions of the state are not always neatly harmonized.
- A model suggested toward the adoption of constitutional-democratic principles at the global level of law and politics to decrease the chances of terrorism must also take into account the manner in which effective control of terrorism is currently accomplished by international cooperation among public police agencies.

QRS

Environmental Protection, Free Trade, and Democracy

David M. Driesen, Syracuse University College of Law

Background   Environmental and free trade laws both have some capacity to aid development of democracy, but that relationship is somewhat complex.
- International environmental law often addresses problems with roots in some of the unfortunate by-products of private productive activities.
- Because international environmental treaties often address problems from private conduct, treaties start—rather than end—the establishment of an environmental rule of law. International environmental law encourages the development of domestic environmental law.
- Free trade law grew out of the GATT, which encouraged friendly commercial relations among the developed countries.
  - Free trade is an essential element in efforts to spread the blessings of economic development to poor countries.
  - It discourages states from banning imports and enacting discriminatory tariffs to protect domestic industries.

Changes in the   Until recently, international trade law and international environmental law
1980s   proceeded along separate tracks.
- The separation between trade and environmental law began to erode in the 1980s. Disputes involving matters such as the disposal of hazardous materi-

als affected trade, which had been unrestricted before the environmental concerns.

- Some of the free trade decisions led to charges that institutions, like the WTO, are antidemocratic.

NOTE: This raises the question as to what, if anything, international law on the environment and law on international trade have contributed to democracy.

Democracy

Generally, a case can be made that environmental protection and free trade coincide with democratic government.

- It is not so clear that either of these bodies of law creates democracy—it might just be that democracies tend to favor free trade and environmental protection.
- International rule of law, as conventionally conceived, exists in some tension with democratic ideals.
- Democratic legitimacy only comes from consent by processes offering some possibility for citizen participation.
- The rule of law and the idea of democracy sometimes reinforce each other but sometimes exist in tension with each other.
  - The rule of law needs adherence to laws, even if the particular application is unpopular and thus appears, in a sense, antidemocratic.

National-Level Law and Democracy

On the national level, the relationship between international law, international environmental law, and democracy is also complex.

- Nation-states influence each other's law through means other than formal treaties—international conferences and other mechanisms for sharing ideas can lead one country to emulate another.
- For example, countries have adopted variants of the U.S. National Environmental Policy Act (NEPA)—a preaction assessment of environmental consequences that requires public participation.
- The spread of ideas like NEPA might be seen as international environmental law spreading democratization—although local conditions such as economics and culture may inhibit this process.

Strengthening Democracy

Environmental law may strengthen democracy.

- If it does, it must do so through creating public participation possibilities that strengthen the engagement of civil society with the creation of law.
- Environmental protection can sometimes motivate a demand for democracy where none exists, as in the case of then-Czechoslovakia.
- The failure of existing institutions to protect the environment can produce demands for democracy.
- While environmental issues may be a catalyst for democracy, often human rights and economic issues prove more central.

International Trade Laws

The picture regarding international trade is equally complex.

- Free traders argue that free trade aids democracy because it builds wealth. But perhaps it is the other way around: democracy creates conditions for free trade as a viable policy.
- If people want protectionist policies, then the rule of law undermines democracy, at least in the short term.
- Free trade obligates national governments to avoid protecting domestic industries, even if their people want that protection in particular cases.

Global Business: Oversight without Inhibiting Enterprise

John Philip Jones, Syracuse University

Background	This article discusses what regulations should be imposed, country by country, to encourage legal and ethical conduct by international firms. • Abuses can be controlled through tighter scrutiny of foreign direct investment (FDI) at a local level—abuses must be policed in the foreign country despite any official corruption. • Local politicians and bureaucrats, who issue licenses, must be motivated by concern for public welfare and nothing else.
Libertarian View	Libertarians see global business as an extension into the international sphere of the principle of the division of labor, which provides economic efficiency. The arguments in favor of global business are • It provides work in overseas markets at wage rates usually above the prevailing rate. • Goods are produced relatively cheaply, which is of great value to everybody, including American consumers. • American workers displaced by foreign labor move on to expanding industries and better jobs—from the rust belt to the sun belt. NOTE: Global business needs to be scrutinized in a way that its excesses are detected and corrected without inhibiting the enterprise of the system.
Benefits	Data demonstrate the overall benefits of global business. • The idea that globalization is to the exclusive benefit of rich countries is a fallacy. • Firms must show themselves as good citizens in foreign countries or they lose in the long term; this benefits the locals.
Problems	In the field of international business there are two broad groups of problems. • Those derived from different and less stringent controls over foreign than over home operations. • Those stemming from investment and financial policies.
Overcoming Abuses	Traditional response to problems has taken the form of • Generally weak legal regulations within the individual countries where global businesses are established. • Sanctions imposed by the companies themselves—self-regulation.
Sanctioning	The potential abuses need to be more strictly investigated than they are at present. • The logical forum to address problems is the United Nations, although the UN is presently not capable of strong sanctioning. • A model would be the Better Business Bureau in the United States.
FDI	FDI is in the interest of both the investor and the receiving country. • Investors want to put up the money only if the proposal meets commercial criteria.

- Receiving countries know it is good for employment, income, and tax reve-nues—there are exceptions where foreigners are limited in percentage of ownership of any one enterprise (xenophobia).
- FDI plans should be subject to tough negotiation.
- FDI is always regulated by the receiving country.
- FDI can make an almost immediate difference to the economic health of developing countries.
- Problems must be dealt with rigorously and proactively.
- Safety standards and marketing policy should be applied uniformly across all parts of a company—in the home country and the foreign subsidiaries.

NOTE: If receiving countries are to avoid disasters, politicians must think exclusively of the economic and social welfare of their people.

The "Good Governance" Concept Revisited

Ved P. Nanda, University of Denver College of Law

Background   In the debate surrounding the issues of debt forgiveness and increases in aid, experts, policy makers, and observers stressed the need for governance reform and policy changes to ensure transparency and rule of law, accountability in public finances, improvement in governance standards, and creation of a pro-ductive private sector.

- To spend new aid productively, suggestions were made to increase aid beyond its current levels to countries with good governance and to give debt relief only to countries with good performance and tolerable political accountability.
  - The UN objection to the above was that debt relief for the very poor nations makes sense and should be extended regardless of bad governance.
- As there is no consensus on how to measure good governance, the term remains ambiguous and the result is imprecise.

World Bank   As a condition for lending, the World Bank requires the recipient government to show effective performance and to promote further reforms.

- The rationale is that when a government combats corruption, nepotism, bureaucracy, and mismanagement, it uses aid to reduce poverty.
- Traditionally, the Bank has not considered political issues to decide to undertake aid programs in the recipient state.
- Public sector reform aimed at efficiency and economic growth remained the Bank policy and practice until a shift in the 1990s after a crisis of governance in Sub-Saharan Africa showing a lack effective use of aid in the region.
  - Thus, good governance appeared on the Bank's agenda in 1991.
  - Governance was to be an indication of how power and authority are exer-cised for development in the management of a country's economic and social resources.

Governance   A UN paper suggests that the new mandate for governance arrived when growing doubts regarding the purpose and effectiveness of the international financial institutions (IFI) seemed to threaten their funding.

- The Bank's governance discourse reflects the tension between economic and political aspects of governance without, at the same time, providing precise criteria for good governance and for evaluating a recipient country for the appropriate conditions for allocation of aid.
- One of the key aims of the Bank's designing a good governance approach was state-market relationships characteristic for Western neoliberal systems.
- Internally directed conditionalities address the structuring and operation of the aid recipient country's institutions and are aimed at rolling back the state systems of many developing countries.
- While the emphasis has been on the economic dimensions of good governance and the state's capacity to effectively use the aid, the Bank continued its apolitical approach to reform by focusing on efficiency in public administration, the rule of law, and transparency and accountability as the major elements to ensure economic growth and development.
  - Ignoring the question of how legitimate a government and its power structures are, the Bank did refer to citizen participation and the role of the state as pertinent governance factors having a bearing on development.

Allocating Aid After a few years, it became apparent to the Bank that sociocultural and political contexts in the recipient countries—not the Western donor's preferences—primarily shape the agenda.
- Little change occurred because of resistance from entrenched socioeconomic and political interests.
- Acknowledging that conditionalities have failed to induce reforms and good government, the World Bank and the donors have shifted their focus from conditionality to selectivity in allocating aid.
  - The World Bank says that the governments better able to use aid are those with good economic performance, and aid should be linked to performance in countries with effective institutions and sound policies.
- A critic, Jan Pronk, said, "Policy improvement and better governance should not be seen as pre-conditions for development aid, but also as objectives themselves."
- Graham Harrison asserted that the Bank has a liberal worldview, which it has imposed on African states in promoting governance reforms. These prescribed reforms, he says, cannot succeed because, although the African states make cosmetic changes in response to the Bank's demands, not much in fact changes.

NOTE: Based upon past experience and current trends, for governance reforms to succeed the history and culture of the recipient country matter the most.

IMF In the 1980s, the number of developing countries seeking assistance grew, the World Bank/IMF intrusions grew, and hence the number of structural adjustment programs (SAPs) became the norm and conditionality expanded.
- The IMF felt that in inducing capital flows and enhancing market confidence, it was acting as a catalyst.
- By the late 1980s, there was a backlash against the SAPs, and by the 1990s, more than half of IMF programs were failing implementation—this in the face of research that showed conditionality does not work.

- Two factors are mainly responsible for the Fund's governance agenda:
  - The rise of capital account openness.
  - The difficult political consequences of its adoption of structural adjustment.
- The Fund's governance policy did not necessarily reflect the primacy needs or interests of those the IMF purported to help, but rather of Western countries and Western NGOs who were far less affected.
  - Decision making at the Fund about the direction of its agenda in each country must be responsive to the country's cultural and political traditions, preferences, and sensitivities.

The United States

The National Security Strategy of the United States in 2002 provided the rationale and framework for new U.S. development assistance under a new Millennium Challenge Account (MCA).

- Noting past failures, the president said that the MCA is for projects in countries whose governments rule justly, invest in the people, and encourage economic freedom.
- The Center for Democracy and Governance in 1998 had already organized its work in five areas—democratic decentralization, legislative strengthening, government integrity, policy implementation, and civil-military relations.
- The U.S. Agency for International Development (U.S. AID) said it will work in a complementary fashion with another agency, the Millennium Challenge Corporation (MCC), "employing principles of selectivity based on commitment and performance in countries that can aspire to MCC eligibility or are good candidates for transformational development."
  - U.S. AID identified nine principles of development and reconstruction assistance to achieve objectives.
  - The MCC uses sixteen indicators to qualify countries to pass the test they must rule justly, invest in people, and establish economic freedom.

NOTE: In 2005, there was consensus on linking assistance to performance, measuring results, and evaluation and "ownership." A country's commitment to change and its allocation of resources are important factors to assure effective use of aid in reducing poverty.

Conclusion

Conditionalities have not necessarily brought about policy reforms that are sustainable over the long term.

- For reforms to succeed, domestic support, ownership, and commitment are crucial—otherwise aid dependence had a negative impact during 1982 to 1995 on corruption, rule of law, and quality of governance.
- Selectivity as a form of ex post conditionality should not penalize least developed countries by concentrating aid on good performers, most of which are middle-income countries.
- Past performance cannot be an effective indicator or guide to future performance; rather governance reforms must be the guide.
- The good governance agendas are being refined—although impossible to have a clear-cut demarcation between economic and political aspects of governance, the current confusion and ambiguities need to be further clarified.